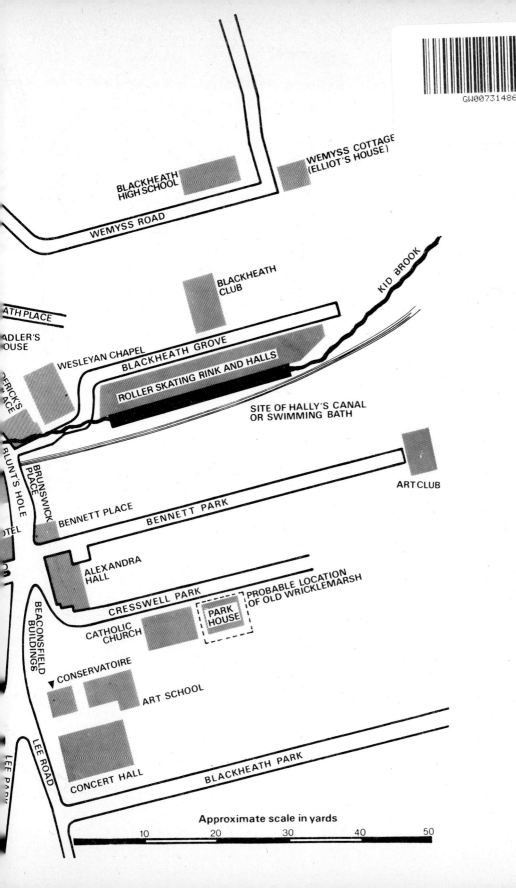

BLACKHEATH VILLAGE
AND ENVIRONS

Volume I:
The Village
and Blackheath Vale

By the same author:

Blackheath Centenary 1871-1971.
    (Greater London Council. 1971.)

The Consumer Wakes Up
    (Pergamon Press. 1968)

The Greenwich Theatre Book (with Hilary Evans)
    (Greenwich Theatre. 1969)

Make Me Understand Pregnancy and Childbirth
(with Dr. Hazel Egan)
    (Dickens Press. 1969)

A Scottish Painter and His World - Gordon Gunn
    (Impulse Publications. 1972)

Martin House: A Short History of the Blackheath
Literary Institution
    (Blackheath Preservation Trust. 1975)

BLACKHEATH VILLAGE AND ENVIRONS
1790 - 1970

Volume I:
The Village
and Blackheath Vale

by
NEIL RHIND

Bookshop Blackheath Ltd.
Blackheath, London · 1976

To the memory of

William Webster (1856-1910)

Alan Roger Martin (1901-1974)

Two men to whom Blackheath owes an incalculable debt and without whose efforts one of London's most pleasant suburbs would be a poorer place.

William Webster

ISBN 0 9505136 0 1 (Clothbound)
ISBN 0 9505136 1 X (Half leather)

First published in Great Britain 1976

Typography by John Gabriel Beaumont
Dust wrapper and titles by Peter Griggs

Offset litho printed by E. & E. Plumridge, Linton, Cambridge
for Louis Leff, Bookshop Blackheath Ltd., 74 Tranquil Vale,
Blackheath, London, SE3

Contents

Preface

This book was intended to be a short history of the suburb of Blackheath to match, to some extent, a pamphlet on the history of the Heath, commissioned from me by the Greater London Council in 1971 to celebrate the centenary of public ownership of Blackheath Common. But like so many projects, the Village history grew in scope and detail. I found that it was impossible to write such a history without investigating the background and ownership of the estates which bordered the Heath and were developed for the people for whom the Village itself, as a commercial centre, was built.

Thus, the simple scheme grew into a two volume work, for it was decided in the Spring of 1976 that a single tome encompassing the history of the Village and the estates of Blackheath would not only be too large but prohibitively expensive both to produce and to buy. Also, the task of writing such an extended work was pushing publication dates further and further away and there seemed a good chance that the author would join that long list of local historians whose research was endless but who never found time to write the major work to which end their investigations were taking them.

Encouraged by my publisher, Louis Leff, I decided that I must be bolder than my distinguished predecessors in the field and publish what had been done, risking the errors and apologising for any omissions. No local history book can ever be complete, nor can it ever be wholly accurate. I ask my readers for their indulgence now, in the hope that while they may forgive me any mistakes or oversights, they will at the same time inform me of these so that subsequent editions will be more complete and more reliable.

Volume 1 covers only the Village and Blackheath Vale; Volume 2 will cover the Heath and the estates facing the Heath. It has not proved possible to define the Village with accuracy. I have included Wemyss Road, but not Montpelier Row; I have included the north west end of Tranquil Vale, but not Eastnor House; I have included Collins Street, but not John Ball School. I came to these decisions, not to make the task easier but simply because I had to draw a boundary somewhere, and all those houses and places close to the Village which are not included in this volume, will be covered in detail in Volume 2. Blackheath Vale is included because it was developed in parallel with the Village and because some of the major Village institutions were to be found there.

I must add a few paragraphs to explain the dedication printed earlier in this book. William Webster, biographical details of whom appear in Chapter 16, gave much money, an immense amount of time and considerable expertise to establishing the major cultural institutions in Blackheath at the end of the 19th century. It was no flaw in Webster's vision that the last war put a temporary stop on some of his enterprises, and it is to be hoped that eventually all of them will be restored to public use. Webster was a versatile man of genius, generous and public-spirited, who died as a result of his unstinting benevolence in demonstrating X-ray apparatus of which techniques he was an early pioneer. I hope that this book will serve as a reminder of his work and interest and will go some way towards keeping his spirit alive.

Alan Martin FSA, was a distinguished local historian whose friendship I enjoyed during the last few years of his life. Like Webster, he devoted himself unceasingly and unselfishly to the welfare and preservation of Blackheath, the suburb of his birth and his home for all his life, and of whose history he was the undoubted authority. Alan Martin was a founder member of both the Blackheath Society and the Blackheath Preservation Trust, and fought long and hard to prevent the destruction of the elements which make up the character, atmosphere and appearance of Blackheath. He was not able to win all the battles but there can be no doubt that without his efforts Blackheath would be a less attractive place than it is today. From the historian's viewpoint, Alan Martin's most significant act of generosity was the donation, shortly before he died, of a wealth of material relating to the history of Blackheath, Greenwich, Lewisham and Lee to the London Borough of Greenwich Local History Library. This valuable collection has added much to the content and accuracy of this volume and has provided historians of south east London with a unique collection of source materials.

Alan Martin was cautious when it came to publication, for although he compiled many notes towards a local history, he wrote little in his later years, his best scholarship seeing print before the 1939-1945 war. It is possible that he was saving further authorship for his retirement, but when that came he was suffering from poor eyesight, which worsened each year, and he was obliged to retire from public activity.

Alan Martin should have written this book, but because he was prevented from doing so, I have taken on the task. I hope that he would have been pleased with the result.

NEIL RHIND

9 Pond Road

Blackheath, SE3

Acknowledgements

During the research and writing of this book I was greatly helped and encouraged by many kind people, a number of whom went to considerable lengths to supply me with information, the sum of which appears in this volume.

I was assisted by the librarians and staff of many public institutions and I would like to record my gratitude for the time and patience with which they answered my enquiries and willingly produced books and other materials. It is not possible to mention everybody and I ask that, should anyone be surprised not to find their name in the lists below, they will regard this as an oversight and not a discourtesy.

I would like to thank the staff of the following: The British Library; British Rail (South Eastern Division - in particular Terry Heslop); Companies House; the library of the Royal Institute of British Architects; Greater London Council Record Office, and Fire Brigade head quarters; Guildhall Library (in particular Ralph Hyde); Guildhall School of Music; Kent County Council Archives; London Borough of Lewisham Local History Library (in particular Mrs J. Read); Maidstone Public Library; Public Record Office; and Westminster Public Libraries.

I am most grateful for the encouragement given by the Councils, Managements and members of the following organisations: the Blackheath Society; the Blackheath Conservatoire of Music; Blackheath Preservation Trust; the Greenwich & Lewisham Antiquarian Society; Westcombe Society.

The following supplied varying amounts of information and assistance, all of it extremely valuable: Charles Alister; R.W. Auld; William Bonwitt; Thomas L. Brown; John Butcher; Mr & Mrs James Cockburn; John Cockburn-Mercer; Martin Edmunds; R.P. Jenner of Messrs Ackermanns; Hazel Jordan; David Leggatt; Mr & Mrs Keith McKenzie; W. Marshall; Joan Martin; Leslie Monson; J.P. Parsons of Messrs Matthews Ltd; Miles Preston of Radcliffes & Co; Eric Rabson; Doris Rhind; John Spruyt; Reginald Edwards; Donald McDonald.

It gives me much pleasure to acknowledge the help of Hilary and Mary Evans as well as to thank them for their encouragement and enthusiasm for the project, with a special word for Mary whose remarkable picture library - by now a Blackheath institution - contains so many of the rare illustrations used in this book. Also, there must be a special tribute to Celia and Stephen Moreton-Prichard who have gone to endless trouble to produce the excellent modern photographs, with further thanks to Stephen whose extraordinary ability to copy old, damaged and faded Victorian photographs and give them new life, contributes much to our knowledge of the past.

Words cannot express my thanks for the immense help and kindness given to me over the last few years by the staff of the London Borough of Greenwich Local History Library at Woodlands, Mycenae Road. Julian Watson, Barbara Ludlow, Frances Ward, and Veronica Morgan have contributed more to this work than they may realise and there can be no doubt that without their skill, professionalism and limitless knowledge of our local history and its sources, this book would be considerably poorer.

I must record my warmest thanks to Louis Leff, my publisher, who had the faith both in the project and in my ability to produce it as well as the courage to sponsor the work - no light undertaking in the expensive and often disastrous game of publishing. More thanks to John Gabriel Beaumont who not only typeset the text but saved the author from a number of dangerous errors of syntax and spelling; Geoffrey Barrow, who compiled the index; David Bonsall, who drew the maps; E. & E. Plumridge, our kindly and skilful printers; Peter Griggs who prepared the art work for the chapter headings, the title page and the dust wrapper.

A special thanks, with love, to my wife, Liz, who not only read manuscript and proofs, but who tolerated my obsessional neurosis for the past five years, and to my children Alexandra and Iain, who have rarely complained.

But perhaps above all, the most important tribute is to the people of Blackheath who have accepted my enquiries and intrusions with little complaint. For this book is about their Village and I hope that they will not be disappointed.

Index of Plates

Illustrations

10. Montpelier Vale (west) in 1976: No. 23 on the right of the picture. (Stephen Moreton-Prichard)

11. The heart of the Village as it was by 1849. The lost stone portico to the north of the Station can be seen on the left of the picture. The photograph could date from the late 1850s. (Author's collection)

12. Postcard view looking towards Brunswick Place. Osborne Place on the left; Spencer Place on the right. Voller's shop became Hanreck's tailoring business in 1916. (Author's collection)

13. Shopping in the Village in about 1905. Note the liveried coachmen. (Postcard in author's collection)

14. Osborne Place in 1938, by then renumbered part as Montpelier Vale and part as Tranquil Vale. (A. R. Martin)

15. Park House, later the Presbytery, built for Capt Thomas Larkins in 1787 out of materials salvaged from Wricklemarsh House. (Stephen Moreton-Prichard)

16. Plan of the Bennett Park Estate as the basis of a redevelopment lease to the Bennett family in 1860 from Albemarle Cator. The Bennetts had held the lease from 1825. (London Borough of Greenwich)

17. Postcard view of the heart of the Village, c1890. Brunswick Place is on the right, before the shop fronts were built forward, and Burnside's shop (20 Tranquil Vale) still as built in the late 18th century. (Mary Evans Picture Library)

18. Rebuilding of 18 & 20 Tranquil Vale in 1903. (London Borough of Greenwich)

19. Frederick's Place before 1860. Hally's shop was replaced firstly with Bank Buildings, and then with the present Barclays Bank in 1888. This photograph may date from as early as 1855. The advertisement for a furniture sale, which can be seen on the steps, is in the name of Kirkman and Engleheart, whose partnership broke up in 1856. (Author's collection)

20. Bank Buildings, erected in 1863 on the site of John Hally's nursery shop. This photograph was taken after 1878. In 1888 Bank Buildings were replaced by the present 16 Tranquil Vale (Barclays Bank). (Provenance unknown)

21. John Hally's nursery before the railway line was laid in 1849. From a billhead once in the possession of the late W. F. Dyer. (A. R. Martin)

22. The Wesleyan church in Blackheath Grove, destroyed by bombing in March 1945. This picture was taken in the late 1860s by Henry Morton, the photographer who traded at 47 Tranquil Vale from c1866 to 1871. (Mary Evans Picture Library)

23. The ruins of the Wesleyan chapel in 1946. (A. R. Martin)

24. Blackheath Grove in late 1860s, shortly after erection. The houses to the left were destroyed or ruined beyond repair in March 1945. Photograph by Henry Morton. (Mary Evans Picture Library)

25. The Post Office in Blackheath Grove, built in 1910 on the site of the old Rink Hall. (Stephen Moreton-Prichard)

26. The Lee Road leading from the south into Blackheath Village, in the 1870s. The house on the right, Hillside, Cresswell Park, was demolished for Beaconsfield Buildings in 1882. Photograph by Henry Morton. (Mary Evans Picture Library)

27. Brunswick Place, Bennett Place, and No. 1 Beaconsfield Buildings in

the late 1930s.   (A. R. Martin)

28. Beaconsfield Buildings - now 1-13 Lee Road - before 1910. John Hinds standing outside his first shop.   (Postcard: Mary Evans Picture Library)

29. The 1779 plan of John Collins' Blackheath Estates. See Chapter 9 for details.   (Provenance unknown)

30. Multon Lambert's shop in 1852 when known as 1 Spencer Place. An advertisement from Mason's Blackheath Directory of 1852.

31. Spencer Place in the 1970s - now known as Nos. 3-9 Tranquil Vale. (Stephen Moreton-Prichard)

32. Spencer Place (right) and Osborne Place (left) in 1905. (Postcard: Lewisham Public Library)

33. Nos. 19-21 Tranquil Vale just before the last war.   (A. R. Martin)

34. South Vale, later 23-35 Tranquil Vale, in the winter of 1939-40. No. 27 Tranquil Vale, then a private house, although used as a doctors' surgery.   (A. R. Martin)

35. The same buildings as illustration No. 34, but in the 1960s, after restoration.   (Stephen Moreton-Prichard)

36. Tranquil Vale (upper) in 1874. Morley's shop is now part of Two Steps antique and curio shop. (Postcard view)

37. Collins Square. The three remaining late 18th-century cottages after redecoration.   (Stephen Moreton-Prichard)

38. Nos. 45 & 47 Tranquil Vale and The Crown public house. No. 47 was the Village post office from before 1811 to 1850. Photograph taken in 1939 by A. R. Martin.

39. The Crown in the 1830s. From an oil painting.   (Provenance unknown)

40. No. 1 Collins Street. Built in 1869 on the site of Hollis' Cottages. (Stephen Moreton-Prichard)

41. Collins Street (west) in 1970.   (Stephen Moreton-Prichard)

42. South Vale Terrace. Built on the grounds of South Vale Cottage in 1871.   (Stephen Moreton-Prichard)

43. Camden Place (site of All Saints' Church Hall) the morning after the Zeppelin raid, August 14 1916. (From: Adventures of a School Master by Hubert William Ord, and reproduced by kind permission of Mrs K. Ord)

44. Nos. 63-65 Tranquil Vale - the remaining fragment of Lamb's Buildings. (Stephen Moreton-Prichard)

45a. Tuck's Corner in the early 1850s. An engraving by Richard Rock. (Author's collection)

45b. Tuck's Corner in the early 1870s. One of Henry Morton's photographs, and an early, although unsuccessful, attempt to capture movement on film. The blur in the middle is a pony and trap.   (Mary Evans Picture Library)

46. Tuck's Corner shortly after the redevelopment in 1885. Appleton owned the Central Supply Stores from about 1889 to 1891.   (Mary Evans Picture Library)

47. One of the Rock engravings. These were drawn by Richard Rock during the period 1845-1855; he lived at 103 Lee Road and sold some of his work at Brown & Webber's shop at 9 Tranquil Vale. This view of Tranquil Vale is probably of the late 1840s.   (Author's collection)

48. The lower section of Tranquil Vale, built in 1822-3. This photograph,

a Henry Morton picture, is probably of the same vintage as Illustration 45a - early 1870s. (Mary Evans Picture Library)

49. A postcard view of Tranquil Vale c1872-4. Edward Norman was at No. 54 Tranquil Vale until c1875. Nicholls held the lease of the Three Tuns from 1853. (Author's collection)

50. The same view as Illustration 50, but after the rebuilding of the Three Tuns in 1885. (London Borough of Greenwich)

51. Tranquil Place (58-74 Tranquil Vale) in 1874. The only known detailed picture of this section of the road before the 1879 re-development of 70-74 Tranquil Vale. (London Borough of Greenwich)

52. Scene outside 70 Tranquil Vale in 1904. (National Maritime Museum)

53. Highland House (70-74 Tranquil Vale & 17 Royal Parade) in about 1910. Postcard. (London Borough of Greenwich)

54. Blackheath Congregational Church in the 1860s. A Henry Morton photograph. (Mary Evans Picture Library)

55. South Vale House in the 1920s. Demolished 1952. (By kind permission of Mr. Reginald Edwards)

56. Bath Place cottages in 1904. (London Borough of Greenwich)

57. School for the Sons of Missionaries, in 1857. An engraving by Richard Rock. (Author's collection)

58. Blackheath Railway Station shortly after it opened in 1849. An engraving by Richard Rock. No. 4 Brunswick Place in the background. (Author's collection)

59. Blackheath Railway Station in the 1970s. The booking hall level was built over a footbridge in the mid-1860s. (Stephen Moreton-Prichard)

60. The Blackheath railway sidings before the last war. The fields in the background behind Eliot Place were meadows attached to Heathfield House. (A.R. Martin)

61. Blackheath Proprietary School before 1857. Pencil drawing by unknown artist. (London Borough of Lewisham)

62. Selwyn Court during building work in 1937, on the site of Blackheath Proprietary School. (A.R. Martin)

63. The Art Club, Bennett Park. (Stephen Moreton-Prichard)

64. The Alexandra Hall, built in 1863. Converted in 1928 for Lloyds Bank. Photograph taken by A.R. Martin in 1938. The shops were subsequently removed.

65. Blackheath Literary Institution in 1846. An engraving by Richard Rock. (Authors collection)

66. The original plans for the Blackheath Concert Hall, published in 1893 in the Blackheath Local Guide.

67. Talbot Houses, Blackheath Vale, December 1939. War damaged and since demolished; Goffer's House is now on the site. (A.R. Martin)

68. East Mill Cottage (Foy House), demolished in the mid-1880s. The All Saints' Vicarage is now on the site. (Author's collection)

69. The windmills on Blackheath. The mill on the left is now Talbot Place; the mill on the right is near the site of the present Mill House and Golf House. (From water colour by R.H. Lucas, 1829, in the Martin Collection, London Borough of Greenwich)

70. All Saints' Church before 1884, i.e. before No. 21 Montpelier Row (Alverstoke House) was built. (Author's collection)

71. A postcard vignette, much enlarged, of the south end of the Village; showing the Alexandra Hall, now Lloyds Bank, c1905. (Author's collection)

Introduction

Unlike the majority of English villages the history of Blackheath goes back
little further than the latter part of the 17th century. It did not grow up
like the neighbouring villages of Charlton and Lee around a manor house or a
parish church. It was never, in the true sense, a village at all, for when
it finally came into being it was sited at the meeting point of four parishes:
Greenwich, Charlton, Lee and Lewisham - a division still perpetuated in
that between the London Boroughs of Lewisham and Greenwich. It thus
never formed the centre of any single parish and, until comparatively recent
times, its population attended four separate parish churches, one of which,
Lewisham, was about two miles away.

It is a fact that the Village abutted eastwards on the ancient lands of
Wricklemarsh, which may have been the estate mentioned as a distinct manor
under the name of Witenemers in the Domesday Book of 1086, and there was
probably a manor house on this estate from mediaeval times. Although it
was probably re-built at least once in its history, there is nothing to suggest
that the site of the manor house was ever changed until Sir Gregory Page
built his splendid new mansion on the crossroad of Blackheath Park and
Pond Road in 1723-4. It is one of the puzzles of Blackheath history that no
record has come down to us which gives a clear view of and accurate siting
for the old Wricklemarsh house, although it survived the death of Lady
Morden in 1718 and was described, when sold to Page, as being untenant-
able. It is extremely unlikely to have stood on the site of the Page
mansion, which was designed by John James (c1672-1746) and erected at
great speed and equally great cost. Mediaeval and Tudor houses
were rarely built on high ground, as their owners preferred the valleys,
which were more sheltered and usually held a stream which ensured a
clean water supply.

I hold the view that the most likely location for the old house was somewhere in the vicinity of Bennett Park and Cresswell Park, and possibly on
the site of Park House (now the Catholic Presbytery) which was built in
1787. Some slight support for this theory is provided by the fact that in
the 17th century the well of the Village (the site of the present railway
bridge) was known as Blunt's Hole - after the then owners of Wricklemarsh -
the Blunt (or Blount) family. In the early 18th century the name was
Dowager's Hole or Dowager's Bottom, after the Dowager Lady Susan Morden,
the last occupier of the old Wricklemarsh house. It is perhaps worth noting
here that in the 17th and 18th centuries the term 'Bottom' had none of the
smutty connotations it has today.

The siting of the Wricklemarsh kitchen gardens in Blackheath Grove from
at least Blunt's time and even after the building of Page's house, must
surely indicate an ancient use, especially as vineyards were planted here
on the sunny, south facing slopes of the banks of the Kid Brooke. One other
piece of evidence can be found in John Flamsteed's book of astronomical
theories and observations, Historiae Coelestis, published in 1712. A plate
in this work entitled Prospectus Orientalis is of a view looking south from

the observatory in Greenwich Park. Two houses can be identified, one is Charlton House and the other, also a Tudor mansion, is roughly on the site of what became Cresswell Park.

It is perhaps of interest to note that it is possible to project a straight line from the Queen's House on the north of Greenwich Park, through the Park at the Blackheath Gate, across Blackheath and through the middle of All Saint' Church and the Presbytery (Park House) in Cresswell Park. Whether this has any significance I do not know, but it surely cannot have been wholly accidental.

Be that as it may, the presence of the old Wricklemarsh house in the vicinity seems to have had little influence on the development of the Village, which hardly existed when Page had the old mansion demolished in 1722.

There were however two or three houses on the Wricklemarsh estate in the early 18th century. The property, about 250 acres, had been purchased by John Morden (1623-1708) in July 1669 from the Blunt family, in whose hands the land had been held since the early years of the 17th century. During Morden's time the Manor of East Greenwich was surveyed by Samuel Travers and his findings have since been published. Whilst this Manor did not encroach on much of Wricklemarsh - the greater part falling into Charlton Parish - there is enough of the south side of the Heath in Travers' plan to show the present site of The Paragon, Montpelier Row, and the central triangle of the Village. The footpath and bridge leading to Morden College are marked, and so is the Queen Elizabeth Well on the south side of Tranquil Passage. The only houses in the vicinity are Sir John Morden's "two new tenements" on the site of the Princess of Wales public house, and a house occupied by one Elliot, on the site of the building known today as Wemyss Cottage, at the east end of Wemyss Road. During Morden's tenure and that of his widow, Lady Susan Morden (1638-1721) at least two other substantial houses were built on the Village boundary of the Wricklemarsh estate: a house known as The Six Chimneys and occupied by John Clowser, which may have been the above-mentioned "two new tenements", but seems more likely to have stood at the top of Montpelier Vale on the site of 34-36 Montpelier Vale; and a house roughly on the site of 12 Montpelier Vale, which was occupied by Edward Sadler as early as 1710. Sadler's house was later occupied by Thomas Felstead.

But three houses do not make a Village and it was not until the Morden estate had been purchased by Gregory Page (1689-1775) that any major changes were made, these taking the form of the demolition of old Wricklemarsh and, to judge from John Rocque's London Survey of 1746, the two new tenements as well.

After Gregory Page's death his principal properties passed to a great nephew, Sir Gregory Page Turner (1748-1805), but Wricklemarsh did not pass to Page-Turner until 1781, on the death of Page's sister-in-law, Juliana. This delay made little difference to the management of the estate because it was certainly let for grazing and other agricultural purposes and the formal parkland attached to the big house probably constituted only a small portion of the whole.

In 1781 Page-Turner obtained consent by Act of Parliament to sell the Wricklemarsh estate and the mansion, the auctions being conducted at various dates between April and August 1783. The estate was purchased by Beckenham land-owner, John Cator, for the paltry sum of £22,550, although it was not the relatively straightforward purchase that has sometimes been claimed. Not only did the Page-Turner family keep back a valuable plot with a frontage on the Village (the site of Edward Sadler's house and garden) but a considerable length on the Heath frontage was not part of the Page freehold. This included most of the land now covered by Montpelier Row and Wemyss Road and part of the site which became The Paragon. These lands were held on lease from the Lewisham Parish, admittedly for 1000 years originally, but the lease was for herbage rights only and this had given Page the opportunity to advance the line of his estate to a neat boundary with the public highway.

It is sometimes held that Cator purchased Wricklemarsh, pulled down the old house and then laid out the estate in building plots almost within a few months. He certainly demolished the house, starting in 1787, probably because it was far too expensive to maintain and he owned a perfectly good property at Beckenham. It is also certain that he granted a lease for the site of the old Wricklemarsh house in Cresswell Park to Capt. Thomas Larkins (see Chapter 6). But further building work was very slow. Other than leases for some of Montpelier Row towards the end of the 1780s, and another to Michael Searles by the end of the 1790s for The Paragon, John Cator leased the rest of his new estate as farm land. The demolition of Wricklemarsh moved slowly (some ruins still remained in 1808) and it was not until 1794 that any further building leases were granted, this being one for Frederick's Place, now 16 & 18 Tranquil Vale, described in Chapter 7.

The building work on Montpelier Row resulted in John Cator having to pay a fine for encroachment in the form of charitable donations to the Parish of Lewisham, based on the value of his rents. When he died in 1806 his Wricklemarsh estate was, with the exception of the Heath frontage and a small part of the Village, much as it was when he purchased it in 1783.

The west side of the Village is poorly documented for the period before 1779. All that is known is that in 1779 the $16\frac{1}{2}$ acres with a frontage to Lee Terrace and Tranquil Vale was held by John Collins and that in 1783 the land tax records show that he had purchased the freehold by that date. Details of Collins' ownership and subsequent developments here are given in Chapters 9 & 10. The only earlier evidence is that there were buildings on the site of The Crown public house and in the vicinity of Collins Square which were marked on Rocque's survey of 1746.

The central triangle of the Village, bounded now by Tranquil Vale, Montpelier Vale and Royal Parade, was part of the Manor of Lewisham and, as such, held by the Barons, later the Earls, of Dartmouth from 1673. As Lords of the Manor they were also the freeholders and could grant development leases. But other than Dartmouth Row and half a dozen properties at the edge of the Heath and, possibly, the lease for Richardson Headly's house (The Three Tuns), there is no evidence that the Dartmouths exercised their privilege very much before the 1770s. The fact that development in the centre of the Village did take place may be because of the location of a public well here - Queen Elizabeth's Well, which is marked on the 1695 Travers' survey. There is no evidence that the well had any connection with Queen Elizabeth I and the name may simply imply that it was there in Tudor times and that it was the traditional spot for those using the Heath for sports or other purposes to refresh themselves. Its position can be plotted accurately from a lease of 1804 from the Earl of Dartmouth to Thomas Miller for two small pieces of land near the Three Tuns. The text reads, in part: "...except and always reserved under George Lord Dartmouth, his heirs, and assigns the well adjoining to the hereby demised premises and the way or passage thereto which said well is to be used only in common by him the said Thomas Miller with the rest of the tenants of the said Earl".

There can be little doubt that this was the old common well, still in use in 1804. It was outside the boundary of the Three Tuns site as it then existed, for its position is clearly marked on the lease plan with a 33ft long passage leading to its head. At the expiry of the Miller lease in 1851 the present library building in Tranquil Passage was erected on the site and the well enclosed to the south east boundary of the plot, behind the shops in Montpelier Vale, and in a small yard at the back of the library - built as a school room. The playground of the school is about eight feet lower than the road and when the Miller buildings were demolished it is likely that the well head was removed and the funnel of the well filled in and consolidated.

So far as we know, the Three Tuns site was the only building in the centre of the Village before the late 18th century, and Blackheath Vale was no more than a sand pit until the 1770s when two windmills were erected at either end of the northern edge of the pit.

Thus, in 1780, Blackheath Village - not yet known by this title - was nothing more than a handful of properties on either side of roadways linking Greenwich with Eltham, Lee and Lewisham. The land on each side was in agricultural use but the first signs of change were apparent and, within the next 20 years, the Village as we know it today would be clearly defined by buildings, many of which have survived. And that is what this volume is all about.

Author's note: I have repeated some basic information at various places in the text in an attempt to improve this book's value as a work of reference. I hope that, in so doing, I have not spoiled the work for those readers who prefer a straight narrative.

1   Phoenix House and Phoenix Place

According to details in the early 19th-century Dartmouth Estate leases
the section of the triangle of the Village south of the Three Tuns and
presently bounded by Tranquil Passage and Montpelier Vale was part
of the garden ground attached to the old pub. The land to the north bounded by Royal Parade and the north east run of Montpelier Vale, from the
present Nos. 25-49 Montpelier Vale, was enclosed by 1800 and may have
been taken from the waste before that.

    The Three Tuns garden development is dealt with elsewhere (see Chapter
11) and this section covers the early development of the lands presently
25-49 Montpelier Vale and Royal Parade: that section of the Village known
until about 1862 as Phoenix Place and Phoenix Vale. The use of the name
Phoenix, almost certainly derived from the house which stood on the site,
may indicate that there was, albeit briefly, an earlier development here
although maps of 1695 and 1746 show nothing in the vicinity other than a
building roughly on the site of the Three Tuns. It was not uncommon in
the 18th-century to use the name Phoenix for a house which had been
built on the site of a previous building destroyed by fire, but whether this
applies to the house in Blackheath Village can only be conjecture now that
so few accurate records survive.

    What is certain is that a lease for the present site of 25-49 Montpelier
Vale and Royal Parade was granted to Matthias Ingram in 1800. The
lease refers to existing stables and coachhouses and Ingram's intention to
erect a new property and to improve existing buildings and other premises.
Ingram was a coachbuilder and coachmaster and this may indicate that
there were substantial stables and outhouses here. The Ingram lease was
for 61 years from 29 September 1799 but, although Matthias was still in
Blackheath in 1808, there is no record thereafter. By 1817 George
Ingram is listed as a coachmaker at High Street, Borough, and William
Ingram was a coachmaster on the Greenwich Road in 1824.

    But there is no doubt that a substantial house was built at the top of
Montpelier Vale, with its garden ground on the line of Royal Parade Mews,
and that it was called Phoenix House almost from the outset. Because its
address would have been nothing more than "Phoenix House, Blackheath",
occupying as it did such a prominent position on the edge of the Heath, it
is not possible to be sure of its tenants before the 1841 census. By this
time the occupier was McGregor Laird, an Africa merchant and
explorer (1811-1862) who later lived at 8 The Paragon. In October
1841 Phoenix House, the yard at the rear and the head lease of the row of
cottages known as Phoenix Vale, was offered for sale, in other words the
whole of Ingram's lease. We do not know who purchased the property but
it is unlikely to have been Laird for he had left Phoenix House by 1844.
His tenancy was followed by that of Colonel James Wood (1797-1874) of
the 5th Dragoon Guards, who had once lived in Lee. His wife,
Mrs. Fanny Wood (1816-1860) was the daughter of the Reverend Charles Parr
Burney, the schoolmaster of Crooms Hill. Previously Colonel and Mrs.

Wood had lived at 31 Shooters Hill Road (from 1840-1845) and were amongst the first tenants of the new houses there.

There must have been some strong disadvantages in living at Phoenix House for none of the tenancies seem to have lasted long. Colonel Wood was succeeded by Mrs. Elizabeth Borradaile, a widow born in 1797 whose son was an income tax collector; in 1855 the house was occupied by William Campbell Gillan and, by 1860, Mrs. Maria Stidolph who used the house for a day school for girls. Mrs. Stidolph was the widow of William Stidolph who had lived at 2 Brunswick Place between 1831 and 1839 and who combined the businesses of music master and book-selling with an estate and insurance agency.

By 1861 the original lease on Phoenix House and the surrounding ground had expired and the Census for that year lists only a carpenter in residence acting as caretaker. In June 1861 a large quantity of Portland Stone and 8000 pantiles, as well as other building materials, were sold on the site and it seems clear that Phoenix House was being demolished at that time.

On the north side of the property, facing across the Heath, was a row of ten wooden cottages known at various times as Phoenix Vale, Washerwoman's Vale or Washerwoman's Row. This terrace was probably built at the same time as Phoenix House, i.e. about 1801-1805, as Ingram's lease included this ground. The cottages were very small, and do not appear in the commercial directories because they were inhabited by artisans, servants and laundresses - facts confirmed by the Census returns of 1841-51-61. They had certainly been built by 1814 when one of them was used as a place of worship for Greenwich and Blackheath Wesleyan Methodists before any formal churches had been built by the movement.

It was because these cottages were occupied by a number of laundresses, including the redoubtable Mrs. Sarah Martin who occupied Nos. 1 & 2 at the south west end of the row, that the nick-name Washerwoman's Vale or Washerwoman's Row was given to these houses. During the early 19th-century the ground opposite was a pit left over from 18th-century gravel digging and was much used by local laundresses as a drying ground - thus the name Washerwoman's Bottom for this section of the Heath. There were waterpumps here and, from time to time, a small pond in the middle which attracted much activity. After the cottages were demolished, Washerwoman's Bottom was still a centre for the drying of laundry and many other public activities, including bonfires, public meetings and sports and games, especially quoits. But with the development of Royal Parade after 1862 and the increasing waspishness of the middle classes during the 1860s and 1870s pressures were applied on the Metropolitan Board of Works and the Lord of the Manor (custodians of the Heath) to remove the drying rights for the laundresses and thus the eyesore of the washing poles. Blackheath people were split on this issue: the washerwomen, for as long as anyone could remember, had dried clothes on the Heath and there was no doubt that the clothes had to be dried somewhere. The opposing faction felt that Blackheath Village was the centre of an attractive suburb and that the approach to its commercial centre should not be sullied by a handful of washerwomen. This faction was encouraged by the adoption of the Heath by the Metropolitan Board of Works in 1871 who, in the rules and regulations governing the common, forbad the erection of posts and the draping of washing on the furze. In the end a compromise was reached and annual licences were issued, but washing and posts had to be cleared away before noon and there was to be no dry- ing on Sundays and public holidays. The effect of these regulations was probably less severe than might be imagined because, by then, the washerwoman was being replaced by commercial laundries outside the Blackheath district and by the late 1870s only a few laundresses remained in the Village, principally in the cottages at Camden Row and Bath Place. The last licences to dry on the Heath were issued in 1893 and then only on the understanding they would not be renewed.

Phoenix Place was a street name which, although it covered only a few yards, was an important section of the Village in the early development of Blackheath as a commercial centre. It covered those shops presently numbered 25-35 Montpelier Vale, and included what may have been the first ever shop in Blackheath.

By 1799 a trader called Robert Dalton (1765-1838) had opened a shop on the site of 25-27 Montpelier Vale where he carried on a business as a general grocer and oilman. This seems to be, insofar as accurate rec- ords survive, the oldest shop site in the Village, although it may have been contemporary with 12 Montpelier Vale which could have been trading as early as 1800. Dalton's shop in Phoenix Place sold china, in addition to groceries and lamp oil, and he probably ran what we would call a general shop or village store. As the Village developed he concentrated more and more on groceries and cheesemongering. His daughter Mary (1790-1841) married James Watson, the butcher from 12 Montpelier Vale (q. v.) so that when Robert Dalton died in 1838 his estate was held in trust by his son-in-law to be divided between Dalton's children on the death of his wife, Mary (b. 1766) which event took place in 1843. Robert Dalton's son, John, continued in the grocery business at Phoenix Place after his father's death, married Sarah Stambury in January 1839, the daughter of the then late Isaac Stambury (1784-1831), landlord of the Princess of Wales from 1824-1831, and took leases on other Village shops in an effort to expand his share of the growing trade.

In 1841, when the Ingram lease on Phoenix House and Phoenix Vale was sold, a lease was granted to William Seager (1801-1857), the local builder responsible possibly for the development of Nos. 2-20 Shooters Hill Road and a row of cottages at the east end of Lawn Terrace, to rebuild or develop part of Phoenix Place. Seager already held leases on some of the houses in Tranquil Passage at the rear of Dalton's shop and his new lease gave him the right to build eight houses on a small plot roughly on the site of the present Brigade Street. As a result Dalton's shop was joined by four more on the site presently numbered 29-35 Montpelier Vale. They were originally numbered 1-4 Phoenix Place with Dalton's shop taking the title 5 Phoenix Place - the numbers running from north to south.

Dalton's shop remained much as it had been in 1799 but in 1852 a new lease was granted to John Dalton for 31 years and it seems likely that Seager made substantial alterations to the premises shortly afterwards, converting it into two shops. In 1854 Dalton's lease and business were up for auction, being offered to "...grocers, cheesemongers and others ...the present proprietor and family have traded here for up to 50 years." This marked the end of John Dalton's commercial activity in Blackheath but as he was then 53 and, no doubt, quite well-off financially, he probably retired. His son, also John, continued in business in Montpelier Vale for a few years thereafter but by the 1860s the family disappear from the records.

After the Daltons had sold their shop at Phoenix Place the premises were divided into 5 & 6 Phoenix Place and the outhouses and rear section of the building occupied by separate tenants, remaining in this state until the whole terrace was redeveloped in about 1882.

The new buildings at Phoenix Place not only provided Seager with a base for his activities but also provided premises for his son, also William (b. 1821) who set up as a coal and corn merchant at No. 4 (now 29 Montpelier Vale). Unfortunately the departure of Dalton, coupled with the development of other parts of the Village, turned Phoenix Place into something of a backwater and there was a large turnover of tenants in the new shops. It was the service trades, which relied less on casual shoppers, that proved more successful than fresh food shops.

It is difficult to be precise as to who the early tenants of Phoenix Place were because the directories at that time rarely gave a number to the houses, but they were all occupied before 1845 and remained so until the whole terrace was re-built. The occupants were as follows:

1 Phoenix Place (35 Montpelier Vale)

Initially this was the residence of the Seager family and it may have been the offices as well, for by the 1840s Seager was employing 10-15 hands and there would have been much administration to cope with. By 1851 he had moved house to 18 Montpelier Row, just across the road. At this date the Phoenix Place house was occupied by Mrs. Elizabeth Goodwin (b. 1802 or 1805) who ran the premises as a boarding house. She was succeeded in about 1875 by George Taylor, a bootmaker, who occupied the shop although the upstairs rooms were still let as rooms and by the 1880s were in the control of Mrs. Elizabeth King. Taylor moved his business to Tranquil Vale by 1882 probably as a result of the redevelopment of Phoenix Place. The new shop was firstly occupied by George Gray, a draper, who was followed in 1892 by Frederick William Warner, a builder who had been in business at 66 Tranquil Vale from 1885. In 1899 Warner's lease was assigned to Collins Bros., electrical engineers, who were heavily engaged in laying electricity cables and wiring to Blackheath houses and shops in the early years of the present century. They did not stay long in these premises but managed in their short stay to alter the appearance of the Village quite dramatically. One of their ventures involved the installation of electric street lighting on this stretch of Montpelier Vale and Royal Parade - the first section of electric street lights in the district. It created such a sensation that the shopkeepers whose businesses were illuminated in this novel manner forgot their differences and, for a brief while, promoted themselves collectively rather than individually. In 1901 they pressed the London County Council to rename this section of the street "Electric Parade" but the LCC ignored the plea and, instead, added the first section of Royal Parade to Montpelier Vale as part of a widescale renumbering order in 1903.

After Collins Bros. had left Blackheath their old premises were occupied in 1911 by William Henry Gomer, a builder and decorator, and grandson of William Henry Gomer who had settled in Blackheath Village in 1808 where he set up in business as a cowkeeper and dairyman. Old Gomer's son, also William Henry (1830-1909) traded as a greengrocer elsewhere in the Village. The grandson's building business operated from 35 Montpelier Vale until the last war but in recent years the shop has been used as an office, initially by Woodgate (Blackheath) Ltd. and presently by Product Resources (UK) Ltd.

2 Phoenix Place (33 Montpelier Vale)

From 1841 to the 1850s this house seems to have been used primarily as a private residence, but in 1855 the shop had been opened by Delmar Bros. wine merchants. By 1862 the trade had changed to that of millinery (Mrs. Anne Brett) and in 1866 there was another change and the house was occupied by William Barnard Pinhey, a surveyor and builder who put up much of the housing on the Page estate lands at Lee Park. During the years from 1870 until the rebuilding in 1882 there was no retail use of the premises although Frederick Allen and his Blackheath Dye Works are listed for this address. This may have been a temporary move during the upheaval for the redevelopment of Phoenix Place because Allen, and later his widow, traded from 25 Montpelier Vale throughout the same period. The new premises were leased in 1886 by the Misses Mansfield (d. 1891) and Perratt, milliners. A year after the death of Miss Mansfield the business was sold to Miss Prangley who traded here until 1909. From 1912 until well after the last war the shop became a laundry receiving office - The Home Laundry Ltd. In recent years it became, like other buildings in this group, a light engineering works, trading as Norman Walpole Engineering Co. Ltd. until 1974.

3 & 4 Phoenix Place (31 & 29 Montpelier Vale)

The Seager development of 1841 placed two shops on this site but the rebuilding in 1882 linked the shop units together mainly because of the type of trade then carried on at No. 4 which used the yard entrance to the south. This was the corn factoring business established by William Seager jnr soon after the shop was built. It does not seem to have been a successful venture in that by the mid-1850s when Seager was still a young man (he was born in 1821) and with a young family to support he had surrendered the lease, possibly because of bankruptcy. In 1858 the premises were taken by Alfred Fox who combined the corn merchant's business with that of Smith & Withers, coal merchants. Alfred died shortly afterwards and his 22-year old son, Thomas, was in charge until 1887, clearly more successful in this trade than in his other investment - property. In 1863 he took on the unexpired lease of some hovels in a court known as Russell Square (now Brigade Street). Although these had only been built around 1839-1841 they were poorly constructed, ill-drained and lacked water. Why Fox purchased these must remain a mystery because, by then, laws governing drainage and water supply were in force and the local Boards of Health were taking the action statute forced upon them. Fox was summonsed and fined part of the cost of repairs and rehabilitation of the houses. By curious irony it was the Seager family, their fortunes now recovered, who took on the new lease for Russell Square and Tranquil

Passage in 1871 and tore down all the old cottages, but this is dealt with elsewhere in this book. Thomas Fox maintained his Phoenix Place shop until 1887, moving into the new premises in 1882-3, but in 1888 the lease and the goodwill of the business had passed to Wensley & Co., although Fox stayed in their employ until at least 1904.

At the end Fox was trading from the newly built double shop, 29 & 31 Montpelier Vale, although No. 31, previously 3 Phoenix Place, was a separate shop from 1841 to 1882. Initially it was conducted as a school by Miss Martha Wilkins but by 1851 the shop was held by Jacob Bizzell, a coal merchant, born in 1818, who also advertised his services as a waiter for dinners and functions. The Phoenix Place establishment may have been Bizzell's home address for he also held premises from about 1868 to 1875 in a small office attached to 45 Tranquil Vale (q.v.). The family later moved to 23 Tranquil Vale where father's coal business was conducted alongside the family's hat making company.

Bizzell was followed, at Phoenix Place, by Miss Charlotte Scott who restored the house to its earlier use as a school for girls, but on the expiry of the lease she departed, the premises were rebuilt and the link with No. 29 Montpelier Vale made permanent.

The corn merchant's business closed soon after 1904 and the shop remained empty until it was taken in about 1907 by Bussey Brothers, motor engineers, the first of their kind in Blackheath although not the first local tradesmen to sell motor cars. In 1910 the business was taken over by William Henry Nurton (1863-1935) & Sons who not only did sell cars but opened a garage in Paragon Place. After the last war their business passed to F.E. Hewlett Ltd., motor engineers and metal workers, in whose hands it remains.

5 & 6 Phoenix Place (27 & 25 Montpelier Vale)

After Dalton had sold his lease on the old shop in 1854 the building was occupied in three separate parts. The yard at the back, entered from Tranquil Passage, was in the hands of Thomas Smith, a builder, plumber and painter, until 1869, whilst the front shops were held by John Charles Sullivan, a bookseller and stationer who moved to 4 Montpelier Vale in 1870 and by Richard Whittaker, a watchmaker and jeweller who moved at the same time to 11 Tranquil Vale.

No. 6 Phoenix Place and the yard were then taken by Frederick Allen for his Blackheath Dye Works; 5 Phoenix Place became a dairy. Allen remained here until 1882 but the dairy had become William Godding's fruit shop by 1874 in which use it remained until the rebuilding. In 1883 the new shops were joined as one by S.G. Linnell, the Direct Dairy Supply Co. and provision merchants who, as well as conducting retail business (they had shops at Lee Green and Lewisham) supplied all the equipment needed for small dairymen and cowkeepers. Although Linnell's name had gone after 1886, the identity he gave to the two shops remained until 1904: 5 Phoenix Place (27 Montpelier Vale) continued trading as the West London Dairy Co. with No. 6 Phoenix Place (25 Montpelier Vale) remaining a provision merchant's, firstly under George Pinnock and from 1890 to 1896 under the management of James Carter.

In 1897 the Allen family returned to 25 Montpelier Vale and re-established the dyeing and cleaning business; by 1908 it passed to Messrs Eastman &

Son. In 1958 the complete premises were taken by Messrs Wookey & Co., estate agents. Edgar Wookey (1861-1932) came to Blackheath in 1917 when he purchased the business of estate agent Herbert Low at 2 Charlton Road - a business which had been founded by R.J. Suter in 1882.

After the West London Dairy had left 27 Montpelier Vale it passed through a variety of hands between 1914 and 1934 trading variously as florists, haberdashers and general shopkeepers. In 1934 the premises were re-opened as a grocery store by Messrs G.R. Saxby and W. Fish who succeeded so well that they were able to move their business to 4 Montpelier Vale in 1938. In recent years the shop at 27 Montpelier Vale had been used by R.J. Norris, the upholsterer and, in 1975, was re-opened as a branch of a Dutch-owned flower and plant retailers. They left after only a few months and it is now a hand-knitted woollen clothes shop.

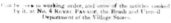

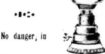

2 Royal Parade

Until 1860 commercial development in Blackheath had been built on a relatively small scale with shops of two or at most three storeys in height. Bulk and grandeur were the hallmarks of the private houses edging the Heath and on the Cator Estate or Aberdeen Terrace. The Village, comprising the shops and cottages of the working people was, so to speak, in a subservient position, punctuated only by the churches and the School for the Sons and Orphans of Missionaries to remind the inhabitants where their greater loyalties lay.

The building of Royal Parade on the site of 10 damp cottages and a crumbling mansion changed the appearance of the Village more dramatically than any previous development in that its sheer size and position blocked the view between the Heath and the heart of the Village. It gave a hard edge to the northern boundary and provided a sizeable increase in shop premises and housing.

Royal Parade presently comprises only those shops facing the Heath and running westwards from the north east corner of Montpelier Vale to the entrance of Brigade Street. The tea shop known as Christy's is included in Royal Parade (No. 17) but is dealt with in the section covering Highland House, Tranquil Vale (q. v.). But originally Royal Parade included Nos. 37-49 Montpelier Vale and these premises are described in the following pages.

The original parade and the mews behind stands on the ground occupied by Phoenix House and Phoenix Vale until 1861. These had been built at the beginning of the 19th century on a 61 year lease granted in 1800 by the Earl of Dartmouth to Matthias Ingram, a coachbuilder. With the expiry of the lease the Dartmouth estate took the opportunity to encourage the redevelopment of the site for commercial purposes.

Building leases were granted to Lewis Glenton (1815-1873) a Charlton-born speculator who was responsible for much of the development of Hyde Vale, Lansdowne Place, Kidbrooke Park Road, and many important groups of buildings in the district. Glenton was so successful that he was able to build and endow three local churches, help float the local bank and, probably as a result, influence most of the major land owners in Blackheath and Greenwich to grant him building leases.

Glenton completed the first section, i.e. 8-16 Royal Parade, in November 1861 and the leases were then assigned to his nominee Thomas Miller Whittaker (1823-1899) the silk mercer who traded from 5 & 7 Tranquil Vale. By the following April a similar transaction had taken place for the group 1-7 Royal Parade (presently Nos. 37-49 Montpelier Vale).

Originally the development was to be known as Phoenix Parade, following the existing nomenclature of this part of the Village but the betrothal of the then Prince of Wales (later Edward VII) to Princess Alexandra of Denmark in 1862 generated an enormous wave of monarchist fervour throughout the land. Glenton, along with many other builders in London, used the opportunity to adopt a name for his buildings which reflected his enthusiasm for

Queen and Country - and Phoenix Parade became Royal Parade almost overnight. The name stuck, which is more than can be said for the building on the corner of Cresswell Park which was dubbed Alexandra Hall in 1863.

Royal Parade was the last extensive site to be re-built in Blackheath Village until the post-war (1939-45) developments by local authorities, with the exception of the redevelopment in 1937 of the old Blackheath Proprietary School. Even these last works tended to be on open land or areas of bombed housing and did not involve large scale demolition.

The motivation behind the development of Royal Parade must have been to capture some of the growing volume of business which Blackheath retailers were handling by the 1860s. So great was this trade, that Greenwich shopkeepers were alarmed at the decline in their own turnover and a number either moved to Blackheath or opened branches in the Village. But it seems apparent that Royal Parade was not the hoped-for success. Whilst the builder covered his costs and Whittaker disposed of leases almost as soon as the scaffolding was down, the indications are that the high class shopping boom was over - for Blackheath, at least. The growth of commercial centres in the suburbs of Lee Green, Old Dover Road and the Lewisham High Street meant that there were rival claimants for the housekeeping moneys which had traditionally been spent in Blackheath Village. Furthermore, many of the London stores were expanding their territory outwards, offering inducements and daily deliveries to account customers, particularly the type of customer who lived in the large villas of Blackheath and supported households of 10 or 15 persons including three or four servants.

The Montpelier Vale section of Royal Parade - it was re-numbered in 1903 as 37-49 Montpelier Vale - was more successful initially than the section facing the Heath, possible because a sizeable proportion of the local shopping population could see it as they walked to and from their houses in The Paragon, Shooters Hill Road and the then newly built Vanbrugh Park. Even so, it was a struggle and although some of the shops kept to specific trades for quite long periods the turnover in proprietors was much greater in this area than elsewhere in the Village.

1 Royal Parade (37 Montpelier Vale)

This was a grocery and wine shop for more than 100 years, although its first tenant was Alfred Richardson, an auctioneer and estate agent who may have been given the task of finding lessees for Whittaker's investment. By 1870 the tenant here was Titus Wray, a wine merchant and grocer and possibly a relative of Alfred Wray, the bookseller at 9 Tranquil Vale until 1872. Titus Wray's business passed to a T.B. Young for a brief period but the shop was taken over by William Henry Pettengell (1829-1899) in 1874. Pettengell was the first grocer to establish a branch at 24 Tranquil Vale - a tradition which continued on and off until 1947. In 1885 and 1886 the Royal Parade shop was held by Douglas Bean but in the following year it was a branch of the Thorpe Bros. business and named Parade Stores, allied to the shop at 24 Tranquil Vale which was then called the South East Stores. More detail concerning the Thorpe family will be found in Chapter 5 and for the reasons described there the Thorpe's shop at Royal Parade was taken for three years from 1892 by Ernest Turner. In that brief time

Turner established himself as a retailer to be treated with respect as well as custom. He expanded his trade rapidly and took on leases for Nos. 4 & 5 Royal Parade - as it proved for not much more than 18 months - the former to sell hardware and the latter for fruit and vegetables. Turner spent a fortune on promoting his business, with full-page advertisements of lengthy copy going beyond simple announcements of goods for sale and expounding his views on food quality, Blackheath people, and quoting the comments of his customers. In 1894 he was particularly proud that he had sold two and a half tons of his home-made marmalade in a month and the newspaper readers must have wondered if Blackheath people ate anything else for their breakfasts.

Turner's success, although short-lived, for over-exertion brought on ill-health and he retired in 1895, was probably based on cash customers, low profit margins and very tight credit. He purchased in bulk and sold in large lots - the marmalade was retailed in seven pound jars for example. His successors at Royal Parade, H. W. Baynes-Smith from 1895 to 1897 and Henry Knapp from 1897 to 1899 kept the name Modern Supply Stores, but clearly lacked Turner's enterprise and drive. In December 1899 the Royal Parade shop split from 24 Tranquil Vale and both premises were leased by established companies who, thereafter, traded with a greater degree of continuity than before.

No. 1 Royal Parade was leased by William H. Cullen & Co., as their branch No. 50. Cullen's grocery empire had been founded in 1876 and had grown rapidly, taking over ailing groceries and bringing modern management techniques and the benefit of bulk buying in order to cut overheads. Cullens were certainly more successful here than the previous lessees and remained (for many years in the capable hands of branch manager George Goldring) until 1947 when they moved to their present address at 24 Tranquil Vale, taking over Dannatt's lease and thus re-establishing a link with that shop.

Cullens were succeeded at Montpelier Vale by Lovibond's, the Greenwich brewer and wine merchant which had been founded in 1826, but when Lovibond's sold out in 1965 to the London Rubber Co. Ltd., then diversifying their trading interests, the shop became a branch of Wineways. This venture was not wholly successful despite an aggressively modern marketing technique and by 1970 the shop had been converted into offices for Falconwood Estates Ltd., thus ending the 100 year span during which this shop sold wine.

2 Royal Parade (39 Montpelier Vale)

This shop started its retail life as a grocery under the proprietership of Ferdinando Martin Briggs with the offices of the Blackheath Domestic Registry at the rear or in upstairs rooms. But in 1871 the whole premises were taken by Benjamin Giles (1834-1901) a hot water and sanitary engineer. The shop sold the usual ironmongery but Giles specialised in other trades, including bell-hanging, and patented a number of lavatory cisterns and sewer pipe schemes. He even managed to obtain the approbation of some distinguished householders in Vanbrugh Park and used this in his advertisements for a patent sanitary system which vented noxious sewer gases over the roof tops of the houses in which it was fitted.

His business passed on his death to John Peter Power (1865-1912) in whose family it stayed until the early 1920s. It was then conducted for a year or two by Ralph Alan Jackman, the son of Lambert Jackman, the managing foreman for the Cator Estate, but in 1927 the Royal Parade shop became a chemist's shop, initially owned by Douglas S. Mitchell MPS, FCS, but through various proprietors until well after the last war. In the 1950s the shop was converted into a motor showroom and has remained in this use ever since.

3 Royal Parade (41 Montpelier Vale)

There have been four quite different trades here: drapery, bootmaking, a toyshop and a restaurant. Its first tenant was Elizabeth Ann Keell & Sons, drapers, who had taken the premises in September 1865, although the shop was used as a repository for about 18 months before that. By 1871 the sole proprietor was William Ealing Keell (b. 1832) who shortly afterwards assigned the lease to George Taylor, a bootmaker. Taylor's business was taken over by 1878 by John Chinneck who remained here until 1883. In 1885 the trade changed back to drapery and this line was carried on by a number of proprietors up until the last war, the last from about 1922 to 1945 being "Pamela", a dress shop.

In 1946 the shop was opened by Mr. and Mrs. Keith Mackenzie as Raggity Anns, "the new toyshop", who remained here until 1950 in which year the business moved to 26 Tranquil Vale. The trade pattern then changed once more, this time to food, when P.I. Dexter re-fitted the shop and, in December 1950, opened the Silver Horseshoe Restaurant. No. 41 Montpelier Vale has remained a restaurant ever since although changing proprietors. In 1969 it was acquired by the owners of La Goulue at 17 Montpelier Vale who converted it into a bistro-style restaurant of the type then popular. In 1975 fashion dictated a change and it was renamed The Gatsby Room and redecorated in a style reminiscent of the 1920s.

4 Royal Parade (43 Montpelier Vale)

This shop started as a china and glasswarehouse under the proprietorship of Francis Burdett (1827-1892) whose business flourished, and he remained trading here until 1890. When Francis retired his son moved the contents of the shop to 32 Tranquil Vale and the Royal Parade premises stood empty until 1894 when they were used by Ernest Turner of 1 Royal Parade as a department for brooms and buckets and other hardware until 1895 when Turner retired from business. Once more 4 Royal Parade was empty but in January 1900 it was re-fitted as a drapery shop, titled Wemyss house, by William Eve. Eve had worked for Thomas Whittaker at 5 & 7 Tranquil Vale but had set up a business of his own in 1886 at 46 Tranquil Vale; he spent the last few years of his life at Royal Parade, retiring in 1902. By curious chance the stock of Eve's business was bought out in July 1903 by Messrs Whittaker & Brown, the successors to Thomas Whittaker, Eve's old employer.

The closure of Wemyss House proved timely for Burnside, the stationer at 20 Tranquil Vale who had to seek temporary premises during the re-building of his old shop as part of Highland Mansions. He took a short lease on 43 Montpelier Vale and refitted the shop as a booksellers and stationers so as to secure some continuity in business. Whether this effort was justified we do not know but it may have caused the financial problems which led to Willam Burnside's suicide in 1903. When Burnside's returned to Highland Mansions the temporary premises at Royal Parade were taken by another wandering trader - this time a Mr. Newton, one-time secretary and catering manager for Stephen Jobbins at 7 & 9 Blackheath Village (q. v.). Newton had been declared redundant during a period of recession and Jobbins had decided to involve himself more closely with the day-to-day work of his, by now, expanding company. Newton set himself up in competition at 43 Montpelier Vale, opening a café in November 1904, adding the upper rooms above No. 45 as an extension and even opening a "roof garden" above the shop frontage the following year - almost exactly what Jobbins had done at 7 & 9 Blackheath Village a few years earlier. But, unlike Jobbins', Newton's venture did not last and the business closed in 1907 or 1908.

For some years afterwards the Royal Parade shop stood empty although a childrens' clothes business flourished there in the early 1920s. By 1927 it had re-opened as a restaurant once more, this time as The Cake Shop under the proprietorship of Miss E. Davies who kept the business going until well after the last war. By the 1950s the business had changed to cater for the growing do-it-yourself market and traded as Woodcraft under the proprietorship of Mr. R. H. Milne until his retirement in 1975. For more than 20 years Mr. & Mrs. Milne and their staff must have influenced the progress of many owner-restored houses in Blackheath.

5 Royal Parade (45 Montpelier Vale)

These premises have principally been occupied by milliners and greengrocers but started with a mixed tenancy. From 1866-1870 Balfern Bros., dyers and cleaners, operated from this address although the principal retail tenant was usually a milliner, initially Miss F. Colville and, by 1869, Mrs. Caldicott and her family who made straw hats. In 1874 the shop was in the hands of one R. Slagg, a general draper but by 1878 the business had passed to George Gray who remained here until 1883. Briefly, in the late 1880s, it was the retail premises of M. Page, a bootmaker, but after a long period when it was empty it finally re-opened in 1893 as a branch of Ernest Turner's company (see 1 Royal Parade) for the sale of greengrocery. In December 1894 the business was sold to Dight & Co. ("of the West End") but in 1898 the lease was acquired by Walter W. Wood (1863-1925), a greengrocer who specialised in local produce mostly from Kidbrooke Farm, Manor Farm at Horn Park and Shroffields Farm on the Shooters Hill Road. Wood remained in business here until 1913 when he transferred to 34 Tranquil Vale. During much of the Great War the shop remained unused but by the 1920s it was operating once more as a greengrocery, the Montpelier Fruit Stores, one of the shops owned by Henry Leon Samuell (1888-1944) who also traded at 17 Tranquil Vale from 1937 to 1944 and from a small shop tucked into the south portico of Blackheath Station. After Samuell's death the Royal Parade shop continued to sell greengrocery but was eventually to be turned into a motor caravan showroom allied to the business at 2 Royal Parade. It is now a furniture shop.

6 Royal Parade (47 Montpelier Vale)

Although 47 Montpelier Vale was leased as a shop and works by Robert
Payne, a brushmaker, it was taken over early in 1869 by George Sowter,
a chemist from Duffield, and stayed in this trade until 1916. Sowter's
business was acquired by Edward Francis Froyd by 1874 but within the
year had passed to John Polley who combined the dispensing of medicine
with the supply of alcoholic beverages (for which he had to apply for a
licence) as the agent for Messrs Gilbeys. In 1881 the shop was taken over
by Daniel Charles Cadman MPS (d. 1898) who added George Howard's pharmacy at 20 Delacourt Road to his company in 1887. After Cadman's death
the business was continued by his family but in November 1912 all the
Cadman shops were acquired by John H. Bailey who, by then, had another
shop at 61 Old Dover Road. Bailey stayed at Royal Parade until 1916,
although the running of the business here was in the hands of J. H. Fletcher
MPS, DBOA, but closed the Blackheath branch in that year. In 1920 part
of the premises (47a) had been taken as a studio by Miss Hattie Hancock,
a photographer and, although she stayed until the last war, the main shop
had a number of tenants, including the Blackheath Kennel until 1936 and,
by 1937, Knight and Anderson, hairdressers, whose successors remained
here until the 1970s. The present tenant, The Villager, sells what the
Victorians would have called fancy goods.

7 Royal Parade (49 Montpelier Vale)

The corner shop of Royal Parade, seemingly a key site for a retailer, has
not, in fact, stayed in any one trade although the lengths of tenure have
been considerable. Until the 1970s the shop was occupied by service trades
rather than retailers relying on casual customers. The first occupier was
Frederick William Cash (1826-1897), a furnishing ironmonger and bell-
hanger who kept a small factory in Royal Parade Mews. On Cash's
retirement in 1891 the whole business passed to Luck & Co., ironmongers
who were trading at 10 Delacourt Road. Luck stayed in the Village until
1901 and by the following year the Royal Parade shop had been converted
into a café-restaurant by a London-based Italian company, A. Conceprio
& Son, in whose hands it stayed for the next eight or nine years.
    With the outbreak of the Great War the shop was trading as the St. Peter's
Motor Works and Garage - by the end of the war its name had changed
to the Blackheath Motor Works although by June 1919 this had changed
again to the Montpelier Motor Works. The company left Royal Parade in
1928 when they opened a service and filling station at 6 Stratheden Road,
which still operates in the hands of their successors.
    The next tenant could not have been more different - Mr. D'arcy Denny's
Health Food Stores. Denny (d. 1947) called himself a psycho-dietist. The
son of William Evans Denny who had purchased 44 Granville Park in 1874
and whose daughters conducted a school there for many years, he named
his shop The Cabin and traded there until the last war. Blackheath people
were probably no more or less interested in health foods than any other
middleclass townspeople in England at the time but Denny's shop would
have been encouraged by the presence of the nationally-known maternity
home Stonefield in Kidbrooke Grove, which was run on vegetarian lines.

After the 1939-1945 war 49 Montpelier Vale reverted to the motoring trade when it became the workshops for R.H. Harris, automobile and electrical engineers; towards the end of the 1960s the pattern of trade switched from batteries to car tyres (Watling Tyre Service) but on the departure of the latter to Lee High Road in 1972 the Royal Parade shop was refitted as a showroom for pine furniture.

THE HEATH FRONTAGE

In the renumbering order of 1903 the LCC retained the original house numbers for that section of Royal Parade facing the Heath - Nos. 8-16 inclusive.

This terrace, whilst providing much needed housing for the shopkeepers or their sub-tenants, proved less profitable commercially and it was soon clear that the service trades, relying to a lesser extent on the casual shopper than other forms of retailing, survived longest.

There were exceptions of course, but these mostly relate to the period before 1900. The difficulty for shopkeepers in this section of Royal Parade was that it was not a route for pedestrians passing through the Village. On holidays, when the Heath was crowded, trade would be attracted, but otherwise, with no houses nearer than Blackheath Vale and Grotes Place and out of sight for shoppers in Tranquil and Montpelier Vale it was a melancholy fact that a shop here had to offer a unique service in order to do well, and this kept shop rents low. There was the additional advantage that the shopkeeper or his manager could live on the premises or sub-let the upper rooms to ensure a regular income. The commercial value of Royal Parade was small, as demonstrated when the whole terrace was sold to Whittaker's executors in 1923 for only £1600.

8 Royal Parade

This shop, at the east end of the terrace and probably the least commercially attractive was occupied by milliners from 1862, firstly by Mrs. Ann Stephenson and, from 1884, by Mrs. Elizabeth Butler Willis. In 1891 the lease was granted to James Davies, a hairdresser who had traded from 1 Tranquil Passage. At the end of his term in 1894 he was unwilling to move and the landlord was forced to seek a possession order. Over the turn of the 19th/20th century the shop was occupied by Alfred Pairpoint, an antique dealer whose son, Neville, exhibited at the Summer Exhibition of the Royal Academy in 1904. From 1909 to 1917 the shop became a servants' registry passing through various proprietors including, from 1914 to 1918, Mrs. E. Gordon Williams. The principal use thereafter was as a bookshop, owned firstly by H. Gray & Co. and, from 1935, Miss L. Mears. In recent years the shop has been a branch of Jay-Cee Glazing (at 14 Royal Parade) and, since 1974, a branch of the arts and crafts shop at No. 9 Royal Parade.

9 Royal Parade

This shop started in 1861 as an office for Charles and George Frederick Wenborn, land agents whose successors were active in Blackheath and Kidbrooke as late as the early 1900s. Thereafter, 9 Royal Parade was used as a greengrocery, stationers and toy shop until the mid 1880s when it was taken by Samuel John Barlow (d. 1913), a trunk and luggage maker who advertised his wares in the local newspaper with a series of carefully-engraved pictures of suit cases, trunks, portmanteaux and brass-bound boxes. Barlow left Royal Parade in 1893 and the shop remained empty until 1899 when it was leased by Frederick Knowler, a saddler and harness maker who worked here until he moved to 16 Royal Parade in 1907. He was followed at No. 9 by Hylton Cock, an antique dealer who had been educated at the Blackheath Proprietary School and enjoyed some skill as a sketch artist. As such he was employed by Village shopkeepers to design advertisements for them and his work appeared in this form for many years in the Blackheath Local Guide and District Advertiser. He filled his own advertisements with small vignettes of the type of antique and curio he wished to buy, but these drawings were quite poor compared with those commissioned by his fellow tradesmen. Cock left Royal Parade in 1911 and the shop seems to have lacked a retail purpose until about 1922 when the premises were taken by the first of a series of electrical engineers who worked from here until 1965: the first was M. D. Boddy until c1926; in 1927 the business was run by Charles Henry Petitt and, after 1934, by his widow Mrs. F. Petitt until 1946. When she retired, the shop was transferred to Alec Schofield who traded here until 1965. Thereafter the shop became an art gallery (The Wren Gallery, run by Paul Branson) but since 1973 has been an arts and crafts business.

10 Royal Parade

For more than 70 years the business conducted here was a ladies and childrens outfitters, opened initially by Mrs. Esther Terry in 1862. By 1865 the shop and stock had been taken over by William Henderson Jones (1839-1884) who named the premises Alexandra House. On his death, the business was continued by his widow, Lydia, and afterwards by his children until 1932. From 1933 until the last war the shop was occupied by Mrs. Margaret Stephens, an artist, but except for a brief spell as "Number Ten", an art gallery, there had been no retailer here for many years, although at the time of writing the shop had been totally refitted as a Turkish restaurant, the Köy Lokanta.

11 Royal Parade

In 1862 Mrs. Ellen Spence, a hairdresser from Nelson Street, Greenwich, transferred her business to this shop. Sometimes styled The Blackheath Toilet Club it remained in her hands until 1875 when the name of Eugene Unwin ("late 24 Piccadilly") appears at this address as proprietor until 1877. He was followed, briefly, by John Thomas Shayler, a milliner, and he, from 1880 to 1888 by George Rhodes, a dairyman. Rhodes was probably the father of William and Jesse Rhodes who owned the Queen's Park Dairy at 9 Lee Road between 1890 and 1895. From 1891 to 1895 the Royal Parade shop was George Lane's Berlin wool warehouse and F. W. Cooney's provision shop, but in 1895 the trade changed and until the mid-1950s was run as a cycle works, firstly by John S. Bell until 1912 and then by Arthur Simmonds through to the last war. In 1948 the business was in the hands of E. S. Dale. By the 1960s the shop was selling glass ware.

12 Royal Parade

Although the first tenant of No. 12 was a plumber, Nathaniel Vaughan, he may simply have been here in a caretaking capacity because, by 1865 the shop was run as a Berlin wool repository by Miss Kezia Saunders. In 1869 the business was taken over by Sarah Ann Knowles who remained here at least until 1888. For a couple of years afterwards the shop was used by Ingle Golding as an upholstery works but by 1895 the trade had gone back to something nearer its previous use, and became Mrs. S. Johnson's millinery shop. In 1903 the business passed to Miss Louisa E. Francis (1878-1954) and stayed in the family, latterly with Ethel Francis until 1964. In the 1970s the business became a dress shop, trading under the name Collards.

13 Royal Parade

This shop started its life as a boot and shoe warehouse and stayed with this trade until the early 1950s. The first owner was Charles Squire Cross but by 1866 the business had been taken over by Alfred Baldry (1838-1910) who had settled in Blackheath in 1856 to set up a shoe making business. He worked at Royal Parade until his death upon which the shop was sold to Colbert Hartley Philpot (1876-1931), who boasted three generations of cordwainers and shoemakers on both sides of his family. Philpot worked here until 1931 although the business continued under the direction of his wife, Mrs. Clara Ellen Philpot until she died in 1953 aged 75. The shop then became a music store, principally selling gramaphone records, in which use it remains today.

14 Royal Parade

No. 14 was, traditionally, a bakery and from the outset and until 1892 in the hands of a succession of bakers and confectioners led by the Morson family until 1880 but followed in rapid succession at one or two year intervals by James Baker, George Pettifer, Miss Emily Alice Ford and lastly Thomas Brooks. In 1896 the dairymen left and the shop was used by John Waddell & Son, coal merchants, as an order office and by Arthur King, a tailor. The shop as such remained unused from about 1905 to the end of the Great War, not re-opening until the early 1920s as the first premises of The New Argosy, a picture framing and art materials enterprise run by Frederick C. Colman. The art supplies side of the business moved to 32 Montpelier Vale (q.v.) in 1937 and by 1949 the picture framing department at 14 Royal Parade was taken over by J. Calveley, trading as Jay-Cee Glass and Glazing Ltd., which firm has remained here ever since.

15 Royal Parade

This shop started its retail life as a combination of dairy and pork butcher's shop and remained in these trades up until the last war. The first tenant was John Polley, the father of John Polley jnr, who traded as a dispensing chemist at 47 Montpelier Vale (q. v.) in 1875. Polley snr, who must have been near the end of his working life - he was born in 1811 - sold the business to William Prescot Gurney before 1878 although by the following year the shop was known as the Alderney Dairy and was in the hands of F. Edwards. Edwards and, subsequently, his widow, Clara, stayed here until c1910. By 1912 the shop was taken by John Pallett, a butcher. There seems to be no record of a commercial tenant here from 1915 to 1923 but in 1924 the shop had been re-opened as a dairy once again, this time by Leonard Frederick Clarke, his brothers and their sons. The Clarke dairy traded successfully until the beginning of the last war when it was absorbed by The Express Dairy Company mainly because the government of the day encouraged the retail dairies to consolidate manpower and cut back on wasteful competitive milk rounds. As a result the Express and the United Dairies swallowed up many of the small local dairy companies and then carved London into various sections over which one or other would have the retailing monopoly on door-to-door deliveries. The Clarke family had achieved no small distinction in the Village by fielding a team of cricketers (all named Clarke) and they regularly played matches against local clubs and against Malcolm Christopherson's eleven (mostly called Christopherson).

After the 1939-1945 war the old dairy lost its separate identity and was converted with 16 Royal Parade into a single shop.

16 Royal Parade

Although 16 Royal Parade was a corner shop it was, in fact, quite small, with most of the building more suitable for workshops and domestic accommodation. From the outset the building was the premises of Edward Smith Earl, an upholsterer by trade, whose business as a furniture remover soon took precedent over his other activities. He had started his trading activities in Blackheath at 59 Tranquil Vale as a music dealer with William Drewett. They moved to 26 Tranquil Vale but the partnership dissolved and Earl traded from various addresses thereafter. Earl also leased some of the stabling and workshops in Royal Parade Mews as a repository and called his business The Blackheath Pantechnicon. Although Earl was joined by his son in 1878 the business did not continue long after Edward's retirement in 1897 at the age of 78, for, by February 1899, the whole business was advertised for disposal and it was purchased by Ebenezer Smith of 43 Tranquil Vale (q. v.). Smith took on only the repository buildings in the Mews and the shop was re-opened by the end of 1899 by the Royal Victoria Cycle Co. By 1907 the bicycles had gone and the shop had been leased by Frederick Knowler, the saddler who had previously worked from No. 9 Royal Parade. He remained until the onset of the Great War but until the early 1920s the shop was not used as such until it was taken by R. Carter & Sons Ltd., builders.

No. 16 Royal Parade returned to retail use after the last war as Deeprose Bros., motor cycle dealers, but in recent years it has been run by Deron Products Ltd. as a hardware store.

Note: 17 Royal Parade (Christy's) is dealt with as part of Highland House in Chapter 11.

3   Montpelier Vale (east)

Montpelier Vale presently can be divided into three distinct sections all of
which enjoy this appellation for administrative convenience rather than
because the buildings on either side of the road had any particular cohesion
in their development.

The west side, which starts at the apex of the central triangle of the
Village and ends at the corner of Royal Parade, falls well within the boundary of the parish of Lewisham, the Manor of Lewisham and the old Dartmouth estate. The history of the east side is more complex in that much
was part of the Page estate and only the section from Nos. 12 to 36 was
eventually conveyed to the Cators in the late 19th century; the site of Nos.
2 to 10 remained with Page's successors.

There are further complications in that Page and, subsequently, John
Cator encroached into Dartmouth land when they fenced or granted leases
for the development of the east side of Montpelier Vale. The strip of land
involved was small in width but it was enough to force Page and Cator to
negotiate separate leases on behalf of themselves and their lessees.

The west side of Montpelier Vale is dealt with in the chapter following;
the south east part of the road, Nos. 2-10 Montpelier Vale, is covered in
Chapter 5: Osborne Place.

The present buildings and back lands on the north east section of Montpelier
Vale stand on the site of the houses and gardens which were known to exist
as far back as the 17th century when the Wricklemarsh estate was held by
John Morden. The northern end may have been the site of a house called
The Six Chimneys. This property was in the tenure of a John Clowser as
early as 1710. John Clowser was a yeoman farmer, and the Charlton Parish
churchwarden's account books show that he held some of Lady Morden's land
from at least 1710 to 1718. In 1720 the same land charge is being paid by
Richardson Headly, who married Clowser's daughter, and it can be presumed
that Clowser died about 1719 and that his son-in-law took over the tenancy.
When Gregory Page purchased Wricklemarsh from Lady Morden's executors
he took on the responsibility for paying the land taxes so it is not possible
to be sure of his agricultural tenants during his ownership of the estate
which then bounded on Montpelier Vale.

South of The Six Chimneys, roughly on the site of 12 Montpelier Vale,
was Edward Sadler's house, and this property, like the Six Chimneys, was
in existence by 1710.

By 1800 the Land Tax returns support the existence of eight to ten houses
of various sizes probably clustered at the top of Montpelier Vale in a small
hamlet. It is not possible to be sure who then lived at the largest property
on the Six Chimneys plot although it may have been Henry and Edward
Ledger. Sadler's house was by then the home of Thomas Felstead and long
after the house was demolished for 12 Montpelier Vale the garden ground
(Which was not built over until 1839-40) was listed in the tax returns as Mr.
Felstead's garden.

The most accurate piece of information to survive concerning the occupiers of this part of Blackheath Village can be found in the Dartmouth Estate lease books. This records a lease dated June 1809 for an encroachment on the north east side of Montpelier Vale granted by the Earl of Dartmouth to Thomas Poynder and William Tunnard for a period of 61 years from 29 September 1800 at 2/6d a year. It is unlikely that Poynder and Tunnard would have leased a thin strip of land in isolation and it can be assumed that they had been granted a similar lease for the sites fronting Montpelier Vale held by Sir Gregory Page Turner. Furthermore, the Dartmouth lease refers to "all buildings and improvements that shall or may at any time hereafter during the term be erected and built thereon."

The tithe schedules of 1845 show that Sir Gregory Page Turner was the freeholder of the buildings facing Montpelier Vale, and John Cator owned the group of cottages known as Bath Place (q.v.) at the rear.

The Dartmouth family granted further leases and renewals on the encroachment, the most recent being in 1894 and 1915 and the Page-Turner trustees had sold their interest in Nos. 16-32 Montpelier Vale to the Cator Estate by 1894.

The author is driven to the conclusion that Poynder and Tunnard were granted building or re-development leases for the north east section of Montpelier Vale by Sir Gregory Page-Turner sometime between 1800 and 1809 but with the lack of any record surviving of the Page estate transactions this must remain conjecture. That there were houses on the site before 1800 is proved by the Land Tax Returns of 1780 to 1810 but it is certainly safe to assume that no trace of these buildings now survives except perhaps at foundation level.

The present buildings numbered 12 to 36 Montpelier Vale have all been rebuilt at various times during the 19th century and Nos. 12-18 were totally rebuilt after the 1939-1945 war. But, of the remaining shops there are clearly traces of the early 19th century structures and in Nos. 20 and 22 we may be able to see a building erected c1809 as the result of the lease granted to Poynder and Tunnard.

The rear elevations of the entire group were rebuilt after the extensive damage caused by the rocket bomb on the Wesleyan chapel in Blackheath Grove in March 1945.

It is difficult to be precise in naming the tenants of the individual properties before 1830 as no rate books exist and the Land Tax Returns give the names of the person who paid the tax and not, necessarily, the tenant. In many cases the taxpayer listed was long dead and clearly the money was being paid out of his estate by his executors.

Further, because most of the buildings were erected as private houses the tenants do not appear in the commercial directories except as living in "Blackheath" or, at best, "Montpelier Vale, Blackheath", for the name had been established well before 1802.

The present numbering dates from 1886; before that the houses were numbered from 1-12, starting at the north end, thus the present 36 Montpelier Vale was No. 1 and the present No. 12 was then No. 12, a happy coincidence which has made the task of matching tenants to premises less difficult than for some of the Village streets.

12 Montpelier Vale

This building replaced a war-damaged shop in the 1950s. The original shop was a two storey brick building probably erected in 1800-1801 on the front garden ground of Edward Sadler's house. By 1801 the property was in occupation of Thomas Watson, a butcher from Leicester, and this may prove that 12 Montpelier Vale is one of the oldest shop sites in the Village which we can establish with any certainty, other than the public houses.

Little is known of Thomas Watson but by 1815 the business seems to have passed to his son James Watson (1788-1867) who remained here until 1853, having negotiated a new lease for 99 years in 1836. James married Margaret (also known as Mary, 1790-1841), daughter of another early Blackheath shopkeeper, Robert Dalton of Phoenix Place, now 25 Montpelier Vale (q.v.). Watson's shop, as was common in those days and into the early years of this century, boasted a slaughter house and the passageway for cattle is still defined by a service entrance between Nos. 10 and 12 Montpelier Vale.

James Watson gave up his business between 1853 and 1854, possibly on retirement, and the shop passed to William Parsons of Deal, Kent, who, despite much local competition at the time saw his business prosper. By 1861 he was employing six staff and eventually built a two storey addition to his premises which later took the number 14 Montpelier Vale. When William Parsons died in 1891 at the age of 72 he had spent more than 37 years in business in Blackheath and was so much respected that the village tradesmen closed their shops on the day of his funeral as a mark of respect. Parson's son, Bernard William Parsons (1847-1926), not only continued his father's business in Blackheath but set about building up a chain of butcher's shops, reaching 100 shops by 1914 and becoming one of the largest multiple butchers in the country at that time. The Blackheath shop was left in the capable hands of the manager, William Baker, who joined Parsons in 1905 and remained working in the shop until 1949 when he retired at the age of 91.

Nos. 12 and 14 Montpelier Vale were so badly damaged in the last war that, after temporary repairs, it was decided to totally rebuild and this was completed by the early 1950s to the designs of W. Braxton Sinclair ARIBA, in the style of the nearby surviving terrace. Sinclair took advantage of the site to build three storeys high, more than doubling the usable space but without compromising the architectural character of Montpelier Vale.

One result of the war was a decline in the fortunes of the Parson's empire, and in 1962 the company merged with Messrs Matthews, an Epsom-based company and now one of the largest retail butchers in the UK. But even today the link with Parsons of Blackheath is not lost - one of Bernard Parsons' grandsons works for the parent company and Mr. Dutnall, manager of 12 Montpelier Vale since 1951, was still in charge of the Blackheath branch in 1976.

14 Montpelier Vale

The original shop on this site was, in fact, a small two storey addition to No. 12, probably built by William Parsons before 1886, and used as a residence, latterly for his widow, Sarah Ann, who died in 1904. After Mrs. Parsons' death, the house was converted into a shop and from 1906 was used by a variety of trades from fishmongers, through umbrella makers, insurance brokers, art dealers and motor engineers. From the mid 1930s until it was damaged in the war, 14 Montpelier Vale was used by Doric Motors as a car showroom and was owned by Capt. C. F. Bird, FCA, who moved his business to Rotherfield, Sussex in October 1939.

16 Montpelier Vale (was 11 Montpelier Vale)

This shop, which was rebuilt with No. 18 in 1963, may date back to the late 18th century when a Mr. Henry Couchman paid land tax for a sizeable property on or close to the site. Couchman was a builder and resident here as early as 1799. By 1809 he is listed in commercial directories as trading with a Mr. Abraham Ansell in Montpelier Vale. Further, there is no doubt that Henry's son William Couchman was in business as a carpenter and upholsterer from 1826 to 1832 in the shop which survived until 1945. Members of the Couchman family traded here continuously until 1899, claiming in their advertisements that they were the oldest firm in Black-heath having been established in 1790. In fact the Couchmans were a unifying link in a series of partnerships which pursued the allied trades of building, carpentry, upholstery, decorating and, by 1838, undertaking. In 1802 it was Couchman & Cuthbert; 1809, Ansell & Couchman; 1826-1832, William Couchman; 1838-1860, Henry Couchman (b. 1811) who employed 19 hands; from 1861 to 1869 it was Couchman & James Hampshire, then aged 24; in 1870 the company was in the hands of James Gunton Couchman, an upholsterer, although from at least 1874 and until the turn of the century Couchman & Co. offered the full range of house building and decorating skills. By 1905 the Couchman family united with Messrs Blow, another Blackheath building firm whose origins were almost as time-honoured in that the Blows had traded as carpenters and builders in Blackheath Vale in the early 1800s. With the death of Catherine Couchman in 1911 aged 64, the only daughter of Henry Couchman (fl. 1838-1860), the business passed entirely to E. F. Blow & Co.

With the rebuilding of Nos. 16 & 18 Montpelier Vale in 1963 the company was wound up and what had been Blackheath's oldest business ceased to exist, although by the 1930s it had passed to G. Martin, later to his widow, and had long ceased to have connection with either Couchman or Blow by name.

The new shops were leased from the outset by Messrs Lyons, the food company, trading as the London Steak House. They opened the Blackheath branch in August 1963 and fed allcomers for the first three days entirely free. This policy seems to have paid off, for the Steak House remains to this day.

18 Montpelier Vale (was 10 Montpelier Vale)

This was a small two-storey building, used by 1826 as a greengrocery by William Moore. By 1851 the trade had changed and it was occupied by Mary Ward, a hosier and linen draper, and it stayed in this use until 1881; Mary Ward was followed in 1855 by Thomas Pilkington but from 1857 to 1874 the proprietor was William Peploe. In 1880 the business was taken over by Thomas Hale, the silk mercer and linen draper who traded from 32 Montpelier Vale from at least 1869 to 1899, probably to acquire some extra stock at bargain prices. In 1882 No. 18 was leased by Luther Norman, a bootmaker who had started his business at Collins Street and South Vale

Road. Luther (1846-1930), and his son Edward traded here until 1914 but transferred their interest to a branch shop at Westcombe Hill thereafter.

After the Great War 18 Montpelier Vale became a sweet shop, principally in the hands of Arthur M. Seear. In 1958 the lease expired and it was embraced with No. 16 and re-built as part of the London Steak House.

20 Montpelier Vale (was 9 Montpelier Vale)

This was almost certainly built as a private house and was not occupied by tradesmen until 1841 when it was held by Edward Moore, a shoemaker. After Moore there is a gap in the record and it is not until 1849 that we can be certain that the lessee was Joseph Henry Taylor, a shoemaker, born in 1820. Taylor was trading in Tranquil Vale in 1847 but remained at 20 Montpelier Vale until 1852. His son, also Joseph Henry, ran a business at 6 Montpelier Vale from 1878 and details of the family will be found under that heading.

Taylor was replaced in 1854 by Arthur John Spackman, an oil and colour man who described his shop as an Italian warehouse, which meant he should have sold olive oil, spaghetti and other Italian foods, but it is more likely as an oil and colour man that he concentrated on lamp oil, soap and paint, which cannot have pleased the Eastmure Brothers next door at 22 Montpelier Vale, who sold the same type of goods. Spackman's business was taken over from 1895 to 1901 by Goater & Co. of 26 Montpelier Vale. In 1904, and for the next 11 years, the shop was owned by Harry Summers who maintained the oil side of the business. It passed in April 1915 to the Bond family who called the shop the Blackheath Oil and Domestic Stores and remained here until 1936.

In 1937 the shop was re-opened as a radio and electrical dealers by Roland Hopwood, one time radio manager for Morley & Son, the piano and music dealers at 23 Tranquil Vale. This was an amicable arrangement because Morley's found that more and more space in their shop was being taken up with radios and gramaphones. Hopwood's business did not survive the war and during the post war years No. 20 Montpelier Vale has been occupied by confectioners or used, as at present, as a dress shop.

22 & 24 Montpelier Vale (were 8 & 9 Montpelier Vale)

It is not unlikely that 22 and 24 Montpelier Vale were originally built as one house, with the front door on the right, and that it was one of a pair with the present Nos. 26 & 28. But so many alterations have been made, especially since the last war, that it is not possible to arrive at firm conclusions from superficial architectural evidence. For example, the house frontage of 24 Montpelier Vale has had the projecting window and an extra half storey added since the last war, the parapet line was raised and now hides the pitch of the roof, but the alterations have been so well made that it is hard to believe that these premises are not as they were originally built.

No. 22 was originally a double-fronted shop, with trading interests as early as the 1820s when William Church and later his widow Catherine worked from here as plumbers and glaziers. By the mid 1850s the shop had been taken over by the Eastmure Brothers as an oil and colour business but during the years 1860 to 1867 the building may have been turned back into a private house or office because the tenants included Henry Morley, professor of music, later at 23 Tranquil Vale, Frederick Chinner, a schoolmaster and, for a short period Benjamin Octavius Engleheart, the auctioneer and surveyor who had offices at 18 Tranquil Vale until 1863 when he went bankrupt. The fact that he is listed for 22 Montpelier Vale in 1866 and 1867 presumably indicates that he obtained a discharge. By 1869 the shop was in the occupation of Robert Rodwell, a shirt and collar maker, but from 1871 to 1879 had passed to John Steel Knights, a cheesemonger, who advertised for sale the 16½ year unexpired portion of his lease in March 1879.

The man who purchased this lease was the dairy-shop pioneer, George Barham, managing director of the then Express Country Milk Co. Ltd., whose business success had a profound and lasting effect on the retail sale of milk in London.

Barham was the son of Robert Barham (1807-1888) a dairyman who had taken over a shop in The Strand in 1840 and brought to it progressive methods of food shop hygiene for those days. His son, George, although apprenticed in the building trade, started a milk distribution business from a shop off Fetter Lane when he was 22. Alarmed by the impurity of London's milk (most of it came from cows kept in back yards and urban stables) George pioneered the transport of clean, country milk by railway train. The business was helped by the great cattle plague of 1865 when every cow within the city and inner home counties had to be slaughtered. Barham was, by then, transporting milk from as far away as Derby and his attitude towards the cleanliness of his wares was revolutionary.

Although his business expanded in that he supplied hundreds of other retailers by the 1870s, Barham had only one retail outlet, the shop in the Strand, and the head offices, now in Museum Street. His first retail branch dairy was opened in June 1880 at 22 Montpelier Vale principally because Blackheath was a fast-growing and prosperous suburb and there were large farms, at Kidbrooke for example, close to hand. The new dairy was intentionally designed to be the butter and cream factory for the company, and the whole policy paid off. Purpose-built processing and packaging plant was installed in the Wemyss Road depot and 22 Montpelier Vale was, without doubt, the then most up-to-date dairy shop in the country. The pattern established at Blackheath was used, even to the design of the shop fronts, at the other company branches opened later at Hampstead, Muswell Hill and Herne Hill.

The shop in Montpelier Vale was novel and the processing plant, creamery, cheese and butter factory open for public inspection. The Express could boast before the turn of the century that Blackheath had the "most ornate dairy in South East London", and that "...(the) Dairy was probably unequalled for completeness of detail, perfection of sanitary arrangement and general equipment."

The manager of the Blackheath branch, Peter Newbould, must have played an important part in the success of the Express in Blackheath, for when it opened there were many cowkeepers and dairymen in the Village, boasting that their milk was best because it came from local cows and was not transported by rail over long distances. Newbould died in 1898 aged 57 and George Titus Barham (1860-1937), George Barham's son and eventually Chairman of the company, attended the funeral.

Newbould, who lived at 15 Wemyss Road, had entered into the activity

of the Village with enthusiasm. He was instrumental in raising funds for
the erection of the drinking fountain at the top of Tranquil Vale in 1897 to
celebrate Queen Victoria's Diamond Jubilee, and he was able to lend 15
horse-drawn milk floats for Royal Birthday parades, no doubt encouraged
in 1895 by the news that the Express was entitled to add the Royal Warrant
to its livery.

The Express did not acquire No. 24 Montpelier Vale (now integral with
22 Montpelier Vale) until 1899, so that the stone-faced triple-arched
facade, with its cow horn decorations at the top of the pilasters - only
recently and unnecessarily removed - must date from about 1900. No. 24
had been occupied by one Edward Kreckler (1814-1898), the son of John
Jacob Philip Kreckler, a harness maker, who had lived in Blackheath Vale.
Edward pursued the trade of saddler and set up his own business in Blackheath Vale but moved to 24 Montpelier Vale in 1845. He stayed there for
53 years, selling leather work, toys and other knick-knacks. His last
thirty years were spent as a recluse and he suffered the agony of torment
by the small boys of the Village. He made no improvements to his shop
which was described when he died as "one of the oldest in the Village",
and its condition when the Express added it to their premises next door
must have been indescribable.

26 Montpelier Vale (was 6 Montpelier Vale)

This small building was probably a private house until the late 1840s when
it became the premises of Henry Hopkinson, a young grocer and tea dealer.
Hopkinson was joined by Francis Goater in about 1868 and the partnership
traded as family grocers and Italian warehousemen until 1875 when Goater
took over the business entirely. The Goater family, successively William
James and then his widow Lucy Goater, ran the business here until 1911,
bottling their own fish sauce and selling a "Blackheath" blend of Ceylon tea.
The Goater stock and goodwill were acquired in October 1911 by William
A. Orton (1864-1923) whose grocery business at Delacourt Road had made
him one of the most influential businessmen in Blackheath. Nevertheless,
Orton only stayed in Blackheath during the years of the Great War and in
February 1920 the business was sold to John P. Miles (d. 1948) who had
been Orton's branch manager. Miles traded from here until his death although
for the last few years he was in partnership with a Mr. Laing. In 1951 the
Royal Arsenal Cooperative Society took over the shop - the first and only
incursion by the Co-op in Blackheath Village - but in recent years they have
abandoned the groceries and use 26 Montpelier Vale as an off-licence.

28 Montpelier Vale (was 5 Montpelier Vale)

The first commercial tenant of this building was probably John Bailey
Capper, a chemist, who had established his dispensary by the year 1841.
Although the proprietors trading here changed many times the shop stayed
as a chemists and druggists until 1974 - a run of at least 133 years in the
same trade.

Capper was here until 1851 but in 1855 the business was in the hands of
William Thomas Ashwin. In 1859 the shop was re-opened by Thomas
Howard Lavers, a "chymist" who had conducted a business in a shop near
St. Mary's Church in Lewisham from before 1838 and, as was common in

those days, added dentistry to his dispensing skills. The Lavers family stayed in Blackheath until 1896: Thomas was joined by his son, Thomas F. Lavers (1840-1915) who was working for his father as a druggist's assistant in 1861. Lavers jnr developed the dental practice and was advertising in the 1880s and 1890s: "... surgical and mechanical dentistry in all its branches. Teeth stopped, sealed and extracted. Artificial teeth from 5/- a tooth; sets from £3.3s.0d."

Young Lavers retired towards the end of the 19th century and the business passed to a Mr. Bloodworth, very briefly, for he had sold the premises to John Butler Davis by November 1898. Why Bloodworth's stay was so short we don't know but the event was marked by the suicide of his assistant, Guy Castell, who swallowed a bottle of prussic acid almost in the same week as Davis took over. Davis stayed at 28 Montpelier Vale until about 1905 when the business was acquired by the first of a series of partnerships which lasted until 1974. Edward Ellison Grimwade MPS was the senior partner from c1908 until his retirement in 1950; he was joined by Mr. Hayward in 1927 who took Mr. Twyman into partnership in 1950. On the death of Mr. Hayward the business ceased and although attempts were made to sell the shop as a going concern partly to achieve historical continuity, it was a sad fact that independent retail dispensing in a world of multiples was less commercially successful than hitherto. The premises, a charming example of a small mid-Victorian shop, were empty at the time of writing.

30 Montpelier Vale (was 4 Montpelier Vale)

Up to 1945 this shop had sold bread, books, bicycles and watches, and boasts one of the longest recorded tenures as retailers in Montpelier Vale that can be proved with accuracy. By 1826 it was the bakery of one John Hudson although he disappears from the records by 1830 and the baker in residence from at least 1838-1855 was Edward White (1808-1857). After White's death the shop was re-occupied by the Hudson family, this time John G. Hudson (fl. 1808-1861) who, with his brothers George and William (1813-1868), sold their bread until 1868 when the goodwill, equipment, and, no doubt, the lucrative delivery rounds, were acquired by George Frederick Jobbins who was then trading from 21 Montpelier Vale, directly opposite.

Jobbins had no need, then, for further premises and the shop was taken in 1870 by John Charles Sullivan, a bookseller and stationer whose father, also John Charles, had been in a similar business at 5 Phoenix Place (q.v.) from 1862-1869. Sullivan remained at 30 Montpelier Vale for about 12 years; the shop then being taken by R.P. Cornish, a bicycle maker. In December 1892 the trade changed when the premises were leased by Percival Kendall, a watchmaker who had taken over the business conducted by one Carl Schonhardt then at 3 Seagers Cottages (in Lawn Terrace but since demolished) from 1875. Kendall's first shop was at the other end of the Village, at 53 Tranquil Vale; his move to Montpelier Vale was permanent and he remained in business at No. 30 until 1945, only retiring because his shop had been damaged by bomb blast in March of that year.

The front of the shop was subsequently re-built and the interior fitted as a butcher's shop, in which use it has remained, presently in the hands of Messrs John Manson Ltd.

32 Montpelier Vale (was 3 Montpelier Vale)

Unitl 1935 this shop housed a succession of drapers and silk mercers; and from 1937 until 1972 was the much respected and well-patronised New Argosy Gallery. Its subsequent use has not always been so well received and in 1975 the frontage was rendered hideous with magenta paint.

As far back as 1823 a draper traded from here, but it is impossible to be sure of the name until the census of 1841 which records the tenants as Horace and Henry Catt, possibly twins, as both were aged 25. Because of their comparative youth it is doubtful whether they were in occupation much before the late 1830s and they do not appear in the directory of 1838.

By 1851 only Horace Catt was in business here and by 1855 the shop had been acquired by George Buckingham (b. 1825), a widower, and he sold the shop in 1868 to Thomas Hale (1843-1924), then only 25, who established himself as a silk mercer, linen draper and hosier. Although Hale's shop was smaller, he rivalled the business of Thomas Miller Whittaker at 5 & 7 Tranquil Vale and managed, in a competetive trade, to stay in business in Montpelier Vale until 1899. It is his advertisements that boast that his shop had been trading as linen drapers since 1823 and as that date was in living memory at the time, it is likely to be correct.

In July 1900 Hale's business was bought out by Percy Afford, who traded here until 1935.

In the autumn of 1937 the shopfront was completely re-made and opened up so that the window display area was thrown in with the shop floor. For in that year the lease had been acquired by Frederic and Hilda Colman, trading as the New Argosy Gallery. The Colmans already owned an arts and crafts and framing shop at 14 Royal Parade and the new shop at Montpelier Vale gave them greater scope for display and exhibitions. The New Argosy specialised in well-designed glass, china, pottery, wood and metal work and introduced good "modern" design to Blackheath. One of the first exhibitions shown at Montpelier Vale was a collection of photographs compiled by the newly-formed Blackheath Society to illustrate Blackheath's past, its present, and, using illustrations of some developments then taking place in the Village, what the future could hold.

The Colman's interests ranged wide: from Medici Society Christmas Cards to fabrics and furniture imported from Scandinavia and Finland - it was possible in 1940 to buy chairs designed by Alvar Aalto (1898-1976) for as little as 24/- (£1.20) each and small tables for less than £1. Despite the difficulties brought about by the 1939-1945 war, with the inevitable cut-back in imports, the New Argosy survived, although seriously damaged by blast. The new shopfront was more robust and the bow windows inserted at that time while not in architectural harmony with the original building, have proved quite successful.

The Colmans retired in 1960 and the shop passed to S. H. Palmer (d. 1972) who remained proprietor until 1972, although by the mid-1960s the stock was less consciously modern than it had been in Colman's day.

From 1972-1975 32 Montpelier Vale was the shop window for a furniture importers, Ambiance, but in 1975 they ceased trading and the shop was empty for a period. In 1975 Messrs Sargent's, stationers, moved in, remained open for business for no more than three weeks, then shut down, establishing what must be a record in short-period trading for Blackheath Village. It is presently a hairdressing salon.

34 & 36 Montpelier Vale (was 1 & 2 Montpelier Vale)

The present buildings on this site are, in no part, the original buildings here, although there is a long record of unbroken trading stretching back to at least 1839.

Before that date and even before the end of the 18th century there was a building near here, occupied by a Mr. Cook between 1790 and 1803, and Peter Tart from 1804 to 1824. It was probably at the latter date the building was converted into a shop. The earliest known commercial tenant was Richard Collins, a fruiterer whose premises would have been roughly on the site of the present 36 Montpelier Vale. At that time there was no building on the site of 34 Montpelier Vale, only a passageway and yard, and it is probable that this was in occupation of Andrew Wilson, a builder and bricklayer. In 1841 the fruit shop had passed to George Goldsmith and he remained here until 1847; his name appears in the 1843 Tithe schedule as the tenant of both house and yard.

When the fruit shop was rebuilt to form the present 34 and 36 Montpelier Vale is not clear but there were two distinct shops trading here in 1845: Goldsmith's, fruiterers, and Samuel Payne, fishmonger.

34 Montpelier Vale

Samuel Payne (1811-1870) was a fishmonger and dealer in game who claimed that his business had been established here in 1843 and that it was "the oldest-established highclass fishmonger in Blackheath". Unfortunately, the last claim was not quite accurate, in that the fishshop at 13 Tranquil Vale had been trading as such since before 1838 - five years before Payne's shop was established, if his claim were true in that respect as well. Certainly the 1843 Tithe schedule does not bear him out and there is no trace of Samuel Payne before 1845 in the commercial directories.

After Payne's death his widow, Eliza, continued to sell fish from here, but on her death in 1892 the shop was taken by John Green until 1904. The lease was then assigned to Charles Benjamin Bacon (1870-1909) possibly because Green was near retiring and he had lost his wife in 1902 and his son Edward in 1904 at the age of 29. Bacon added the merchandising of ice to fishmongering and game dealing. Although Bacon died in 1909 the shop continued to bear his name until the end of the Great War. It was then taken over by the Watts family from 1920 to the mid 1940s, who saw the shop's centenary as a fishmongers in 1943 or 1945, depending upon the accuracy of their predecessor's claim.

From the late 1940s to the present date the shop has traded as a green-grocery, initially under the control of F. A. Redden although it is presently called Leslies.

36 Montpelier Vale

Although George Goldsmith had left this shop by 1847 the trade here cont-inued as a fruiterers and greengrocers until 1916: after Goldsmith, the proprietor was a John Brown, but from 1855 to 1887 the business was in the hands of Joseph Alfred Wenham, who was also a market gardener and sold his own produce. In 1888 the shop was taken over by Robert Keech who was succeeded by his son Thomas (1865-1919) from 1896 to about 1906.

1.   An aerial view of Blackheath Village and Blackheath Vale in the mid-1960s.

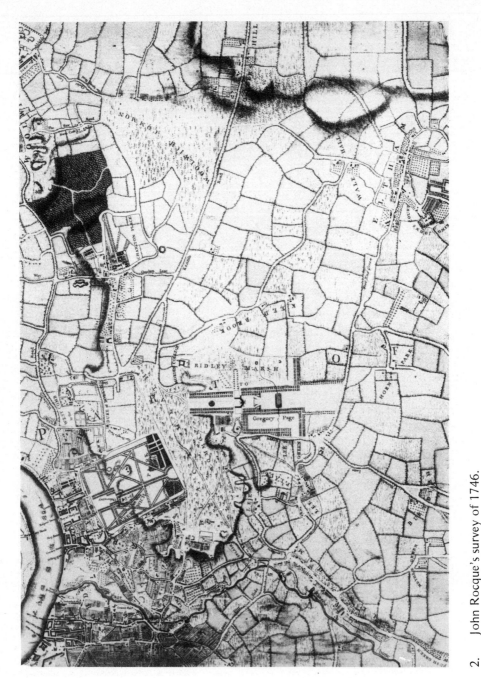

2. John Rocque's survey of 1746.

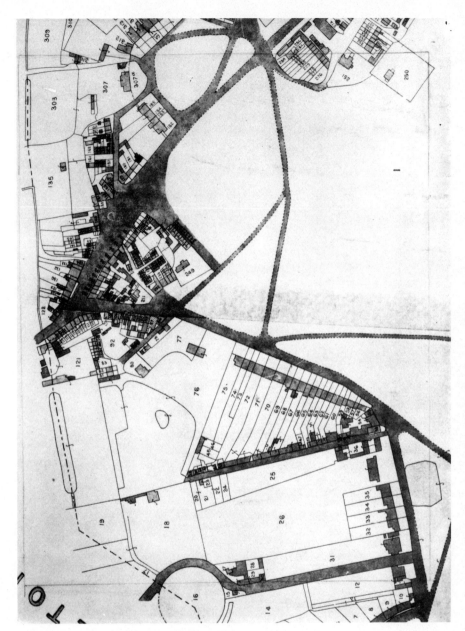

3. The Tithe Schedule for the Parish of Lewisham in 1843.

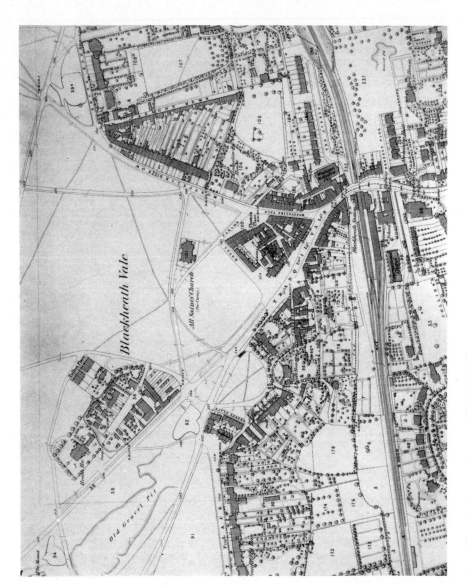

4.   The Ordnance Survey of 1863-1867

From 1909 to 1916 the shop was owned by Frank Skinner.

In 1912 the upstairs rooms were rented as workshops by W.M. Parkin, a tailor, and he took over the shop as well in 1916. Parkin's business passed to the Specterman Bros., but in the early 1920s the shop was being used for its present purpose - as a newsagents and tobacconist - held, successively by Charles Keeling, Herbert Barker, James Rolph from 1935, and, for the last two decades until 1976, by A.H. Stowers.

29

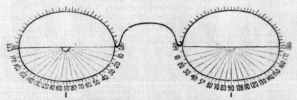
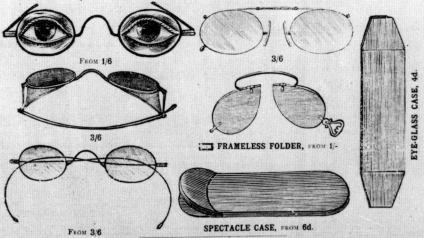

4 Montpelier Vale (west)

The west side of Montpelier Vale was developed in two quite distinct sections:

Nos. 1-11 - built 1822/3; rebuilt 1885
Nos. 13-21 - built 1851

Until approximately 1869 the buildings on the west side of Montpelier Vale were without street numbers and it is difficult to be precise in compiling lists of tenants before that date. Further, the 1822 development of the site presently occupied by Nos. 1 & 3 Montpelier Vale was part of Tuck's Corner and the premises here were sometimes held by the lessee of 38 Tranquil Vale as part of his lease.

The 1822 Development

In September 1822 the Dartmouth estate issued a building lease to Joseph Jackson of Kidbrooke, for the development of what had been, until then, the garden ground of the Three Tuns Public House. The site had frontages in Tranquil Vale and Montpelier Vale and was the ground for what became, subsequently, Nos. 36-50 Tranquil Vale (q.v.) and Nos. 1-11 Montpelier Vale.

The lease was to run for a term of 61 years from 29 September 1822 for an annual rent of £8. Jackson, who was living in Blackheath at the time, but not then at Kidbrooke Lodge, St. Germans Place where he lived from 1838 to 1840, leaves no other record as a speculative builder and this development in Blackheath may simply have been an investment. Little is known of him and after 1840 his name does not appear in the easily available records other than that he was a liberal in politics and served as a magistrate and Overseer to the Poor in the Liberty of Kidbrooke during the 1830s.

The first building in the Montpelier Vale section of Jackson's development was part of the corner site redeveloped as 36 & 38 Tranquil Vale and the present 1 & 3 Montpelier Vale. At some time before the redevelopment (in 1885) the Montpelier Vale frontage was divided into separate shop units and took the numbers 13 and 14 Montpelier Vale, following on the sequence established with the shops on the other side of the road.

No. 13 was the family entrance for 38 Tranquil Vale, but No. 14 had been sub-let by 1851 to Henry Piggot, a gardener who had lived at 11 Tranquil Vale from 1839-1845. During the early 1860s the tenant was a tailor, Thomas Arthur. It has not been possible to establish further tenancies until 1874 when the shop was taken, for the sale of hats, by Charles John Bond jnr, whose father had established a tailoring business in Tranquil Vale in 1830. It was Charles Bond who was granted the re-development lease for this section of Montpelier Vale in 1884 and his origins and activities are dealt with below, but to complete this section it must be recorded that he, and his mother, Mrs. A. Bond, kept this shop until 1885 and returned after the re-building.

5 Montpelier Vale (was 15 Montpelier Vale)

The little shop on this site combined a coal agency with a straw hat factory from approximately 1838 to the early 1870s. Jane Dennen was making hats in 1839 but by 1845 the tenant was Miss Deborah Layton who worked here until at least 1872. Working with her was her sister, Joanne Huggett, whose husband John (1805-1870) traded as a coal merchant for the last ten years of his life but may well have been the John Huggett who kept a small school for boys in Camden Row in 1845 and acted as librarian to the Blackheath Literary Institution off Tranquil Vale from about 1843 to 1856.

7 Montpelier Vale (was 16 Montpelier Vale)

The first known tenant here was John Willis, a shoemaker, (b. 1786) from about 1837 to 1852. From at least 1860 until the building was demolished the house was tenanted by members of the Moore family, in particular Thomas Moore, a carpenter, and later, George Moore, a bricklayer. There is some evidence that George Moore's grandfather had a hand in the actual building of these houses in 1822 but this was based on family reminiscence at the end of the 19th century and cannot now be proved.

9 Montpelier Vale (was 17 Montpelier Vale)

We can be more certain of the tenancies here between 1822 and 1884 than almost any other shop in this stretch of Montpelier Vale because of the lengths of tenure stretching to a time when records were more precise. Samuel Whittle, a shoemaker (1788-c1845) had a workshop here from before 1826 and was still a tenant in 1841. By 1851 the shop was held by the first of a line of greengrocers: John Hopkins was here until about 1858; he was succeeded by William Henry Gomer (1830-1909) the son of William Henry, the milkman at 13 Montpelier Vale. By 1869 the shop had been taken over by William Hinds (b. 1834) who remained here until the shop was demolished but re-opened his business at the newly built 1 Montpelier Vale in 1886 for a short while.

11 Montpelier Vale (was 18 Montpelier Vale)

This building was the corner house of the group, with a passageway to the north east leading to a stable building at the rear. By 1830 the premises were used by Richard Newland, a coachmaster, who ran one of the many private horse buses which took Blackheath men to and from the City each day. Newland was probably put out of business by the railways but he also doubled as an upholsterer and from 1839 to 1845 traded as both although his name was sometimes mis-spelled as Richard Newlyn. From the 1850s to the 1870s the house was occupied by the Moore family, builders and carpenters, some members of which lived at 7 Montpelier Vale. The tenant at No. 11 in 1851 was Elizabeth; in 1861 it was her son Thomas, born in 1812, a carpenter; but the commercial occupier of the house and yard during the 1860s and early 1870s was William W. Moore, who had been

born in Blackheath in 1804 and was probably Thomas Moore's brother.
During their tenancy some of the rooms, and perhaps the shop room, were
let to dressmakers, in particular Miss Mary Ann Baker, who cut and
sewed here from as early as 1866 until 1882 and probably left only when
the lease expired and the shop was pulled down. Miss Baker notwithstanding,
part of the shop was rented by Walter Payn as a fancy repository and a
branch of his main business elsewhere, but only for two or three years
until 1882 when he returned to concentrating on his drapery at 18 Delacourt
Road.

The 1885 Development

Jackson's lease of 1822 was for 61 years but had been assigned by the 1860s to
James Watson. On its expiry the lease was not renewed and it reverted to
the Dartmouth Estate as freeholders. In August 1884 new leases for the
whole plot exactly as in Jackson's lease of 1822, were granted to Charles
John Bond jnr (1836-1916) to allow re-development. Once tenants had been
found Bond nominated them for 99-year leases direct from the Dartmouth
Estate, retaining only No. 3 for himself.

Bond was a draper, hosier and hatter, the son of Charles John Bond snr
(1811-1879), who had established his business at 50 Tranquil Vale in 1830
but who moved to 44 Tranquil Vale by 1850 and remained there until 1874,
when he retired. Bond jnr then took the business to the shop at 3 Montpelier Vale, essentially as a hat shop for his mother, because he took a lease
on 8 Montpelier Vale by 1875 where he worked as a hosier, hatter and
shirtmaker until he retired at the end of the 1890s.

The most fundamental change caused by the redevelopment in 1885 was
the loss of "Tuck's Corner" which was replaced by three separate shops:
36 & 38 Tranquil Vale and 1 Montpelier Vale, but otherwise the new terrace
matched the old buildings almost exactly.

1 Montpelier Vale

When the building was completed by 1886 the first occupier was William
Hinds who had traded as a greengrocer from about 1869 at 9 Montpelier
Vale, but by 1890 he had gone and the shop was embraced by the tenants of
the corner shop, 36 Tranquil Vale, as an extension for the grocery business
re-established there. But when Messrs Foster took over those premises
they did not take No. 1 and it was occupied for a year or two from 1904 by
Coryton & Co., florists, and from about 1908 to 1912 by Arthur Pettit, in
the same trade.

In the 1920s the lease was held by the Dry Cleaning and Dyeing Co. and
the shop remained in this trade until 1974, latterly as the Vogue Valeting
Service. In 1975 it was re-united with 36 Tranquil Vale as part of an
estate agent's premises.

3 Montpelier Vale

The Bond family retained the use of this shop until 1890, mainly as a hat
shop for Mrs. A. Bond, but from 1891 until 1928 it was held by a succession
of ladies trading as milliners and dressmakers, who not only stressed that
their creations were exclusive but that there was some, undefined, link with

the Continent either in their names or in the style of the goods available: from 1891-1906 Madame Frohock's Modes de Paris; 1899-1903 Madame Courtenay, court milliners; 1905-1916 Madame Compton; from 1918 to 1928 Mrs. Florence Roberts, milliner, but upstairs would be found Madame Willoughby, exclusive dressmaker.

All that had gone in 1929 when Miss Anne Darby opened an arts and crafts shop "Anne's Shop" which survived until 1935 when the premises lost all pretensions and became a greengrocers owned by Cecil Fenner. Fenner's stayed here through the war and up until 1964. In recent years the shop has been Brantiques (antiques) and, presently, a health food store.

5 Montpelier Vale

This shop was a confectioners from 1886 until 1925, and a ladies outfitters from 1927 to 1973, when it was put up for sale.

The first confectioner here was George Johnson in 1886, who was succeeded by R.J. Johnson in about 1907-8. In 1915 the business was taken over by the Misses Alice and Flora Pullen who sold sweets and ice creams here until about 1925. In 1927 the lease was acquired by Annie Barr (d. 1936) (Madame Barr) a ladies outfitter who had taken over Miss Standage's shop at 3 Blackheath Village in 1901. In 1907 she moved to 3 Lee Road and traded successfully from there until 1927 when the Westminter Bank took over the shop as an extension to their premises. The Montpelier Vale shop flourished until 1973 when the then proprietor retired and the stock sold to Messrs Reeve & Jones at 31 Tranquil Vale. In May 1976 it re-opened, still called Madame Barr, but with a more fashionable stock than before.

7 Montpelier Vale

After 1918 No. 7 was linked with No. 9 Montpelier Vale as Cave Austin's grocery shop, but the original lease had been assigned in 1884 to William Butcher (1840-1903) the chemist at 33 Tranquil Vale. He probably took the premises because he needed the space at 35 Tranquil Vale then occupied by his sister, Miss Martha Butcher, who owned a Berlin repository. Martha moved her stock to 7 Montpelier Vale when the building was completed and she stayed there until 1888, or thereabouts, because the business had passed to the Misses Robinson by 1890 and they remained at 7 Montpelier Vale until 1916.

In 1917 Butcher's trustees were given permission to combine Nos. 7 & 9 into one shop and both were then occupied by Cave Austin until 1974.

9 Montpelier Vale

In 1885 Edwin Mason, a hairdresser, opened a bright new salon here, after six or seven years of having to conduct his business in upstairs rooms in Tranquil Vale and Montpelier Vale. There was a large risk in setting up as a quality barber in Blackheath Village in the late 19th century, in that the greater proportion of the carriage trade patronised T.W. Smith at 25 Tranquil Vale. Add those to that portion of the populace who never had their hair cut or who patronised back street low-price barbers, and the remaining trade was quite small, probably not enough to support the shop at Montpelier Vale, and Mason had left the district by 1891.

His successors at No. 9 were the brothers James and Alfred Austin, grocers, who were building up a small chain of stores which had started at 33 Lee High Road before 1878, and by 1888 had grown to seven branches in Lee, Lewisham and Rushey Green. The Austins were taking a great risk by opening a store in Blackheath Village when they did, for there were a dozen grocery stores established there and about the same number had come and gone in the previous five years. Nevertheless, the Austin Bros. survived and, in 1899, were trading as Cave Austin & Co. Ltd., having merged with Cave and Son, of Lee High Road. In 1917 they took over the next door needlework shop at 7 Montpelier Vale and traded from both until 1974 although before the end Cave Austin's had been swallowed by large retail multiples and ended as a branch of Moore's Stores of Liverpool.

In 1975, 7 & 9 Montpelier Vale re-opened as a wine bar.

11 Montpelier Vale

When this site was redeveloped in 1885 the alleyway to the north had long gone. The first tenant was Mrs. Janet McLean who ran the shop as a fancy repository for two years, but in 1888 the lease had been assigned to Miss Emma Pryer, French milliner, and this business survived here until the last war, trading in this name but clearly not with the original proprietor. In recent years the shop has been used as a receiving office by Messrs Achille Serre, dyers and cleaners.

The 1851 Development

Nos. 13 to 21 Montpelier Vale were built in 1851 on the site of two houses and some waste ground between them and the entrance to Tranquil Passage.

The building lease was granted to John Pound, the third son of Thomas Pound, landlord of the Three Tuns, who had established himself as a builder and brickmaker in Burnt Ash. He left his mark on Blackheath not only with the development of these shops but also in the building of the west end of St. John's Park.

Although Pound held the building lease there is evidence that Couchman & Co., whose offices were at 16 Montpelier Vale, opposite, may have been the actual contractors, and the leases assigned to Pound's nominees. All these leases were roughly for the same term, 61 years, but vary in their commencing dates between 25 March 1851 and 25 March 1852.

Two buildings were demolished for the development: to the south was a small house used by William Henry Gomer, a cowkeeper and dairyman who had started his business in the Village in 1808 and may have built the house shortly afterwards. Gomer moved into the newly built 13 Montpelier Vale in 1851 but had gone by 1859, the cows being sold to Matthew Arthur Ivison. The building to the north was a private house and it has proved impossible to be sure of the tenants, although it may have been used by the Gomer family.

13 Montpelier Vale (was 5 Montpelier Vale)

The new building was leased to William Henry Gomer II in 1851 and he may have lived here for a short while. By 1857 the shop had been let to Mrs. Emma Eaton Fielding, a watchmaker and probably the widow of Alfred Fielding, a jeweller of Nelson Street, Greenwich who had compounded with his creditors in 1854. Mrs. Fielding died in about 1889-90 and the business was continued by her son Robert (1850-1934) who before his death was one of the last surviving pupils of the old Greenwich Proprietory School. Fielding claimed the business had been established in 1824 but this cannot refer to its foundation in Blackheath. When he retired, the shop was sold to James Nicholson Clark, an optician rather than a watchmaker, but he combined both jobs equally and traded here until the last war. After the war the shop became a hairdresser's, in which use it remained until 1976.

The upstairs rooms at 13 Montpelier Vale have long been used for commercial purposes and for the first half of this century they were the offices of a succession of servant's registries and employment agencies.

15 Montpelier Vale (was 4 Montpelier Vale)

This shop was built by Francis Webb, a carpenter who lived at 67 Tranquil Vale when it was still Lamb's Buildings, on a lease for 61 years from Lady Day 1851. The first commercial tenant was Joseph Taylor, a boot and shoe maker, born in 1820, who had set up a shop at 20 Montpelier Vale by 1849. Taylor remained at No. 15 until about 1859 when the business was taken over by Frederick Marmaduke Marsden who, although a young man, enjoyed sufficient success to employ five shoemakers here. Marsden may have died by 1874 for his name is missing from the records for that year, but by 1878 the shop is firmly in the hands of his widow, Elizabeth Jane Marsden, who kept the shop going until 1885. In 1886 the trade had been sold to Walter Flack but he stayed in Blackheath for only four years, after which he concentrated on his business interests in Cambridge. The lease of the shop at Montpelier Vale was still held by the Taylor family and Joseph Taylor jnr added No. 15 to the business already well established at No. 6. In 1914 the lease was transferred to his widow, Rachel Taylor, but by 1917 the shoe trade left 15 Montpelier Vale, albeit temporarily. By 1904 half the shop had been sub-divided and let to a Mr. White of the Dry Cleaning and Dyeing Company who moved at the end of the Great War to No. 1 Montpelier Vale. Thereafter the shop supported a number of varying interests: from 1920 to 1923 the proprietor was Alfred Moyes, a toymaker; in 1924 and up until the late 1930s the proprietor was Harold Avenell, who sold sports goods and riding outfits, but, of greater importance for the small girls of the district, he ran a doll's hospital here for many years. After the last war the shop successively housed Jenny Wren, a baby clothes shop run by Mrs. Sylvia Mackenzie, the shoe department of Vanity Fayre (at 25 Tranquil Vale), Fantasia, a leather goods business and, the present users, the Kingsway Wallpaper Stores.

17 Montpelier Vale (was 3 Montpelier Vale)

John Pound, who built the terrace, kept the head lease of this shop, but assigned it almost immediately (1852) to Mrs. Elizabeth Esther Walker, a milliner, who traded from here until the early 1860s. She sold the business to the Dent family and the shop remained with Mr. & Mrs. William Henry Dent until 1880, but selling ladies and children's clothes instead of hats. From 1882 to 1899 the proprietor was Edwin Fancourt but in September 1900 the last 12 years of the original lease was sold. No. 17 was then opened as a Photographic and Art Stores, the proprietor from 1904 being John William Hodges, FSMC, DBOA, (1874-1926), an optician and keen photographer who supplied many of the illustrations for the 1909 "Borough" Guide to Blackheath Village. In March 1914 the shop was taken over by Butcher, Curnow, of 33-35 Tranquil Vale (q.v.) as their photographic department. Hodges became manager of the optical department, a position he held until his death in 1926. Butcher, Curnow, closed down the branch at 17 Montpelier Vale in March 1915, due to wartime staff shortages. In 1917 it was taken, briefly, as temporary premises by C.J. Irish, the saddler, who had been bombed out of Camden Place (q.v.) at the end of 1916.

After the 1914-1918 war the shop was held by the North Kent Corn and Seed Co., who sold poultry food and dog biscuits etc., but in 1931 was conducted as a grocery by various owners including A. & P. Shave, a family often confused with the Shoves who had traded from 22 Tranquil Vale from 1844 to 1913. The upstairs rooms were used by dressmakers, the best known of which, Mrs. Annie Leech, was here from 1904 to 1920 when she moved to 8 Montpelier Row. From 1928 until the last war this was the premises of the hairdressers, Elaine et Cie.

After 1945, 17 Montpelier Vale was principally a dress shop until 1966 when it was opened as La Concorde, the first restaurant in the Village to which the epithet "foreign" could be applied. Shortly afterwards, it was acquired by new proprietors who kept the French flavour, but changed the name to La Goulue, by which title it is known today.

19 Montpelier Vale (was 2 Montpelier Vale)

From the outset, 19 Montpelier Vale was a butcher's shop and remained so for more than 70 years. The original lease was granted to one Warner, probably Samuel Warner, a plasterer at 23 Tranquil Vale who was employing twenty men in 1851. Although Warner's lease was granted in March 1852 it had been assigned, or the shop sub-let, to John Charles Covell, a butcher. By 1860 the shop had been taken over by Thomas Kimber and William Edward Slark of Greenwich. Slark was trading on his own by 1874 and continued to do so until about 1883-84. By 1885 the shop had been taken over by the Walker family, initially by George Edward, but in 1886 by Thomas Henry Walker. Thomas traded here until 1896, claiming that his shop was "By Appointment to the Prince of Wales". In 1896 he would have lost the Royal Warrant because he went bankrupt and had to be fetched from Plymouth where he was found boarding a steamer for foreign parts. He was jailed for contempt, principally for failing to forward £1000 in cash as he had promised to the bankruptcy court, but instead taking a first class ticket and much heavy luggage to Devon.

During Walker's absence the shop was run by Alfred Middleton until a new lease was granted to Miss Susan Poulter (later Walker) in 1912 for a further 14 years. Mrs. Walker's name appeared on the signboard until 1923 when the lease was surrendered. For a brief while the shop was used by William Stevens, an upholsterer, although it remained empty between 1927 and 1930. In 1931 it was re-opened by Messrs Stone and Marten, furriers, and this business remained until 1973. The shop was then totally refitted in a contemporary manner for its use as a dental surgery.

21 Montpelier Vale (was 1 Montpelier Vale)

The shop at the corner of Montpelier Vale was built by John Dalton, the grocer of Phoenix Place (q.v.) and leased to him for 61 years from 25 March 1851. He conducted his grocery and tea dealing business from here for a few years, probably to keep the trade during the rebuilding of the Phoenix Place premises, but in October 1854 the new shop was being advertised for sale with the lease available of "a recently erected and let to John Dalton, grocer and tea dealer, spacious lofty corner shop and fine spring water." This last asset may have been why George Frederick Jobbins decided to take on the lease of the premises.

Jobbins (1817-1895) was a master baker, born in Holborn, and by 1850 the owner of a successful business in Old Bond Street. He clearly felt that there was a good trade to be had in Blackheath despite the fact that there were already a number of bakers trading there.

Within ten years Jobbins had been proved right - building developments in the 1850s and 1860s had added a large number of rich households to the Blackheath population who, although they may not have paid their accounts very promptly, did so sufficiently well for Jobbins to employ seven bakers at Montpelier Vale. In 1880 George Frederick handed over the control of his business to his son Stephen, who not only called the shop "The Model Bakery" but also acted as an agent for domestic staff and could supply all the catering needs for functions and entertainments, supplying everything from knives and forks to conjurors and dance orchestras.

By 1897 Stephen Jobbins had taken over the bakery of the Riddington family at 7 & 9 Blackheath Village and, for a few years, ran both bakeries in concert. But in 1900 Jobbins assigned his lease of 21 Montpelier Vale to Sidney George Birdseye (1861-1954), a hosier and outfitter who had taken over Bond's business at 8 Montpelier Vale in 1899.

Birdseye did not stay long at 21 Montpelier Vale, although his business flourished elsewhere in the Village, and the premises were taken over in 1907 by Edgar W. Lethbridge, a tailor, who shut down in 1916 when his son Ernest (1878-1917) joined the army. At the end of the Great War the shop re-opened as the Western Dining Rooms; by 1924 the style had changed and it was Mrs. R. Pidgeon's restaurant. At the end of that year the business had been taken over by Alderton's of Plumstead, and for the next six years as Alderton's Café, supplied Blackheath ladies with dainty teas, light luncheons and meals of a sort that required small appetites and extremely refined table manners.

In 1931 the shop once again became a bakery - this time under the control of E. & A. Allen who remained here until the 1939-1945 war. Shortly after the war the shop was re-opened by D.A. Webb for the sale of bicycle and motoring accessories and remains in this use today.

23 Montpelier Vale

This number was designated to what is, really, the back door of No. 21 Montpelier Vale. It has been occupied as a separate unit but sometimes held with No. 21; from at least 1866 until the mid 1870s it was the premises of a Miss Braddock, a milliner, but essentially No. 23 has been residential accommodation.

5   Osborne Place

The last development in Blackheath Village which filled up private garden ground was the erection in 1840 of a terrace of twelve shops then called Osborne Place. The present nomenclature splits Osborne Place between Tranquil Vale and Montpelier Vale and this decision in 1886 was not only eccentric but has, subsequently, not helped the local historian. The numbering of Osborne Place began at what is now 10 Montpelier Vale and ended at what is presently 22 Tranquil Vale.

The terrace was built on a lease granted in August 1836 by an Order in Chancery for Sir Gregory Page Turner, by then declared a lunatic. It was the development of a site which had included James Watson's butcher's shop (12 Montpelier Vale), a cottage, stable, slaughter house shed and other outbuildings which were "late in the tenure of John Oddy and James Judd". All this ground was, in fact, the old garden of Edward Sadler's house, a late 17th or early 18th century property which had been demolished early in the 19th century, probably before 1810, for the development of the north east side of Montpelier Vale.

The butcher's shop detailed in the lease was then held by Watson and he acquired the additional 1836 lease on a term of 99 years from 1840. In this new development Watson encroached on the strip of land which did not belong to the Page Turner family but was part of the Dartmouth freehold. It was not much more than a few feet at its widest but it became necessary for the Earl of Dartmouth to issue separate leases in 1842 and 1854 and the matter was not resolved until the transfer of the freehold much later in the 19th century.

It is also of interest that the site for Osborne Place was not sold to John Cator in 1783 as part of the Page estate, and this may have been because it had been the subject of dispute between the Parish of Lewisham and Sir Gregory Page as far back as 1741. Page certainly leased land on the north and west boundaries of his Wricklemarsh estate which did not become his freehold and were still on lease and retained when the Page estate was sold to Cator. Whatever the reason, the Osborne Place site and lease were vested in the Polhill branch of the Page family and remained so until well after the last war.

To judge from the details in the lease we must credit James Watson with the development of Osborne Place as the first terrace of purpose-built shops in the Village. The name of the builder is not recorded and it is doubtful whether an architect, in the modern sense, actually designed the terrace, for it is a simple group, much in the style of many other terraces of its date. A good master-builder would have been able to cope with such a structure from his general working experience. But what is remarkable is that it has remained generally unspoiled to the present day and that it fitted so well into the scale and harmony of the Village that when, in March 1945, it was much damaged as a result of bomb blast, it was skilfully restored although some of the Victorian shop fronts and fittings were replaced in the interests of modern retailing practice.

Osborne Place was built during 1839 and 1840; it comprised twelve matching three-storey shops, with a service yard at the rear entered between Nos. 11 and 12 (24 & 22 Tranquil Vale). Initially there was no piped water and supplies had to be drawn from pumps and wells. Why this group was called Osborne Place has not been discovered. It was common then, to name groups of buildings either after the builder or after the owner. More rarely a distinguished local resident or Royal personage would lend their name, but the author can find no trace of a local builder or house proprietor called Osborne and he can only assume that the name was taken from that of the ground landlord Sir Gregory Osborne Page Turner. This theory is weak because Watson could have just as easily named the terrace Page Terrace or Turner Terrace. By curious coincidence, an employee at 22 Tranquil Vale from 1844 to 1909 was one Joseph Osborne. He started work there as an errand boy and it is extremely unlikely that the new shops would have been named after him.

1 Osborne Place (10 Montpelier Vale)

This was built as a pub - The White Hart Beer House. It was licenced as a beer house and remained as such until the early 1960s - a unique survival of a period when beer-only licences were issued to small pubs in an effort to reduce the sales of spirits and reduce drunkenness, although it failed in both respects. The first tenant was William Evans from 1840 to 1847, when his widow took over the licence. She was followed by John Burles (d. 1860) and his widow Susan until 1862. The house then transferred to the Devon-born Digory Denbon Weeks (1823-1874) and on his death the licence passed to John Burles jnr until 1887. Thereafter there was a string of licencees who made no particular name for themselves but simply got on with the job of selling beer: 1887-1893 Charles Guy; 1895-1901 George Carlisle; 1904-1909 Sidney Herbert Smith; 1910 Arthur Stone; 1911-1917 James Evans; 1920 William Ornes; 1923-1936 George Benson; 1937-1938+ David James.

When the pub closed in the early 1960s it was refitted as an ordinary commercial shop and opened for the sale of carpets, in which use it remains today.

2 Osborne Place (8 Montpelier Vale)

This shop has sold clothing of some sort since it was first occupied in 1842 by Charles William Strutt, a hatter, born in Deptford in 1811. Strutt, true to his name, was an aggressive man who appeared in court on at least one occasion for his abusive manners. Nevertheless he stayed in business here until 1875 when the business was acquired by Charles John Bond jnr (1836-1916) a hosier, hatter and shirtmaker who took over his father's business which had been founded in 1830 at 50 Tranquil Vale although it subsequently moved to 44 Tranquil Vale. Bond jnr. also traded at No. 3 Montpelier Vale (q.v.) from 1874 to 1888 and was responsible for the redevelopment of that site in 1885.

The sale of the Osborne Place shop was precipitated by the death of George James Bond (1845-1899) second son of Bond snr, and the impending retirement of Charles Bond jnr. The new proprietor was Sidney G. Birdseye, a hosier who, in 1900, took premises in addition at 21 Montpelier Vale. Birdseye (1861-1954), later with his son Herbert (d. 1913) stayed here until the years of the Great War although the business was taken over in 1913 by William Morley Cheesewright (1883-1961). Until 1919 the company traded as Birdseye & Cheesewright but thereafter the shop traded solely as Cheesewright's until 1961. After Cheesewright's death the business was acquired by H. H. Wagstaff Ltd. in whose hands it remains at the time of writing.

3 Osborne Place (6 Montpelier Vale)

This shop has had only two names over its door since it opened as a boot-makers in 1841: the first proprietor was George Pugh (1805-?1870) who also had a business at 105 Regent Street. Pugh specialised in ladies shoes but by 1878, when the shop was held by George Pugh jnr (b. 1832), the business passed to Joseph Henry Taylor (1852-1913), advertising as a court and military bootmaker established in 1850*. Taylor was the son of a Village shoemaker of the same name who had owned shops at 20 Montpelier Vale from about 1849-1851 and 15 Montpelier Vale until 1858. There is no trace of either Taylors as bootmakers between 1858 and 1877 and we can assume that the old business had closed down because Taylor snr had died and Taylor jnr would have been too young to set up on his own account; as it was, his sister had married into the Norman family, also bootmakers, who worked at 18 Montpelier Vale from the 1880s to the 1890s, and would have become Joseph Taylor's rivals in business.

After Joseph Taylor jnr's death in 1913 the business passed to his son, Harry Taylor, who remained here until 1950 (his wife was killed when the shop was bomb blasted in 1945) and it then passed to a Mr. Millet, his nephew. In 1969 the shop was acquired by the present proprietor, Mr. Spring, trading as J. H. Taylor (Blackheath) Ltd., thus ensuring an unbroken run as a shoe shop of more than 134 years at the time of writing.

4 Osborne Place (4 Montpelier Vale)

The pattern of trading here has been quite mixed but it has nearly always been allied to food of some sort. At the outset it was the premises of James and Angelina Moore, confectioners and pastrycooks. In 1853, the business passed to Richard John Morley (1827-1893) who earned a high reputation by selling sweets and cakes to boys from the Blackheath Proprietary School on their way to and from lessons. Morley's shop boasted a tiny tearoom and he also sold wine, aspects of the business further exploited by Edward Symons who purchased the shop from Morley's executors in 1895. This venture lasted only until 1899 and, except for a short period when it was owned by the Bodega Co. in 1904, the shop remained empty until it was taken over by Silverstone, the tobacconist who traded at 1 Lee Road and, until 1913, from 11 Tranquil Vale as well. By the mid 1920s the business was part of the W. Findlay group but in 1938 the shop was acquired by Messrs G. R. Saxby and W. Fish, and called the Blackheath Bacon Shop. Saxby and Fish had started their company at 27 Montpelier Vale in 1934 but moved to 4 Montpelier Vale because of their trading success. The Blackheath Bacon Shop survived the war and flourished until 1964 when it allied to Hale & Partners Stores Ltd., who. soon afterwards, were

* Some advertisements say 1851.

41

swallowed by the Key Markets group and the shop was turned into a small self-service store, presently trading in the name of David Greig.

5 Osborne Place (2 Montpelier Vale)

These premises were a tailor's shop and workshop from 1840 until the last proprietors retired in 1975. It was opened in 1840 by the young William Voller who had started business in Lee Green in his very early twenties and, by 1839, had taken premises at 1 Lee Road. This must have been a temporary stay because, by the age of 25, Voller had set up in 5 Osborne Place where he remained until his death in 1892.

The business continued in that name until 1913 when it transferred to 30 Budge Row, Cannon Street. In 1913, 5 Osborne Place was taken by William McKnight & Sons, also tailors, for a couple of years. In 1916 the premises of Alfred Hanreck at 53-55 Tranquil Vale were bombed and the family took over the then empty shop at 2 Montpelier Vale. Hanreck (1879-1961) was British-born although of Russian origin and was obliged to publish notices of that fact in order to allay rumours at the outbreak of the 1914-18 war that he was a German spy. He also found it necessary to remind his customers that their suits were made entirely by British labour. Alfred Hanreck survived the scandalmongers and was followed into the business by his sons Lionel and Stanley, who kept the shop at 2 Montpelier Vale until their retirement at the end of 1974. It was particularly unfortunate that the family were affected by German bombing for the second time in their lives when the Montpelier Vale shop was severely damaged in March 1945. For more than six years the tailoring business was sustained from their home in Vanbrugh Park until the brothers returned to their restored premises in 1952.

From the 1860s the shop was used solely as retail premises and the upper floors let out; for a brief while there was a homeopathic dispensary here, but from the 1870s the rooms were traditionally used by hairdressers, firstly by Joseph Cook and, later, by Edwin Mason who opened his own shop at 9 Montpelier Vale in 1885. More recently the rooms have been used by chiropodists.

6 Osborne Place (34 Tranquil Vale)

The building here is divided into two retail units and has been since at least 1925. Yet, as a single shop, it enjoyed much prestige until 1904 as the oldest established ironmongers in the district. It was opened as a branch shop by William Marshall (1788-1864) of London Street, Greenwich, at the end of 1839 as an ironmongery and tinsmiths, selling a wide range of goods from gas stoves to gas mantles, including a patent cooking and heating stove known as the Blackheath Kitchener. Marshall's business was purchased from his son by George F. Keed in 1869 but rapidly resold to Henry Richard Smith who combined the management of the roller skating rink in Blackheath Grove with serving in his ironmongery shop. Smith advertised that his shop had been founded in 1791 and hung a huge model padlock with this legend over the door. We must assume that he was referring to William Marshall's Greenwich shop as there is no evidence that either Marshall or Smith were in Blackheath before 1839.

Smith's shop closed by 1906 and the shop remained empty until 1913 when it was taken by Walter William Wood (1863-1925), the greengrocer previously at 5 Royal Parade, but for two years the premises were shared by W. S. Shove, coal merchants, who had just left 22 Tranquil Vale after 72 years. After Wood's departure 34 Tranquil Vale was converted into the Victory Restaurant - it was opened in May 1919 - although when it was owned by Mrs Sharland (from August 1920 to 1923) it was sometimes known as The Victoria. In 1924 the shop was divided into two: 34a and 34b (south): the first tenants were J. Puller & Sons, cleaners and dyers at 34a, and R. Bowyers & Sons, dairymen at 34b. Pullers became part of the Eastman's group and the Bowyers sold out to Thomas Jones in 1937. As a result of the bomb damage in 1945 there was a fundamental change in that Eastman's went over into 34b and 34a eventually became a branch of Clark's, a Catford bakery. More recently 34b has become a wool shop and 34a was opened in 1975 as the Blackheath Gallery, for the exhibition and sale of local artists' work.

7 Osborne Place (32 Tranquil Vale)

The shop here enjoyed the soubriquet "The Blackheath Bazaar" for many years during the 19th century although the name was applied to other shops from time to time, in particular to William Carson's Bazaar at 74 Tranquil Vale. Nevertheless, 7 Osborne Place was the Blackheath Bazaar and the most popular traditional toyshop for the Village. It was opened as a fancy repository by Mrs. Alice Marshall in 1841 but the business passed to Miss Charlotte Mary White in 1849, who added toys and ladies' outfits to the fancy goods sold here. In 1865 the shop was taken by Mrs. Susannah S. Wood, wife of George William Wood, the fishmonger at 13 Tranquil Vale. Mrs. Wood continued to sell clothes for children as well as the toys but when the shop passed, in 1873, to Mrs. Sarah D'Almaine Dell, the emphasis was firmly on toys and gifts - she even erected a large rocking horse above the shopfront to make it quite clear where her interests lay. In 1884 the business had been sold to a Mrs. Lewis Woodhams but after a few years the Bazaar "established 50 years" was advertised for sale in April 1892. The next owner, William Smith Burdett, cleared away the toys and concentrated on china and glass, following the trade of his father whose business had flourished at 43 Montpelier Vale from 1866 to 1891. Young Burdett lasted only two years at 7 Osborne Place and in 1896 the shop passed to Annie Jackson (1850-1929), who dealt in second hand furniture and antiques, the family remaining there until Eleanor Annie Jackson (1900-1936) died.
    After an empty year the premises were re-opened in 1938 by E.R. Simpkins & Sons, confectioners, who had run a shop at 22 Tranquil Vale for 11 years previously. Simpkins was the last confectioner in the Village who made his own sweets and chocolates and the shop kept the family name, latterly under the control of Charles Harold Simpkins (d. 1976) until 1974. In 1975 the premises were re-opened by K. & A. McKenzie, of 5 & 7 Tranquil Vale, for the sale of lingerie and scent, but retaining the distinctive mahogany fittings of the old shop.

8 Osborne Place (30 Tranquil Vale)

The history of 8 Osborne Place is uncomplicated - it has been a chemist's shop since the 1840s, first appearing in the directories in 1845 as the dispensary of Samuel Long Hiscox, chemist and druggist. In 1849, the business was purchased by Charles Beyfield Miller, a dispensing chemist (1823-?1896) from Saffron Walden. After Miller's death the shop kept his name although the practice was owned by J. A. West until the last war. By 1944 the lease was assigned to the Nottingham-based wholesale and retail chemists, Boots & Co., in whose hands the shop remains, still dispensing prescriptions 130 years after the pharmacy first opened.

9 Osborne Place (28 Tranquil Vale)

This shop, perhaps more than any other in the Village, represented one of the qualities so cherished by Blackheath people from mid-Victorian times and almost to the present day - stability. No. 9 Osborne Place was Bennett's the clock and watch maker, and the name stayed over the door from 1840 to 1963. When a Blackheathen who had chosen to leave his native town returned, and that might be twenty, thirty or even fifty years later, Bennett's with its huge clock on the parapet of the shop would still be there, unchanged in a changing world. But Bennett's did change, and change frequently - in fact the family ceased to have anything to do with the business after 1870, although their name was kept for the next 90 years.

This particular shop was opened in 1840 by Mrs. Elizabeth Bennett and her son George Weedon Bennett, who had started the Blackheath business at 3 Blackheath Village in 1835. The Bennetts were directly related to John Bennett, the Cheapside watch and clock maker who had purchased the lease of seven acres of ground in Blackheath Village fronting on to Lee Road. More about this family and their tenure is given in Chapter 6 and, for the sake of simplicity, only their occupation of 9 Osborne Place is touched upon in this part.

Mrs. Bennett's name was associated with the Osborne Place shop until 1845 and from 1847 to 1861 the business was firmly in the hands of George Weedon Bennett, who died in September 1861 at the early age of 45, worn out perhaps, by a lifetime of involvement in the community as well as a successful career as a clockmaker. The Bennetts also owned a shop in Greenwich which George closed in January 1859 because he wished to con-centrate on Blackheath "... to which a mistaken policy has transferred a large portion of the trade of this town." After George's death the stock and lease were taken up by his brother, William Cox Bennett, a poet of whose verses Ruskin wrote "... a gentle loving mind is displayed in them..." but whose interest in clocks declined until, by 1870, his affairs were in the hands of trustees, and a manager, William H. Smith, was effectively running the business.

In 1874 the shop had been taken over by James Jackson Davies, who stayed here until 1894. Mr. Smith left Bennett's and set up his own shop at 47 Quentin Road, Lee, in 1895, and a new manager, G. S. Hughes, was put in charge. By 1898, another manager, Harry Jennings Cooper, had been appointed, and he acquired the business in 1905, although the Bennett name continued to be displayed over the facia. The trade was helped by the fact that in the early 1860s the Bennett family had erected an enormous clock on the top parapet of the building. This monstrous timepiece could be seen from great distances and gave Blackheathens an accurate time check as they hurried to the station from almost any direction. It was taken down for a major overhaul in 1910 after working well for nearly 50 years

WEST MILL

EAST MILL HOUSE

22/23 MONTPELIER ROW

PHOENIX VALE

PHOENIX HOUSE

TRANQUIL PLACE

LAMB'S BUILDINGS

EASTNOR HOUSE

GROTES PLACE

HARE AND BILLET

ELIOT PLACE

1.   Blackheath Village as seen from Whitefield's Mount in 1808

2.   Nos 25-35 Montpelier Vale; the site of Phoenix Place

3.   Nos 39-49 Montpelier Vale in 1903

4.   Nos 8-16 Royal Parade about 1910

5.   Montpelier Vale (east) in 1938. No 12 (right) the old butcher's shop

6.   Nos 12 & 14 Montpelier Vale in 1938

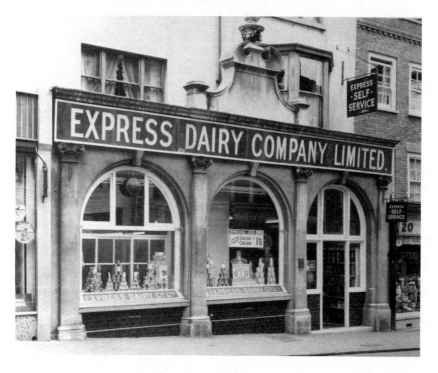

7.   The Express Dairy in the early 1960s

but by 1933 Harry Cooper had to plead for subscriptions to maintain the clock, principally on the grounds that it had become almost a public utility but was much too expensive to maintain privately. It continued to work well until 1945 when it became a casualty, along with the shop, of the blast from the rocket bomb which destroyed the Wesleyan chapel in Blackheath Grove.

After Cooper's death in 1949 the business stayed in Blackheath for another 14 years, owned by Cooper's daughter and son-in-law, Mr. & Mrs. Peter Kingwill, but early in 1963 the proprietors purchased the shop of Walter C. Joel & Co., at Richmond, and moved there to continue trading under the new name. Bennett's had gone - after 128 years in Blackheath.

With remarkable speed the shop was altered and re-fitted as a retail bakers, Broomfield's, part of the Garfield Weston group who, only the same year closed the branch of Hemmings, within the group, at 37 Tranquil Vale, for lack of custom. Broomfield's was more successful and occupies the premises at Osborne Place at the time of writing.

10 Osborne Place (26 Tranquil Vale)

Although it is now a toy shop, this building was, for most of its life, a stationers and booksellers. It was opened in 1840 by William Drewett and Edward Smith Earl for stationery and sheet music - they had started their venture in 1838 at 59 Tranquil Vale when they were both very young; Drewett aged 22 and Earl just 19 years old at the time. By 1945 only Earl was still trading at 10 Osborne Place, now describing himself as a music seller although the 1851 census lists him as a Professor of Music; in 1861 he was trading as an upholsterer and piano dealer from a room above 22 Tranquil Vale but eventually made a firm reputation at 16 Royal Parade (q.v.) By 1857 the business had been taken over by William John Martin who relied less on the sheet music sales and more on the lending library he established here - "The English and Foreign Library", a 10,000 volume collection known to the subscribers as "the local Mudie". One of his assistants in 1871 was the 21-year-old Ebenezer Wilmhurst who later opened his own shop across the road at 9 Tranquil Vale. Just over thirty years later Martin's successor at Osborne Place took over the stock and staff of Wilmhurst's shop when the latter retired in 1905. Martin's business in Tranquil Vale was sold in 1879 to David Edgar Neve. Neve had been born in Brighton in 1846 and trained for the family bookselling business in that town, but left for Blackheath when he was 33. He followed the Martin tradition by enlarging the library and expanded his trade by means of offering large discounts for cash payments and publishing some of his own material, particularly maps and guide books. He was an enthusiastic cyclist, a founder member of the Cycling Tourist Club and an amateur artist of no small ability. His brothers, Drs. Ernest and Arthur Neve, were missionaries in Kashmir and Edgar was not slow in keeping the press informed of their deeds and work amongst the heathen.

In 1893 Neve changed the name of his shop to WESALP - a mnemonic made up from the letters of Neve's advertising slogan: "West End Stock at Lowest Prices" - and this proved so successful that new customers assumed that the proprietor must be Mr. Edgar Wesalp and the name stuck until the shop closed in 1945. Neve's interest was principally in newspapers; he "lent" The Times, stocked the Paris dailies and even opened a special reading room for ladies in 1895 where, for a small annual subscription and 2d a visit, ladies could read the daily newspapers including The Guardian "an expensive paper to buy", in decorum and peace. This was an act of enlightened self-interest on Neve's part for he was trying to rescue the enthusiasm and goodwill left over from an attempt to establish a ladies reading room elsewhere in the Village, which had to close after three years because of difficulties with the lease (see Chapter 8).

Neve retired in 1922 and died in March 1932, aged 88, but his shop continued under managers until the last war, closing only when it was severely damaged in 1945. In 1950 it re-opened as Raggity Ann, a toys and sports goods business which had been started by Mr. & Mrs. Keith McKenzie at 41 Montpelier Vale in 1946.

11 Osborne Place (24 Tranquil Vale)

This shop has always been a grocer's store and was one of the first shops in Osborne Place to be completed and let. It was opened in 1839 by Joseph Millington (b. 1801) but by 1849 had been taken over by John Dalton jnr., son of John Dalton, the grocer at 21 and 25 Montpelier Vale and grandson of Robert Dalton of Phoenix Place (q.v.). Dalton jnr also opened a grocery shop in 1846 at the then newly-built 1 Spencer Place (q.v.) but he left Tranquil Vale in 1853 and the business was sold to a Thomas Taylor. Taylor did not stay long and by 1859 the shop was owned by William Walters (1806-1872?) who remained here until his death. His tenure was followed by 1874 by Matthew Wright and by 1877, the widow Elizabeth Smith - who went bankrupt. Her successor, William Henry Pettengell (1829-1899) not only did very much better than Mrs. Smith but also opened a branch at 1 Royal Parade (q.v.) and established a link with that shop which survived till 1899. On Pettengell's retirement he sold the business to the Thorpe Brothers, who named the Osborne Place shop the South Eastern Stores. The Thorpes were not without their problems: in 1891 their father, George Thorpe, of Shepperton House, Lee, was committed to trial for falsifying the accounts of his employers, Sir Henry Peek & Co., for whom he had worked since 1854 and from 1879 acted as chief cashier. Thorpe snr fled to Australia with one of his sons but was extradited when Peek's accounts were found to be short by £2,829. At his trial in September 1891 it was revealed that he had milked the company of close on £15,000 over a period of ten years, using much of this to establish his sons in business in Blackheath. He was sentenced to ten years penal servitude and the shops had to be sold.

The new proprietors of the South Eastern Stores had similar problems in that their manager in 1893, Alonso James Appleton, was indicted on a petty fraud charge, although, being a first offender, he escaped with six months probation.

In 1899 the problems at 24 Tranquil Vale were ended when Messrs Dannatt and Williams, respectable and successful grocers of Greenwich, took on the lease of the shop. They already traded from 3 Tranquil Vale (q.v.) - biographical details will be found under that heading - and stayed at both shops until 1947. For business reasons the shop at 24 Tranquil Vale changed its name to The Blackheath Village Stores in 1917 although remaining in the hands of Dannatt & Co. and their executors until 1947. In that year it was sold to Messrs W. Cullen, the chain of grocers who had traded from 1 Royal Parade (37 Montpelier Vale) from 1899. Cullen's, who have been at this shop ever since, also took over Dannatt's lease on 3 Tranquil Vale but did not trade from there, surrendering the lease in 1950.

12 Osborne Place (22 Tranquil Vale)

The southernmost section of Osborne Place, now 22 Tranquil Vale, has occupied an important place in the commercial history of Blackheath in that its first and its present tenants were long-established Blackheath companies providing services in which they were almost unrivalled. Although 12 Osborne Place had been completed by 1840 it is shown as un-occupied in the 1841 census and the first tenant is not listed until 1843. This was William Spencer Shove (1816-1882), a coal, corn and seed merch-ant, a member of the Shove family of London Street, Greenwich, whose business origins stretched back to the 18th century when Ambrose Shove set up as a coal and corn merchant. His sons, William Spencer and John Shove followed their father, with John taking over Ambrose's shop by 1852 and William setting up in Blackheath in 1843.

The rapidly developing suburb in the late 1840s and 1850s provided William with as many customers as he could cope with, and the demand for horse feed and coal must have been enormous. When Blackheath Station opened in 1849 Shove was one of the first to establish a coal depot there, only a minute's walk from the shop. It was not long before the shop was in the hands of managers and William Spencer Shove could give his time to public service, as a participant in church affairs and on the boards of the local administrators, be they vestries, boards of works, guardians, or charity committees. On his death at The Maples, 44 Lee Road, the business passed to his son Spencer Shove, although the company was then being managed by Joseph Osborne, who had started with the family as a 17-year old assistant in 1844 and died, in harness, still manager, in 1909. His death somehow coincided with the death of the trade which had made Shove a rich man for, by then, Blackheath was converting its stables into motor garages and the demand for horse-feed was falling fast, and whilst there was still a need for coal it was not necessary to maintain a large shop as an order office. In August 1913 Shove's shop at 22 Tranquil Vale closed and the coal agency moved to smaller premises, initially at 34 Tranquil Vale and, in June 1915, to the half shop at 38b Tranquil Vale where it remained until the last war, eventually being absorbed by Rickett, Cockerell & Co.

William Shove's son Harold branched out into the bakery and catering trades and established a lively business at 44 & 46 Tranquil Vale using his father's name, but this had nothing to do with the trading pattern at 22 Tranquil Vale.

Shove's old shop remained empty for a period but was re-opened in 1916 by the Misses C. and Annie Joyes (Annie Joyes 1867-1920) as confectioners. In 1927 this business was taken over by E.R. Simpkins & Sons, makers of high-quality confectionery, and they stayed at 22 Tranquil Vale until 1938 when they moved to 32 Tranquil Vale.

In 1940 the shop was taken by the estate agents Dyer, Son & Creasey, who had been bombed out of the premises at 17 Montpelier Row which they had occupied since 1826. The story of Dyer's will be found in more detail in the forthcoming second volume of this work, but a few words on their history are appropriate here.

Although the Montpelier Row property had been occupied by the firm since 1826, the home agency had been founded six years before in 1820 and established in a small house and shop (since demolished) next to the Princess of Wales public house. The founder was George Felix Gilbert (1791-?1860) who was a book seller, house agent and auctioneer, the first of this profession in Blackheath. Gilbert acted as agent for many of the local landowners and his business prospered so well that he was able to move to 17 Montpelier Row in 1826. Gilbert had six children, of whom only George jnr (1823-1903) entered the business; Joseph Francis (d. 1855) became an inventor, specialising in ordnance; Albert (b. 1826) was an architect; but John (1817-1897), an artist, achieved real distinction, being awarded a knighthood in 1872. He was principal artist for the Illustrated London News for more than 30 years, President of the Water Colour Society in 1870 and a Royal Academician in 1876. From 1864 until his death he lived at 11 Vanbrugh Park Road West (Ivy House, since demolished) and left a fortune of nearly £232,000.

In 1857 George Felix Gilbert sold his business to John Dyer (1832-1910), by then a business associate, and the company remained in the Dyer family until the 1960s. John Dyer was succeeded by his son William John Dyer (1857-1932) who took John Hilton into partnership in 1882. In 1913 the third generation of the Dyer family joined the board - Capt. William Fanstone Dyer (d. 1962) - and the firm kept the title Dyer, Son & Hilton until 1917, when Hilton retired.

After the Great War the company expanded and John Rogers Creasey (1886-1950) and his brother, Robert Douglas Creasey, were taken into partnership in 1922. Although the trading name Dyer, Son & Creasey has remained over the agency door ever since, the control of the company passed, after the death of William Dyer in 1962, to the Barwick family. But Dyer's can still claim to be the oldest estate agency in Blackheath, having traceable origins going back at least 156 years.

6 Park House and the Bennett Park Estate

The eastern edge of the main road cutting through the Village marked the boundary of the old Wricklemarsh estate which passed successively from the Blunt family, to John Morden and, eventually, to Gregory Page.

Although Page was responsible for the demolition of the old Wricklemarsh house there seems to be enough evidence to show that he kept the kitchen garden, nurseries and vinery on their traditional sites so that when Cator purchased the estate from Page's legatees there were clearly defined sections of the property that lent themselves for development. The principal plot was an 11 acre parcel of ground which stretched roughly from the present line of Blackheath Park to Blackheath Grove to the north and was bounded on the west by what is now Lee Road and Blackheath Village and on the east by the back garden walls of the houses on the west side of Pond Road.

Cator had purchased Wricklemarsh in 1783 and, so far as we know, the first lease he granted was to Captain Thomas Larkins (c1746-1794) for the plot as described above. It was for a term of 90 years and commenced at Michaelmas 1787 at an annual rent of £83.10.0. Larkins, an East India Company Commander and part ship-owner, built a house on the crest of the high ground on the south of his 11 acre plot - Park House, now the presbytery of St. Mary's Roman Catholic Church in Creswell Park. This house was built with materials salvaged from Page's Wricklemarsh, which Cator started to pull down in the same year. An unidentified newspaper cutting of September 1787 confirms this: "Captain Larkins has purchased a large quantity of materials (of Sir Gregory Page's mansion) and is now building a house on the brow of the hill 200 yards to the west of the late mansion."

Some authorities have claimed that Larkins built the house for his own use but the facts almost certainly confirm that the project was nothing more than a speculation for, by 1788, he was advertising the house to be let or sold. For this transaction the ground attached was only seven acres - whether Larkins retained the other four acres for separate development or had surrendered part of the lease back to John Cator is not known. We do know that some of the kitchen garden and nursery ground on the site of what is now Blackheath Grove and the railway line had been let for horticultural purposes as early as 1784 when it was held by Christopher Fell and rated as "part of Mr. Cator's garden". Thomas Larkins let his new house but only enjoyed its proceeds for a further six years, for he died early in 1794 after a visit to the London Tavern where "he was seized with a fit and taken into a coffee house where every effort was used for his recovery but in vain." (Gentlemen's Magazine)

The new tenant for Park House was Francis Easterby, a director of the

East India Dock Co., who initially rented the property but took over Lark-in's lease from the latter's executors in July 1806. Easterby (d. c1834) lived in Blackheath until 1824 but in May 1807 he changed his name to Cress-well. This was his wife's maiden name, she was the daughter of John Cresswell of Cresswell, Morpeth, in Northumberland, and Francis prob-ably took the new name to satisfy the conditions of a legacy or inheritance.

In November 1825 the unexpired portion of Larkin's original lease was assigned by Cresswell to John Bennett, the Cheapside and Greenwich watchmaker and manufacturer of scientific instruments. Bennett (fl. 1770-1830) did not live in the house, but he used this new property to increase the family fortunes and, as a result, he left a legacy in bricks and mortar which have long survived any memory or appreciation of the man and his family.

In order not to break the continuity of the narrative the Bennett develop-ments are described later in this chapter under the headings of the present street names.

Park House, which in Cresswell's occupancy had established the name Cresswell for the park and the road leading from the Village, was by 1825, subject to the headlease assigned to John Bennett. It was sub-let to Nath-aniel Brown Engleheart (1791-1869) a proctor of Doctors Commons and son of George Engleheart (1752-1829), the miniature painter to George III and pupil of Sir Joshua Reynolds (1723-1792). In fact, when Engleheart snr was 75 years old he came to live with his son in Blackheath and died at Park House in 1829.

Nathaniel entered into the spirit of the growing Blackheath community and his name frequently appears in the records of local charitable and cultural activity, for he was what we would call an all-round man. He was an amateur carpenter and carver and even set up his own printing press at Park House where he produced at least three books: "Reminiscences of former happy days...by a Septuagenarian...printed by N.B. Engleheart at his extensive printing Establishment at Blackheath, 1863"; "Omnium Gath-erum - from an old portfolio, in 1864; and two editions of "A Concise Treatise on Eccentric Turning", first published in 1852, but reprinted with Engleheart's name on the title in 1867.

Nathaniel Engleheart married Mary Jane Curteis (1795-1859) and they produced 15 children, eight sons and seven daughters: many of the boys followed their father's profession and became lawyers, and some practised in Blackheath, but the three eldest all pre-deceased their father.

Nathaniel Brown (1815-1853) was a proctor and died at 85 Lee Road; George Edward (1818-1853) became a barrister and lived on Guernsey; Benjamin Octavius (1825-1892) was an auctioneer and estate agent and con-ducted a business at 18 Tranquil Vale from about 1852 to 1863, some of this time with Arthur Kirkman. This Engleheart was declared bankrupt in 1863 but he seems to have recovered his financial standing because he was in business again from 1865 to 1867 at 22 Montpelier Vale. William Hayley (1816-1853) was in practise as a lawyer at 27 Tranquil Vale in the early 1850s.

Of Nathaniel's daughters, the eldest, Mary Jane (1813-1873) married Pelham Richardson (1804-1860) the bookseller who lived firstly at 97 Blackheath Park and later at 15 Morden Road.

On Nathaniel Engleheart's death the surviving members of the family quit Park House and the lease was surrendered to the Bennett trustees.

By then the park land once attached to the house was in the process of development so that the next tenant of the big house found a considerably reduced garden area, mainly confined to the large lawn to the south which fronted on to Blackheath Park. This arrangement proved quite suitable, for the new occupier of Park House was Dr. William Todd (1820-1887) who, although born a protestant and ordained in Dublin, had been converted to Catholicism and ordained into the priesthood of the Roman Catholic Church. His first ministry was in the Catholic diocese of Southwark and his parish was at Chislehurst. Todd's abiding concern was with orphans and he founded St. Mary's Orphanage for Boys at Chislehurst during the 1850s. The location quickly proved inadequate and Todd moved the home to Crooms Hill in 1860 to a house borrowed from Canon North, the then Rector of Greenwich. According to the history of the Blackheath church, Todd and North quarrelled and the Catholic was forced to find new premises very quickly if his orphanage was to continue. There was, by this time, a sizeable congregation of local catholics, worshipping at Our Ladye Star of the Sea, built in Crooms Hill in 1851, despite much anti-popery. Todd knew that he would receive support for his orphanage and when he found Park House empty he purchased the remains of the lease and opened the orphanage there in 1870. The boys were largely the sons of clerks, doctors, service officers and professional men and Todd's list of subscribers grew in eminence to include many of the Catholic bishops and the Dukes of Norfolk. One of his first acts was the building of a small chapel on the site of the present parish hall and the erection of a two-storey school with a refectory and playroom abutting Park House. The existence of the chapel caused problems in that Dr. Todd offered Mass to Catholics not resident at the orphanage and this took worshippers away from the congregation at the Crooms Hill church. The difficulty was resolved and Blackheath became a separate district of the diocese in 1873.

The next major change to Park House came during the ministry of Father Francis J. Sheehan (1859-1935) in 1890-91. Sheehan had served as curate at the Blackheath church and returned as the fourth priest in 1888, and soon after his appointment plans were laid for the building of a new church in Cresswell Park. The financial impetus came from the Butler family who lived at 50 Lee Terrace and had been unsuccessful in agreeing terms with the freeholder (the Page Estate) to build a Catholic church on the sites of 50 & 52 Lee Terrace.

Because the orphanage lease had, by then, another 60 years to run, it was decided to build the church in the grounds at Cresswell Park, and the new church - Our Lady Help of the Christians - was opened on July 11 1891 by the Roman Catholic Bishop of Southwark. It was built in Kentish ragstone, to the design of the architect A. E. Pardic, by Messrs Smith & Sons of Norwood, and cost £4,147. It was enhanced with a small, proportional tower incorporating a statue of the Patroness of the church.

With the new church, the Blackheath congregation grew and has remained a secure part of the community ever since, surviving not only the 1939-1945 war, but also the general decline in religious observance.

After the dedication of the new church in 1891 the old building, erected in 1870, was turned into a church hall. This hall suffered badly in the war and it was demolished; the present parish hall was not built until 1955.

The garden ground to the south of the church and Park House (facing into Blackheath Park) had been leased with Park House as early as 1807 and has remained part of the title ever since. The freehold of both the Church and Presbytery now belongs to the Church authorities.

THE DEVELOPMENT OF THE BENNETT ESTATE

When John Bennett purchased, in 1825, the unexpired portion of the old lease granted to Larkins in 1787, the total ground was about seven acres. Larkins' lease had referred to 11 acres and the author, for the lack of positive evidence, can only assume that Cator took back some of the land fronting Blackheath Park and Lee Road and some of the frontages in what is now Cresswell Park.

Be that as it may, the matter is further complicated because the Larkins lease was surrendered before its expiry, due in 1877, and a new 99-year lease issued in 1860 to the Bennett trustees. The new lease included not only all that area covered by the 1825 assignment but embraced a small but important parcel of land known as Frederick's Place, now the site of Nos. 16-20 Tranquil Vale. In order to keep the narrative as clear as possible, the history of Frederick's Place and Blackheath Grove is dealt with at the end of this section.

The developments on the Bennett Park estate can be split into two groups:

Group 1: Cresswell Park - 1828
     Brunswick Place (now Nos. 1-9 Blackheath Village) - 1828

Group 2: Bennett Place (now Nos. 11 & 13 Blackheath Village) - 1862
     Bennett Park - 1863
     Alexandra Hall - 1863
     Frederick's Place - rebuilt 1863
     Blackheath Grove - 1864

Cresswell Park

Although it is possible that the development of Cresswell Park in 1828 was not undertaken by the Bennett family, it is convenient to deal with these houses at this point.

The developer was probably one John Grice, who built a row of 6 three-storey houses, in the form of three pairs of semi-detached units - to the west side of Park House along what is now the east-west line of Cresswell Park. The surviving houses - 1 to 4 Cresswell Park - looked northwards across the valley of the Upper Kid Brook, towards the Heath, over the roof-tops of the small shops then recently erected on both sides of Mont-pelier Vale. The western pair of Grice's houses faced into Lee Road and were subsequently demolished for the erection of Beaconsfield Buildings in 1884-1887.

From the outset Grice was the ratepayer for all his houses, although he was probably an absentee landlord, living perhaps only at No. 4 (the house nearest the Church) until 1831, after which all the houses had been let or sold. The numbering of the properties changed over the years and what is now No. 1 was No. 4 Cresswell Park and, further, at some time Nos. 1 & 2 were held as a single unit. The present numbering seems to have been established in 1845.

Initially, Nos. 1 & 2 Cresswell Park were linked in that they were both rented by Major William Richardson (1771-?1847) who had been licensed to take boarders attending the new Blackheath Proprietary School built in 1831 in the Village on the west side of the Lee Road. Richardson conducted the boarding house for approximately 16 BPS pupils until 1844, at which date he seems to have relinquished his interest in 1 Cresswell Park. His successor at this address was a schoolmaster, John Glover, but whether he conducted a school here is not recorded. A later tenant from 1874 to 1878 was a Captain Marshall Hall, the father of G. W. L. Marshall Hall then a student at the Proprietary School but later a distinguished advocate.

From the early years of this century until the last war the house was used as a hostel for employees of Messrs Hinds drapery shops in Lee Road; both 1 & 2 Cresswell Park remain in the freehold of Hinds successors, Hinds of Eltham Ltd., but in recent years No. 1 has been the offices of a publishing company.

No. 2 Cresswell Park was held by Major Richardson until 1847 when he gave up his duties as a boarding house master because of death or retirement. Thereafter it passed through a number of brief tenancies but in 1856 it was used by Miss Mary Tatlock as a boarding school until 1861. From 1869 to 1872 it was the home of the Reverend Christopher Cyprian Fenn MA, then Secretary of the Church Missionary Society and curate at St. Michael's Church in Blackheath Park where his father, Reverend Joseph Fenn was incumbent from 1828 to 1876. In 1873, No. 2 Cresswell Park was taken by Miss Jane Caroline Corbett and she, and subsequently her relatives, remained in the house until the death of Francis Mary Corbett in October 1940 - a single family occupancy of 67 years.

Nos. 3 & 4 Cresswell Park were purchased in 1838 by the McLeod family: John Crofton McLeod and his son, Joseph, a solicitor, lived from 1838 - 1845 at No. 4, and both properties remained with McLeod jnr until his death in 1878 when they were sold. But after 1845, No. 4 was rented by (Sir) John Hollams (1820-1910) a solicitor who became President of the Law Society in 1878-79 and was knighted in 1902. Hollams left Cresswell Park in 1851 but lived at Paragon House, South Row, from 1860 to c1875.

From 1892 the tenant was Lt. Col. James L. Ratton (1845-1924) of the Indian Army Medical Service, who was succeeded here on his death by his son-in-law Col. I. E. F. D'Apice, DSO, RA, (1878-1952) who was still living here up until the 1939-1945 war, completing a family occupancy of more than 48 years.

Of the tenants of No. 3 Cresswell Park none seem to have achieved distinction and few stayed in the house for more than two or three years with the exception of John Harris and, later, his widow Elizabeth Harris, who lived here from 1855 to 1887.

Alpha House and Hillside

The two houses in Cresswell Park which faced Lee Road were markedly different from Grice's other properties and their position made them attractive and convenient buildings to occupy.

Hillside, the northern half of the pair - part of which can be seen in an early postcard view of the south end of Blackheath Village - was completed by the end of 1830 but not occupied until 1833 when it was rented by Thomas Marshall (1781-1855), a retired Lieutenant of Marines. He was succeeded by Barber Tuck (1809-1865) the grocer whose business at 36

Tranquil Vale was one of the most prosperous in the Village; after his death Mrs. Sarah Tuck remained in the house, but in 1874 the property had been leased to Edward Belleroche, a Belgian by birth, who lived in Blackheath for more than 20 years. Like many outsiders he was able to observe the British at their best and worst and made a reputation for himself with his campaigns for improvements in the management of the district, especially for the less bureaucratic control of the Heath and in pressing the railway company to widen Blackheath railway bridge. He was not successful in this last and when he returned to Belgium the Directors of the South Eastern Railway Co., although not his fellow Blackheathens, must have been relieved. Belleroche was the last tenant of the house, quitting in 1882, the year before its demolition.

Alpha house was the largest of the Cresswell Park development and, for a time, was divided into two dwellings, 6 & 7 Cresswell Park. But by 1840 the two units were rated and tenanted as a single dwelling. From 1841 to 1845 the house took the address Cresswell Park Hill and was occupied by William Moberley, but on his departure the building was occupied by the first of a succession of school-owners who leased the house until it was demolished in 1882-3.

The first was Miss Anne Chapman (b. 1805) who used Alpha House as a preparatory boarding school; she was followed in 1857 by Robert Haynes who ran it as a boys' school. In 1866 Mrs. Shaw altered the pattern and only took day pupils, but within a year the business had been purchased by the 30-year old Mrs. Kate Gibbs who restored the boarding element. By 1871 there were eleven resident pupils here and Mrs. Gibbs conducted a respected preparatory school for boys between the ages of six and 14, until the lease expired in 1881. The house was torn down the following year and Mrs. Gibbs moved her school to 1 Leyland Road in Lee.

Brunswick Place

At the same time as John Grice was building his houses in Cresswell Park another development was under way on the Bennett Estate, this time on the important Lee Road frontage. It was a seven-house terrace of three storeys and was given the name Brunswick Place, no doubt to honour the memory of Caroline, Duchess of Brunswick, Queen to George IV, who had lived at Montague House on the south west corner of Greenwich Park. Caroline was much loved by the people of Blackheath and during her lifetime they not only named a pub in her honour (The Princess of Wales) they even set fire to the Heath on her birthday.

Brunswick Place was built as a terrace of private houses, but the loss of Nos. 1 & 2 for the railway metals, the addition of two buildings at the south end of the terrace, and the subsequent conversion of the buildings into commercial premises in 1893 has not helped towards the conservation of what must have been a group with much charm and interest.

Further, the terrace has suffered four changes in name and numbering which, even today, can cause some doubts in the minds of Blackheath residents as to the correct postal address: "The group opposite the station" is likely to mean more than 1-9 (odd) Blackheath Village, as can be seen below.

1828-1884	1885	1886	1929
1 Brunswick Place (demolished 1848)			
2 "	"	"	"
3 "	"	"	" - rebuilt 1858
	{14 Tranquil Vale	1 Lee Road	1 Blackheath Village
4 "	" 12 "	" 3 " "	3 " "
5 "	" 10 "	" 5 " "	5 " "
6 "	" 8 "	" 7 " "	7 " "
7 "	" 6 "	" 9 " "	9 " "

The building of Brunswick Place on land previously sub-let to the Hally family as a nursery garden was an important part of the development of Blackheath Village, for it completed a chain of developments which stretched from the north west corner of Blackheath Park through the Village along Montpelier Row and ended with The Paragon. There were subsequent changes but these entailed re-building over existing foundations; thus, to all intents and purposes, Blackheath Village was completed with the erection of Brunswick Place in 1828. The addition of the railway station in 1849 helped turn the southern extremity into the heart of the town.

In its original form Brunswick Place was divided from the building which pre-dated the present 16 Tranquil Vale (Barclays Bank) only by a footpath. The cutting of the railway along the line of the Upper Kid Brook meant that Nos. 1 - 3 Brunswick Place had to be demolished only twenty years after they had been built, and this upset the harmony of the terrace which had been developed as a scheme rather than simply as a string of identical houses. The central pediment over the present 3 Blackheath Village (the tobacconist) indicates the middle of the group and it is probably safe to assume that 1 & 2 Brunswick Place were identical to the surviving houses.

The terrace was certainly built as housing, but before long they had been taken by shopkeepers and other commercial users and the front drawing rooms adapted for retail use. Nevertheless, it was not until 1893 that Brunswick Place became aggressively commercial and the present shop fronts extended over what had been private front yards or gardens.

Consent for the conversion of domestic housing into shops by the process of adding one storey shop fronts was not given lightly in the 1890s, principally because it was felt that there were enough shops but not nearly enough housing. The Brunswick Place development was approved no doubt because the buildings had been in commercial use for almost 50 years and the designs submitted were of a better quality than most, having been designed by an architect - John Rowland - as an overall scheme rather than piecemeal development. The work was completed in August 1893 and reported as "... several improvements of more or less public interest..." The most remarkable aspects of this work were those extensions designed for Jobbins at Nos. 6 & 7 Brunswick Place and for Wayland at No. 2 Bennett Place (q.v.).

The terrace was included in the new lease granted to the Bennett trustees in 1860 and it was the expiry of this as well as the neglect caused by the war in 1939-1945, that brought Brunswick Place to a poor condition by the 1950s. In 1961 plans were submitted for the replacement of the whole group with an ambitious scheme of shops, flats and offices, partially built out over the railway cutting. The scheme was rejected by the then London County Council principally on two grounds: firstly, that the scheme did not contain enough residential accommodation and, perhaps more importantly, that part of the new development would be in the way of the projected motorway suggested by the Greater London Development Plan. Thus, because the LCC did not wish to make a decision which would increase the value of the site and push up compensation rates when the motorway was built, Brunswick Place was saved. But, at the time of writing, the motorway plan has been scrapped and because the present leases on Brunswick Place expire in 1980 the future of the terrace will, once again, be in doubt.

1 & 2 Brunswick Place

The two houses at the north end of the terrace were demolished for the building of the North Kent Railway in 1848/9 although both were empty at the time and no tenants had to be dispossessed. No. 1 was the home of James Sterry (1780-1848), a carpenter, whose death must have been most convenient for the railway company.

No. 2 was first occupied by a Mrs. Smith, but by the summer of 1831 the tenant was William Stidolph, a versatile entrepreneur who combined the activities of concert promotion with those of selling books and music, stationery, life insurance and property investment. He was also a teacher of writing and his wife Maria returned to Blackheath in 1860 and ran a girls' school at Phoenix Place for a short time.

Stidolph left Brunswick Place in 1839 and his house was taken by Miss Isabella Royal (b. 1781) for a girls' school. It was very small but with a high teacher/pupil ratio of 3:1 (there were only nine students, and two governesses to assist Miss Royal) and it had closed by 1846.

3 Brunswick Place (now 1 Blackheath Village)

Although built in 1828, the first tenants here did not move in until 1830 and the house became, for three years, the home of James Bunce (1790-1858) who became Master of the Queen's Bench Court, and moved in 1834 to 8 Pond Road. Until the demolition in 1848 the leaseholders included William Voller, the tailor who moved to 2 Montpelier Vale in 1840, and Frederick Wrake, a bookseller, in 1841. He was followed by a Mrs. Leadbitter, but from 1845 to 1848 the house was rented by Samuel Warner, the plasterer, who moved to 23 Tranquil Vale at the end of his tenancy.

By the mid 1850s the railway company released some of the land they had acquired for building. Blackheath had been one of the main centres for the work and more land had been taken than was eventually needed, particularly on the south side of the permanent way. In 1858 3 Brunswick Place was re-built as a single storey shop, probably because the railway embankment was not strong enough to support a more substantial structure.

For the next 25 years the shop was occupied by a succession of estate agents and surveyors, a highly-profitable business during the years 1855-1885. The original company was started by Arthur Abraham Kirkman (1825-1867) who had opened an office at 18 Tranquil Vale in 1852 and was, briefly, in partnership with Benjamin Octavius Engleheart there. On Kirkman's death the Brunswick Place office passed through a series of partnerships: 1867-1873 Edward Thomas Coppinger, who was joined in by Edwin Shalless in 1870; Shalless (d. 1876) was on his own by 1874 but was joined by Alfred Budds who traded as Shalless and Budds until

1884.

In 1885 the estate agents were replaced by tobacconists, initially by John Goslin (1827-1901) who traded at 50 Tranquil Vale from 1850 until his old shop was redeveloped in 1885. Goslin's business was acquired by John Silverstone & Co., who owned the tobacco shops at 11 Tranquil Vale and, later, 4 Montpelier Vale. Eventually the shop was acquired by W. Findlay & Co. but by 1935 they had moved next door and 3 Brunswick Place became Bon-Accord Antiques, in 1937 Blackheath Kennels and, during the last war the coal order office of Rickett, Cockerell & Co. In recent years it has been a shoe mender and a greengrocery.

4 Brunswick Place (now 3 Blackheath Village)

Probably no shop in Blackheath Village has enjoyed such a variety of tenants as 4 Brunswick Place, not only because of the trades they followed but also because many traders established important reputations here or in other Village premises after starting their commercial careers in this shop. This movement was encouraged by the sub-letting of the upper rooms for commercial use and the addition of a workshop at the rear.

The first tenants of any interest arrived in 1835 when Mrs. Elizabeth S. Bennett, widow of John Bennett who owned the headlease of the premises, continued the family clock and watch making business; in 1839 the company had been taken over by George Bennett, but he moved to the new shop at 28 Tranquil Vale in 1841. The Bennetts were followed by Thomas William Smith (1809-?1890) the hairdresser whose shop enjoyed a high reputation when he moved to 25 Tranquil Vale (q. v.); at Brunswick Place Thomas was sharing the premises with his wife, Ann, who made straw hats. In 1850 the shop became a milliners, firstly owned by Jane Trill, probably the daughter of silk mercer William Arthur Trill of 5 & 7 Tranquil Vale, but later in the hands of Margaret Sarah Clark. By 1854 the Clark family (George and the Misses Jane and Catherine) had abandoned the hats and were offering a wide range of linen goods. From 1858 to 1860 the premises were taken by William Hasler & Sons, tailors.

A major change was effected in 1861 when the shop was leased by Edgar Drewett, a photographer by profession but a man who dabbled in property management, and once described himself as a brick maker of Burnt Ash Lane. To judge from the printed directories Drewett (sometimes spelled Drouitt or Drouett) left the photography to assistants: in 1871 George Edwards; 1875 Joseph P. Sterling; 1880 Frederick Potter; and Henry Cocking in 1882; while the owner indulged in his other interests including the management of the Alexandra Hall (q. v.) of which he is recorded as proprietor from 1864 to 1868 and again in 1872.

For the want of other evidence it is likely that Drewett built the workshop extension at the back of the shop in 1868 and this was let to James Jennings, a letterpress and copperplate printer and the first printer of any note to set up a press in Blackheath Village. Some of the earlier stationers claimed to be printers but almost certainly they could handle little more than cards and letterheads and placed more substantial work elsewhere. Jennings' steam-operated presses could cope with books, magazines, including the magazine of the Blackheath Proprietary School, and even a newspaper - The West Kent Courier - which he published between 1880 and 1883.

Drewett's lease expired in 1887, although he quit the previous year; and no doubt the term of his sub-lease to Jennings expired at the same time

The new tenant of the front shop introduced a new trade - she was Mrs. Jane Standage, a ladies and childrens' outfitter, and she remained here until June 1901 when she sold her business to Madame Annie Barr (d. 1936) of Birmingham. Madame Barr moved to more spacious premises at 3 Lee Road in 1907 but in the short stay at Brunswick Place established a reputation which was retained until the 1970s by her successors.

After Madame Barr had left 4 Brunswick Place the shop section passed through a variety of tenancies: from 1908 to 1913 it was the offices of the auctioneers and house agents, Richardson & Booth; for a brief time in 1914/15 it was the Blackheath branch of Howard Percival, a hosier; but from 1916 to the early 1930s it was the showroom of the Singer Sewing Machine Co. By 1935 the shop had become a branch of the tobacconist group Findlay & Co., but in recent years has traded as Suzy, tobacconist and confectioner.

The upstairs premises had been let separately as early as the mid 1870s when they were used by Mrs. Mary Mackins, a dressmaker, and for a year or two, as the offices of the local branch of the Church of England Young Men's Society. In more recent years, from 1908 to the end of the 1920s, it was the surgery of the dental surgeon Leonard Ta'Bois LDS.

Reverting to the workshop at the rear, when Jennings left Blackheath, the goodwill and equipment of the printing company were acquired by Charles North (1847-1915), a printer who had set up his press in what was then 39 Turner Road, Lee, in 1881, and traded as The Blackheath Press. North, who was the son of James North (1815-1899), came from Buckingham and served his apprenticeship with Harrison & Sons, the printers in St. Martin's Lane, WC2. His arrival in Blackheath was timely, for with the growth in the district of every conceivable association, club and learned society, there was an enormous demand for print. Jennings was a straightforward jobbing printer - Charles North was a highly-skilled exponent of his craft, a sound businessman and deeply committed to the aims of many of the learned societies for whom he worked. His first major job had been the printing and production of F.H. Hart's History of Lee in 1882. North became the official printer for the Lewisham Antiquarian Society, printing for them not only their transactions but a series of volumes of lasting antiquarian interest which are a tribute not only to the scholarship of their compilers but also to the quality of North's presswork.

But perhaps Charles North's greatest monument was the Blackheath Local Guide and District Advertiser, a newspaper founded by him in January 1889. Initially it was little more than an advertising medium, 7" x 9½", only eight pages, with details of the local omnibus and train timetables, church services and a few paragraphs of local news. It was published fortnightly and delivered free to every household in the district, possibly the first of its kind in the country and much imitated. Within five years the circulation had reached 5000 and the number of pages had grown from 8 to 60, a remarkable achievement which allowed North to install new equipment and, for lack of space forced a move in 1892 to larger premises at the old Alexandra Hall on the corner of Cresswell Park.

The print shop stayed empty for some years but in 1917 a dancing teacher, Miss Duncan, was forced to leave the rooms she used at the Art Club building at the end of Bennett Park then under military requisition. She took over the workshop at Brunswick Place and she, and her successors, Miss Doris Idle from 1929 and, in recent years, Barbara Stow, have taught the various dance steps regarded as socially necessary over the years.

5 Brunswick Place (now 5 Blackheath Village)

As a private house this building was first occupied by Mrs. Nash from 1829 to 1831 and then by Mrs. Penson from 1832 to 1836. In 1837 the occupier was John James Hudson, a hatter, and this established a commercial use for the premises. Hudson left in 1843 to open a stationery shop in London Street, Greenwich, and the shop at Brunswick Place passed to Paul Hack in 1844 and Thomas Bincker in 1849, both dealers in Berlin wool, although Hack was a glover by trade.

In 1853 the house was taken by Frances Roe, a governess and school-mistress who opened a school here. Miss Roe (1825-1890/91) took boarding and day pupils, charging 25 guineas a year for the former and 1 guinea a quarter for the day girls. Each was required to bring a silver spoon, knife and fork and six towels. The school moved to 4 Bennett Park in 1872 where it remained for a further 18 years.

Miss Roe's successor at Brunswick Place was the Village tailor and mercer Charles John Bond, then in retirement after 40 years trading at 50 Tranquil Vale (q.v.) and elsewhere. Bond died in 1879 but his widow lived on at No. 5 for another year.

The Bond's successors at Brunswick Place were builders and sanitary engineers and made considerable alterations to the frontage of the property, firmly establishing it in commercial use. The company was started here by Samuel Hider in 1881, but by the following year he was in partnership with George Allen & Son, of Lee High Road. In 1885 Hider retired and the business was pursued solely by the Allens, who were joined in 1899 by Ernest Pink, an electrical contractor and a necessary ally at that time when no self-respecting builder dare admit to ignorance of the new means of illumination.

George Allen dabbled in estate agency and this may account for the fact that the upstairs rooms were let to surveyors from time to time, including J.D. Edmeston, the architect involved in the development of Westcombe Park and part designer of the Blackheath Concert Hall and Conservatoire of Music in 1895-6. For a brief while L. Spiers, the district surveyor, kept an office here but by 1908 there had been a complete change and 5 Brunswick Place was used as a servants' registry by Mrs. Davies and a coal order office by Thomas R. Huntley & Co. In 1913 the premises were taken over by the auctioneers and house agents, Richardson, Booth & Maynard. In 1914 the company was run by Edward W. Maynard and David Davidson, and they operated from here until July 1921 when the business was acquired by Messrs W. Laurence Foster & Horace G. Foster. The Fosters remained in Blackheath until 1964 when the business was sold to Victor W. Hindwood & Co., estate agents then with offices at 1 Charlton Road. Shortly afterwards the company was renamed Hindwood, Clarke & Esplin, in whose hands the shop remains today.

6 Brunswick Place (now 7 Blackheath Village)

Since 1897 6 Brunswick Place has been linked with No. 7 as a single retail unit, but prior to that date it followed the pattern of the other houses in the group. It was first occupied in 1830 by George Ramsey who was succeeded in 1833 by a Miss Tyler. From 1836 to 1853 the tenants were the Misses Elizabeth Morgan and Matilda Jewell, milliners and dressmakers. They left the house in 1854 and were followed, for two years, by William Heasler. For the two years 1858 to 1860 the premises were used by Henry Morley, the music dealer from Crooms Hill whose business had been established in 1828. Brunswick Place was a temporary stay for Morley for he moved to 45 Tranquil Vale in 1861 and to 23 Tranquil Vale (q. v.) in 1888 where the company remained until 1942.

For the years 1861 to 1882 6 Brunswick Place was a doctors' surgery, occupied by a number of prominent local medical men as a branch of their main practices: from 1861 to 1867, Drs. Finch, Moon and Duncan of London Street, Greenwich; from 1868, Robert Finch (1825-1881) who was joined by Dr. Elphinstone in 1874. In 1878 Finch was in partnership with Dr. Peter Cooper (1854-1927). Finch and Cooper were best known for their practice at Stainton Lodge, 35 Shooters Hill Road, and the Brunswick Place rooms were probably not their main base.

With the expiry of the lease the doctors left No. 6 and for the five years 1885 to 1890 the premises were used by Mrs. Caroline Allen, a dyer and cleaner. It was during the occupation of Mrs. Allen's successors - Mr. & Mrs. Peter Newbould, who ran a scholastic and servants' agency - that the shop front was built forward in 1893, but the work cannot have been much use to the Newboulds and they left in 1896. The following year the lease was acquired by George Riddington Hutchings, the baker who traded from 7 Brunswick Place, and the shop has remained part of those premises ever since.

7 Brunswick Place (now 9 Blackheath Village)

The first tenant was a Mrs. Eliza Cudliph (1766-1845), who moved here in 1829, one of the first tenants of Brunswick Place. After her death the house passed through various hands, including Alfred Walker from 1846 to 1850, and Mrs. Elizabeth Warner, a milliner, in 1851. From 1854 to 1858 the occupier was Samuel Warner, probably the plasterer who lived for some years at 23 Tranquil Vale (q. v.)

It was in December 1859 that the property was adapted for a bakery by Stephen Riddington (1811-1882) and this is the use to which the shop has been subject ever since, although bread is no longer baked on the premises.

The Riddington family came from Colnbrook, Berkshire, and by 1839 Stephen had opened a bakery on the Lewisham High Road to the south of St. Mary's Church. In 1845, his brother, Joseph, had set up as a butcher at 60 Tranquil Vale. His success, no doubt, encouraged Stephen to open a branch of his business at Brunswick Place despite the fact that there were other bakers in Blackheath Village, including Smith's bakehouse at 63 Tranquil Vale which had been the principal bakery in the Village since 1800. Riddington's shop was well-sited commercially, close to Blackheath Park and the newly-developed Lee Park, and the business prospered. On Stephen's death the business was controlled by his widow, Frances Riddington, but for the last ten years it was supervised by his son, George, who had added the additional surname of Hutchings. In 1897 George Riddington Hutchings leased the next door premises and created the double-fronted shop we know today. In 1893 Hutchings had been an enthusiastic participant in the scheme to extend the shop fronts of Brunswick Place and the plain house front disappeared behind an "artistic and elaborate" facade and the interior was re-fitted and "luxuriously furnished in the oriental style". The bakery now offered teas, luncheons and ice creams, and Riddington's started catering for outside functions, in particular for weddings which, by this date, seem to have been used by Blackheath families mainly as demonstrations of financial opulence.

In 1898 Riddington-Hutchings sold out to Stephen Jobbins (1852-1912), by then his principal rival not only in baking but in general catering as well. Jobbins was the son of George Frederick Jobbins (1817-1895) who had opened his Blackheath bakery at 21 Montpelier Vale (q.v.) in 1856. Stephen Jobbins kept the Montpelier Vale bakery for two more years but in 1900 he concentrated his attention on the double shop at Brunswick Place.

He increased the space for the restaurant side of the business, calling this section "The Luncheon and Oriental Tea Rooms", and fitted ladies and gentlemen's lavatories and a hot and cold shower bath "for use of football clubs, etc." An awning was erected over the flat roof of the front extension so that patrons could enjoy their tea in the (partial) open air and watch the life of the Village flow before them. It was plain teas for 9d. and additional "creature comforts" for 1/-, and very popular they were. By the turn of the century Jobbins had five branches in the vicinity, at Lewisham, Lee, Eltham and Mottingham, and was set on the path of expansion, eventually taking over Barrett & Sons shops in Tranquil Vale. In 1926 the company not only employed the ex-patissier from Harrod's in Knightsbridge, but also a general manager. It was inevitable that Jobbins would be taken over, and from 1931 it came under the control of E.J. Hall (1886-1948). Over the next few years, and by a process too complex to explain here, the Blackheath bakery, founded in 1856, had become by the late 1950s part of Rank's and a branch of one of that company's satellites - Ackerman's. The whole is now part of the Rank-Hovis-McDougall bread and flour empire who have not, it is pleasing to relate, imposed the dead hand of uniformity on Jobbins, and allow the Blackheath shop to continue trading under its original name. It is of interest, perhaps, to note here that James Thomas McDougall (1843-1919), the flour merchant, and one of the forebears of the company which now owns Jobbins, lived at 12 Morden Road from 1886 to 1916.

Bennett Place and Bennett Park

John Bennett's lease on the Estate was due to expire in 1877 but it is now clear that the family was negotiating a new lease from the Cators from about 1855.

Old John Bennett had died about 1830, not having lived in Blackheath, but his three sons, John Bennett (1814-1897), George Weedon Bennett (1816-1861) and William Cox Bennett (1820-1895) pursued the family business of making clocks and watches, and were firmly established in Cheapside and Stockwell Street in Greenwich.

Mrs. Elizabeth Bennett, old John's widow, opened the Blackheath branch at 4 Brunswick Place (q.v.) in 1835. She worked here with son George, but after her death he took more substantial premises at the then newly-built 9 Osborne Place (28 Tranquil Vale) in 1840.

John Bennett jnr remained in London although he lived at Cresswell Park for a short while in the 1850s, probably to be on hand during the reorganisation of the family finances. The Bennett shop at Cheapside was his concern and through it he achieved some distinction in City circles, moving through the Court of Common Council, to be elected Sheriff and receive a knighthood in 1873. Despite spending money in the proper places - he advertised on the front page of the Catalogue to the Great Exhibition in 1851 at a cost of £150 - he failed to become an Alderman because, although three times elected, each election was annulled.

Brother William lived in Greenwich and earned no small reputation as a poet and journalist. He was active in local politics and persuaded his fellow Greenwich Liberals to adopt William Ewart Gladstone (1809-1898) as their prospective MP in 1868. When George Bennett died in 1861 his shop was taken over by William, but it was left in the hands of trustees and finally sold in about 1870. He became London correspondent for Le Figaro.

To return to the chronology of events, by the 1850s the Bennett family held a lease on an estate which had been partly developed with the building of Cresswell Park and Brunswick Place in 1828.

They also held the lease on Frederick's Place (q.v.), and the remainder of the ground had been let as nursery gardens to John Hally. In 1849 the north end of the estate had been cut off by the new railway line so that Captain Larkins' miniature country park must have presented a not altogether sylvan appearance by the 1850s.

In May 1855 the Bennetts offered 25 guineas for a block plan for the laying out of the Park for building purposes. It has not proved possible to discover all the details which brought about the development of the Bennett estate but a new 99-year lease was granted by the Cators to run from June 1860. Building went ahead after that date, in that the south west corner of Frederick's Place was re-developed and, by 1866, the Wesleyan church and houses in Blackheath Grove, a few houses in Bennett Park, and Bennett Place had been completed. A building lease was granted for a large site on the corner of Bennett Park and Cresswell Park which had resulted in the Alexandra Hall in 1863.

In August 1866 there was a major sale of the estate properties by order of the executors "of the late Mrs. Bennett, deceased" which included the unexpired leases of most, but not all, of the buildings then completed. It could be that part of the deal with the Cators was that the Bennetts should let off the plots to assignees who would then enter into separate agreements with the freeholder (Cator) but that the Bennetts had kept a number of properties for themselves.

Be that as it may, in January 1871 an Order in Chancery directed the sale of many of the houses in Blackheath Grove and Brunswick Place, because of a testacy dispute (Jenkins v John Bennett and another) and creditors of George Bennett (who had died in 1861) were invited to submit claims. This marked the end of any active interest in the Blackheath estate by the Bennett family, with the exception of John.

The sub-leases on the various properties on the estate changed hands many times whilst the freehold remained, for the most part, with the Cators. But even some of these were sold as the years went by so that when the headleases expired in 1960 there was no possibility for a major re-building scheme to be put in effect, and the broad plan of the old Bennett

Estate has survived.

The paragraphs that follow describe the developments here and the tenancies for those sections of Bennett Park built after 1860.

Bennett Place (Now 11 & 13 Blackheath Village)

To the south of Brunswick Place was a plot of ground which lined up neatly with the boundary of the field at the rear. In 1862 a building lease allowed the erection of two houses which became known as 1 & 2 Bennett Place. The names and numbering have changed at least three times:

1862	1885	1886	1929
1 Bennett Place	2 Tranquil Vale	13 Lee Road	13 Blackheath Village
2 Bennett Place	4 Tranquil Vale	11 Lee Road	11 Blackheath Village

No. 1 Bennett Place was a substantial three storey house, built for Dr. Robert Stark Tate MRCS (1818-1880) who used the building as his home and consulting room. Tate's daughter, Eleanor Gertrude Tate (1875-1929) was one of the founders of St. Helen's, a distinguished girls' school which operated from 81 Vanbrugh Park until 1939.

Dr. Tate's successor at Bennett Place was Dr. Robert McKilliam MD (1837-1915) a homeopathic physician with as much interest in souls as in the physical body. He was a religious zealot, the editor of a church paper called The Morning Star, and deeply interested in missionary work. From 1891 he leased the Alexandra Hall (q.v.) using part for a pharmacy and part for religious worship. In 1896 McKilliam left Bennett Place and moved to 6 Grotes Buildings, and the old surgery closed. The building was then much altered. The original entrance, in Bennett Park, became a front door for the upper rooms, and the Lee Road frontage altered for commercial use. It should come as no surprise that such an important site was taken by John James Sainsbury (1844-1928) for one of the links in his fast-growing chain of grocery shops. Sainsbury, who had worked as a lad for Henry Jeans, an oil and colour merchant at Green's End, Woolwich, had started his own business in 1869 at the age of 19. The branch at Blackheath was just one of the 100 opened between 1892 and 1914, and it remained here until February 1959 when the policy changed to concentrating on large supermarkets in the major shopping districts like Lewisham and Woolwich.

After Sainsbury's departure the shop remained empty for many years, the dusty black roller shutters subject to the attention of the fly posting fraternity. In 1965 it was re-opened by Design Studios Ltd. for the sale of contemporary furniture and fabrics, but this venture did not last and in recent years the occupiers have been Blackheath Travel Ltd., travel agents.

No. 2 Bennett Place was opened in 1862 as the consulting rooms of the Blackheath Homeopathic Dispensary, which cannot have pleased Dr. Tate, next door. The idea behind the Dispensary was to offer an inexpensive medical service to the poor, and for 1/- a week, or 2/6d a month, members could have all the advice and medicine they needed. It was possible to buy books of shilling tickets to distribute to the poor and needy and possibly some of the more tight-fisted households in Blackheath used these to obtain cut-price treatment when their servants were ill. John Urell was the dispenser and the medical officer was Dr. R.M. Theobald, MA, MRCS; to keep an eye on the funds Major General A. Clarke was appointed treasurer. Alas, the Blackheath Homeopathic Dispensary did not last and the consulting room gave way to the drawing room of Charles Dawson Philpot, manager of the South East Banking Co. Ltd. in 1865. The South East Bank had opened a branch at 19 Tranquil Vale in June 1864, Philpot had been appointed manager, but the Bank failed in 1866 and Philpot left the district.

From 1867 to 1878 No. 2 Bennett Place was occupied by auctioneers, estate agents and surveyors, principally Alfred Richardson from 1867 and Ernest Richardson from 1873. From 1871 to 1872 the house was used as the offices of William Charles Green, the estate agent then developing part of the Manor Way on the Cator Estate. From 1878 to 1883 the upper rooms were let to a firm of solicitors and the shop frontage to Riddington's, the bakers at next door 7 Brunswick Place.

A new lease was granted in 1886 to Henry Wayland (?1856-1922) a photographer who took on the role abandoned by Edgar Drewett of 4 Brunswick Place in 1885. Wayland built a studio in the garden and quickly established himself as the Village photographer. By 1890 he was in huge demand, recording for posterity every birth, marriage, and social occasion, birthdays, betrothals, coming of age, anniversaries, in fact any event which could be recorded for the family photograph album. These were sepia-tone pictures, recorded on glass negatives and printed on eighth-inch thick card, the reverse emblazoned with Wayland's signature, blocked in gold. Henry and his assistants travelled the district, taking official photographs of sports' clubs and amateur dramatic groups, and even sought the rights to take photographs of distinguished people shortly to visit Blackheath. These last, especially royalty, would then find their images peering at them from shop windows, Henry Wayland having produced copies in quantity to sell to the local patriots.

In 1893 Wayland joined the tenants of Brunswick Place and built out towards the street. In his case, the extension was across a nine foot garden but it was so narrow it was nothing much more than an extended portico, but created in a rich late Victorian manner, with red, brown and gold paint, a handsome dome and much stained glass. The window was decorated with potted palms but to the south Wayland retained the open path to his front door, shutting out the public with a wrought-iron gate in which his name had been worked in facsimile of his signature. The gate survives to this day but the attractive and curious design scheme of Rembrandt House, as Wayland called his shop, has been lost in recent years under plastic facias and purple paintwork.

Wayland worked here until the early 1920s but ill health drove him to an early retirement and he died in June 1922. The company continued under the same name but in the proprietorship of Herbert William Bayzand who kept the shop going until the 1939-1945 war, at the end of which the studio at Rembrandt House was empty. It is one of the small tragedies in the social history of Blackheath that after the war Wayland's records - the glass plate negatives of virtually every photograph he took - were shovelled into the back of a lorry and taken away to rubble tips.

For the next twenty years 2 Bennett Place was used as a radio and television showroom, initially by Butcher, Curnow of 35 Tranquil Vale, later as a joint venture by Butcher and Miskin and, finally by Messrs Keating & Miskin who subsequently moved to 18 Tranquil Vale.

In June 1965 the shop was opened by Jeff Banks as Clobber, for the sale of fashionable clothes for young women; this use continues at the time of writing but the name is now Jane and I.

Bennett Park

One year after work commenced on the building of Bennett Place plans were approved for a large meeting hall and swimming bath on the corner of Cresswell Park and Bennett Park. This was the Alexandra Hall, an important addition to the public facilities in the Village and a necessary replacement for the inadequate Blackheath Literary Institution next to the railway station. The history of the Hall is related in Chapter 16.

Linked with the Alexandra Hall, in that they were built at roughly the same time, were the first eight houses on the south side of Bennett Park, now numbered 2-16 (even) but originally Nos. 1-8 Bennett Park. They were built by a Mr. H. Bond, on plans submitted to the local Board of Works in April 1864. Before they were completed they were offered for sale as 9-roomed carcases - a common practice at the time in that the builder would obtain a short lease for the basic construction work and sell the unfinished house to a nominee in whose name the freeholder would issue a long lease.

Possibly because of the legal problems attached to the Bennett family estates nothing further was built on the south side of Bennett Park until 1875, when Henry Couchman built No. 26 (Gunton Cottage). The final group, Nos. 26 to 46 (1-10 Brunswick Villas) were not completed until 1884-1885, with the higher numbers being ready for occupation first. This piecemeal development did nothing for architectural harmony of the road, and none of the buildings approach the quality and pleasing appearance of Nos. 2-16 Bennett Park, built in 1864.

There was one oddity on this side of the road. Between Nos. 16 and 18 a plot was leased to the Plymouth Brethren for a meeting house, and this was erected in 1871. In 1920 the Brethren had gone and the building was taken over by the Christian Science Church, then a relatively new movement in this country although the church had been founded in Boston, USA in 1876, by Mary Baker Eddy. In 1938 the Blackheath Christian Scientists moved to Meadowcourt Road to their own purpose-built church, the 10th Church of Christ Scientist, London.

The building in Bennett Park then became the local centre for the Jehovah's Witnesses (The Watchtower Bible & Tract Society, founded by Charles Taze Russell). Unfortunately the Witnesses' Hall was burned down in 1958 in somewhat mysterious circumstances and it was replaced with a block of secular flats.

The earliest development on the north side of Bennett Park came in 1869-70 when Nos. 1-11 (odd) were built and given the name 1-6 Leamington Villas. These were followed, in 1871, by Nos. 13-19, built by John Land as 1-4 Sunbury Villas - Land called No. 19 Sunbury House and he lived here until his death in 1878. He died intestate and the Sunbury Villas were sold in May of that year, although his widow remained at Sunbury House until 1881.

No. 21 was completed early in 1871 but Nos. 23-29 Bennett Park not until 1873. The remainder of the north side of the road was completed between 1879 (No. 31) and 1880 (No. 41) - a row of houses not particularly distinguished, and some remained empty for several years after the builders had finished work.

No. 45 Bennett Park - The Art Club Studios - facing west towards the Village, was built in March 1886 and is dealt with in Chapter 16 of this book.

Bennett Park, like Blackheath Grove and, to some extent, Wemyss Road, proved quite early in its history to be a failure, in that the houses were of a size to appeal to comparatively well-off families but the road lacked the facilities and amenities that had attracted Londoners to the more generously designed estates of Kidbrooke, Vanbrugh Park, Granville Park and St. Johns Park. The Bennett Park gardens were tiny, there was no mews or back lane for stables and, later, garages. Further, although the properties were extremely handy for the station and shops they were also only too close to the railway line. As a result there was a great turnover in tenancies and by the beginning of the 20th century many of the houses in the road had become boarding houses or had been split into flats and apartments, thus attracting a shifting population.

By 1904 there were complaints that the road was drab, ill-swept and the entrance littered with refuse thrown about by flower sellers, hawkers and street vendors. The Village end of the road was lined with broughams, carts and the stalls of unofficial traders, and its proximity to the service mews behind Brunswick Place did not help. Nevertheless, Bennett Park has played an important role in the social history of the neighbourhood if only because the various art and music schools which flourished in the district found their first homes there. The Blackheath Club established itself at No. 17 in 1881 before moving to purpose-built premises in Blackheath Grove; at No. 41 the Blackheath, Lee & Lewisham Government School of Art was founded in 1881, moving to No. 27 in 1883 where it stayed until it merged with the art school at the Alexandra Hall in 1892. The Blackheath Conservatoire of Music started its life at No. 28 in 1881, extending into No. 30 in 1889 and No. 32 in 1891.

Much of the environmental decline that took place in Bennett Park was caused by the 1939-1945 war and the austerity which followed it, combined with the running down of the headleases, a good number of which expired in 1959. In April 1960 more than 22 properties in Bennett Park were auctioned, mostly on the south side, but this gave the opportunity for a period of reconditioning and it is pleasing to write that the great demand for housing in Blackheath has led to the restoration of a good number of the houses, although many are still divided into flats.

7 Frederick's Place;
Hally's Nursery and Blackheath Grove

The well of the Village, marked now by the railway bridge, has always been its heart, certainly by the 17th-century and probably long before that it was marked by a footbridge and some form of dwelling. For this was the meeting point of the roads from Greenwich and Woolwich with the roads to Eltham, Lewisham and Lee. Further, it was the meeting point of a number of important estate and parish boundaries. On the west side, now the site of the railway station, was the Manor of Lewisham, the Village frontage of which was owned by John Collins in 1783. On the east was the boundary of the Wricklemarsh Estate which in itself was split between the parishes of Charlton and Lewisham - the line running approximately through the Village from the south and turning westward along Blackheath Grove.

One of the first results of the sale of the Page estate to John Cator in 1783 was the latter's swift decision to let the nursery plot on the western edge of the old Park. Some of this land had either been leased from the Earl of Dartmouth or the Lewisham Parish in Page's time and had either been built over or cultivated before Gregory Page purchased Wricklemarsh from Lady Morden's executors in 1721-22. One site in particular had, by tradition, become the kitchen gardens and vineries of the Wricklemarsh Estate and we know from John Evelyn's Diary that Colonel Thomas Blunt made his own wine from the grapes grown there. This garden area is now covered almost exactly by Blackheath Grove, the railway line and the ground by and behind Nos. 1-13 Blackheath Village (Brunswick Place). Horticulturally the choice of this plot made sense: there was a southern facing slope, the ground on the east shelved upwards and there was a size-able stream in the valley, flowing from east to west - the Upper Kid Brook. There was a public road to the west side, now marked by Montpelier Vale and Tranquil Vale, which meant estate worker's cottages could be built facing the road. In 1695 the north eastern corner of the gardens was marked by a building known as Elliot's House, the site of which is occupied today by Wemyss Cottage at the east end of Wemyss Road. On the west edge of the garden there were three or four houses which had been built early in the 18th century, including one occupied by Edward Sadler which was large enough to enjoy a garden which covered the ground now occupied by 22-34 Tranquil Vale and 4-10 Montpelier Vale. It was during Sadler's occupation that Sir Gregory Page altered the watercourse (the Upper Kid Brook) and "raised a bridge" on what was regarded as the boundary of Lewisham Manor at Dowager's Hole or Blunt's Hole. He was ordered by the court at the Bowling Green (the Green Man public house on Blackheath Hill) to restore the line of the stream or pay a penalty of £10.

Towards the end of the 18th century, Sadler's garden, if not his house, was in the hands of Thomas Felstead. And, in 1784 and 1785, much

of the old kitchen garden attached to Page's mansion had been let by John
Cator to Christopher Fell. Fell's tenancy passed to a Mr. Mason and then
to a Mr. Miller. In 1792 the ratepayer was Thomas Seagood. It was in the
following year that Cator must have granted a building lease for the site
now occupied by 18 and 20 Tranquil Vale, for two houses were built here
which took the name Frederick's Place. They were three-storey plain
brick dwellings, probably built by James Grice who was in residence at 1
Frederick's Place in 1794 - the year both properties first appear in the
rate books. The John Grice who built Cresswell Park may have been
James' son but otherwise little is known about the Grice family. They may
have been employed for building work by Captain Thomas Larkins who held
11 acres of ground attached to Park House in Cresswell Park (q.v.) on a
lease from Cator in 1787. That Larkins may have been the developer of
Frederick's Place is unproven but when his lease passed eventually to the
Bennett family they certainly held the headlease on those properties.

Because these buildings have occupied an important place in the history
and development of Blackheath Village they are dealt with in some detail
below, and are followed by an account of John Hally's nursery which
survived until 1860 on this site.

1 Frederick's Place (now 20 Tranquil Vale)

James Grice lived here from 1794 to 1799 and was probably responsible
for giving the new houses their name, possibly as a tribute to Frederick
Augustus, Duke of York (1763-1827) then commanding the English army in
Flanders.

Grice was followed by a number of short tenancies up until 1817, principally by members of the Jennings family. From 1817 to 1825 the house
was held by a Mrs. Miller; from 1826 to 1838 by Mrs. Mary Docker but in
1839 only by her daughter, Elizabeth. In 1841 the property was altered for
commercial purposes when Henry Burnside, a bookseller, took the lease.
He died within a year and his son William (1806-1872) took over and set the
business on a comfortable and profitable course which lasted until 1903,
although the family name remained above the shop until the 1950s. William
Burnside was an Ulsterman, deeply religious and sufficiently commercial in
his mind to judge accurately his customers' needs and tastes. He built a
front extension to the house for the shop premises and styled his business
The Blackheath Circulating Library. William, helped by his wife Mary
Ann (1812-1874) when she wasn't pregnant, served in the shop but on fine
days he would stand at the door, dressed in a black frock coat and white
cravat, beaming at his customers, many of whom he would have known
from the various parish and charity committees on which he served.

After William's death the shop was taken over by his son Henry (1847-
1903) who had worked with his father since he left school; another son,
Frederick, became a clergyman and eventually editor of the Church of
England Yearbook.

Henry Burnside continued on the same lines as his father, selling more
and more stationery, and handled printing in a small way. He advertised
widely, especially at Christmas, with much emphasis on the theological
stock. He was able to boast in 1893 that he would obtain any book in print
on the same day if ordered before 1 p.m. and he would allow a discount of
3d in the 1/- if the customer paid in cash. Like his father before him,

Henry Burnside was keen on self-education and improvement and he achieved some praise, but not financial success, by mounting a series of specialist lectures at the Blackheath Concert Hall in the late 1890s - subjects like "Around the World on a Bicycle" attracted his fancy, but unfortunately these lectures were not profitable, and this, coupled with other financial burdens, led to Henry's suicide by drowning in September 1903. Part of the trouble may have stemmed from the fact that the old shop was re-built in 1904 as Highland Mansions and between the demolition of the old premises in March 1903 and the re-opening at 20 Tranquil Vale in April 1904 Henry was committed to a lease on temporary premises at 43 Montpelier Vale (q.v.). This must have been expensive for he went to the trouble of fitting out the shop and completely stocking it as though it would remain for the next five years.

When Burnside died his financial affairs were in disarray but, such was the affection in which he was held by his customers and fellow-shopkeepers, that they collected more than £2,000 for his widow, Marianne (1843-1929), as a testimony to their sorrow.

The shop continued to trade as before, keeping the name although the control was vested in the hands of managers - until 1936 Mr. W. Dickinson and from 1937 to 1963, Mr. S. Spendlove. But during Spendlove's time the shop was acquired by Messrs Hatchards Ltd. and they in turn were to become part of the Wyman, Marshall group and then John Menzies & Co. Ltd., a Scottish-based chain of booksellers and stationers who are now allied to W.H. Smith & Son.

2 Frederick's Place (now 18 Tranquil Vale)

Unlike the next door house (1 Frederick's Place) this property kept its purpose principally as a private residence until it was re-built in the early 1860s. But that was primarily because the tenant for many years was the owner of the shop on the other side.

When it was completed in 1794 the first tenant was a Jonathan Sleede. Sleede was followed by no less than eleven names between 1796 and 1830, none staying long here with the exception of John Mather who completed a tenancy of nine years between 1807 and 1816. From 1820 to 1823 the house was taken by Dr. George Birch who moved to 27 Tranquil Vale in 1824 to establish a medical practice which lasted, through different partnerships until 1916.

From 1828 to 1830 2 Frederick's Place was held by Stevens Lewis, but on his departure the house was taken by John Hally, the nurseryman at 3 Frederick's Place, and it remained with that family until 1860 when it was demolished.

Although this building was used essentially as a domestic dwelling, the Hally family let out at least one room, initially to Jane Trill, the milliner, but from 1849 to 1863 the front rooms were used by estate agents and surveyors; from 1849 to 1858 James Collis, the district surveyor, had an office here and from 1852 to 1863 Alfred Abraham Kirkman (d. 1867) and Benjamin Octavius Engleheart (1825-1892) operated their Blackheath Estate Agency and Auction office from here until the house was rebuilt.

The new house was a three-storey brick and stucco building, integral with Bank House on the corner of Tranquil Vale and Blackheath Grove, and was built as a shop in 1863. It was leased to the tailor, Charles John Bond

(1811-1879) whose business had been established in 1830 and who in 1860 was also occupying a shop at 44 Tranquil Vale. Bond's activities and family fortunes are dealt with elsewhere in this book, in particular under the details on 8 Montpelier Vale (q.v.), for his sons followed their father in the tailoring business. Charles Bond's second son, George James (1845-1899) took over the Frederick's Place shop on his father's death and continued to trade here until his death.

In 1899 Bond's shop was taken by Sidney G. Birdseye of 8 Montpelier Vale (q.v.) but solely to dispose of the stock, for in November of the same year the shop premises were leased by Frank William Smith, also a tailor who owned a shop at 72 Tranquil Vale. Smith (d. 1922) had been manager to T. Mills at the Tranquil Vale premises since 1881 and had taken over the company in 1895. After the re-building of 18 Tranquil Vale in 1903 he surrendered his interest in 72 Tranquil Vale and concentrated his efforts solely at No. 18. As well as being a quality tailor Smith was a self-educated authority on china and furniture, creating a veritable museum above his shop. On his death in October 1922, his art collection (not counting the pictures he bequeathed to the British Museum) fetched £5,000 at auction.

After Smith's death the business continued to trade under his name but in the hands of D.H. Seddon, and it was not until the late 1950s that the familiar, slightly old-fashioned shop window, with its discreet bolt of dark cloth, distinctive blind, and metal scroll work, were removed and the premises re-fitted for Messrs Keating and Miskin as a radio and television showroom.

3 Frederick's Place (16 Tranquil Vale)

The present 16 Tranquil Vale (Barclay's Bank) was built in 1888 on the site of a short-lived block known as Bank Buildings. This last had been built in 1863 as the result of the expiry of the lease held by John Hally, the nurseryman who cultivated a large tract of land covering, roughly, Black-heath Grove, the railway land to the east of the railway bridge and the present railway sidings and car park.

The origins of this nursery have been described above and it was in 1795 that the tenancy passed to Richard Hally (fl 1770-1830). Hally's nursery prospered through the early years of the nineteenth century and in 1826 he built a one-storey wooden shop for the retail sale of plants, flowers and seeds - 3 Frederick's Place. Business must have been brisk, for the Village now boasted a large number of new shops and houses in Tranquil and Montpelier Vale, and the first large-scale developments were taking place on the Cator Estate. The Cator houses were substantial, with large gardens, and the then enthusiasm for gardening and arboriculture would have ensured a good demand for seeds, plants and equipment as gardeners in the new houses would not have had time to build up their own stocks and establish greenhouses and potting sheds.

John Hally (1798-1879) took over his father's business in 1831 and was a man of much enterprise, building cottages for his staff (Hally's Cottages) and a small house for himself on the site of the present Post Office. He did not live in that house for long, choosing to reside at 2 Frederick's Place, next door to the shop.

The nursery garden was irrigated by a large sheet of water, an overflow basin for the Upper Kid Brook, and known as The Canal. It was one of a chain of small reservoirs which stretched from the round pond in Pond Road (which was used primarily as a reservoir for the cisterns at Wricklemarsh) flowed behind the west side of Tranquil Vale and eventually fed the lake in the park attached to Cedar Lodge. All that remains of this is the rubbish shoot presently used by Messrs Penfold. These overflow basins were much needed, especially in the winter when the Kid Brook was swollen with rains or melted snow and the lower part of the Village would flood to a depth of three feet.

John Hally, in a reminiscence published in 1878, records that in 1809 he had to be carried through the flood from his father's house which stood near the present Post Office, and that the Villagers would build snow dams, ten to twelve feet wide at the base, to contain the flood waters.

In 1836 John Hally took advantage of his canal, extended and cleaned it and, in the May of that year, announced the opening of "...a capacious and commodious swimming bath...with 20,000 gallons of clear water of peculiar softness, supplied by a placid stream, an accumulation of some of the purest natural streams. An important utility for schools and invalids for whom cold bathing is recommended." The Kentish Mercury wrote: "...beautifully situated and tastefully laid out gardens and nursery ground...an addition of no mean importance contributing to the health and convenience of the residents...a swimming bath of first rate excellence in every respect. A single inspection will satisfy the most fastidious. Mr. Hally deserves extensive encouragement for his proof of public spirit."

Such was Hally's success that he built sizeable greenhouses as well as the cottages. The nursery was sufficiently attractive for it to be opened to the public on high days and holidays and it must have presented a most pleasant scene in the growing Village, with gardens on either side of the main highway, then carried by a small wooden bridge over the stream. The large traffic had to splash through the brook which was easy enough in summer but must have caused much difficulty in a bad winter.

Because much of Hally's land, especially on the east side of the Lee Road was included in the lease assigned to the Bennett family in 1825, it was inevitable that some would be taken for building. In 1828 the road frontage was developed as Brunswick Place (1-9 Blackheath Village) leaving only a small footpath between 3 Frederick's Place and the first of the new houses. This took away some of Hally's nursery but far greater damage was caused by the introduction of the railway in 1848 and 1849. This swallowed up not only land on both sides of the main road but also the swimming bath. The railway engineers had taken advantage of the undeveloped marshy valley for their permanent way, needing to demolish only five properties between Lewisham and Shooter's Hill Road, but were forced to channel the Upper Kid Brook into a conduit between the Pond Road basin and the new railway station. This had the effect of draining out Hally's swimming bath for, with the excavation of the railway embankment, it had been left at a higher level than the stream. No doubt Hally cultivated new land, replacing some of his lost holdings by renting fields in Lee Park, and he retained the use of some land by the railway towards Heath Lane and behind the houses shortly to be erected on the elbow of Granville Park.

By the late 1850s the Bennett trustees had surrendered their lease and sought a new agreement which gave them the right in 1860 to develop the remaining land to the east of the Lee Road.

Hally's underlease must have expired at this date as well, for Nos. 2 and 3 Frederick's Place were demolished, along with the gardeners' cottages, and the ground from the Village to the west boundary of Pond Road was cleared for building.

The site now called Blackheath Grove was then developed with a street of three storey houses, built as pairs, and a number of public buildings which were to play no small part in the social and spiritual life of the district: a bank, a Wesleyan church, a roller-skating rink and meeting hall and, eventually the Post Office. These are described below, starting with the bank because it was part of Frederick's Place.

After Hally's shop had been demolished, the ground of 2 and 3 Frederick's Place was let on short lease to the directors of the newly-established North Kent Bank Ltd. The North Kent was founded in 1864 by Blackheathens for Blackheath with a capital of £100,000 in 2,000 shares of £50 each. Not all the capital was subscribed but this did not prevent healthy progress, so that by 1868 the Directors were able to announce a sixth consecutive half year dividend at eight per cent. Almost every person attached to the enterprise lived in the district, from the Trustees, Dr. William Carr of Lee Grove, the Rev. W.H. Drew from 22 Montpelier Row and James C. Traill of Morden Hill, down to the auditors and brokers. The members of the Board changed from time to time but included Lewis Glenton, the Charlton born property magnate, Thomas Fox, a Blackheath corn merchant of Phoenix Place and John Dyer, the house agent from Montpelier Row. The overall direction was in the hands of Chairman H.B. Farnall of the Manor House at Lee, aided by the manager Frederick Keeling Holdsworth.

The North Kent was not the only bank in Blackheath Village. Within three months of the opening of the North Kent, the London and County Banking Co. had established a branch at 11 Tranquil Vale (q.v.) in June 1864 - whilst building work was still in progress at Frederick's Place. The London & County prospered and became, eventually, part of the National Westminster Group; the South Eastern at 19 Tranquil Vale, allied to the English Joint Stock Bank, failed in May 1866. The remaining two banks had sufficient business for both, and this was the state which persisted until 1928 when Lloyds Bank took the old Alexandra Hall (q.v.) on the corner of Cresswell and Bennett Park.

The North Kent traded until 1878, when it went into liquidation and all its branches passed to the London and Provincial Bank. There seems to be no evidence that the North Kent failed, although a debtor's summons had to be served on the Blackheath manager, Frederick Holdsworth. One can only guess that the growth in banking - in volume, technique and risk - made it difficult for small banks to work with any degree of security yet offer their customers the services supplied by the large banks. The London and Provincial Bank Ltd. traded under that name until 1921 when it was drawn into the rapidly-expanding Barclays Bank group.

When Bank Buildings were erected in 1863-4 the rooms at the rear and facing into Blackheath Grove were taken in part by the Post Office for one of its London District telegraph offices. Shortly afterwards the postal office and sorting rooms were transferred here, thus bringing an end to the system of employing sub-postmasters in Blackheath which had operated since before the 1820s.

The rooms above the PO were let as offices, mainly to lawyers and accountants, but by 1884 these had been rented by the YMCA as hostel accommodation.

The proposed re-building of the Bank had by 1887 encouraged the Post Office to seek more suitable premises, which they found at 3 Beaconsfield Buildings. The new bank block on the corner of Blackheath Grove, in its distinctive red brick and white stone dressings took the number 16 Tranquil Vale, but this has rarely, if ever, been used.

John Hally was in his early sixties when he surrendered the Blackheath Village nurseries, but he continued to work as a market gardener on smaller nursery grounds in the district. As with so many semi-retired businessmen he engaged in small property speculations, particularly on the ground in Granville Park which he held on a nursery lease. This was on the site of 41 to 45 Granville Park, set on the outer elbow of the road and the last substantial ground in Granville Park not developed by the mid-1860s. A success with No. 41 (Hamilton Lodge), which had been built by Hally and an experienced developer, Joseph Russell, encouraged Hally to work alone on the rest of the plot and he was granted a development lease for Nos. 43 and 45 Granville Park. The venture must have failed, for Hally petitioned for his own bankruptcy in 1869. His failure does not seem to have brought him much disgrace for he remained in the district, a respected elder tradesman, until his death on 21 December 1879 at the age of 81.

Blackheath Grove

Whilst the prime commercial site on Hally's nursery was that occupied adjacent to Frederick's Place, the best land for a housing speculation was along the line of the old Canal which was, by 1860, overlooking the railway cutting.

Amongst the applicants for building consent from the Bennett trustees were the congregation of the Wesleyan Chapel sited behind Nos. 62 and 64 Tranquil Vale (q.v.). Wesleyan Methodism had its origins in Blackheath as far back as the time when John Wesley (1703-1791) and George White-field (1714-1770) had preached open-air sermons on the Heath. Indeed, Whitefield's name had been attached to the mound previously known as Wat Tyler's Mount. The Blackheath Methodists had met in formal worship as early as 1814 in one of the cottages facing the Heath and known as Washer-woman's Row. In 1847 Thomas Allen, a solicitor, had paid for the erection of a Chapel in his garden in Tranquil Vale (q.v.), its entrance being a doorway set between Nos. 62 and 64 Tranquil Vale. As it could seat only 400 and, possibly, because it was abutting some extremely unsavoury cottages, the decision was made to build a larger, more imposing, church. A lease was secured on the ground behind Bank Buildings and the foundation stone of the new chapel was laid on 14 October 1863 by Francis Lycett; John Jacob Lidgett (1820-1869) of 6 St. German's Place, one of the leading Methodists in Blackheath, presided over a "dejeuner" for 100 people at the Alexandra Hall after the ceremony.

The new church was completed by the end of November 1864 although the old chapel was kept until its demolition in 1866. The difference between the two was enormous, with the new church seating more than 1,000 and costing over £6,500. It was built in what was then described as "the middle pointed period of Gothic" to the design of James Wilson FSA. There were Kentish rag and Bath stone dressings, a seven-light traceried window and a Bath stone reredos. Overall, a 120-ft tower with clock and bells looked down on the Village. The roof line was 50 ft above ground and it was supported by shafts of polished Red Devonshire marble. It may come as no surprise to the reader that the contractor, a Mr. Streeter, went bankrupt and that the Church fathers were involved in legal dispute in 1866 because the surveyor's fees had not been paid.

The Methodist chapel changed the appearance of the Village, for its tower and spire dominated every aspect. Whilst this has proved most useful to local historians in dating early photographs, it must have enraged the Anglicans whose All Saints had been built on the Heath in 1857 partly for the lack of a suitable site in the Village within the Parish of Lewisham.

Whether the Blackheath Wesleyan Church lived up to its expectations it is hard to say. The congregation found the money to build a substantial Sunday school at the back of the church and a sizeable house for the Minister in 1870, but none of the incumbents stayed long, the preachers mostly being supplied by the Circuit. In 1929 the then minister, Revd. Charles G. Danbury, took 15 Shooters Hill Road as the parsonage and the original Blackheath Grove house was sold and became a guest house known as Avenue House. The church itself was the principal victim of a V2 rocket bomb which hit the Village on 8 March 1945, destroying the main building, although not the whole tower, and the old parsonage, the school room and houses in Blackheath Grove and Wemyss Road.

The congregation thereafter met for a time in the Church Hall of St. Michael's, Blackheath Park, and then in Winchester House, Independents Road (q.v.). When the lease on the original site in Blackheath Grove expired, the remains of the church were demolished and a row of plain two-storey shops built on the frontage of the site; they opened for trade in July 1961.

The ground occupied by the schoolroom and parsonage was turned into a car park, and the only vestige of the Wesleyan occupation of the site is the footpath which leads from Wemyss Road to the car park.

When the domestic stretch of Blackheath Grove was built in 1863 it was given the name The Avenue, Bennett Park. This was kept until 1871 when the name The Avenue was generally adopted because of the confusion with Bennett Park proper. Some early directories referred to the road as Bennett Park Avenue, which must have made matters even worse. The use of the title Blackheath Grove was not imposed until after the last war.

Nos. 1-12 and 15-22 Blackheath Grove were completed by 1865 and offered for sale in 1866 by Mrs Bennett's executors but because of legal difficulties the sale did not go through and the whole was offered for sale again in 1871. This time they were purchased by Henry Richard Smith along with the ground opposite on which he built a roller skating rink (see below).

Although many of the houses are presently not in first class condition externally, they were intended to be superior villas and a number of well-established shop-keepers lived in Blackheath Grove in order to be close to the business centre. But, like Bennett Park and Wemyss Road, this street possessed too many disadvantages in that the houses had small gardens for their size and the front rooms were too close to the railway line. As a result they appealed to neither the middle class because they lacked amenity, nor to artisans because they were too large and expensive to maintain. By the 1920s practically every house had been converted into flats or one-room apartments and this use, combined with the running down of the leases, helped towards a general decline in quality by the 1940s. The development of the post office in 1911 and the conversion of the old skating rink into industrial premises in 1916 did not help.

Nos. 1-4 were bombed beyond repair in 1945 and replaced by the police flats (Wyatt House Annexe) in 1955.

Nos. 15 and 16 became the Blackheath Nurses Home between 1909 and 1927. This was an important adjunct to the much-respected Blackheath Institution for Supplying Hospital Trained Nurses, founded by Miss Duncan in 1888 at 9 Montpelier Row. The organisation did exactly what its title proclaimed, for those who could afford to pay for private nursing. Miss Duncan retired in 1921, after 34 years, and her successor Miss D. R. Gillbee RRC, continued to run the Institution here until 1927. A similarly-titled venture flourished at 15 St. John's Park from 1929 up until the last war, but the need for such agencies has since somewhat declined.

Of all the houses in Blackheath Grove probably Nos. 13 and 14 are of most interest. This pair were not built until 1879, long after the rest of the street, and they were especially erected for the Blackheath Club. The Club had been founded in 1877 and took 17 Bennett Park as its first premises under the secretaryship of Samuel McCall. The aim of the body was to provide a gentleman's club on the same lines as the more distinguished clubs in London's West End and the subscription income was clearly sufficient to sustain a mortgage on the substantial premises they built in Blackheath Grove. It was a club of deep armchairs, large billiard rooms with a man to mark the cues, copies of the leading newspapers and periodicals - somewhere for Blackheath gentlemen to escape the demands of their families. The members could pretend they were in Pall Mall without taking the tiring journey to town. The husbands and older sons of most of the leading Blackheath families joined and the Blackheath Club met their needs for more than 25 years. Alas, the interest then declined and in 1905 the mortgagees foreclosed and the lease and the contents of the house were sold in June of that year.

Because it was custom-built, the building remained empty for several years - the rooms were too large for domestic use and no takers could be found to put the buildings into institutional use. By 1924 the building had been divided into flats and re-titled Avenue Mansions.

The Roller Skating Rink

Blackheath people in the 1860s and 1870s were always hungry for novelty, quick to take up a new fashion - equally quick to drop it once it became unfashionable. But once they decided to do something they tried to do it well. It was not simply a matter of pride, but many of the local residents were rich and there was no shortage of men of influence and competence to ensure that few ventures foundered for lack of financial or professional help.

Therefore it is not surprising that the novelty of roller skating seized the Village in 1875. Ice skating was popular on the ponds on the Heath and in the grounds of the large houses, especially in Pond Road, at Brooklands, and at Cedar Lodge on Belmont Hill. But this activity was, of necessity, governed by the vagaries of the weather and the social set to which you belonged. Thus, when the mania for roller-skating crossed the Atlantic in the early 1870s Blackheath was quick to buy skates and a Blackheath tradesman equally quick to take commercial advantage.

The prime mover behind the establishment of the Blackheath Rink was Henry Richard Smith, an ironmonger who traded from 34 Tranquil Vale (q. v.) and purchased the leases of a number of houses in Blackheath Grove. His Rink was built on a narrow strip of land between the houses in the Grove and the railway line. It was designed to cope with the British climate and constructed in two sections: an open area 250ft by 50ft, and a closed section 125ft by 50ft, which was sheltered on three sides by a wall. At the Village end was a large hall - The Rink Hall - and the offices. Part of the structure survives in the Holmes Plating Works but the Rink Hall and the covered section were lost when the Post Office took over the premises in 1911.

It would not be right to credit Blackheath with the first British purpose-built roller skating rink, although in February 1876 it was described as "one of the first opened in the suburbs of London". Initially, Smith leased the rink to a William Morris who is listed in the rate books as the proprietor, but by 1878 Smith's name reappears and, despite changes in management of the roller-skating section, it remained with him until 1909.

The advantage of the Blackheath Rink was that its covered section could be converted into a ball room, meeting hall or concert room without much difficulty. From the outset the Rink became the venue for most of the public and private functions for which, previously, Blackheath Village had lacked space. Although the Alexandra Hall had displaced the old hall of the Blackheath Literary Institution in 1863, it was clearly neither large enough nor suitable for every event.

In February 1876 there were newspaper reports of a "brilliant skating party" with the enclosed section transformed into a "brilliantly lit ballroom" with the band of the Horse Artillery providing the musical accompaniment. To encourage the patrons the Rink provided a resident orchestra, skating instructors, and employed professionals to give demonstrations. "Lewisham" Curtis, a distinguished skater who raced in a demonstration match at the newly-opened rink at London's Olympia in 1890, made his reputation during the 14 years he worked for Smith at Blackheath.

Although Henry Smith promoted skating attractions, including, for example, a star turn by the "Six Hagen Sisters" in 1877 and skating prom-enade concerts, he was far-sighted enough to promote the non-skating facilities well in advance of the rapid decline in popularity for the wheeled sport. In 1878 the Rink was let for tennis in the mornings, skating being reserved for the afternoon and evening sessions, and Smith had started a hire company, providing everything needed for dances, dinners and concerts, from knives and forks and table linen, to chairs and music stands. It was this aspect of the business that prospered until the Blackheath Concert Hall opened in 1895 at the south end of the Village. It is likely that the skating mania was over-catered for: in March 1876 a rink had been opened in King Street, Greenwich, opposite the Royal Naval College, and in the following month a large rink was in use next door to Lee Station, and these were followed rapidly by rinks in Deptford, Bromley and Chislehurst. Such was the craze in South London that a wag wrote that skating rinks and spelling bees were the new foot and mouth disease.

Blackheathens put their Rink Hall to better uses than spelling bees: in 1877 the newly-reformed Blackheath Dramatic Club staged its first product-ions there, concert promoters were more and more interested in its

8.   Montpelier Vale (east)

9.   Montpelier Vale (west) in 1906

10. Montpelier Vale (west) in 1976

11. The Village as it looked in 1849

12. The Village in the 1870s: Osborne Place (left); Spencer Place (right)

13. Shopping in about 1905

14. Osborne Place in 1938

facilities, and Blackheath was added to the lecture circuits. For the next 20 years the Rink Hall became the centre for every type of meeting, concert, display and entertainment. In 1880 the Australian General Tom Thumb with Commodore Knutt drew the crowds; the Blackheath Orchestral Society under the baton of Alfred Burnett performed some of the conductor's compositions although the audience was not as large as it might have been "because the Lewisham Bicycle Club concert was taking place in the nearby Alexandra Hall".

In 1889 Colonel Gourand demonstrated "the marvel of the age" in his lecture on Mr. Edison's perfected phonograph, which was asked "to speak for itself". There were poultry and pigeon society meetings; the escaped Nun, in a lecture tour sponsored by the South East London Protestant Alliance, regarded the Rink Hall as an important place in her programme. She had "escaped" from a convent in 1870 and spent the rest of her life lecturing on the iniquities of the Catholic Church.

It was claimed that the Rink Hall, at its maximum, could seat nearly 1,000, probably in some discomfort, and more than 200 performers crammed onto the portable stage. This encouraged the formation of the Blackheath Philharmonic Society and the Blackheath Amateur Operatic Society, and performances of Gounod's Faust, Mozart's Requiem, and other works of an essentially sacred rather than a secular nature. Performances of Wagner and Gilbert and Sullivan caused a split in the ranks of the choir on the grounds that music of a non-sacred nature was profane, but the bigots were left behind and the music groups grew in stature, built a Concert Hall, and flourished until the years of the Great War of 1914-1918.

Henry Morton Stanley (1841-1904) came to Blackheath to lecture on his 23 years in Africa - but was experienced enough to arrive earlier than advertised to avoid the crowds waiting at the station to catch a glimpse of the great man. Padarewski and Sarasate, at the serious end of the spectrum, and George Grossmith and Charles Dickens jnr at the other, entertained capacity audiences. In 1893 there was a meeting of The Brethren, with 650 for lunch and 800 sitting down for tea. Mdme Adeline Patey made her "positively last appearance on her farewell tour" at the Rink - which was more true than she probably expected, because she died a few weeks later.

The list is endless, but it is worth recording that the local schools took the Rink Hall for speech days and prize givings. Two series of events stand out for their curiosity value: in 1883 the Blackheath Proprietary School, then with a distinguished record in classical studies, produced two performances of Aristophanes' Archanians at the Rink Hall. What made this unusual was that the school performed the play in ancient Greek and in costume. How many Blackheathens sat through, let alone fully understood the comedy, is not recorded but the classicists and educational theorists who attended were most impressed, and the performances pre-dated the now hallowed tradition of Bradfield College which mounts Greek drama in the vernacular as part of the school curriculum.

Moving down market somewhat were the annual concerts displaying the musical talents of the pupils from Nelson and Collingwood Colleges in Lee. These all-day musical marathons were described by the press as events "with innumerable items calculated to satisfy all but the absolutely insatiable." Every child who could play an instrument was pressed into the performance, so that some of the classics would be arranged for ten pianos, or fifteen cellos. There would be duets for 14 hands at 7 pianos, trios arranged for 6 pianos and 18 hands, to be repeated immediately by a different 18 hands. The list and permutations was near endless.

George Grossmith returned by popular demand in 1893; Albert Chevalier first appeared in July 1894. It was at this last performance that controversy occured between rival bands of stewards. It had been the practice for local people to act as stewards for formal evening entertainments, but some of the best-known performers hired men from outside Blackheath, probably for their greater muscle-power. Chevalier's appearance attracted more than 1,000 to the Rink Hall and because outside stewards were employed many of the Blackheath amateurs struck in protest.

This was not the only difficulty encountered by impresarios hiring the Rink. Firstly, the chairs and platform had to be erected for each event and, because there was no rake to the auditorium it was not unknown for a small person to be seated behind a woman in a large floral hat and have no view of the proceedings. More annoying, especially for the performers, was the proximity of the railway line. Train drivers adopted the habit of blowing off steam and whistling as they passed the Rink Hall and a number of poignant moments in song recitals were ruined by the zeal of employees of the South Eastern and Chatham Railway. To make matters worse, in 1891 "a new terror" arose in the shape of an assertive clock in the tower of the then newly-erected church in Cresswell Park. "Not content with striking hours," wrote the Blackheath Local Guide, "it chimes the quarters in an irritating minor third, much to the annoyance of both performers and listeners."

After the opening of the Blackheath Concert Hall in 1895, the building went into decline, despite attempts by Smith to keep his rink and hall busy with an expensive advertising campaign. The pattern of events staged there changed and the Hall was used by charities or for dog or flower shows sponsored by groups who could not afford or did not need the elegance of the new Concert Hall.

In 1896 the Blackheath Bicycle Supply Co. of Tranquil Vale hired the skating rink to teach ladies how to ride their machines in privacy. It became cheap enough to hire the Rink for evangelical meetings which stretched out over 7, 10, and even, on one occasion, 16 days.

Smith had disposed of all his business interests in Blackheath by 1909. The skating concession was taken over in the April of that year by a company called Skating Rinks Ltd., run by Lennox Barry, who spent much money on renovating the Blackheath Rink, laying down a new floor and employing an orchestra for three daily sessions, with teas in the lounge and professional demonstrators. Skating Rinks claimed there were over 100 devotees in Blackheath and that the sport had become as fashionable as it had been thirty years before. But this venture was unprofitable and the Rink closed on 24 July 1909. An advertised attempt by a new manager, Frank Ormond, to mount a spectacular skating carnival in the following November does not seem to have taken place.

This closure was probably welcomed by the Village residents and those whose houses overlooked the Rink. It was noisy - the sound of 300 pairs of skates rushing round the floor accompanied by a band playing at top pitch must have been fearful - and many church goers felt that the young people who attended regularly were in moral danger by exposure to popular tunes played over and over again.

In September 1910 the Rink Hall was advertised for sale or long let and the Post Office, which had had an eye on the site for some while, took the main hall for its new offices and sorting depot.

The history of Blackheath's post offices is dealt with below, but to bring the Rink story up to date it must be recorded that the Post Office only took the Rink Hall. The open and partly covered sections of the roller skating rink were not immediately sold. It was next used for industrial purposes, in February 1916, when it was acquired by Oliver Hone Pearce for the manufacture of a construction toy something like Meccano. Hone Pearce (1872-1948) worked here until 1936 although "the local toy factory" found more profit in making furniture and, eventually, breeze blocks for building. In 1936 the premises were taken over by Holmes Plating Co. Ltd., who have remained here ever since although many alterations have been made. The company was founded by J.H. Holmes (1884-1953) who acquired the freehold of the site from the Cator Estate in 1949.

The Post Office

The history of the Blackheath Post Office until 1866 is also the history of two Village shopkeepers who acted as postmasters: Ebenezer Larwill at 47 Tranquil Vale (q.v.), and William Charles Roe at 46 Tranquil Vale (q.v.) who took over from Larwill in 1852.

With the redevelopment of Hally's shop at 3 Frederick's Place in 1863 and the erection of Bank Buildings, the Post Office opened a telegraph office there in 1866. The post receiving and delivery office remained with Roe's widow until 1869 but in the following year all post office business was conducted from Bank Buildings although the rooms were inadequate and there were many complaints at the slow service and late deliveries. Nevertheless, the Post Office were to stay in Blackheath Grove until 1885 and only moved when Beaconsfield Buildings was erected. This move should have solved their problems but so rapid was the increase in postal business in the 1880s and 1890s that the premises at 3 Beaconsfield Buildings quickly proved too small.

In 1906 the Post Office started looking seriously for a site to build not only a new office but a sorting room and accommodation for the postal-workers as well. The search ended when the old skating rink and its hall were put up for sale and the PO purchased the hall and the covered rink area at the rear. This was by 1910 but the new building, designed by John Rutherford of HM Office of Works, was not opened for public use until September 1911. The new premises in Blackheath Grove (still in use) were a great improvement, with a public area 30ft by 20ft and a sorting office of more than 3,500 sq ft. Blackheath had lost a roller skating rink but had gained a post office large enough to cope with all local needs.

80

8   Beaconsfield Buildings

When in 1825 the Bennett family took over the 1787 lease of land granted
to Capt. Thomas Larkin, the western boundary of the plot stretched from
the corner of Blackheath Park along Lee Road to the corner of Blackheath
Grove. In 1828 building leases had been granted for houses in Cresswell
Park and six villas were erected there, including a semi-detached pair
of houses facing into Lee Road. The underleases of these two houses
expired in the early 1880s and the opportunity was taken to develop the
site, a narrow triangle of land tapering to a point where Lee Road and
Cresswell Park meet. Alpha House and Hillside - described in Chapter
6 - were demolished in 1882 and were replaced by a terrace of nine shops
above which were three storeys of office and residential accommodation.
The new terrace was called Beaconsfield Buildings, almost certainly
named after Benjamin Disraeli, 1st Earl of Beaconsfield (1804-1881). It
was built by Edward Nathan of Sutton; the contractor being a Mr. Nicholls.

The building work took four years, from 1882 to 1886, and was completed
in four sections, the north section being of only one storey, and the southernmost was a pair of shops built in Dutch gable style and set back from
the road to the same building line as Park Place, a row of early 19th
century houses which stood on the site of the present Blackheath Conservatoire of Music and Blackheath Concert Hall.

Beaconsfield Buildings were part of what were known colloquially as the
"Blackheath Improvements" and were one of a series of out-of-character
developments in the Village which included the Barclays Bank site opposite
the railway station, and Highland House at the Heath end of Tranquil Vale.

The development was encouraged by two major institutions seeking new
premises in Blackheath - the Post Office and the London & County Banking
Co. - and they had probably signed their leases before the first brick was
laid. But the speculation was not well-timed and possibly because the
country was passing through one of its cycles of depression, the newly-built
units remained empty for some years and it was not until 1888 that all nine
shops were let.

Beaconsfield Buildings were re-numbered in 1929 as 1-17 Lee Road (odd)
but subsequently the numbering was altered because of the re-structuring
of some of the shop fronts. Further, by 1914 every shop in Beaconsfield
Buildings, bar Nos. 1 & 2, bore the same name: Hinds & Company.

Because of these two factors the history of this block follows the original
numbering and the story of the Hinds development and expansion is given at
the end of the chapter.

1 Beaconsfield Buildings (now 1 Lee Road)

The first section of the terrace to be completed was the segment which became Nos. 1 & 2, and it was completed by 1882 as new branch premises for the London & County Banking Co., who had outgrown their old home at 37 Tranquil Vale (q.v.)

The London & County had opened its first Blackheath branch in July 1865 at 11 Tranquil Vale (q.v.), three months after the North Kent Bank had opened in a purpose-built office on the corner of Tranquil Vale and Blackheath Grove. The London regarded the Tranquil Vale shop as a temporary home and acquired a vacant plot higher up the road (now 37 Tranquil Vale) early in 1869. The building there was most imposing from the outside but the interior was small and the Bank rapidly outgrew this office. The development of Beaconsfield Buildings gave them the much-needed space but allowed them to remain within the commercial heart of Blackheath. Initially the Bank took only No. 1 Beaconsfield Buildings - No. 2, later incorporated with the Bank, was leased as a separate retailing unit. The London & County moved here late in 1882 under the then manager Walter J. Caffin (1844-1907) and the old banking hall was put up for sale. Caffin served the bank for 40 years, starting as a ledger clerk in Greenwich in 1866, succeeding John Thomas Edwards in 1876 as the Blackheath manager and remaining in charge of the Village branch until his retirement in 1906.

2 Beaconsfield Buildings (now 3 Lee Road)

Although this unit was later incorporated with the bank it was used as a shop at the outset, initially by Edward Nathan as an ironmongery. In 1890 the business passed to a Harry Prescott but in 1892 the shop was taken over by Corteze & Co., who were carvers, gilders and frame makers and found much work from the students of the nearby Blackheath School of Art. They traded here until 1906. In 1907 the lease was assigned to Madame Barr, ladies outfitter and corsetière. Annie Barr (d. 1936) had purchased Mrs. Standage's shop at 3 Blackheath Village in 1901 and moved to Beaconsfield Buildings where she remained until 1927, when the old shop lease expired. In 1927 the Bank took over her premises and she moved to 3 Montpelier Vale where her distinctive shop continued to serve a devoted clientele even after her death, not closing until 1973.

Meanwhile, the London & County Bank had grown, swallowing and being swallowed by other banking houses: in 1909 it became the London, County and Westminster Bank; in 1921, the London, County, Westminster & Parrs Bank; finally, in 1923, the Westminster Bank.

Caffin had retired as manager of the Blackheath branch in 1906, to be succeeded until 1911 by Walter Curtis, and from 1912 to 1919 Walter Newcomb; the manager from 1920 to 1926 was Clyde Adlington Forsdyke.

When Madame Barr gave up her shop the Bank set about the re-fitting and the enlargement of both shops, joining them as a single unit and forming the banking hall as it is today. This work also saw the end of the subletting of the back rooms of No. 2 although the rooms above the terrace took the title Westminster Bank Chambers and added in no small measure to the amount of office accommodation in the Village, particularly for solicitors and building societies.

3 Beaconsfield Buildings (now 5 Lee Road)

This building was earmarked at the outset for the new Village post office and sorting rooms. From 1865 the local PO had been in a small section of Bank Buildings on the corner of Blackheath Grove and Tranquil Vale. The lease on these premises was due to expire in 1888 and the PO took the opportunity to seek larger and better premises, so the development of Beaconsfield Buildings seemed an ideal answer. But it was not a good move in that almost immediately the PO had to rent additional space at No. 2 Beaconsfield Buildings for a sorting office and, by 1906, was once more hunting for new offices. The search took five years and it was not until the old Rink Hall in Blackheath Grove was up for sale that the PO found a site large enough for their numerous services.

They moved in 1911 and their old premises at No. 3 Beaconsfield Buildings remained empty until the end of 1913 at which date the premises were acquired by Hinds & Co., the latter with this act completing their ownership of the whole terrace.

Before Hinds took over No. 3 the upper rooms had been let on occasion and one example of local social enterprise is worthy of note. This was the establishment of a ladies reading room and tea room at No. 3 in 1892. The aim was to provide for the women of Blackheath what was already available, in some measure, for their menfolk at the Blackheath Club in Blackheath Grove (q.v.) and the West Kent Carlton Club at Point House on Blackheath Hill - somewhere to escape from family and domestic matters. The Ladies Reading Room was well-organised, with a notable governing body that included Miss Florence Gadesden (d. 1934), head mistress of the Blackheath High School for Girls in Wemyss Road from 1886 to 1919.

The Reading Room flourished and within a year boasted more than 200 members at a subscription of 10/6 a year. "The best papers and magazines ..." were provided and the tearoom did brisk business. Alas, the venture was forced to close in 1894 because of difficulties over the lease and the group had been unable to find suitable accommodation elsewhere. Edgar Neve offered a solution by setting aside a room at his shop (Wesalps) at 26 Tranquil Vale but the spirit of the enterprise was broken and it faded away.

4 & 5 Beaconsfield Buildings (now 7 Lee Road)

No. 7 Lee Road was originally designed as two retail units. The tenants of No. 4 were headed in 1888 by George Knight who kept a toy shop and fancy bazaar, but this soon changed into Madame Cecile's dressmaking establishment from 1892 to 1895.

No. 5 was occupied from 1889 to 1898 by a succession of cigar and tobacco importers, trading under various names including Dennis & Co., the Beaconsfield Cigar Stores, and Albert & Co., tobacconist. The upstairs rooms were used as offices, principally by a solicitor, J.E. Shaw, who acted as secretary of the Blackheath Conservative and Lee Conservative Clubs, and later by the YMCA.

In 1899 both shops were merged into one by George Alexander Rose, a baker and confectioner who owned shops at 40 Old Dover Road and also, subsequently, at 179 Lee High Road. Rose was an enthusiast for his trade, often winning cups and medals for his bread and cakes at national baking competitions. But he never quite broke the trading monopoly of Jobbins' and Barrett's in Blackheath and he assigned his lease to Hinds & Co. in 1911.

6 Beaconsfield Buildings (firstly 11, now 9 Lee Road)

There was no tenant in this building until 1888 when it was taken over as temporary premises by the London and Provincial Bank during the re-building of their offices at 16 Tranquil Vale in that year.

From 1890 to 1897 the shop was used by dairymen, principally as the Queen's Park Dairy Co., owned by William and Jesse Rhodes, and in 1896 and 1897 as the Cambrian Dairy of David Williams, which moved to 53 Tranquil Vale (q.v.) at the end of that year. In 1898 the lease was acquired by Hinds & Co.

7 Beaconsfield Buildings (now 11 Lee Road)

Messrs Hinds were not able to take over this shop until 1903 when they bought out the lease of Charles Perry who had opened a hosiery shop here in 1887. Perry (1839-1922) had started business at the age of 23 in Woolwich in 1862 and moved to Blackheath in 1886. When Hinds purchased his lease in 1903 Perry took over No. 70 Tranquil Vale and traded from there as a gentleman's outfitter until his death in 1922, having worked for himself for more than 60 years.

8 & 9 Beaconsfield Buildings (was 15/17, now 13 Lee Road)

The story of these buildings is also the story of a remarkable enterprise which began in March 1887 when John Prichard and John Hinds (1863-1928) with one assistant opened a drapery shop in Blackheath. In 1889 they took over the next door premises (9 Beaconsfield Buildings) and it was probably on that date that the single storey extension towards the road was added.

John Hinds had been born in Carmarthen and had at 14 years of age been apprenticed to a local draper. In 1882 he came to Regent's Street in London as a shop assistant and, with this experience and probably some cash in hand, teamed up with John Prichard and settled in Blackheath. Why they came to Blackheath has not been recorded but they must have had great faith in their marketing abilities because the Village boasted at least a dozen drapery shops in 1887.

In fact the venture went well, although in March 1891 Prichard left the partnership and the 27 year-old John Hinds became sole proprietor.

In 1894 trade was brisk and Hinds added a sizeable extension at the rear for the workshops where he manufactured ladies underwear and baby clothes. He was joined by his brother Charles Pugh Hinds (1877-1953) and, in 1898, took the first step in the process of acquiring all the shops in Beaconsfield Buildings with the exception of Nos. 1 & 2 then held by the London & County Bank. They began with the purchase of No. 6 and in 1903 took over Charles Perry's shop at No. 7. In 1907 further workshops and additions had to be made at the back of the premises and a mess room added for the staff, which had now reached more than 100. Hinds was forced to lease houses in Cresswell Park and Bennett Park for staff dormitories, for in those days drapers were bound apprentice and usually lived on their employer's premises.

The progress of John Hinds' business was remarkable by any yardstick and not a year went by without new departments being added and new shops being opened or re-structured in the house style. For example, in 1909 the Company took on the lease of Whittaker & Brown's old shops at 5 & 7 Tranquil Vale. Hinds had bought up the stock when Brown retired in 1908, but waited a year before embracing the premises at, no doubt, advantageous terms.

Nos. 5 & 7 Tranquil Vale (q.v.) included a substantial workshop at the rear - the old Blackheath Literary Institute building - and this added more than 3000 sq. ft. to Hinds manufacturing space. When the Company celebrated its 25th anniversary in 1912 its buildings occupied more than half an acre, it traded from 50 departments through the whole range of drapery and household requirements, and employed more than 200 staff. A new house livery was implemented for the Beaconsfield Buildings shops and a large new sign erected on the south elevation of No. 7.

By this date John Hinds was leaving much of the day-to-day running of his shop to others, particularly brother Charles, although residing as he did at 30 Lee Park he was able to keep a close watch on the business. In March 1910 he was returned as Liberal MP for West Carmarthen, a seat he held until 1922 when he relinquished it owing to ill-health. Hinds was drawn more and more into political activity, trade associations and free-masonry, and held office in numerous associations and orders in his home county or with a Welsh or Anglo/Welsh interest. In 1917 he was rewarded with his appointment as Lord Lieutenant of the County of Carmarthen, no doubt as a result of his political loyalty to fellow Welshman and friend, David Lloyd George (1863-1945).

John Hinds died on 23 July 1928 of heart disease and the results of an appendectomy, and his passing plunged Carmarthen into mourning. The biggest wreath at his funeral was sent by Lloyd George who delivered the oration at the memorial service held at the Welsh Baptist Church in London's Eastcastle Street.

Initially, Hinds' death little affected the progress of the Company. Brother Charles was Chairman of the Board and continued to develop the interests his elder brother had established so firmly. In the early 1930s a branch store was opened in Eltham and there were links with other department stores elsewhere in the suburbs, in particular, Shinner's of Sutton. But there was no second generation to take over control - John Hinds' son, W.P. Hinds, had been killed on active service in February 1916, and the Company tended to draw its directors from long-serving members of the staff. The outbreak of the World War in 1939 and the resultant shortage of raw materials, coupled with the expiry of the lease on 5 & 7 Tranquil Vale, saw the fortunes of the Company dwindle. Hinds had been formed into a limited liability company in 1927 and had purchased the freehold of their shops in Beaconsfield Buildings in 1924.

In 1944 the Company consisted of three department stores and had a pay-roll of more than 200 - ten years later the company known as Hinds of Blackheath had gone. The retirement of K. Morris James, the managing director, in September 1950 after 41 years with the company and the death of Charles Pugh Hinds in December 1953 at the age of 76, hastened the end. By 1953 all but two of the Blackheath shops had closed and in 1954 the original premises at 8/9 Beaconsfield Buildings (13 Lee Road) were leased to a house furnisher trading as Edward Evans Ltd.

Hinds branch at Eltham passed to different proprietorship and although the name remains, the store has no connection with the original company.

The Beaconsfield Buildings shops remained empty for some years after Hinds' departure. No. 3 opened in 1961 as Victor Sefton, an ironmongers and builders' merchant; and was re-opened in 1970 as Florian's delicatessen in which name it still trades. Nos. 4-5 became a launderette in 1961.

No. 6 was opened as an army recruiting office in November 1961. No. 7 Beaconsfield Buildings was fitted out as a showroom for Norwegian products - Norsk Design - in December 1963, but became a recruitment office for the Royal Navy and Royal Air Force in 1972.

9   The Collins Estate in Lewisham

Of all the early developments in Blackheath Village none has lasted so well as that on the western side of Tranquil Vale which comprises some of the oldest surviving buildings in Lewisham.

But, unfortunately, this very section is not well-documented for its early years. This is almost certainly because its freehold had been acquired by a Greenwich house owner, John Collins, at least by 1783, and no records of his leases and assignments have survived. Because the Lewisham parish ratebooks for the period have been destroyed the local historian must rely on the not always accurate Land Tax Returns and early county directories. But even with this fragmentary information it is possible to construct the broad outline of its history for the period from Collins' purchase to the 1820s when the commercial records begin to be credible.

From the little information we have it is known that John Collins I (1741-1787) was once the tenant or freeholder of an area of $16\frac{1}{2}$ acres, divided into five large fields, sited on the west side of the public highway which ran north and south through the centre of the Village. The Collins estate fronted Lee Terrace on the south, Blackheath Village, and Tranquil Vale as far north as the Crown public house. It included the sites eventually sold for the railway station, the Blackheath Proprietary School premises and the School for the Sons and Orphans of Missionaries in what is now Independents Road.

The property stretched across the parish boundaries of Lee and Lewisham (marked by the line of the Upper Kid Brooke) but whether Collins' land had been part of the Manor of Lewisham or one of the manorial holdings in Lee is not known. Further, there is no surviving legal record of the landowner from whom John Collins purchased the land, only a note in the Land Tax Returns for 1783 that land in Blackheath had passed from a Mr. Heath to Mr. Collins and that this land was to the south of the Crown public house. In the Blackheath Local Guide for March 7 1925 (Vol. XXXVII. No. 5) some brief notes on the history of the Village were published by John Hodges (1874-1926), supported by a photograph of a plan of the Collins holding in Blackheath. This plan (reproduced in this book) was dated 31 May 1779 but whether it indicated Collins' tenancy or his freehold is not recorded. In addition, no buildings are shown and there is no indication of the stream flowing east to west through the centre of the holding. All that can be deduced is that there was a gravel pit on a site now marked by Selwyn Court. Another puzzle raised by the map is that we know from Rocque's survey of 1746 that buildings existed to the west side of Tranquil Vale on the site of The Crown and the present Nos. 45 & 47 Tranquil Vale. This is confirmed by the map published in Hasted's History of Kent of 1778.

There is a further element of mystery in that in 1946 the then directors of the Collins estate claimed that the land had been purchased by Collins in 1787, the year of his death. If this was the case then the 1779 survey was probably made to establish formally the area of the conveyance then under negotiation, but the correct date is more likely to be 1783 as noted in the Land Tax Records. It is also possible to conjecture that John Collins I held the land on lease and that on his death enough capital was released from the sale of other properties for his son, John Collins II (1766-1826) to purchase the freehold and take over the existing tenancies, but this seems unlikely to have happened so quickly. Further, John Collins II held only half the interest - the other two quarters going to John Collins' sons-in-law, John Harris and John Matthews.

John Collins I was a builder and property owner, but not on a large scale. His will, which was proved on 27 July 1787, refers to a number of lease- hold and freehold houses in Greenwich, Lewisham, Deptford and Wimpole Street, London; the Collins family home was at King Street, Greenwich, and they owned the house next door which they let to a gentleman with the delightful name of George Luncheon. John Collins II was urged in his father's will to sell the leasehold properties and apply the money to the residue of his estate which was to be enjoyed by John jnr and daughters Mrs. Mary Harris, Mrs. Catherine Matthews, and Julia and Ann Collins, and held by them in common. It is not unlikely that some of these monies were used for developments and that leases were granted for Tranquil Vale - there were at least 14 houses there by 1798 - and elsewhere.

John Collins II was the only son; he worked at the Navy Pay Office, Somerset Place, and never married. On his death he was buried, near his father, at St. Alfege's Church, Greenwich. The Blackheath estate then passed to his sisters, two of whom lived in Blackheath Village until they died - Ann (1786-1848) and Julia (1780-1864) who resided at South Vale Cottage (q.v.) which was demolished four years after Julia's death for the development of the present South Vale Road.

It is quite unlikely that there will ever be much more added to this brief history of the development of the Collins estate during its early years. Certainly before 1780 there was a pub at the north end called The Crown, and Nos. 45 & 47 Tranquil Vale and the three cottages which survive as Collins Square may date from about that time and are typical of the period. There is, furthermore, no doubt that Nos. 23, 25, 27, 31 and 33/35 Tranquil Vale as well as some cottages behind Nos. 33/35 had been built and were occupied by 1798.

The land that lay to the south of the Kid Brooke was in use as market gardens during the early 19th century and those fields and meadows which sloped down from Lee Terrace to the stream in the well of the Village were probably used for grazing and orchards. There is no record of any housing on this section before 1800 although there could have been farm buildings. The fact that the Upper Kid Brooke was prone to flood and overflow its banks in the winter months may have dictated the slow pace of development.

About 1800 and certainly by 1802 a Mrs. Sarah Kerl is shown in the Land Tax returns as paying for a group of four cottages in Tranquil Vale, and these are probably the shops numbered 13-17 Tranquil Vale which were known until 1885 as 5-8 Spencer Place.

The death of John Collins II in 1826 may have given encouragement to granting of building leases for the then undeveloped section of the street, now

occupied by Nos. 39-43 Tranquil Vale, as well as for the eventual development of Lee Terrace between Blackheath Village and Lawn Terrace.

The most fundamental change to the structure of the Collins estate
probably occured in 1848 when the South Eastern Railway Company built
their north Kent line from London Bridge, via New Cross and Lewisham
to Blackheath, Charlton and Woolwich. Armed with compulsory purchase
powers the railway companies were able to acquire comparatively large
amounts of land. At Blackheath they were able to do this without much
demolition of property because the route of the metals lay along the valley
of the Kid Brooke through Hally's nurseries. The railway company established at Blackheath one of their central depots for equipment needed in
the tunnelling process which was necessary in order to avoid damage to
Morden College. They also channelled the Kid Brooke into a pipe. This
helped to control the annual inundations and, as a result, drained much of
the nearby land and released it for development.

After the railway had been established the Company did not release its
holdings on land purchased from the Collins estate and, once the metals
and station buildings were completed, leased a large plot to the south of
the new station to Sir Henry Meux who was building pubs next to railway
stations as fast as he could clinch deals and obtain licences. The Railway
Hotel was opened in 1851; by 1853 more land had been sold to the elders
of the Blackheath Congregational Church for their new place of worship,
and a further plot behind the Railway Hotel was sold in 1856 to the Trustees
of the London Missionary Society for a new school for the sons and orphans
of missionaries. Another tract of land between the east boundary
of The Glebe, Lee Terrace, and the site of the Congregational Church had
been sold in 1852 to G. S. Herbert, who built South Vale House on the plot in
the same year.

By the end of the 1850s the Collins Blackheath estate had been fully
developed. And although two short sections were rebuilt for different
reasons in 1927 and 1937, the present appearance of the west side of Tranquil Vale was established by 1849.

By this date, partial ownership of the Collins estate was passing, through
the law of gavelkind*, to more and more descendants through the marriage
of John Collins I. The management until the 1880s was effectively in the
hands of his granddaughter, Elizabeth Harris (1798-1888) and the Misses
Julia and Sophia Harris (d. 1919) thereafter. Sophia, at her death owned
more than half the estate but her will divided this into many fractions and
introduced several new owners. The Law of Property Act 1926 required
the appointment of trustees and by May 1928, E.D. Weippert and Walter
Humphrey had been appointed to represent the owners. In May 1934 the
estate was vested in Collins Properties Ltd., and remained thus until 1950
when the remaining freeholds were sold and the company went into voluntary
liquidation.

*gavelkind: whereby an estate is divided equally between sons, or daughters
if no sons. As a result the individual holdings get smaller and smaller
with each new generation. Abolished by law in 1925.

Tranquil Vale as a street name was not imposed in its present form until about 1886 and further changes were made in 1929. Nevertheless, the name has been used to refer to this section of the Village from the early 19th century although not for a specific stretch of houses but as an overall description for the street and, in the 1820s and 1830s usually indicating premises on the east side of the street.

Until the 1860s the buildings on the west side from Nos. 23 to 47 were known as South Vale and the remainder by various appellations, all of which were swept away, officially, in 1886.

Tranquil Vale

Present No.	Original name & No.		Variations
1	Blackheath Literary Institution		
3	1 Spencer Place		
5	2 Spencer Place		
7	3 Spencer Place		
9	4 Spencer Place		
11	5 Spencer Place		
13 South	6 Spencer Place		
15 Vale	7 Spencer Place		
17	8 Spencer Place		1861
19} 21}	9 Spencer Place - later 9 & 10 Spencer Place		1 South Vale
23	South Vale	13 Tranquil Vale	2 South Vale
25 Vale House	South Vale	12 Tranquil Vale	3 South Vale
27	South Vale	11 Tranquil Vale	4 South Vale
29	South Vale	10 Tranquil Vale	5 South Vale
31	Waterloo House, South Vale	9 Tranquil Vale	6 South Vale
33 35	South Vale	8 Tranquil Vale	7 South Vale
-	South Vale		8 South Vale (demolished 1868)
37	South Vale	7 Tranquil Vale	9 South Vale
39	South Vale	6 Tranquil Vale	10 South Vale
41	South Vale	5 Tranquil Vale	11 South Vale
43	-	4 Tranquil Vale	12 South Vale
45	South Vale	3 Tranquil Vale	13 South Vale
47	South Vale	2 Tranquil Vale	
49 (The Crown)	-	1 Tranquil Vale	14 South Vale
South Vale Cottage			15 South Vale (demolished 1869)
51	1a Camden Place		
53	1 Camden Place		
55	2 Camden Place		demolished after bomb
57	3 Camden Place		damage in 1916
59	4 Camden Place		Site of All Saints Church Hall
61	5 Camden Place		
-	6 Camden Place		

			1871
63	3 Lambs Buildings		1 Lambs Buildings
65 (Melford)	2 Lambs Buildings	demolished 1888/9	2 Lambs Buildings
67 (Braeside)	1 Lambs Buildings		3 Lambs Buildings

For a short period in the 1870s Nos. 23-35 Tranquil Vale were included in
the Spencer Place sequence:

23 Tranquil Vale	11 Spencer Place
25 27 } Tranquil Vale	12 Spencer Place
29 Tranquil Vale	—
31 Tranquil Vale	13 Spencer Place
33 Tranquil Vale	14 Spencer Place

The following account of the individual buildings in this road is divided into
sections, usually the group of buildings as they were developed originally.
To aid the reader, the current street number is given first with any previous
principal appellation given in parenthesis.

1 Tranquil Vale

This street number has been attached to various buildings on this side of the
Collins estate; in 1885 it applied to the Railway Hotel. But the use lapsed
and in 1929 the number was given to Blackheath railway station. In 1975 it
was allotted to Martin House, a new building erected by the Blackheath
Preservation Trust Ltd. on the site of the old Blackheath Literary Institution.
The building is dealt with in Chapter 15 of this book.

3-9 Tranquil Vale (was 1-4 Spencer Place)

This terrace of shops, occupying a curious, almost triangular, piece of
ground was the last part of Collins' Tranquil Vale frontage to be developed.
Built in 1845-6, possibly by one of the Suter family, the terrace was
designed as shops and built as a speculation. No. 4 was auctioned by a Mr
Stow in July 1846 and described as "a newly-erected house and shop in the
most eligible part of Blackheath, being 4 Spencer Place, Tranquil Vale".

Despite their proximity to the Kid Brooke with its propensity to flood,
the Spencer Place shops were soon occupied and quickly established themselves as some of the most important and prosperous retail units in the
Village.

Unfortunately they were damaged during the last war, in October 1941,
and this was so close to the expiry of the headlease that Nos. 3, 5 & 7
Tranquil Vale remained empty and in a dilapidated condition for some years
In August 1950 the freehold was acquired by the Blackheath Preservation
Trust Ltd. from the trustees of Collins Properties Ltd., then in voluntary
liquidation. The Trust restored the buildings, following as far as sensible,
their appearance as revealed in old photographs.

3 Tranquil Vale (was 1 Spencer Place)

For more than 100 years this shop was one of the best-known Blackheath grocers, held by a succession of proprietors, sometimes as a branch of a business elsewhere in the Village.

The first tenant was John Dalton the younger, son of John Dalton who had owned grocery shops at 21 and 25 Montpelier Vale (q.v.). Dalton did not stay long at 3 Tranquil Vale but transferred his business to 24 Tranquil Vale (q.v.) in 1849, and the shop at No. 3 passed to Multon Lambert (1811-1889) who traded as a cheesemonger and grocer from here until his retirement in 1883. Lambert, who had started his business in 1840 at 61 Tranquil Vale (5 Camden Place) was the typical Blackheath shopkeeper of his time. He was an enthusiastic supporter of the local literary institutions, a church elder, he lived above the shop but did not marry until the business was well-established. When he retired he moved to 44 Bennett Park, then newly-built, where he lived in the bosom of his family until his death in 1889. His son, Charles William Lambert became a missionary in the Far East, but was killed by thieves at the American Baptist Mission in Burma in 1895. Mrs. Harriet Lambert (1830-1899) survived her husband by ten years, and their spinster daughters, Harriet Mary (1855-1927), and Margaret Caroline Payne Lambert (1859-1927) continued to live at Bennett Park until their deaths. When Multon Lambert retired in 1883 the business at Spencer Place was taken over by Dannatt & Co., the cheesemongers of Nelson Street, Greenwich, whose family business had been established by George Dannatt (1826-1901) at 20 Nelson Street in 1847. This business was so successful that Dannatt retired in his middle age and devoted the rest of his life to religious and public works. The grocery shops were then under the control of his son, George Herbert Dannatt (1854-1929) who took into part-nership the 21-year old Henry Williams (1847-1929). This partnership lasted more than 60 years, eventually embracing half a dozen retail shops in prime commercial positions. In 1899 they took over the failing South East Stores at 24 Tranquil Vale and the company controlled both Blackheath shops until 1947. In 1917 the shop at 3 Tranquil Vale was registered as The Blackheath Village Stores Ltd. and it traded in this name until 1946 when the Dannatt & Williams shops were acquired by Cullens Stores Ltd. Cullens have traded ever since at 24 Tranquil Vale but surrendered the lease on the war-damaged shop at 3 Tranquil Vale soon after they acquired it.

After restoration by the Blackheath Preservation Trust the old Village Stores became, initially, a showroom for gas appliances but in 1963 was re-opened for the sale of paint and wallpapers and has remained in the same use ever since.

5 & 7 Tranquil Vale (was 2 & 3 Spencer Place)

Although built originally as two shops these premises have been linked as a single retail unit from their first occupation in 1845 by William Arthur Trill, a silk mercer and draper. The Trill family, led by the brothers Stephen and Thomas Trill, had established a drapery at 31 Tranquil Vale in 1832 and they and their children opened a bewildering number of shops in Blackheath and Greenwich over the next 15 years. None of their ventures seemed to last long although the shop at 31 Tranquil Vale was still in Trill's name in 1844. In the following year they had moved across the road to No. 42 but this time trading as glass and china merchants.

In 1847 the Trill family left 5 & 7 Tranquil Vale and their business

15. Park House, later the Presbytery, built for Capt. Thomas Larkins in 1787

16. Plan of the Bennett Park Estate in 1860

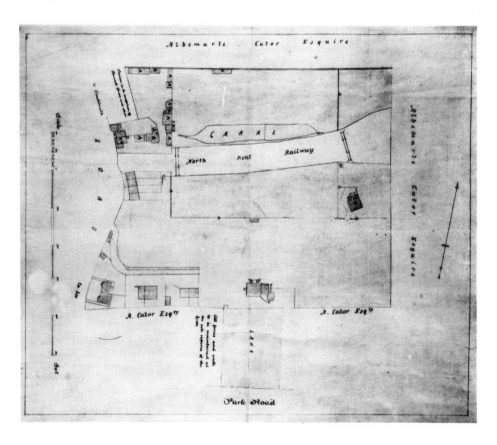

17.   The heart of the Village in 1890

18.   Rebuilding Nos 18 & 20 Tranquil Vale in 1903

19. Frederick's Place before 1860, replaced by Bank Buildings in 1863.

20. Bank Buildings in the late 1870's. Replaced in 1888 by the present Barclays Bank

21. John Hally's nursery before the railway came

22. The Wesleyan Chapel shortly after completion in 1863

23. Ruins of the Wesleyan Chapel in 1946

passed to Thomas Miller Whittaker (1823-1899) a 23 year old Stafford-born draper who was destined to become not only one of the most prosperous businessmen in Blackheath but played an important part in the development of Royal Parade in 1861. Whittaker was a manufacturing draper as well as a retailer, employing a number of apprentices (who lived on the premises) and outworkers to produce many of the smaller lines sold in his shop. At some stage, possibly by the early 1870s, Whittaker took on the lease of the old Blackheath Literary Institution building at the rear of his shop and converted it into a workshop and showroom. By this time the main shop was in the hands of a resident manager who looked after 12 assistant drapers, and Whittaker was living in a large house in the Eltham Road. Like Multon Lambert, the next door grocer, Whittaker was a keen Baptist - he had founded the Dacre Park Baptist Chapel in 1852 - and was active in local politics, eventually being elected to the Lewisham vestry. In 1890, prob-ably due to retirement, Whittaker took Morriss William Brown (1852-1925) into partnership. Brown, who had married Whittaker's daughter, Emily Ann, continued the business with equal success but, in 1908, decided to dispose of the lease. The stock was purchased outright by Hinds, the drapers at Beaconsfield Buildings (q.v.) and the lease on the empty premises taken by Wilson & Co., also drapers. Wilson stayed less than a year and in September 1909 the shop was acquired by Hinds as a branch of their rapidly-expanding business, for the sale of art needlework, curtains and blankets. For the next thirty years Hinds enjoyed a high reputation in the district, employing more than 200 people at their Blackheath shops and workshops, selling a wider and wider range of goods.

During the last war the premises were severely damaged and the company's retailing interests declined, possibly because their lease was due to expire in 1947 and there would have been no future in renovating the Tranquil Vale shop.

After restoration by the Blackheath Preservation Trust the premises once more became a draper's shop, but this time specialising in children's wear, shoes and nursery equipment, when a lease was taken by Mr. and Mrs. Keith McKenzie whose business, Raggity Ann's, had been established in 1946 at 41 Montpelier Vale. At the time of writing Nos. 5 & 7 Tranquil Vale have sold clothing for more than 130 years.

9 Tranquil Vale (was 4 Spencer Place)

This shop has been occupied by only two trades in its lifetime: from 1846 to 1905 it was leased by a succession of stationers and booksellers; from 1905 up to the present time by watchmakers and jewellers.

The first tenants were Messrs Brown and Webber, stationers and book-sellers who traded here from 1846 to 1848. This was not a long stay but they left their mark by publishing a series of engravings of local scenes by Richard Rock who lived at 103 Lee Road during the 1840s and 1850s.

Brown and Webber were succeeded from 1849 to 1852 by Henry Davis who kept to the same trade but does not seem to have made much impact. In January 1853 the shop was re-opened by Alfred Hughes Wray (1823-c1872) as "a useful and ornamental stationers, with the latest novelties, a lending library and servants' registry." Wray was more successful than the previous tenants, and built up no small trade by acting as an agent for the Kentish Mercury, not only selling copies but taking in advertisements for which he would have been paid a small commission. For a period in the 1850s the villagers had another reason for visiting Wray's shop - each Thursday Mr. Pearce, a surgeon dentist, took over one of the upstairs rooms and, for a modest fee, would try to bring relief to sufferers from toothache.

Wray sold his shop in 1873 to Ebenezer Wilmhurst (1850-1906) who had started in the stationery trade at 26 Tranquil Vale when it was owned by William John Martin. Wilmhurst followed the same retailing pattern as had Wray before him and occasionally published some slim books of verse and other ephemera. In 1878 he published a small commercial and court directory of the district, largely to promote his own wares. When he retired in 1905 he sold the stock of the shop to the proprietor of Wilmhurst's apprentice shop at 26 Tranquil Vale, but the lease on the shop at 9 Tranquil Vale was assigned to Horace A. Triggs, a jeweller whose business had been established in Tranquil Passage in 1860 but who was then occupying 29 Tranquil Vale. The business passed to his son, R.A. Triggs, by 1915 and it remained with the family until 1962 when the lease and goodwill passed to Messrs G. Blanshard who are the present tenants although the company is now part of Harvey & Thompson Ltd.

11-17 Tranquil Vale (was 5-8 Spencer Place)

According to the Land Tax records a group of four cottages stood on this site, in the ownership of Mrs. Sarah Kerl, from 1802 to 1825, and prior to 1802 there had been a single small house here, possibly the Kerl's own home. It is not until 1825 that the present buildings appear in the commercial directories as shops and it is possible that the early cottages were originally built as housing and that the conversions were made as the demand for retail shops grew in the 1820s and 1830s.

They form a plain, two-storey brick built terrace with no signs of obvious "antiquity" like the weatherboarding of 47 Tranquil Vale or the Collins Square houses and, perhaps because of this, it is hard to accept they must be over 170 years old. Further, being only two storeys high and quite small, subsequent alterations and changes to the shop facias by successive commercial tenants has always ensured a contemporary appearance.

Because Mrs. Kerl paid the Land Tax it is not possible to be sure of the early residents of 11-17 Tranquil Vale until the shopkeepers took over in the 1820s or afterwards.

11 Tranquil Vale (was 5 Spencer Place)

The first known tenant of this shop was Henry Piggot, a greengrocer and fruiterer who was in occupation from before 1838 until at least 1847, after which he moved to 3 Montpelier Vale. The Tranquil Vale premises were then taken for the next 14 years by Albert and Ann Elizabeth Thies as a drapery and millinery shop. But in July 1865 the premises had been substantially altered and opened as a branch of the London and County Banking Co., with John Thomas Edwards as manager. This was only a temporary stay for the Bank was quickly in negotiation for a site higher up in the Village cleared for the development of Collins Street. In 1869 the new banking hall at 37 Tranquil Vale was completed and the London and County disposed of their lease on 11 Tranquil Vale to Richard Whittaker, a watch-maker and jeweller. His tenancy lasted only until 1874 in which year the shop was taken by the first in a long line of tobacconists which lasted until 1913. Most of these tenancies were brief but in 1895 the shop was rented by Jude Silverstone who imported tobacco from Egypt and Turkey for the manufacture of hand-made cigarettes. Silverstone opened a branch of the business at 1 Lee Road in 1903, taking over the business established by John Goslin originally at 50 Tranquil Vale (q.v.) from 1860 to 1885. By 1909, Silverstone's company had passed to Alfred Kauffman, who may have been his manager and, in 1913, Kauffman moved to 4 Montpelier Vale.

The Tranquil Vale shop remained empty for a year or two but in August 1915 it was opened as the Mascot Tea Rooms. This made little impact, for by the end of the Great War 11 Tranquil Vale was a sweetshop and it remained in this trade until 1945 after which it became a receiving office for Messrs Collins, cleaners and dyers.

In 1971 the premises were refitted by Mr. & Mrs. Irving as Books of Blackheath.

13 Tranquil Vale (was 6 Spencer Place)

This small shop holds a remarkable trading record for Blackheath in that it has been a fishmongers since the mid-1830s. It is possible that the premises were held by Thomas Jones, a cheesemonger, in the 1820s but there is no doubt that William and Phillip Jones, fishmongers, had leased the shop by 1837 and remained there until at least 1847. By 1851 the business had passed to George William Wood (b. 1821) and stayed in the family, latterly under his son's control (also George William and born in Blackheath in 1851) until 1904. In that year the business was acquired by William Goodson but he stayed only until 1915. The following year the shop was taken over by A.C. Burtenshaw of Beckenham and this family traded from here until 1956.

Since then, the shop, presently the only fishmongery in Blackheath, has been owned by W.D. Marshall, and the business has remained with the Marshall family to the present day.

15 Tranquil Vale (was 7 Spencer Place)

This, the third of Mrs. Kerl's cottages, seems to have become a butcher's shop when it first went into commercial use in the mid-1820s. There is some evidence that it was occupied by Charles Brown, a butcher who also worked from 3 Camden Place (q.v.) and later purchased the headlease on Camden Row and Camden Cottages.

But he had left 15 Tranquil Vale by the 1830s and his place was taken by the butcher John Willett Williams (b. 1801) who traded from here until at least 1851. Although the shop was very small, Williams had an outbuilding at the rear, reached by the alleyway between Nos. 9 and 11 Tranquil Vale. This building was used as the slaughterhouse, for it was common practice at the time for even the smallest butchers to kill their own meat. The disposal of offals and refuse was done haphazardly and there were complaints at the stench arising from the back of this shop on many occasions in the early 1850s.

The business passed through two other proprietors before 1868 in which year it was acquired by Thomas Daynes Wood (1836-1912) whose name remained over the frontage until 1920. After Wood's death the business was carried on by his sons, particularly Arthur Thomas Daynes Wood (1869-1920) but when Arthur was killed in a bus accident at the age of 51 the family sold the shop to B. W. Parsons Ltd., the old-established butchers of 12 Montpelier Vale (q. v.). They used Wood's shop as a pork meat department but in 1924 closed these premises

For a brief period 15 Tranquil Vale became an estate agency (John Kelly & Co.) but in 1931 it was re-opened as a restaurant by G. R. Astlett. In 1935 the then proprietor gave it the name The Pagoda Tea Shop and this held until its eventual change of style to Italian cuisine in 1969. In December 1950 the Pagoda was taken over by G. D. Warner of the Welcome Inn at 44 Tranquil Vale (q. v.) on the grounds that "the classes don't mix and I want to cater for the masses."

At the time of writing, the Italian restaurant had closed and the premises re-opened for the sale of take-away Chinese food.

17 Tranquil Vale (was 8 Spencer Place)

Until 1851 this was the last unit to enjoy the appellation Spencer Place. Its first commercial tenant was Jonathon Collins, a tailor (b. 1811) who traded here from c1830 to at least 1847. In 1849 the tenant and trade had changed to John Arthur Smith, who was a plumber and painter, and used the shop as his base until about 1874. From 1880 to 1881 John Hilton, an auctioneer and surveyor set up an office here but in 1882 he was invited into partnership with William John Dyer (1857-1932) and transferred his office to the latter's headquarters at 17 Montpelier Row (q. v.). In 1882 17 Tranquil Vale became a greengrocery - its present use - when it was taken by Thomas Mansell Noble (fl. 1840-1885). His widow Sarah (1837-1912) continued the business which remained with the Noble family until 1934. In 1937 the shop was acquired by Henry Samuell (1888-1944) who had started his fruiterers business at 45 Montpelier Vale in 1927. Since the 1950s the shop has traded as Fenner's.

19 & 21 Tranquil Vale

Although these two shops are relatively insignificant in the broad sweep of Tranquil Vale and appear to be contemporary with Nos. 11-17 Tranquil Vale, they were in fact built in the early 1830s, probably as a single unit. In the 1850s they took the description 9 and 10 Spencer Place but the commercial records show not only considerable variation in the tenancies but shopkeepers moving from one to the other and back again. Further, No. 10 seems to have been occupied by more than one retail business at the same time. To judge by the size of the shops this seems hardly possible and the author is driven to wondering whether there were buildings at the rear which have long been demolished or, that the address 10 Spencer Place was given to the basement of No. 23 Tranquil Vale (q. v.) which was entered from the road close to the present No. 21 Tranquil Vale. This view is supported by census and other records which show Joseph Watson, a shoemaker at 10 Spencer Place from 1832 to 1845, and a census return for the property presently 23 Tranquil Vale as occupied by the same Joseph Watson, a shoemaker.

It seems from the evidence that the building was not split into two separate units until 1866 and that they were both numbered 9 Spencer Place until 1885. It is with this assumption that the tenancy details are listed below.

19 Tranquil Vale (sometimes 9 Spencer Place)

There was a wide variety of commercial tenants here between the years 1839 and its use as an upholsterer's workshop by John Apsley in 1866 and 1867. The first tenants seem to have been Arthur and Jane Berry who combined the trade of plumbing with the running of a small general shop, then known as a fancy repository. During the 1840s it was leased by Miss Naomi Hindwood, a milliner, but by the 1850s it had been taken by John Willett Williams the butcher who traded from 15 Tranquil Vale from the 1830s to 1851. John Williams was succeeded in 1859 by George Williams, who may have been his son, but in October 1863 the shop, with a 19 year unexpired lease was sold to a Mr. Button, a watchmaker, for £610. This was clearly an investment for Mr. Button as he does not seem to have occupied the premises. In June 1864 he let the shop to the South Eastern Banking Co., Ltd. for a new branch. The Bank failed in May 1866 because of its close link with the also bankrupt English Joint Stock Bank. The effect of this failure for those Blackheath residents with accounts at the South Eastern was mitigated to some degree when the London and County Bank - whose Blackheath branch was a few doors away at 11 Tranquil Vale - took over the accounts at 50% of value.

It was in 1866 that the shop must have been divided and the tenants for the north section from this date are dealt with below as at 10 Spencer Place.

The tenant at No. 9 for a couple of years was the upholsterer John Apsley, but in 1868-9 the shop was taken by Douglas Fountain (1841-1895) a hosier and shirtmaker, and he set the pattern of trading here which lasted until the 1940s. On his death the business passed in 1896 to Mills, Baker, and their name remained over the doorway until 1930, at which date the shop was acquired by William Barkway.

In November 1952 it was leased by Butcher, Curnow Ltd., as their optical department under the management of F.A. Bevis who had joined the company in 1926.

21 Tranquil Vale (sometimes 10 Spencer Place)

When this unit was created out of the single shop known as 9 Spencer Place, the first tenant, in 1866, was John Urell, a homeopathic chemist. He had conducted a dispensary at 2 Bennett Place (11 Blackheath Village) from 1863-1864 as part of the Blackheath Homeopathic Dispensary, a quasi-charitable venture which failed to sustain its good intentions. In 1869 Urell's dispensary was taken over by another homeopathic chemist - William Butcher of Regent Street. Butcher was to make an enormous impact on the commercial development of Blackheath and to play, possibly the most important role in the local retail trade. His company survives today, and its story will be found on those pages outlining the history of Nos. 33-35 Tranquil Vale. His main business interests were transferred to 33-35 Tranquil Vale during the 1870s but he retained an interest in 21 Tranquil Vale long after the shop had been let to the Victoria Wine Co. in 1874. Butcher's Analytical Laboratory functioned from here until 1895, offering a service analysing foodstuffs, blood, urine, and any other substance that doctors and the general public wished to examine.

From 1896 the premises were wholly in the occupation of the Victoria Wine Company and they remained at No. 21 until 1948. They moved to 20 Blackheath Village that year and remain in those premises although the name of the company has changed now to Wineways Ltd. The shop at No. 21 Tranquil Vale has been successively a travel agent, theatre booking agency, and stamp and curio dealers.

23-25 Tranquil Vale

These street numbers cover a group of four houses and one in-fill shop which add immeasurably to the charm and character of Blackheath Village. As well as being architecturally distinguished they are also notable for being not only some of the oldest buildings in Blackheath but also a group that has survived relatively unspoiled.

Their exact date is unknown because of the lack of rate records and conveyance documents, but there is no doubt that the four principal properties had been built and were in occupation by 1798.

Initially they were built as private houses but during the 1820s they drifted into commercial use although, at the beginning, rather discreetly as private schools or doctors' surgeries. But once they had become shops their position in the Village attracted, for the most part, shopkeepers who achieved no small success.

23 Tranquil Vale (was 2 South Vale: 13 Tranquil Vale)

This building, by far the best preserved of the group because of the skilful restoration work after the last war, was first occupied by a Mrs. Kitchin from 1798 to about 1804. She was succeeded by 1805 by Mr. John Brewer who seems to have remained in residence until 1823. There were three comparatively short tenancies after that: Mr. Watson (1824-1825), Mr. Creed (1826-1828) and Mr. Hoe (1829-1831).

The tenant from 1832 to 1850 was Joseph Watson, a boot and shoe maker (1789-c1846) and his son James, born in 1816. Whether they used this building as a shop as well as their home is not known and there must be some small doubt that a working cobbler at the time would have lived in quite such a grand house.

In 1851 the tenants were of unquestionable standing, being Samuel Warner, a house plasterer of some status then employing twenty men despite his relative youth, and Thomas Feldwick, a retired ironmaster.

It was at this period that No. 23 was converted into a shop and the tenancy passed to Emma Morley (1823-c1875), a daughter of Henry Morley of Crooms Hill. Emma sold Berlin wool, the fine quality wool for embroidery and decoration, and described her premises as a fancy repository. This probably meant she stocked a wide range of haberdashery and drapery, samplers, cushion covers and the cottons, needles and wools needed to keep the wives and daughters of the Blackheath middle classes from going mad with boredom.

After Miss Morley's death or retirement, the shop was taken over by Joseph Bizzell, the son of Jacob who lived at 3 Phoenix Place (31 Montpelier Vale) and doubled as a coal merchant and part-time waiter. This combination of roles may seem curious – but his son pursued the lucrative trade of merchandising coal with that of millinery. No doubt his wife concentrated on the latter although only until 1882; for the rest of their tenancy until 1887 it is Jacob's coal business that is paramount: he moved to No. 13 Montpelier Vale in 1888 and remained there until well into the twentieth century.

The new tenant at 23 Tranquil Vale was Emma Morley's brother Alfred Morley, a music and musical instrument dealer trading as Henry Morley & Son, music warehouses. Morley's were already well-established in the Village and were probably the principal music dealers in the district. The original company had been founded by Henry Morley in Crooms Hill in 1828 where he built a reputation as a piano dealer and as a concert promoter, especially of instrumental and song recitals at the new literary institutes springing up in the 1840s and at the Green Man Assembly Rooms at the top of Blackheath Hill. In 1858 Henry, or his son Alfred, established a branch of the business at 7 Blackheath Village (then 6 Brunswick Place) which succeeded well enough for them to take premises at 45 Tranquil Vale where they remained until 1887 when the larger shop at 23 Tranquil Vale fell vacant.

The new premises – soon to be dubbed Bach House – became the principal shop for the Morley business, supplying all the musical needs of Blackheath from sheet music, instruments and tutors, to tickets for concerts at the Crystal Palace, Royal Albert Hall, Queen's Hall and, from 1895, the Blackheath Concert Hall. In fact, so important had Bach House become that the Morleys closed down the original shop at 7 Crooms Hill in 1894 and concentrated their efforts in Blackheath Village. When Alfred Morley died, his widow, Matilda Elizabeth (1837-1909) became senior partner and took over the direction of the company. As there were no children of the marriage to ensure continuity of the family company Harold M. Hopwood was taken into partnership in 1913 and the old company flourished under his direction until the outbreak of war in 1939. In December 1937 the radio and gramaphone side of the business moved to 20 Montpelier Vale under the direction of Hopwood's son, Ralph, partly because the music machines were taking up too much space at 23 Tranquil Vale.

War damage to the shop and Harold Hopwood's impending retirement in 1941 forced the company to consider their future in a time of restricted supplies and staff shortages and they were taken over by the Lewisham music dealers and piano manufacturers, Robert Morley & Co. This must have been something of a blow for the Morleys of Bach House – they had spent much money and effort over the previous 40 years denying any conn-ection whatsoever with the Lewisham company of the same name.

The merger was not able to save Bach House and by the end of the war the music shop had closed down.

In 1948, 23 Tranquil Vale was acquired by Mr. & Mrs. E. A. J. Parker, antique dealers, and they effected a magnificent restoration to the premises. There is no doubt that this work encouraged other Village shop keepers to restore rather than re-build their premises after the 1939-1945 War and the example set by the Parkers ensured a high standard elsewhere.

In 1968 Mr. & Mrs. Parker gave up their shop and it remained empty until 1972 when it was purchased for a branch office of the Woolwich Equitable Building Society.

25 & 27 Tranquil Vale (Vale House)

Although there are two postal numbers for these premises they were built
as a single house in 1798 and occupied as such until approximately 1836;
they were partly re-united in 1921 but the double shop front was not installed
until 1956: prior to that date No. 27 had kept the facade of a private house.
In 1959 the freehold of the property was vested with the Trustees of Morden
College.

The principal tenants of the single unit were a Mrs. Pritchard (1798-1802),
Daniel Ross (1803-1804), Mr. Miller (1805-1810) and Mr. & Mrs. Walker
(1811-1824).

In 1824 the house was taken by the first in a long line of medical men -
George Birch, a surgeon. But in 1831 part of the premises may have been
let on a temporary basis as a school room for the newly-founded Blackheath
Proprietary School then waiting for its new buildings to be completed
further south in the Village on the site of what is now Selwyn Court. But this
view was based on the memory of someone not born in 1831 and the evidence
now points to the Prop's first home being at The Crown public house.

25 Tranquil Vale (3 South Vale; 12 Tranquil Vale)

The first independent day school which certainly did occupy these premises
was one conducted by a Mr. Ebenezer Harris from about 1835 to 1840;
he was succeeded by Henry Dodson (b. 1811) who ran the establishment as
a day school for boys, but seemingly with little success, as he had left the
neighbourhood by 1848.

The empty house was then taken by Thomas William Smith, a hairdresser
and perfumer, who had built up a successful trade at 3 Blackheath Village
from 1841 to 1847 where his wife, Ann, had worked diligently as a straw
hat maker. Smith, who had been born in Chelsea in 1810, managed to
capture the carriage trade and he dominated the hairdressing business for
men and women in Blackheath - many others tried to break his monopoly
but failed - and such was his power that, despite partnerships and changes
in proprietorship, his name remained over the door until 1949.

The truth is that Smith had taken Robert Winterbourne into partnership
as early as 1851. Winterbourne's name does not appear after 1870 and at
some stage the business passed to Smith's son-in-law Henry Hodges (1854-
1916), who remained sole proprietor until 1904. In that year the company
was sold to Hodges' manager, Thomas William Drummond, and the shop
remained with the Drummond family until the mid-1950s. Mrs. Smith's
straw hat business had been sustained until the 1860s, but it eventually
closed on her death in 1868. In 1880 part of the premises were let to
Miss Clare Jackson who made lace and artificial flowers. But by the 1890s
the hairdressing department occupied the entire premises and in 1921
Drummond added No. 27 Tranquil Vale to the shop, thus uniting the two
halves of the old house.

In 1956 the style of the shop changed and the new proprietors of No. 27
were Mr. & Mrs. Cockburn-Mercer, trading as Vanity Fayre. They took
over No. 25 in March 1959 for a shoe department and the shop fronts took
on their present appearance at this time.

27 Tranquil Vale (was 4 South Vale; 11 Tranquil Vale)

From 1824 until the 1950s the north section of 25-27 Tranquil Vale was used as a doctor's surgery by a succession of partnerships which included some of the most distinguished names in local medicine. The surgery was established by George Birch who had set up a practice at 2 Fredericks Place in 1820 but moved to 27 Tranquil Vale in 1824. This house was not always the residence of the doctors concerned, nor was it always their principal set of consulting rooms. Rather than describe the tenants in narrative the names of the doctors here before 1914 are set out below with the dates in which they were in practice at 27 Tranquil Vale:

1824-1837:	George Birch (fl. 1790-1840)
1828-1867:	Henry Barnett JP (1805-1873)
1836-1877:	William Carr (1814-1877)
1852-1858:	Dr. Stott
1864-1900:	John Nicholas Miller (1837-1911)
1879-1916:	H. F. Bailey
1904-1916:	F.J. Harvey Bateman, FZS, JP, (1869-1920)

During the middle years of the 19th century some of the rooms were let to members of another profession - lawyers, principally to William Hayley Engleheart (1816-1853) from 1847 until his death, and to Octavius C. Tyron Eagleton who was also the vestry clerk to the Parish of Lewisham.

29 Tranquil Vale (was 5 South Vale; 10 Tranquil Vale)

This slip of building, now an integral part of 25-27 Tranquil Vale, was built on the stable or alley way between Nos. 27 and 31 Tranquil Vale in about 1835. Its first tenant was Robert Mount, a saddler and harness maker who was resident here from at least 1838 to 1845. Before 1850 the premises had passed to Charles John Irish, also a saddler, who was born in Yeovil in 1826. The Irish family worked as saddlers in Blackheath until 1918 but they left 29 Tranquil Vale in 1865 and traded thereafter from 59 Tranquil Vale until 1916 when those premises were destroyed by a bomb. In 1866, 29 Tranquil Vale was leased by Robert Waddington Triggs, a watch and clock maker who had established his business in a small house in Tranquil Passage in 1861. Triggs (1830-1891) was succeeded at 29 Tranquil Vale by his son, Horace Triggs who continued to work here until 1905. In that year he moved to 9 Tranquil Vale and the small shop at 29 Tranquil Vale passed through a number of trades, being held for brief periods by stationers, umbrella makers (H. Wallis) and, in 1914, by H. E. & J. Smith as a health food shop - The National Health Stores. During the 1920s and '30s it was best known as an arts and crafts shop, trading from 1926 to 1936 as the Collis-Boughton Studios, and it remained in this use until after the last war. In 1956 the premises were opened as a dress shop, Vanity Fayre, and the proprietors eventually acquired Nos. 25-27 Tranquil Vale as part of the business.

31 Tranquil Vale (was 6 South Vale; 9 Tranquil Vale)

This building, known at various times as Waterloo House or Albion House, was first occupied in 1798 by a Mr. Ross. He was succeeded in 1805 by a Mr. Barnes who paid the Land Tax until 1824 although he may not have lived there all that time. In 1825 John Collins II was the tenant and he was succeeded by Charles Collins for the years 1826 to 1828. From 1829 to 1831 the tenant was a Mr. Knott, but in 1832 the first commercial users appear in the record. These were the brothers Stephen and Thomas Trill, silk mercers and drapers who leased the shop from 1832 until 1845. The Trill family, who owned a shop in Nelson Road, Greenwich, occupied various premises in Blackheath Village, in particular they were the first tenants of 5 & 7 Tranquil Vale (q. v.) in 1845. Stephen Trill left the partnership in 1844 and set up as a china and glass merchant at 42 Tranquil Vale (q. v.) but had died by 1850. Thomas Trill's wife, Jane, was trading in her own account at 5 & 7 Tranquil Vale in 1847 and it can be assumed that she had been widowed, like her sister-in-law, at an early age.

The Trill business at 31 Tranquil Vale was acquired in 1847 by Henry Goodwin Missing (1812-1862) as a linen drapery. Missing, who gave the name Waterloo House to the building, traded successfully for the first years of his tenancy but by the 1860s found himself in difficulties. His credit rating slumped and he attempted to save the business with a partnership arrangement, but this failed and he shot himself in an unlit railway carriage in the Blackheath Tunnel on 26 April 1862. It was his suicide, amongst other events, that led to pressures on the railway companies to provide lighting in railway carriages.

Missing's shop was taken over by another draper, William Henry Collier, but by 1868 the shop had passed to Robert Acfield Gibbons from Caddenham in Suffolk. Robert Gibbons (1819-c1890) proved a better businessman than Missing and traded here until 1890 at which date the company changed its name name to Mead, Gibbons & Co., remaining at 31 Tranquil Vale until 1897.

In that year the enterprising William Butcher, trading next door at 33 Tranquil Vale (q. v.) as a chemist, took Albion House as a bicycle works and showroom, the Landseer Cycle Works, and remained there until 1901. Whether this was overstretching his resources or not we do not know, but in June 1902 the premises passed to Haycraft & Son Ltd., the ironmongers of Deptford whose origins stretched back to 1777. Haycraft's had a number of branches in south-east London, particularly in Lewisham High Road and Deptford and it was inevitable that they would seek premises in Blackheath, particularly to catch the lucrative bicycle market. Haycraft's established themselves at No. 31 Tranquil Vale, taking over William Butcher's bicycle interests, and traded here for the next 50 years although they totally re-built the shop front in August 1905.

Haycraft's remained in Blackheath until after the last war but closed down in 1953 because of financial difficulties. From 1954 the premises were shared between a drapery business and Keating & Miskin, television and radio dealers, but by 1959 the whole shop had been restored as a single unit by Messrs Reeve & Jones, drapers who had traded at 16-18 Delacourt Road from the early years of this century.

33 & 35 Tranquil Vale (was 7 South Vale; 8 Tranquil Vale)

This was the northernmost of the four 1798 houses built on Collins Tranquil Vale frontage and, even before the building of Collins Street in 1867-1869 there was a footpath here leading to a group of cottages and the nursery garden by the railway line.

The first tenant was a Mrs. Weatherall but by 1805 the house was occupied by John Kempson. From 1829 to 1832 the owner was Michael Bryant but in 1832 the directories show that the shop at least was occupied by Walter Bagnall (1798-1869) who was a furniture broker, cabinet maker and upholsterer. He remained at 33 Tranquil Vale from 1832 to 1855, conducting a most successful business and employed half a dozen assistants in the 1850s.

After Bagnall's retirement the business was taken over in 1856 by William Tyler Bradley (1824-1883) who pursued the same calling as Bagnall but additionally operated as a house agent, auctioneer and appraiser and, like many carpenters, as an undertaker as well.

It was during Bradley's tenancy that the southern half of the retail premises was taken by William Butcher and his family. Butcher (1840-1903) was a Paddington-born homeopathic chemist who had started in business in London's Regent Street in 1862. He had come to Blackheath in about 1868 and set up a dispensary and laboratory at 19 & 21 Tranquil Vale. This was a small shop and he rented rooms from Bradley for the Butcher residence. When Bradley retired in 1878 his shop was leased by the Butchers as a Berlin repository (general haberdashery) for Miss Martha Butcher (William's sister) and William continued to work from 19 Tranquil Vale. In 1885, the premises at the rear, then known as 35 Tranquil Vale, were leased by William Arthur Lloyd, a cycle manufacturer, as The Cycle Trade Supply Co. In 1885 William Butcher moved his principal dispensary to 33 Tranquil Vale and Martha's Berlin repository moved to the newly-built 7 Montpelier Vale (q.v.). All this time William Butcher's business was growing and his interests were extending beyond the dispensing of medicines and the supply of surgical appliances. He was a keen advertiser and promoter of the business, publishing booklets on medical matters which he delivered free to every house in the neighbourhood. Although his sons, William F. and Frank E. Butcher entered the family business in 1889 William snr took into partnership one of the Blackheath employees, William A. Curnow (1855-1916) and from 1895 the company was known as Butcher, Curnow & Company, although Curnow was not made a director until 1904 when the family firm registered as a limited liability company. In 1891 the shop was totally refitted with the then most up-to-date mahoganny furnishings and the latest apparatus for the manufacture of medicines and the printing of photographs - for William's interests in photography had by then grown to obsessive proportions. He had a particular enthusiasm for the magic lantern, hiring these out with a selection of 6 dozen slides for 10/6 an evening to church groups, schools and parties. To celebrate the wedding of the Duke of York to Princess May of Teck a large screen was draped over the front of 46 Tranquil Vale and William Butcher entertained huge crowds with displays of patriotic pictures of the Royal couple and other suitably stirring pictures.

It was the invention of the cinema which seized William Butcher's imagination. Early in 1896 he had entered the manufacturing race and had taken a lease on two floors of a workshop in Brigade Street for the manufacture of camera equipment, an Otto gas engine had been installed and business was brisk. Within a year the company employed more than 60 staff turning out hundreds of cheap cameras, developing and printing kits and all the rest of the paraphernalia needed for the enthusiastic amateur. On January 9th 1897 William Butcher demonstrated some "animated

pictures" on a machine called the Moto-photoscope - the pictures were
half a dozen short films of railway stations, a charge of the German cavalry,
a hand-coloured film of a minuet - all shown on a six-foot screen. The
effect was sensational and within a year no private or charitable event in
Blackheath was complete without Mr. Butcher's films. He added to the
stock and was quick to obtain copies of the film made of Queen Victoria's
Diamond Jubilee procession in 1897.

In no time Butcher was making his own films and handling the distribution
of film through Butcher's Film Service. A further sensation was caused in
November 1898 when he screened films shot in Blackheath Village showing
the arrival of the Eltham omnibus, the railway station, and scenes shot on
and around the Heath, and gave "the first public exhibition in England" of
colour movies made by a process which almost certainly involved the hand-
colouring of every frame.

In March 1900 Queen Victoria paid her first ever visit, so far as the
public knew, to Blackheath, passing via the Village to visit the Boer War
wounded at the Herbert Hospital in Woolwich. Butcher took advantage of
the excitement of the day by hiring the Blackheath Concert Hall and showing
most of his stock in continuous programme.

Additionally, Butcher was enthusiastic about the other mechanical novelties
of the time and was one of the first local promoters of the gramaphone,
selling Edison phonographs in 1898 and His Master's Voice machines in
1900. Meanwhile the factory in Brigade Street was reaching its maximum
capacity and the addition of cinematographic apparatus to the catalogue
meant that Butcher required more space. The answer was found in April
1902 when a lease was taken on a large building on the corner of St. Bride
Street and Stonecutter Street in the City of London, which William Butcher
dubbed Camera House. His payroll was now up to 150 with the dispensary
and cycle works at Tranquil Vale, and workshops in Royal Parade Mews and
at Camera House. The cycle works was the Cycle Trade Supply Co. which
had been started by William Arthur Lloyd and occupied the rear of 33
Tranquil Vale, producing a distinctive machine known as the Landseer.
It will come as no surprise to the reader to learn that Butcher not only
hired the roller skating rink in Blackheath Grove as a cycling school but,
in March 1900, he was advertising that he sold motor cars as well.

Despite the expansion of the company, the involvement of William
Butcher's sons, W. F. & Frank Butcher, and Mr. Curnow's management
of 33-35 Tranquil Vale, it was clear during 1901 and 1902 that the strain
of coping with his empire was having a deleterious effect on William
Butcher. He resigned from a number of local government offices - he was
a Councillor on the Lewisham Borough - and went to Queensland, Australia
for a nine-month holiday. This had little good effect and at the end of 1903
he took another holiday, this time at St. Leonards-on-Sea. On December
20 he flung himself from an upstairs window and died from his injuries
the following day.

Butcher's death was a severe blow to the company but it did not prevent
his heirs pursuing their business ventures with the same vigour. They
encouraged Blackheathens to buy the electrical and mechanical novelties
of the time and took advantage of the mania for photography which continued
unabated until the Great War of 1914.

In 1915 the company took delivery of a stock of gas masks. Realising
that there could not be much demand for these in Blackheath the advertising

line ran: "Send your soldier friend a Portia 104 respirator and a pair of goggles and he is fitted to perfection." But it was the Great War which slowed the pace for Butcher, Curnow in that more and more of their London employees were called to the colours and the company was forced to restrict its activities. In March 1914 they had taken over the photographic and optician's business of John William Hodges (1874-1926) at 17 Montpelier Vale, but were obliged to shut the shop in March 1915 because of staff shortage. Hodges joined the company as manager of the optical department and remained with Butcher, Curnow until his death in 1926. In that year the department was taken over by Mr. F.A. Bevis FBOA, FSMC, who remains with the firm at the time of writing, but as company secretary.

Butcher, Curnow were not slow to show an interest in wireless and television sets and were pioneers in the retailing of these. Early in 1922 the company sold Burndept and Ethophone radio sets and when Marconi House started regular broadcasting in December 1922 Butcher, Curnow offered free listening for customers who had yet to make up their minds. And when loudspeaker sets were introduced the enterprising company was quick to demonstrate the latest novelties being produced by Burndept's radio works in their Grotes Place factory and at Eastnor House.

In 1934 a branch was opened at Sidcup which carried the complete range of Butcher, Curnow products as well as radio, optical and photographic goods and, an extraordinary novelty, a television set for £7.10.0 which was made up from a kit of parts and gave a picture about $1\frac{1}{4}$in square.

In 1976 the company was still controlled by the Butcher family. Curiously, in 1952, they took on the lease of 19 Tranquil Vale - part of the building which had been the first dispensary in Blackheath of William Butcher, who had founded the company in 1862.

37-43 Tranquil Vale

This group of shops is part of a block of buildings erected in the early 19th century between two alley ways. The alley to the south ran down the side of 33 Tranquil Vale to a group of cottages built in about 1798 by John Collins II. These cottages were first occupied by Henry Blow, a builder and carpenter who formed a working partnership with a Mr. Couchman who was working in Blackheath at the turn of the 19th century at Montpelier Vale (q.v.) From the early 1830s the cottages were mostly occupied by members of the Hollis family, led by Robert Hollis (fl 1800-1840) who was a bricklayer but was employed by the Collins family to do odd jobs around the Blackheath estate. One of his annual tasks was to clear the lakes or lagoons formed by the overflowing Upper Kid Brooke on the site of the present Collins Street and South Vale Road.

Robert Hollis was succeeded in the tenancy and in his trade by his widow Mary and his sons James and Joseph.

By 1855 the Hollis family was represented by Joseph and another brother, Henry, who between them occupied two of the cottages; No. 3 was tenanted by Mary Elizabeth Piggott, a dressmaker born in Lewisham and widow of Henry Piggott who had traded as a greengrocer at 11 Tranquil Vale from the 1830s to 1848 and, briefly, at 3 Montpelier Vale from 1850 to 1852.

Hollis Cottages were demolished along with some small outbuildings in 1867 when Collins Street was built.

To make the carriage way for the new Collins Street the alley way had to be widened and this involved the demolition of a small shop on the northern corner with Tranquil Vale - and part of the site was taken by the present 37 Tranquil Vale (q. v.). The old shop had been numbered 8 South Vale and occupied by greengrocers. From 1832 to 1867 the tenants were the Jarrett family, initially Edmund (1801-1848), his widow Jane Jarrett (1801-?1853) in the early 1850s, and thereafter until 1867 by Edmund jnr.

37 Tranquil Vale (was 9 South Vale; 7 Tranquil Vale)

The present building was erected during 1869 for the London and County Banking Co., Ltd. who from July 1865 had operated from a branch office at 11 Tranquil Vale (q. v.).

Prior to that there had been a small, two-storey shop on the land, with a steep-pitched roof and probably no more than three or four rooms in addition to the shop area. Its first commercial use was as a confectioners, owned by one John Harvey from at least 1840 until 1858. In 1860 the premises were acquired by Miss Agnes Townsend and a Miss Quayle who traded from here as milliners. The joint venture did not last long and by 1866 the shop and business had been taken over by Mrs. Elizabeth Caldicott, a widow, who moved to 5 Royal Parade (q. v.) when the Bank took 37 Tranquil Vale, although the original shop was probably being demolished in that year for the works relating to the development of Collins Street.

The new building, completed early in 1870, was superficially a rather grand affair and suited to the dignity expected of a bank. But, in fact, although it is an impressive building from the street elevation it can be seen from Collins Street that it is no more than a modest brick building with a red brick and stonework facade and a fancy bell tower. Nevertheless the London and County Bank directors and their new manager John Thomas Edwards were very pleased and they remained at 37 Tranquil Vale until March 1883 when the volume of business dictated a move to new premises. These were found in the new development to be called Beaconsfield Buildings (q. v.) at the south end of the Village and the London & County moved into No. 1 in 1883. From 1876 the manager was Walter James Caffin (1844-1907) who had started with the London & County in 1866 as a ledger clerk at the Greenwich branch and served them faithfully until his retirement as manager of the Blackheath branch in 1906.

The empty banking hall at No. 37 Tranquil Vale proved a difficult let, possibly because it had been designed as a bank and was not wholly suitable as an ordinary retail shop. From 1886 to 1895 the occupant was G. H. Beaver, a saddler. On his departure the shop stayed empty but in 1899 was taken as an office and depot by the newly-registered Blackheath and Greenwich District Electric Light Co. In 1898 and 1899 the company had been granted permission to lay mains and wiring along most of the major roads in the district although their offer to provide free installation of electric street lighting along Eliot Place, Eliot Vale and Aberdeen Terrace had been turned down. By 1899 their transformers had been installed at various points, including one at the Village end of Blackheath Park, and the company had strong hopes of building their own generating station on the Point at Blackheath "...which should then cut down complaints of low voltage." Electricity was commonplace in Blackheath by 1901, encouraged by the scheme whereby the electricity company offered free installation of six lights if the customer would guarantee to pay 6/- a quarter for their

use and a meter rent of 2/- a quarter. By June 1901 more than 500
Blackheath premises had been fitted, paying 6d a unit compared to 3/- a
1000 cu ft for gas. In 1908 the BGDEL Co. moved to 183 Lewisham High
Street and the shop at 37 Tranquil Vale remained empty for some years,
not being re-opened until after the Great War as Gordon Dent's dyeing and
cleaning office. After the 1939-1945 war the premises were used briefly
by E. Box, a builder, but during the 1950s became a retail bread shop
owned by A. B. Hemmings, a division of the Garfield Weston Bakery group.

In 1965 the shop reverted to its original office use when it was taken by
Gill, Noble & Co., insurance brokers.

39 Tranquil Vale (was 10 South Vale; 6 Tranquil Vale)

In common with the other buildings in the group numbered 37-43 Tranquil
Vale this shop was re-built, probably in the early 1850s - but it has not
proved possible to fix an exact date although the present structure can be
identified in a photograph taken in or before 1858. The original shop, in
existence by the early 1820s was a narrow two-storey building with small-
paned windows on the shop front. From its earliest days up until 1948 it
was a shoemaker's shop. The first known tenant was John Beavis, a boot
and shoe maker who was the tenant here as early as 1826. By 1838 Beavis
was dead and his widow, Sophia, was trading here as a shoebroker. But
by 1845 she had been joined by a cobbler, William Taylor (1791-1874) from
Cleveland, Yorkshire. Taylor named the building Cleveland House and by
1851 was the sole proprietor, working from here until 1874. In that year
the business was acquired by Thomas Wright Simonson (1841-1930) who
advertised that he had taken over an old family business established in
1800. Whether this meant that Beavis had worked in Blackheath since 1800
- for which there is no evidence - or that Simonson's family traded elsewhere is not known. Simonson worked at 39 Tranquil Vale for more than 50
years, although he was joined eventually by his son, Thomas Edmund
Simonson (1868-1951). On Simonson jnr's retirement in 1937 the shop
passed to another shoe dealer, Ralph R. Warne and he traded here until
1948. The following year the freehold of the shop was sold and it became
the S. E. Supplies, an ironmonger's, during the 1950s. In 1963 it was
briefly a bookshop but in 1964 was converted into a Chinese restaurant, in
which use it remains today.

41 Tranquil Vale (was 11 South Vale; 5 Tranquil Vale)

The original shop on this site was occupied from 1827 to at least 1832 by
James Kidman, an ironmonger, but in common with the other buildings of
this group 41 Tranquil Vale was re-built at some date in the 1850s. The
old shop - a small two-storey double-fronted building - and the new were
in continuous occupation by the same tenant from before 1841 until 1888.
In 1841 Moses Eckton (1796-1868), a grocer and cheesemonger, was in
residence here. Eckton moved to 125 Shooters Hill in 1846 and opened a
grocery store there, leaving the Tranquil Vale shop in the hands of his son,
Aaron Eckton (1821-1896). Aaron lived at 21 Bennett Park until 1896 but
sold his business on retirement in about 1889 to Charles Henry Selwood
Morris who stayed at 41 Tranquil Vale until 1907. From 1908 to 1910 the
owner was Harry Summers but in 1911 the grocery shop was acquired by

William Sheppard (d. 1956) who was here until 1936 except for a short period towards the end of the Great War when he left the business in the hands of his wife, having volunteered for the army.

In 1937 41 Tranquil Vale became an off-licence, remaining in this use until 1965, latterly as a branch of Findlater, Prentice & Co. In that year the shop was acquired by F. T. Coultate, the newsagents and tobacconists also trading at 50 Tranquil Vale (q. v.).

43 Tranquil Vale (was 12 South Vale; 4 Tranquil Vale)

There is every possibility that the original building on this site was part of Collins Square, which originally consisted of a small court with nine cottages. Much of the square was demolished for the development of Collins Street and the partial rebuilding of 37-41 Tranquil Vale and it is likely that the house on the site of 43 Tranquil Vale was cleared at the same time. It first appears in the records in 1852 as commercial premises when it was held as a lock-up shop by Thomas Smith, an ironmonger. Smith worked from here as an ironmonger and gas fitter until 1869; the following year the tenant was Henry Richard Smith who followed the same calling and may have been related. Henry moved to 34 Tranquil Vale (q. v.) in the same year and the smaller shop at No. 43 was leased to Joseph Armitage, an upholsterer. This business had passed by 1878 to Robert Crickmore (1844-1924) who traded here until 1899, during which time he built a sound business and a good reputation.

His success allowed him to retire at 55 and he sold the shop to Ebenezer Henry Smith (1872-1933) who had purchased Edward Smith Earl's repository and Blackheath Pantechnicon at Royal Parade and Royal Parade Mews in 1899 when Earl ceased trading. Ebenezer Smith's furniture and upholstery business was to remain in Blackheath until 1965 and Smith himself became an important and much-respected member of the retailing community, active in the Blackheath Chamber of Trade which had been founded in 1900. His shop was mostly left in the hands of a manager: until 1914 under the control of G. P. Baker, who was killed on active service; and from 1918 to 1946, A. G. Shapland who became a director when the firm was constituted as a limited company. On Shapland's retirement the business was controlled by Ralph Ebsworth Smith DSC, Ebenezer's son.

In September 1965 the upholstery business closed down and the shop was taken over by Messrs Findlater, Prentice, the wine and spirit merchants then trading at 41 Tranquil Vale. The company was eventually absorbed by a large retail wine and spirits group and now trades as Threshers Ltd.

COLLINS SQUARE, 45-47 Tranquil Vale and THE CROWN

Collins Square, of which only a picturesque fragment remains in the shape of three restored wooden-faced cottages, was originally part of a small hamlet within the Village which included Nos. 45 & 47 Tranquil Vale and The Crown Public House.

It is impossible to be certain of precise dates but it can be presumed that the Square was not completed until after 1784 when Collins acquired his Blackheath freeholds; also, the Collins Square cottages do not appear as a separate assessment in the Land Tax returns until 1798.

The Crown and 45-47 Tranquil Vale are certainly much older and may date from before the John Rocque survey of 1741-1746 which shows buildings on this site.

Be that as it may, the head lease on the Collins Square cottages was held by Henry Blow, a builder, and a Mr. Green from about 1798 to 1802, and it passed eventually to a Mr. Jennings, probably the farmer who had leased part of the old pits at Blackheath Vale from the Earl of Dartmouth in the early years of the 19th century.

With the building of the shops on the west side of Tranquil Vale between Collins Street and The Crown, Nos. 45 & 47 were no longer considered part of Collins Square. By 1871 only four cottages were left in the Square and subsequently another was demolished, sometime in the early years of this century. There is no doubt that the remaining cottages fell into poor condition between the wars and reached a point in 1961 when the Lewisham Borough Council served a clearance order on health grounds. The result was a public outcry, for it was felt that the Medical Officer was being over rigorous in his interpretation of the bye-laws. This opposition led to the formation of an action group to fight the Borough Council and the properties were reprieved. Restoration work, under the supervision of Neil Macfadyen RIBA, started in December 1963.

45 & 47 Tranquil Vale (was 14 South Vale; 2 Tranquil Vale)

It is likely that from the outset Nos. 45 & 47 Tranquil Vale were one building but by 1861 the south section had been let separately and this situation applied until 1965 when the two shops were once more united.

The first tenant for whom accurate records survive was Ebenezer Larwill (1780-1869) who was trading here by 1810 as a fruiterer. By 1820 his occupation had changed and Larwill was firmly established as a book-seller, stationer and draper and, more importantly, as the Blackheath Village postmaster. He held this office until 1850 and, as a result, became one of the best-known and important Village tradesmen.

The postmaster's task involved the collection and delivery of mail from the posting house at the Green Man public house at the top of Blackheath Hill. In the 1830s the post arrived in a sealed bag and Larwill's duty was to come back to the Village, sort it, and deliver it. This he did in a uniform of "red coat and vest, blue trousers with red stripes, and a high hat with a gold band and gold chords from crown to rim." In those early days it was not necessary to leave the mail at the house of the recipient and letters would be left with neighbours or at local shops and public houses. Parcels would be transported by the local carriers and stage coach proprietors, most of whom had a booking office arrangement with the Village publicans or with a particular shopkeeper.

How long Larwill acted as postman as well as all the other roles he played is not recorded and, as the suburb grew, he must have had help. We know that in November 1839 letters for the Shooters Hill Road area were delivered by one Bob, who in that year alone had walked 10,000 miles in his duties but was paid only 10/- a week. It is no wonder that he complained he was over-worked.

Larwill retired at the age of 70 in 1850, moving to No. 2 Kent Cottages (69 Lee Road) where he lived until 1869 with his four unmarried daughters. As his only son had died in 1826 at the early age of 20 years the Larwill family line in Blackheath ended in April 1883 when the last surviving daughter, Fanny Rosina, died aged 61.

The shop at Tranquil Vale was sold to George Arnott (b. 1803) who continued the drapery and stationery side of the business but did not inherit Larwill's job as postmaster. This office went to William Charles Roe (fl 1796-1860) trading as a chemist and druggist at 46 Tranquil Vale (q.v.).

By 1866 47 Tranquil Vale had passed to Henry Morton, a photographer and stationer, and his wife Sarah who looked after the shop. Morton (1825-1872/3) was not the first commercial photographer in Blackheath Village but he is the first whose work has survived and can be identified as his without doubt. He published a series of carte-de-visite pictures of the Village and some of the nearby buildings, and this book is partly illustrated with examples of Morton's work.

Arnott had named 47 Tranquil Vale Victoria House and the name was retained by the Mortons. After Henry's death Mrs. Morton continued to run the shop here as a fancy repository until December 1885. In that year she took a lease on the then newly-built 38 Tranquil Vale (q.v.) and transferred the business and the house name to those premises.

Between 1887 and 1927 the Morton's old shop was held by a succession of greengrocers or confectioners, starting with Robert Savage, a fruiterer, from 1887 to 1896, to be followed by George Budd and James Hillyard. By 1909 the tenant was Albert William Cranford, a confectioner, whose business passed to Edwin Carter at the end of the Great War.

From 1928 to 1965 47 Tranquil Vale was a branch shop of Ebenezer Smith's upholstering business at 43 Tranquil Vale (q.v.) but in 1965 it was re-united with No. 45 after an interval of more than 100 years by Mr. Ernest Turner as part of "Two Steps", an antique shop.

45 Tranquil Vale from 1861-1965

When George Arnott left 47 Tranquil Vale the southern half of the shop was, by 1861, leased as separate premises. It was then a single-storey shop unit and may have been quite separate long before the 1850s, but there is no evidence to support this.

The first known tenant was Henry Morley, the Greenwich piano dealer who had opened a branch of his business at 7 Blackheath Village (q.v.) in 1858. Morley remained at 45 Tranquil Vale until 1888 when he took over much larger premises at 23 Tranquil Vale. Details of his company's history will be found under that heading, principally because 45 Tranquil Vale was only a branch of his main offices and it was not until the move to 23 Tranquil Vale that the company shifted its major activities to Blackheath.

It was during Morley's tenure, in June 1863, that the head lease on this shop was sold, along with 43 Tranquil Vale and other property, by the executors of Benjamin Smith jnr (1794-1862) the baker of 63-65 Tranquil Vale. This seems to indicate that the separation of 45 & 47 Tranquil Vale was not an informal arrangement and the two shops were occupied independently of each other until after the last war.

Morley was succeeded at No. 45 by Charles Brown, a pork butcher, who opened his business in April 1891 and remained there until 1897. For two years after that the tenant was the British Electric Installation and Maintenance Co. and it is likely that they took these premises solely for the duration of their work for the Blackheath and Greenwich District Electric

Light Co., who were at 37 Tranquil Vale (q.v.).

In 1901 the shop was taken over by Mrs. Gertrude Grey for the sale of stationery and arts, crafts and curios from the orient. The shop quickly became known as Grey's Oriental Stores, and until 1940 you could buy from here oriental pottery, porcelain, lanterns, silk dressing gowns, and all sorts of Chinoiserie. The outbreak of the 1939-1945 war put a brake on supplies and the business eventually closed. The premises were later used as an antique shop - "Two Steps" - re-uniting with 47 Tranquil Vale in 1965.

The small wooden extension to No. 45, between the shop and the alley way which led to Collins Square, had been erected before the 1860s and sub-let to a succession of coal merchants as an order office. The principal tenant for many years was the coal merchant Jacob Bizzell, but towards the end of the 19th century it had been embraced by the user of No. 45 and has remained so ever since.

THE CROWN
(Now 49 Tranquil Vale; was 15 South Vale; 1 Tranquil Vale)

All the facts now point to the Crown public house being the oldest surviving building in the Village, although it has been altered more than once in its history. There is also some evidence that it may be the oldest public house despite the long-held tradition that this honour should be afforded the Three Tuns. But there is nothing in the licensing returns, nor in the Land Tax returns to support the supposed antiquity of the Three Tuns as a pub with the exception of a reference in the Lewisham Parish registers of 1737 which notes the death of Richardson Headley, who was a victualler, of the Three Tuns, Blackheath. But none of the records other than his will refer to him as an innkeeper and his name does not appear in the licensing records.

But by 1780 the name of John Masco appears in the licensing lists and the Land Tax returns for The Crown in Blackheath. Further, Rocque's survey of 1741-1746 shows a building of approximately the same size on the site of the present public house, and this may prove that The Crown was in existence by this time.

Nevertheless, John Masco is the first licencee of which there is reliable evidence, and we know from the Tax Returns that the freehold was held until 1783 by a Mr. Heath and that after 1783 the owner was John Collins I.

The original building was only three windows wide, with a round head door at the entrance. On the north elevation was an extension with a deep square bay window on the upper storey and this may have been the private quarters for the landlord. In 1832 a new lease was issued, to be effective for 31 years from Christmas 1830, to allow improvements to be made. By the 1840s The Crown was a Barclay Perkins pub, selling bottled ales and describing itself as a stout warehouse. There is no doubt that it was also a staging point for a least one of the many horse buses which took Black-heathens to the City each day and that there may have been livery stables nearby.

Of the Victorian landlords little is known but some made a greater impact on the community than others. For example, Richard Drouet was a keen supporter of the Greenwich Tories and he, with his wife, Emma Jane, supplied dinners to the Party faithful of such sumptuousness (including "venison, grouse, beef, and every delicacy of the season") that the local newspapers spent more space in describing the table than reporting the candidate's speech. In the 1860s the District Board of Works always lunched here on the day of their annual inspection of Blackheath Village.

In the 1890s the licencee was William Henry Hailey (d. 1895) who had been an original member of the Brighton Volunteer Fire Brigade and who so loved that town, he was buried there. Why he came to Blackheath at all is a mystery but while at The Crown he revived an old English tradition - pole climbing. A new sign post was erected in June 1892 and the old sign board re-painted. To celebrate the occasion Hailey fixed a leg of mutton to the top of the pole and sold tickets to the local lads for the privilege of trying to climb the pole to take the mutton. A large crowd assembled at the appointed time but before the ceremony could commence an urchin shot from the mob, shinned up the pole like a monkey and was off with the mutton before the ticket holders had stripped off their jackets. There was a near riot, but Hailey saved his reputation by offering another joint of meat, which was won by a fireman from the local brigade. The crowd forgot their anger and the day continued with much jollity and, no doubt, large quantities of Barclay's Entire Ales were consumed.

It was in the late 19th century that The Crown was altered, the roofline raised and the frontage changed to the appearance it kept until 1965. The extension was thrown into the main building and the fenestration of the upper floors regularised and the small door to the wing re-built to match the main entrance to the building. A stone parapet replaced the old facia board and the pub became known as The Crown Hotel.

In March 1965 the building was badly damaged by fire, but the main structure was not over-harmed, the damage being confined to the interior of the bars. Unfortunately there were fatalities but despite these setbacks the then landlords, Mr. & Mrs. James Cockburn, worked with great speed to restore the building and re-open in December 1965. Although there were substantial changes made to the interior the outside remained much as it had been before the fire, with the exception of the round-headed doors which were re-positioned and hidden behind storm porches.

The landlords of The Crown are as given below. Some of them held a direct lease from the Collins estate but, eventually, the lease was acquired by Barclay Perkins (and their successors) and the names given are those of tenant publicans:

1780-1787	-	John Masco
1788-1791	-	Thomas Bird
1792	-	Thomas Bowles
1793-1794	-	William Goldthorpe
1795-1805	-	Isaac Mann
1806-1809	-	Robert Stanhope
July 1809-Nov 1811	-	John Edward Mortimer (on Land Tax lists till 1824)
Nov 1811-1824	-	Edward & Sarah Sibley (later at The Sun in the Sands)
1825-1839	-	John Cooper
1840-1844	-	Joseph & Elizabeth Cooper
1845-1852	-	Charles & Alice Evans
1855-1868	-	Richard Drouet (1818-1867)
1868-1871+	-	Mrs. Emma Jane Drouet

1874	– Octavius Coppinger (previously at Hare & Billet)
1877-1882	– Arthur William Bischoff
1885-1887	– William Chapman (or Chaplin)
1886	– Mrs. E. Lapraik
1888	– Harold William Moseley
1890	– Thomas Merton
1891-1895	– William Henry Hailey (d. 1895)
1896-1899	– Thomas Coppinger (previously at Hare & Billet)
1900-1901	– Mrs. Christina Mackenzie
1904-1906	– Mrs. Clara Louise Holt
1907-1950	– Alexander Macfarlane
1953-1958	– Alec Macfarlane
1958-1963	– Mr. Richardson
1963-1976	– Mr. & Mrs. James Cockburn

South Vale Cottage and South Vale Road

Until 1869 what is now the entrance to South Vale Road was occupied by a house known as South Vale Cottage. Its grounds extended over the whole site of the present South Vale Road and part of Collins Street; two sizeable buildings stood in the garden at a point about 70 yards due south of Camden Row and the estate was enhanced by fountains and an ornamental lake fashioned from the natural overflow pond fed by the Upper Kid Brooke which ran along the south boundary.

There is no earlier record of this property before 1832 when the directories list one Jacob Hulle as the tenant of South Vale Cottage, but it is possible that it was built as a residence for the tenants of the Crown.

Hulle's tenancy was followed, for a brief period, by that of John Oddy, who had occupied premises on the west side of Montpelier Vale earlier in the century, but by 1839 the freeholders, the Collins Estate, had taken South Vale Cottage for their own use. The occupiers from then until 1864 were the Misses Ann and Julia Collins, daughters of John Collins I. Ann (1786-1848) and Julia (1780-1864) lived here until their deaths, clearly unconcerned at being sandwiched between a pub and a group of small shops but perhaps content they could keep an eye on the estate of which they owned a part. With Julia's death the last direct link with John Collins was severed although an interest in the Blackheath properties had been willed to so many different branches of the family, some scattered in the Colonies and the USA, that every lease issued from the 1860s onwards had to be signed by more than 15 interested parties and, after 1903, by more than 20. Julia's control over the estate was probably autocratic and her demise gave relatives the opportunity to develop the South Vale Cottage garden ground. The Collins Street site was dealt with first and it was not until July 1869 that South Vale Cottage was demolished.

The development of this land was undertaken by Henry Reed and most of the present houses in South Vale Road were built between 1870 and 1871. The north terrace (Nos. 19-28) were completed by 1873. From the start there was confusion - the houses in Tranquil Vale from Nos. 23 to 47 had long been known as South Vale and despite naming the new properties South Vale Terrace the postmen, if not others, met increasing difficulties. In 1877 the new South Vale was re-named Stansby Street, almost certainly after the builder Frederick Stansby who was living at 16 Bennett Park at the time of the start of the development of Collins Street and may have had some interest in the plan or construction. The present name for the street was imposed in 1885, by which time the title Tranquil Vale was firmly applied to both sides of the main road.

South Vale Road represents the northern Village boundary of the Collins estate, beyond that the land was part of the Manor of Lewisham and the freehold held by the Dartmouth family.

Camden House and Camden Place (51-61 Tranquil Vale)

Opposite the Crown public house, on the north east corner of South Vale Road and Tranquil Vale (west) is the All Saints Church Hall, built in 1927/8 to the design of Charles C. Winmill, architect, and built to replace the inadequate accommodation used at Brigade Street until that date. The hall was built on a site which had been cleared at the end of the Great War of the results of considerable bomb damage.

The damaged buildings had replaced an earlier house, a mansion of some pretensions - Camden House.

This had been built by 1780 and was occupied from at least 1789 by Thomas Rashleigh (1749-1833) of Hatton Garden who lived there until his death. No detailed view of Rashleigh's house has been found but it probably looked south across the valley of the Village and stood in a small garden fronting onto Tranquil Vale. It was demolished in October 1836 long after work had commenced on a group of shops called Camden Place, which hedged in the old house. From the 1820s the only way in to Camden House was through 3 Camden Place (57 Tranquil Vale). The development seems to have been completed after the demolition of Camden House although the late A. R. Martin held the view that the basic structure of the old mansion survived hidden behind the shop premises. If that were true then all traces were finally removed in 1917.

Camden Place abutted South Vale Cottage to the south, jutted out at an angle into Tranquil Vale and stretched a short way along Camden Row. The shops here, mostly completed and occupied by 1837, included drapers, bootmakers, butchers and other small businesses. They were often the starting place for young retailers whose businesses flourished and who were thus forced to seek larger premises elsewhere in the Village where they became successful and important members of the trading community.

Camden Place was severely damaged by a bomb dropped from a Zeppelin on August 13 1916. The shops and Nos. 1 and 3 South Vale Road were so badly affected that they had to be demolished. Nos. 1 and 3 South Vale Road were replaced by South Vale Mansion in about 1925 and the shops site was used for the All Saints Church Hall which was completed in 1928.

1a Camden Place (51 Tranquil Vale)

This was a stable which was converted into a shop in the early 1870s. The first commercial tenant was George Worth, a coachbuilder, but from 1878 to 1895 the building was occupied by Edwin Rufus Marsden, a carver and gilder. From 1899 to 1901 it was the shop of George Brews, a golf club and ball maker and a Pro at the Royal Blackheath Golf Club, then playing on the Heath. For a brief while the shop was used by Wilfred Parkin, a tailor who had moved to 36 Montpelier Vale in 1912.

1 Camden Place (53 Tranquil Vale)

This shop started its retail life as a greengrocers in the 1830s but passed
through a variety of trades before becoming Alfred Hanreck's tailoring
shop in 1910. From 1855 to 1867 it was a cobbler's shop but in 1869 the
offices for a builder and plumber, Walter Roper. In 1870 the business
was taken over by William John Streek (d. 1905) but he moved to 3 Camden
Place (57 Tranquil Vale) in 1876 and traded from there and other premises
in the Village until his death and his company continued to trade in Blackheath until 1939 under his name, while its successors owned the business
at 42 Tranquil Vale until 1975.
  1 Camden Place then passed to a succession of watch and clock makers,
starting with Carl Schonhardt in 1878, Thomas Bunston from 1881 to 1888,
and finally Percival Kendall in 1889 who moved in 1892 to 30 Montpelier
Vale where he remained until his retirement in 1945. The Camden Place
shop became successively a dining rooms, a dairy and the workshop of
Leonard W. Clarkson, a wood carver.
  In 1910 the shop was rented by Alfred Hanreck (1879-1961) a tailor then
working from his home at 6 South Vale Road. Hanreck was of Russian
origin but British-born - a fact he had to publish in August 1914 to dispel
rumours that he was a spy for the Kaiser - and had been a tailor all his
working life. He achieved some success in his early years in Blackheath
and by 1913 added 2 Camden Place to his shop premises. He traded from
the double shop until Camden Place was bombed in 1916. After a brief
spell working from South Vale Road Alfred Hanreck took over the old
tailoring business at 2 Montpelier Vale (q.v.) where the family worked for
the next 58 years.

2 Camden Place (55 Tranquil Vale)

Although the first commercial tenant here was a hairdresser (John Asker)
for most of its retailing life it was a drapers' or millinery shop. The first
of these traders was a mother and daughter team of milliners with the
extraordinarily appropriate name of Hatfull, established before 1845, and
they were followed from 1847 to 1865 by Miss Martha Bull.
  By 1869 the shop had become an underclothing and baby linen warehouse,
initially owned by Mrs. Emily Eckton but from 1869-70 by Miss Elizabeth
Smith. In 1874 the trade changed and 2 Camden Place had passed to
Luther Norman, a bootmaker, who eventually opened a shop at 18 Montpelier Vale (q.v.) which stayed with the Norman family until 1914. By
1882 the Camden Place premises had become a drapery again, passing from
Miss Isabella Cross until 1887, Alfred Attoe in 1888 and 1889 and then,
after a brief period as a barber shop, it became a tailor's shop. At one
stage it was the offices of the Blackheath Bespoke and Ready Made Clothing
Co., but by 1900 had been taken by Wilfred Parkin. He moved to 1a Camden Place in 1908 and after a period during which it lay empty 2 Camden
Place was added to Hanreck's premises at No. 1 (q.v.).

3 Camden Place (57 Tranquil Vale)

This building was the oldest of the Camden Place houses and had been
built before the demolition of Camden House in 1834. By 1826 the shop
had been leased to butchers and this use continued until 1875. The first
known meat seller here was Charles Brown who had set up his shop by 1826
and remained until 1837. In 1838 he obtained a lease on the whole site of
Camden Place and his old shop, if not the whole complex, became known
as Brown's Buildings. Brown's butchery was then leased to one James
Sprunt (fl 1810-1855). In 1852 the business was taken over by Edward
Gardner Couldery (1814-1875) the son of Robert Couldery, also a butcher
and member of a family of butchers who had traded in Lewisham and Lee
from the early 19th century. The Coulderies held a number of lucrative
contracts, supplying meat to the local Boards of Guardians who were
responsible for feeding those on parish relief. In 1863 the contract was
with Edward Couldery at Blackheath but the quality of the meat was so poor
that the Board withheld payment of £84 on the grounds that the goods
supplied were unfit for human consumption.

This did not seem to deter Couldery and he continued to trade here
successfully until his death in 1875.

With Couldery's demise the old butcher's shop was leased by W. John
Streek, a builder and plumber who had worked from 1 Camden Place from
1870. Streek built up a thriving business, was appointed official contractor
to the local water board - a faded sign to this effect can still be seen from
the station car park on the south elevation of 7 Collins Street - and earned
a respectable place in the trading community of the district. But in 1905
he followed the example of some of the other respectable Village tradesmen
and committed suicide - Streek's method was to swallow a quantity of oxalic
acid. This was not a novel means, for in the year 1902 one of his employees,
Henry James Butters, had ended his life in the same way.

It is unlikely that Streek's self-destruction was brought on by financial
worries because his company continued to trade at Camden Place until its
destruction by the Zeppelin bomb in 1916 and, thereafter, at 63 Tranquil
Vale until the 1939-1945 war.

4 Camden Place (59 Tranquil Vale)

These were the first premises of William Drewett and Edward Smith Earl,
who set up as music sellers here when Drewett was only 22 and Earl only
19. In 1840 they moved to 26 Tranquil Vale (q.v.) and although the partnership was dissolved by 1845 Earl remained in the Village, but shifted
his trading interests from sheet music via pianos to furnishing and upholstery. It was these last two trades which he pursued from the 1860s to
1897 at 16 Royal Parade (q.v.).

The Camden Place shop was occupied for brief spells by a succession
of different trades, many of the proprietors later moving elsewhere in the
Village. Mrs. Martha Bull, who moved next to No. 2, opened a child bed
and linen warehouse here in 1845; she was followed by milliners and
furriers and from 1855 to 1858 by John Bailey Capper, the chemist who
had opened his first shop at 28 Montpelier Vale in 1840. But in 1860-61
4 Camden Place was leased by Charles John Irish (1826-1917) a saddler
and harness maker who had arrived in Blackheath in 1848 from Yeovil and

set up a workshop at 29 Tranquil Vale (q. v.). By the 1860s he had moved
to Camden Place where the business remained until 1916. Charles John
retired in 1898 and was succeeded by his son Charles Edward Irish (1856-
1902); the business continued to function in the hands of Charles Edward's
son until 1917 although war damage had in 1916 forced a move from Camden
Place to 17 Montpelier Vale.

5 Camden Place (61 Tranquil Vale)

This was a cheesemonger's shop from 1837 to 1849, firstly in the hands of
Edmund Rouch (who also sold poultry and offended his neighbours by casual
disposal of offals and feathers), but from 1840 to 1849 held by Multon
Lambert (1811-1889) who moved in 1850 to 3 Tranquil Vale (q. v.) under
which heading further details of Lambert and his business venture will be
found. He was succeeded at Camden Place from 1851 to 1855 by William
Tyler Bradley (1824-1883) who moved to 33 Tranquil Vale (q. v.). Thereafter, until 1874, the shop remained largely empty although from 1869 to
1870 it was occupied by drapers who styled the building Camden House.
But from 1874 to 1890 it was held by Stephen George Wilkins, an ironmonger
who moved his home and business to 46 Vanbrugh Park in 1891. From
1892 to 1905 5 Camden Place became the carpenter's shop of Alfred John
Bastien but by 1908 until the bombing in 1916, the shop was leased by
Streek's, the builders at 3 Camden Place (q. v.).
     At the rear of Camden Place was a small workshop which sometimes
took the number 6 Camden Place, particularly between 1850 and 1875.
But it was never numbered in Tranquil Vale.

LAMB'S BUILDINGS (63-69 Tranquil Vale)

The buildings on the north west corner of the Village, presently 63-69
Tranquil Vale, have their origins in a development in 1789-90 by John
Lamb, who had been land agent to Sir Gregory Page of Wricklemarsh.
Lamb (1734-1801) obtained a lease from the freeholder, the Earl of Dartmouth, and built a pair of houses in 1789 on the site of 67 and 69 Tranquil
Vale. A third house, on the site of 63 to 65 Tranquil Vale, was not built
until 1793 but may have replaced a cottage or similar simple dwelling
house. Whether Lamb was involved in this construction is not known, but
all three houses soon took the name Lamb's Buildings and this appellation
held until 1885, after which the present numbering was imposed. Originally,
the numbering started at the north end, thus:

       69 Tranquil Vale - 1 Lamb's Buildings
       67 Tranquil Vale - 2 Lamb's Buildings
63 & 65 Tranquil Vale - 3 Lamb's Buildings

but in 1871 the census enumerator managed to confuse the issue and reversed
the order so that No. 1 became No. 3 and vice versa. As it was, the
sequence was so short that the simple address Lamb's Buildings, Blackheath, was sufficient for the postmen and compilers of commercial directories.
     Nos. 1 & 2 Lamb's Buildings were demolished in 1888-9 and the present
houses built on the site. But No. 3 (63-65 Tranquil Vale) which had become

a baker's shop as early as 1800 may have survived although the present appearance does not suggest a late 18th-century building. It may have been re-built in 1863, when the head lease on the whole group was sold, but there is no evidence to support this and the author would like to believe, for the lack of other evidence, that the original building survives, albeit altered somewhat during the mid 19th century.

63-65 Tranquil Vale (was 3 Lamb's Buildings)

This double building, with a small shop on the corner facing down Tranquil Vale was probably completed in 1793 and first occupied by Joseph Willings (sometimes spelled Wellings). He lived here until 1799 but in 1800 the premises had been taken by Benjamin Smith (1769-1822) a corn-dealer of Blackheath Vale. Smith may have had some interest in the windmill at Talbot Place, which would be quite reasonable in view of his principal trade, but what is more certain is that he opened Blackheath Village's first bakery at 3 Lamb's Buildings. This shop was one of the first three or four in the Village and between them they could have supplied the retail needs of the few houses then in existence on the south side of the Heath.

Benjamin Smith remained the sole Village baker, so far as we know, until his death in 1822, but his business interests were carried on by his family. His wife, Catherine (1773-1840) took over the corn-dealing trade at Blackheath Vale, helped by the Smith's second son, William (1808-1842). Their eldest son, Benjamin Smith jnr (1794-1862) may have left the neighbourhood after his father's death, for the bakery at Lamb's Buildings was sub-let to a Mr. Hart Wright from 1826 to c1828. By 1828 Benjamin jnr had taken over the shop, and he worked there until 1859, three years before he died, having obtained a renewal of the lease on 1-3 Lamb's Buildings for 31 years from 1837.

In 1861 the new tenant at 3 Lamb's Buildings was Edward Gilbert Kibble (1825-c1890) - also a baker and operating a sizeable business, for he was employing eight men and eleven boys in 1861, and in 1863 purchased the unexpired portion of Benjamin Smith's 31 year lease from Smith's executors; he also arranged to renew the lease on the entire block, for a further 21 years in 1867. Kibble retired from the bakery business in 1882 and a new lease was granted on 3 Lamb's Buildings to Sidney George Barrett. He and his sons kept the bakery going here until 1916 but in that year closed the old bakehouse, transferring their interests to the bakery and confectionery business previously owned by the Shove family at 44 and 46 Tranquil Vale and added to the Barrett stable in 1907. This contraction may have been caused by a shortage of skilled workers brought on by the 1914-1918 War. If this was so it does not seem to have prevented the Barretts from further expansion afterwards and by the 1920s they were part of the group which also owned Messrs Jobbins (their one time rival) at 7 & 9 Blackheath Village.

With the closure of the bakehouse the building was divided, with the shop premises let separately from the domestic accommodation, now firmly numbered 65 Tranquil Vale.

From 1917 to the 1939-45 war the shop was held by Streek & Co. Ltd., the builders (see 61 Tranquil Vale) but after 1945 it became successively and arts and crafts shop, a haberdasher's and, in 1975, an antique shop. From 1923 to 1939 the residential section (No. 65) was the home of Henry

Park Hollis FRAS (1858-1939) sometime astronomy correspondent to The Times.

67 Tranquil Vale (was 2 Lamb's Buildings)

This is the site of the southern half of Lamb's Buildings which was the house occupied by John Lamb from 1790 until his death in 1801 at the age of 67. His widow, Mary (1756-1819) remained in the house after John's death, and their daughter, also Mary (1784-1854) lived here until 1851, only moving away from Blackheath three years before she died.

Thereafter the property was used essentially for residential purposes. By 1869 it had become a lodging house and remained in this use until its demolition in 1887-1888; the last proprietor being Miss Sophia Brenchley who held the property from 1870.

The new house (Melford) built in 1890 was essentially residential but from 1920 to the 1940s was a dental surgery.

69 Tranquil Vale (was 1 Lamb's Buildings)

The original house here was first occupied in 1789 by a Mr. Brown and there was a succession of brief tenancies until the Lucas family rented the property in 1801. Francis Lucas (1762-1820) was the principal tenant until his death but his widow remained at 3 Lamb's Buildings until 1825. By the 1830s, the occupier was John Mascoe, a tailor (1803-c1869) who may have maintained his workshop here. Mascoe gave up his lease in 1868 and the premises were taken by the sisters Isabella and Martha Birkett, who traded as milliners and dressmakers until the mid 1870s, although Isabella married George Moore, a pattern maker, in 1871 and the business took the name Birkett & Moore.

By 1878 1 Lamb's Buildings was leased by Sophia Jones, a dressmaker who had conducted a business in Montpelier Vale early in the 1870s. She remained the tenant until the demolition of the old property. The new building (Braeside) was completed in 1889.

SPECIAL
WINTER PREPARATIONS

THE object aimed at in the preparation of this Food, is the production of an article of High NUTRITIOUS QUALITY, EASY DIGESTIBILITY, one that is agreeable to the PALATE, and ECONOMICAL to the Purse. To obtain these results, the finest cereals are submitted to a process which, while removing everything of an unassimilable character, develops their muscle, nerve, and bone-making elements. The completeness with which its digestion is accomplished ensures a regular action of the bowels, and no one using the Strengthening Food need ever resort to the use of Aperients.

NUTRITIOUS

DIGESTABLE

PALATABLE

ECONOMICAL

Infants' Food or Porridge.
2 lb. PACKETS, 1/- EACH.

RESTORINE is a tonic of great value in cases of General Debility, Weakness, Lowness of Spirits, and Nervous Exhaustion.

RESTORINE improves the Appetite, and gives tone to the Digestive Organs.

RESTORINE acts on the Brain and Nerves, and increases the power for mental and physical exertion.

RESTORINE is a specific in all cases of Neuralgia.

The Glen, Blackheath Hill.

I have very much pleasure in saying that I have found Mr. W. Butcher's RESTORINE a very valuable Tonic.

For Debility and Languor, and for Neuralgia I know of nothing better.

(Rev.) ARCH. CAMPBELL GRAY.

PRICE—1/1½, 2/9, and 4/6 per Bottle, Post Free.

THE great value of Malt Extract consists in the fact that when taken at or directly after Meals, it assists in disposing of the other foods, and thus indirectly as well as directly nourishes and strengthens the whole system. This result depends on the activity of a peculiar substance called Diastase, the presence of which uninjured, is secured in W. Butcher's Improved Extract, by a special process of evaporation *in vacuo* at a very low temperature.

Price 2/- per Bottle.

MALT EXTRACT AND
COD LIVER OIL.
2/6 per Bottle.

FOR CHAPS AND
ROUGHNESS OF THE SKIN

W. Butcher & Son's Glycerine and Cucumber is an excellent Preparation, soon producing a Clear Complexion and Soft, White Skin.

Gentlemen will find it an excellent soothing application after Shaving.

Being quite harmless, it can be applied to the tenderest skin, even that of an Infant.

Price, 1/- per Bottle.

W. Butcher & Son.
Chemists, 315 Regent St., & Blackheath, S.E.

10 The Collins Estate in Lee

When John Collins purchased the freehold of his Blackheath estate in or before 1783 the land included some acres in the Parish of Lee. The boundary between Lee and Lewisham was the Upper Kid Brooke which flowed east to west from Shooters Hill towards the River Ravensbourne.

Collins' holding in Lee can still be defined and was bounded on the north by the railway line, on the east by the main road through the Village (known officially at this point as Blackheath Village), on the south by Lee Terrace, and on the west by a line running down Lawn Terrace behind the gardens of The Glebe, to the railway.

Unlike the northern section of Collins' Blackheath estate, the Lee land remained undeveloped for many years. There is no firm evidence as to what the land was used for but almost certainly it was cultivated as market gardens, and the field roughly on the site of what is now Selwyn Court (20-34 Blackheath Village) was excavated for gravel. Some of the land on the south bank of the Kid Brooke was rented by John Hally, the nurseryman. There was no major building on the site until 1831 and subsequent development was slow. It was not until after 1849, when the North Kent Railway Company purchased, as of right, a sizeable chunk of the Collins freehold between what is now Lawn Terrace and the railway station yard, that the present pattern was established. The railway company took more land than they eventually needed and once the works for the permanent way were complete, sold off plots on the south side of their freehold. Details of the buildings on the Lee Parish section of the Village are as follows:

Blackheath Railway Station - built 1849

Railway Hotel - built 1850

Independents Road: School and Home for the Sons and Orphans of Missionaries (later Winchester House) - built 1857

Blackheath Congregational Church - built 1853

Society of Friends Meeting House - built 1972

South Vale House - built 1852, demolished 1952

Lawn Terrace and Seager's Cottages - built between 1835 and 1863; mostly demolished by 1952

Blackheath Proprietary School - built 1831, demolished 1936 for Selwyn Court

Blackheath Railway Station

The railway came through Blackheath almost by accident although there can be no doubt that even if the lines had not been laid in 1849 they would have linked the suburb to London not many years later.

The opening of the passenger railway between London and Greenwich in 1838 had revolutionised local travel and given south east London a speedy link with the centre which not only took City workers to and from their counting houses but also brought tens of thousands to Blackheath and

Greenwich Fairs on Bank Holidays. Inevitably there had been pressure by the railway companies to run their railway metals from Greenwich to Woolwich, but the simple route, which was across Greenwich Park on the south side of the Queen's House, was opposed with great vehemence. Despite extremely attractive plans and pictorial presentations showing a clean railway train puffing gently across a sylvan park setting over a classical viaduct, the townsfolk of Greenwich, led by the Revd. William Aldwin Soames (1805-1866), vicar of the Parish, and Stacey Grimaldi (1790-1863), the miniaturist, then living at 49 Maze Hill, were unconvinced. As a result of their efforts the enabling bill before Parliament was rejected by the House of Commons in 1836.

This did not deter the railwaymen, and the Kent Railway Co. published a new prospectus in 1837 showing a scheme for a railway from Greenwich to Dover via Woolwich and Gravesend, across the same controversial parkland. The railway, when it came in 1838, stopped at Greenwich.

But in 1844 yet another scheme was announced, this time by the London, Chatham and North Kent Railway for a line between London and Woolwich, but via new stations to be built at Lewisham, Blackheath and Charlton. This plan was not opposed to any degree and the enabling legislation was passed without any trouble.

The railway works had remarkably little effect on the landscape at Blackheath compared to much of the destruction then being wrought in the name of transport progress. Once past Lewisham the line was planned to run through the natural valley of the Upper Kid Brooke from Lewisham to the edge of the Cator Estate at Pond Road and then proceed through deep cut embankments and across the lawn of Morden College. This last plan was amended and, at considerable cost, a tunnel bored not only under Morden College lawn but under the Shooters Hill Road as well, the line being distinctly marked by the present Vicarage Way and a gap between the houses in Old Dover Road.

Work on the new railway commenced in August 1845 but did not reach the area under the Heath itself until September 1847 when 45ft deep ventilation and working shafts had to be sunk through the Heath to aid the tunnellers below. By then Blackheath had lost a handful of houses, including Nos. 1-3 Brunswick Place (q.v.); No. 14 Pond Road (Pond House) was demolished for the embankment in January 1849. The railway engineers, led by George Robert Stephenson (1819-1905) nephew of the illustrious George Stephenson (1781-1848), and then living at 45 Blackheath Park, exercised great care in the building of their line. Although they had acquired an excess of land at Blackheath, principally because this was one of their main depots, the damage they caused to the landscape was minimal and only five houses between Lewisham and Charlton had to be removed. Further, they built a number of stout private bridges to re-link the otherwise severed parts of the Cator Estate and Thomas Brandram's estate, the Cedars, which then stretched from Lee Terrace to the Heath.

By August 1848 the company announced that the North Kent Line would be opened "in six months" with the exception of the Woolwich Station, the building of which was delayed because of the heavy costs of the construction.

By January 1849 the date had been amended to July 1. This was further delayed, primarily because the company had failed to pay the contractors. A court order, in the contractors' favour, despite certain unfinished works, forced the railway company to pay a further £5000 in order that the line be delivered to them for passenger traffic, although engineering trains had been running since June 1849.

Blackheath Station opened on 30 July 1849 as a station on the North Kent branch of the South Eastern Railway. Trains ran half-hourly from London Bridge to Lewisham, Blackheath, Charlton and Woolwich, and hourly to Erith, Dartford, Greenhithe, Gravesend and Strood between 7.30am and 10.30pm; the "Up" service ran half-hourly from Woolwich between 8am and 11pm. The Blackheath fare was 1/- (1st class), 9d (2nd class) and 6d (3rd class); and annual season cost £14 (1st class) and 11gns (2nd class).

The North Kent line was not free of incident in its first few weeks of operation. Before the service began there had been an accident at Charlton when one man had died and many were injured. Within a fortnight of opening a 60-carriage train from Gravesend had stuck in the Blackheath tunnel, lacking the power to climb the gradient, and an extra engine had to be sent to push from behind. During the 35 minute delay many of the passengers were drenched because poorly stopped land springs were leaking through the tunnel roof. On August 19 a woman was killed on the Woolwich platform, then packed with people due to the inadequate amount of rolling stock for the volume of passengers wishing to travel on the new line. But the biggest calamity for the company came in the following week when Charlton station burned to the ground, although this was nothing compared to February 1851 when New Cross station burned down for the third time in nine years. The second time, in 1844, occured the day before King Louis Phillipe of France was due to attend a grand reception and inspect the locomotive works prior to journeying to Dover. Unaware of the disaster the King entered the gate with his party and was, according to the newspapers "completely astounded".

Despite these accidents it was clear that the North Kent would be a reasonable commercial success. Fares paid in the first seven weeks totalled £17,349, and the Phoenix Insurance Co. paid for Charlton Station.

Blackheath Station was probably designed by George Smith FSA, FIBA (1783-1869) who had designed the first station at London Bridge in 1843 in conjunction with Henry Roberts (1803-1876). Smith was a local man, having designed a number of buildings in Blackheath and having served as surveyor for Morden College for a period. He was probably the designer of the Blackheath Literary Institution and more detail of his career will be found under that heading in Chapter 16.

The main building stood, as now, on the up line and was cut into the embankment so that the north elevation opened onto the platform and housed the booking hall, offices and porters' rooms, and the south elevation, seemingly only two storeys, looked like a private house and was, in fact, the official residence for the station master. It stood in a small garden and was reached originally by a pathway running behind the Railway Hotel.

Two elaborate stone porticoes stood on the foot bridge to mark the public entrances to the Station; the north portico led passengers to a staircase leading to the down platform and the south portico led in to the main building.

At the outset the down passengers had to buy their tickets in the present hall on the up line, which must have been greatly inconvenient as they then had to climb all the way up again, walk over the bridge and into the north gate. There were two decorative gas lamps on the bridge to light the way.

The remarkable fact about Blackheath Station is that so much of it has survived almost intact. One of the porticoes was demolished when the down line staircase was replaced by a slope, but the station master's house, presently empty, can still be seen by trespassers who care to look down the pathway between the florist's and the butcher's shops.

The first tenant of the house and Blackheath's first station master was the remarkable Edward Duncan Chapman, who was appointed to Blackheath (with responsibility for Lewisham and, later, Kidbrooke) in 1850 at the age of 30, and remained there for forty-eight years, retiring in January 1898 on full pay, two years before he died in his 81st year.

Chapman must have been a quite exceptional man, for despite an endless catalogue of troubles and complaints against the railway company which started within months of the inauguration of the service, no blame was ever attached to him. For example when, in 1852, a train ran out of fuel, slipped its brake and ran backwards into a fruit train - all in the middle of an unlit Blackheath Tunnel, the grumblers were quick to point out that Mr. Chapman was in no way to blame: "He is unsurpassed by any station master on this, or as far as our experience goes, any other line." Just before Chapman's appointment one angry passenger had complained of "larking blackguardism" amongst the company staff and this was a good enough reason for the complainant to leave the neighbourhood for ever.

Throughout the 1850s the service increased, reaching 21 trains daily with a journey time of 20 minutes to London Bridge, and 22 minutes from the terminus, from which the last train of the day left at 12.30am. Once again, this time in 1852, there was a further scheme to run a railway across Greenwich Park, but, as before, Parliament refused to entertain the notion.

At the end of that decade came the first of many such ceremonies when the excellent Mr. Chapman was presented with a silver salver and a purse of £70 by grateful commuters as a token of "the high esteem in which they held the conduct of Mr. Chapman in the performance of his duties."

The 1860s saw many changes, not the least of which was the addition of a footbridge between the platforms which was extended in about 1865 to hold the booking hall, parcels' office and the bookstall, all of which must have pleased travellers to Woolwich and beyond. The bookstall concession had been granted to W.H. Smith &,Son of The Strand, and had opened in the downstairs hall of the station in January 1863 with Mr. J. Turner as manager. *

Of greater import to the railway company was the opening of Charing Cross station in January 1864, as this considerably added to the usefulness of the line and also increased revenue. Despite the engineering wonders of Hungerford Bridge the problems of the Blackheath Tunnel were not re-solved; in 1861 a portion collapsed and, in December 1864, there was an accident with three fatalities and many injured - subsequent court actions against the South East Railway Company cost them more than £5,500 in compensation payments. One solution was suggested in a petition to the company to open a deep-cut station at Myrtle Place (the Royal Standard area) on the Old Dover Road. The company refused, but new plans were being laid for their old dream of extending the Greenwich line to Woolwich. This was finally published in September 1869 and involved a great change of heart toward the beauty of Greenwich Park - a tunnel was to be bored under Royal Greenwich and a deep embankment cut to the north of Park

*In 1972 W.H. Smith sold off many railway station bookstalls. The Black-heath kiosk passed to the then manager, Mr. R.P. Simmons.

24   Blackheath Grove in the late 1860s

25.   The Post Office, built in 1910

26.   The Lee Road end of the Village before the erection of Beaconsfield Buildings

27.   Brunswick Place, Bennett Place, and No 1 Beaconsfield Buildings in the late 1930s

28.   Beaconsfield Buildings before 1910

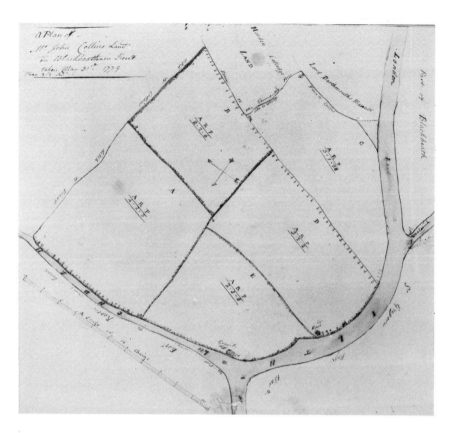

29. John Collins estate in Blackheath, in 1779

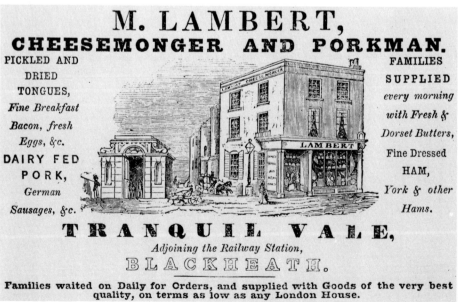

30. Multon Lambert's shop at 3 Tranquil Vale in 1852

Vista. This was approved but Maze Hill station was not in passenger use until the summer of 1876 and Greenwich station had to be totally rebuilt about 12 feet below the then existing railway metals.

The population of Blackheath grew rapidly in the 1860s and 1870s and the pressure on the rail traffic grew in proportion, along with all the concomitant problems and difficulties of running clean trains on time. The railway bridge in the Village was widened in 1877 and the increasing commercial use of the station had necessitated the building of considerable lengths of sidings (now the car park), stables for the company's delivery horses, coal yards for the local merchants, and so on.

But the public were not pleased and, in January 1879, the season ticket holders, led by stockbroker Derman Christopherson (1835-1907) of Kidbrooke Grove and William George Lemon (1831-1897), a barrister and once Headmaster of the School for Missionaries' Sons, convened a meeting at the Alexandra Hall to protest at the increase in fares and season ticket rates and what they claimed was "...the worst mismanagement of a railway in London"; 23 minute journeys were taking 30, 40 even 60 minutes, and out of 231 specific journeys only four had been faithful to the timetable. Sir John Eardley Wilmot (1810-1892), a Tory MP, grumbled at the incomplete waiting room on the up line, the lack of one on the down line, and the fact that complaints were not dealt with. He described the letters he had received from the company: "...bad language and rudeness jostle each other."

It made no difference at that time, any more than subsequent protest meetings right up to the 1960s, but at least Edward Chapman was spared public criticism. And, by a curious irony, the Alexandra Hall was the venue of another railway meeting a year later, when Capt. Thomas Henry Charleton, then at 133 Shooters Hill Road, gave a free supper to 200 railway staff in appreciation of their hard work.

In 1883 the Bexley Heath Railway Company was floated to build a line from Crayford to Lee via Bexley Heath, but political pressures from the South Eastern Railway altered the plan, and Blackheath became the first station of the projected line. This had a relatively small effect on Blackheath Station other than to allow trains which had previously terminated at Blackheath to travel on somewhere else, but its construction did coincide with much-needed improvements at Blackheath. Complaints from passengers had moved from reasonable demands to shrill abuse and a series of verses, "Lays of the North Kent Line", appeared in the Blackheath Local Guide throughout 1891, expressing in simple poetry many of the frustrations of the local commuters. In addition, angry demands were being made to the Railway Company to further widen the bridge in the Village, which had become a dangerous bottleneck principally because of the great increase in omnibus traffic. The Company refused, saying that they would reconsider the matter when the Bexley Heath railway was being constructed; some Blackheathens said they would prefer a wider bridge as an alternative rather than a complement to a Bexley Heath line.

The new line was built between 1891 and 1895. The works required not only a tunnel under part of the Cator Estate, passing slightly to the west of 97 Blackheath Park (Swiss Cottage, demolished in 1963, which was the home of William Rigby, the line's contractor during the years of construction but at the point where the new line left the North Kent rails, a few yards past the Pond Road bridge, a steep concrete retaining wall had to be built to prevent No. 12 Pond Road sliding into the cutting.

In 1897 major improvements were made to the station. The present cast iron canopies over the platforms were erected and the platform on the south side, facing what was then a carriage shed, was widened 5ft. This was one of the last acts by the old South Eastern Railway Company. Although there had always been fierce rivalry between them and the London, Chatham and Dover company (fd. 1860) it was inevitable that they would have to amalgamate if either was to survive. Enabling legislation was tabled as early as 1893 but the merger did not come into effect until January 1899.

The last years of the 19th century also closed two important chapters in Blackheath travel history - the retirement of Edward Duncan Chapman at the end of 1898 and the change in the old South Eastern Railway - both having served Blackheath for nearly half a century - Chapman having worked for the company for more than 52 years.

Length of service at Blackheath was not confined to Chapman: Inspector Daniells served at Blackheath from 1875 to 1898; Mr. Look, the chief booking clerk, worked there from 1874 to 1908, retiring after 48 years with the company; stationman David Anderson, after 29 years at Blackheath, was sent into retirement in 1898 by grateful passengers who put up enough capital for him to open a small business at the seaside; W. Eves, the ticket collector appointed in 1895, stayed at Blackheath until 1935; and in 1937, Clara, a 17 year old white mare, was retired to Warwickshire after many years as a parcel delivery horse at Blackheath.

In 1899 Francis George Giles was appointed station master, with Kidbrooke Station as part of his responsibilities, over-seeing little change from Duncan's day but coping with the common round of floods, bad fogs and late or irregular trains. Once he had to soothe nervous Villagers when news spread that his daughter kept a pet viper in the official residence - it escaped in July 1903 but whether it was ever recaptured was not recorded.

Within 18 months of taking over Blackheath Station Francis Giles was faced with one of the most important events in his career - a Royal visit. In March 1900 Queen Victoria, then aged 81, decided to visit the Boer War wounded in the Herbert Military Hospital on Shooters Hill. It was arranged that she would travel by train to Blackheath and then drive in a carriage to Shooters Hill and Woolwich. The Station was given a spring clean and the Village shopkeepers collected just over £80 towards the cost of flags and bunting to decorate all the shops from the top of Montpelier Vale down to the railway.

Vast crowds collected in the heart of the Village and enterprising tradesmen charged half a guinea or more for the privilege of a view from their upper windows.

The railway company and the Queen's advisers felt that it would be undignified for the frail and diminutive lady to climb the stair from the down platform to the roadway. To overcome the problem an archway was cut through the brickwork of the down platform wall and the Royal carriage waited close by in the Station yard. The Royal dignity was assured and Her Majesty drove out of the Station to the thunderous cheers of an immense crowd.

Shortly before Giles retired in October 1911 after 50 years service, the railwaymen struck for better pay, but the Blackheath men stayed at their tasks and earned not only the gratitude of the passengers but a £30 testimonial towards comforts for the staff room.

In 1913 major alterations were made to the booking hall and the north staircase leading to the down platform was made into a slope. As a result the last vestiges of the elaborate portico on this end of the Station disappeared. Subsequently, the railway company let off a tiny sliver of land under the south portico and this has been damaged and partly obscured ever since. But the 1913 work saw the booking hall painted in the distinctive Southern railway green and cream and the installation of the mahoganny-faced facia to the booking office and parcels office which survived until 1967.

During the first war the traffic increased and the sidings were much extended to cope with the military traffic. Stationmaster Giles had retired in October 1911 and had been replaced by James Thomas Missenden, who was eventually promoted to take charge of Tunbridge Wells in 1917. He was succeeded by William Rusbridge, who had entered the company's service in 1885, and who remained at Blackheath until his retirement at the end of 1922. This was a significant year for it marked the end of the old South Eastern and Chatham Railway which had, along with all the other independent companies, been amalgamated by act of Parliament into four railway regions. From 1 January 1923 Blackheath Station became a suburban station of the Southern Railway and remained such until 1948 when the railways were nationalised. Electrification of the London suburban lines had started in the early 1920s and work commenced on the Blackheath-Bexley stretch in June 1923. The stationmaster then was a Mr. H. J. Christer, and he served Blackheath until 1936 when he was succeeded by James Frederick Archer, a railwayman of 37 years standing.

Archer retired from Blackheath in 1942, having supervised during the difficult years of the 1939-1945 war. In 1941 a bomb was found in his garden, which, if it had exploded, would have destroyed him, his house, Blackheath Station and much of the Village. Once it had been made safe it was displayed on the Station and collected £16 for service funds.

Archer was succeeded by Alfred John Leaper until 1946. The station masters thereafter were: Kennard Alfred Aldous (1947-1952); Charles Leslie Cradduck (1954-1959); Joseph Henry Russell (1960-1962); Thomas James Cliffe (1963-1966)- the last occupant of the station house; and Terence Edward Haines from 1968 to 1971. From October 1971 Blackheath was placed under the control of the Station Manager at Lewisham, William John Brown.

The fall in freight traffic on the railways during the 1950s saw the closure of the Blackheath Station goods yards at the end of 1962. Part of the land (that nearest the Village) was laid down for a municipal car park, but the larger section to the west was sold to Lewisham Borough for housing.

Blackheath Station may not have been one of the most important on the Southern Railway, but there is no doubt that, as with so many suburbs, its coming gave a new impetus to estate development and hastened the inevitable blanketing of fields and meadows with bricks and mortar. Nevertheless, while many suburbs were spoiled by the advent of passenger railway lines, Blackheath was extremely fortunate. Not only was there a natural valley through the Village crossed by an established carriage road under which the metals could conveniently be hidden so that the railway did not have a divisive effect on the community, but the town was well-established, attractive and, for those days, fully-developed. The demand for residences in Blackheath and south Greenwich was from the middle-classes, and from speculators like Lewis Glenton, who was responsible for building much of Kidbrooke and the Granville Park area, and who saw that this market was more lucrative than building rows and rows of small villas. As a result, some extremely fine and generously-fitted houses were built, which have, despite war damage and speculative greed, remained to contribute much to the overall attractiveness of the district.

In the early 1880s the street frontage of the station master's garden was let to tradesmen, in particular, florists. The first flower sellers here were Joseph Garton and his son William, nurserymen of Shooters Hill Road and Stratheden Road. By 1906 the business passed to William John Minhinnick and his name remained over the facia of the shop until 1965 although it had long before passed into other hands. It now incorporates a small office which had traded as a greengrocery or coal office, as 8 and 8a Blackheath Village. South of the florist's shop, now called Harmer's, and next to the passageway by the Railway Hotel a one storey butcher's shop was erected by Messrs Walkers after their lease had expired at 19 Montpelier Vale (q. v.). By the mid-1930s the shop had passed to E. Tucker and has remained in this family ever since.

A long-term rival to Smith's newspaper kiosk inside the station has been the newspaper seller whose pitch is established outside against the south portico. This sales point had been established as far back as the 1870s and held by the Elliott family, father (J.M. Elliott - 1866-1944), son, and grandson (K. Elliott) from at least 1881 to 1962.

THE RAILWAY HOTEL

When the South Eastern Railway Company carved themselves a large chunk of the Collins estate in the middle of the Village they did so because Blackheath was to be a principal depot during the construction of the line. Once the service was in operation, the station and other offices built, the company was left with surplus land to the south of the line. They were not obliged to sell it back to the Collins Estate and, instead, leased it in four main plots over the years 1850 to 1856.

The first plot was already earmarked, principally because it had a frontage to the Village but also because, close on the heels of the railway builders, came Sir Henry Meux, a brewer, who was opening pubs close to all the railway stations on the North Kent line.

The Railway Hotel was opened in 1851 but not without a fight to achieve its licence. Initially the Hotel could only sell beer, and James Moore, the first licencee, had to make a number of applications to gain the right to sell spirits ("malt liquor"). In October 1851 his application was opposed by the landlords of the Three Tuns and The Crown. His counsel claimed that no new licence had been granted in Blackheath for more than 50 years and that the opposition was stage-managed by brewers who wished to retain a local monopoly. The brewers countered by claiming that the local clergy and residents did not want another pub, a view held with especial force by residents of Blackheath Park and Lee. James Moore won his case and "The Railway" settled down to being one of the four Village pubs - without the history or interest of the other hostelries perhaps - but with no apparent harm befalling the inhabitants of Blackheath Park and Lee.

In 1877 the then licencee, Alfred Alexander Cole, decided that it was time his hotel took its rightful place as one of the assets of Blackheath, and created the Blackheath Pandocheion. This was not much more than a luncheon room and buffet but the publicity was an interesting example of mid-19th century public relations. He wrote:

"Whilst fully believing that the partaking of bodily refreshment and pleasant surroundings not only enhances the zest of consumption but ought materially to assist digestion, the process of which requires tranquillity of mind, the new proprietor of the Railway Hotel, Blackheath...considered the old stuffy "parlours" with their uneasy seats and conventional sanded floor in which our forefathers...solemnly discussed their grog and the latest news from The Times, were not...the kind of thing to find favour in Blackheath in the 19th century, and he has, therefore, fitted up his premises in an elaborate style (Jacobean) as luxurious as it is unique in England and adopted for it the euphonious Greek title Pandocheion."

The Pandy, as it quickly became known, did not last long, although the diminutive was used for the Railway Hotel until well into the 1930s, because in 1893 the then proprietor, Joseph Taylor, stripped out the Jacobean fitments and installed a new staircase and dining room on the first floor.

The most radical change took place in the 1950s when the brewers removed all vestiges of the Victorian age and managed to create, with plastic and pastel paint, a pub with almost no character whatsoever. At the same time the Doric porch and columns were removed from the front, possibly because of the narrow pavement here, thus removing the one element which gave the outside of the building some interest.

In the list of landlords and licencees given below, Mrs. Gertrude Alberta Matthews was the most remarkable in that she held the tenancy from 1924 to 1975, a total of 51 years.

1851-1863   -   James Moore (1814-1863)
1863-1864   -   Angelina Sarah Moore (d.1864)
1864-1875   -   Edwin Davis Moore
1876-1886   -   Alfred Alexander Cole
   1887   -   George Henry Summer
1888-1897   -   Joseph Taylor
1897-1898   -   J. Lewis
1899-1900   -   Henry Hunt Sirkett
1901-1904   -   James Saunders Poole
1905-1912   -   William Fox
   1914   -   Messrs Cope & Ashley
1916-1919   -   John Albert Davies
1920-1942   -   Thomas W. Cutmore (d.1942)
1942-1975   -   Mrs. Gertrude Alberta Matthews (1889-1975)
                (Mrs. Matthews was the widow of Thomas Cutmore)

INDEPENDENTS ROAD

The unmade roadway presently called Independents Road (a relatively recent title as the buildings in this road were numbered as Lee Road until 1960) represented the southern boundary of the railway company's holding.

The ground was steep, dropping sharply towards the retaining wall on the south side of the lines. Seemingly of little use, except for a short terrace of small cottages, the site was used by two organisations needing to erect large buildings but lacking the funds for a more open location.

Both were religious foundations and it was this, coupled with the erection of a new meeting house for the local chapter of the Society of Friends, that has given the road its appropriate name.

The three principal buildings in Independents Road are dealt with below in the order not of their construction but as the visitor from Lee Road would meet them.

Winchester House (School for the Sons and Orphans of Missionaries)

This by now rather run down red-brick Gothic building was erected in 1857 as a school for the sons and orphans of missionaries and remained in that use until 1912 when the foundation moved to Eltham.

The origins of the school go back to 1841 when the London Missionary Society resolved to open an institution for the boarding and education of missionaries' sons. A girls' school had been established at Walthamstow in 1837 and the boys' school opened in the same place on January 1 1842.

The government of the school was in the hands of a committee, led largely by the Revd. Arthur Tidman DD (d. 1868) who had been appointed Foreign Secretary of the London Missionary Society in 1841. Despite problems of organisation and finance the boys' school moved to 1 Mornington Crescent in 1852 and a new headmaster was appointed - William George Lemon BA, FGS, LLB (1831-1897) - who was to serve the school as Principal or Secretary until 1882.

Despite leasing the next door property to accomodate the growing number of pupils, nearly 50 boarders, it was clear that the Committee's plans for a purpose-built school would have to be brought forward.

Various sites were considered and Blackheath chosen principally because a committee member, Miss Peek, lived in the district. Her father, James Peek (1801-1879), a resident of Kidbrooke Lodge, St. Germans Place from 1850-1867, and co-founder of the biscuit manufacturers Peek, Frean, had helped establish the Blackheath Congregational Church in Independents Road in 1853. Miss Peek was a member of that congregation and was able to report to the LMS on the vacant plot next to the church from first-hand knowledge.

The Society paid the South Eastern Railway Company £1,800 for the land and commissioned designs from William Gilbee Habershon (1818-1891) whose father, Matthew Habershon (1789-1852), spent most of his architectural practice building churches and town halls. Habershon's school at Blackheath was an impressive structure, demonstrating great architectural and engineering skill in managing to place so large a building on such a small site. Considering the interests of architect and client it was certainly no accident that it resembled a church, with its lofty rooms, lancet windows and lozenge-shaped leaded lights. The foundation stone was laid by the Earl of Shaftesbury (1801-1885) on November 25 1856 and the Illustrated London News described the new building as: "...in the domestic style of the 15th century in the best Kentish brick, and Bath stone dressings on the angles and windows."

The pupils and masters moved to Blackheath in 1857, no doubt pleased with the semi-rural quality of the suburb compared to Camden Town and, initially, not unpleased by the new school. But Habershon and the LMS committee proved not to be men of vision. The building became inadequate as the years went by, it was almost impossible to heat properly in the winter and much of the accommodation was inconvenient, the rooms being either too large or too small. The playground (since built over) was no larger than the ground area of the school.

But none of these factors could diminish the value of the school and its building, while not ideal, managed to blend into the overall pattern of the Village.

Although many of its staff and governors were drawn from Blackheath addresses (Lemon lived at 20 Montpelier Row from the 1860s and Tidman's sons lived at Pond Road and Priory Park) it was not a local school in the real sense. The pupils were boarders, sons of missionaries from many parts of England and Scotland, of many shades of dissenting opinion. Nevertheless, they were supported by the local churches, in particular the Congregational Church next door. Further encouragement came from St. Michael's in Blackheath Park, St. John's in St. John's Park and the Lee Baptist Chapel, near Dacre Park, all of which were keen centres of evangelical and missionary zealotry. But none quite matched the independent fervour of Dr. Robert Mackilliam at the Alexandra Hall, which he ran as a private centre of religious worship with special emphasis on urging young men and women to travel to the far corners of Empire to convert the Heathen.

From the 1870s the few spare places in the classrooms had been filled by day boys - attending what was called Blackheath Grammar School - but by the turn of the century the institution had outgrown its buildings. Changes in educational priorities which necessitated better playing fields, science laboratories and more generous accommodation for boarders were revealing the inadequacies of the Blackheath school.

In 1898 a house had to be rented in Bennett Park for the headmaster's residence and as an overflow dormitory. Attempts to find new premises were enlivened by a Board of Education inspection in 1907 which had condemned the building. In 1892 there had been 49 boarders - by 1898 there were 86, with parents scattered over India, Madagascar, China, Africa, the South Seas and Jerusalem.

In 1910 new premises were found in the shape of the buildings previously occupied by the Royal Naval School at Eltham since 1889 when that body moved from what became the Goldsmith's College at New Cross.

The Missionaries school, after more than 50 years in Blackheath, left in 1912. Few boys and fewer masters were sorry to leave, for the new buildings were a great imporovement on the old. With the move the School for the Sons and Orphans of Missionaries took on a new name: Eltham College, and with that title has flourished ever since as an independent boarding and day school for boys although few of its pupils these days are the sons of missionaries.

The Headmasters at Blackheath were as follows:

1852-1866 - William George Lemon, BA, FGS, LLB (1831-1897)
1866-1868 - James Scott MA
1869-1870 - Charles DuGard Makepeace MA
1870-1875 - Revd. E.J. Chinnock MA, LLB
1875-1892 - Revd. Edward Waite MA (d. 1910)
1893-1914 - Walter Brainerd Hayward MA (1864-1929)

The school moved out of Blackheath during the Christmas holidays 1911-1912 and shortly afterwards the building was put up for sale. There were no takers and the rooms lay empty for more than 18 months, by which time the country was at war.

In October 1914 many Blackheath families were moved by the plight of
Belgium and welcomed some refugees from the German invasion. The
main problem was one of housing and the governors of the Missionaries
school generously offered their empty building for use as temporary accommodation. The Belgians moved in on 16 October 1914, but out again when
the building was requisitioned by the Royal Army Pay Corps, to find new
temporary homes at Mill House on the Heath or at Woodlands in Mycenae
Road, then owned by the Yarrow family.

The Pay Corps remained in the old school until 1921 and, at one stage,
considered purchasing the freehold as a permanent centre for clerical
workers, but, probably as a result of the public efforts to drive them out
of the Concert Hall and other Blackheath buildings after the war, the army
left and the building was once again put on the market.

It was finally sold in July 1923, to Mrs. Jane Robinson Tremlett (1876-
1948), a novelist and widow of Horace Tremlett, a mining engineer.

The Tremlett family re-named the building Winchester House and converted the upper storeys into flats. The lower rooms were used by a variety
of commercial and religious interests for dancing schools, bridge clubs,
reading rooms and so on.

The old playground to the west disappeared under a factory building during
or just after the Great War, passed through a variety of uses including the
manufacture of fruit drinks in the 1930s, and remains (an eyesore) to this
day.

Early in 1972 Winchester House was sold and although a scheme to replace
it with an office block was refused by the London Borough of Lewisham, a
question mark still hangs over its ultimate use.

Blackheath Congregational Church

The Blackheath Independent Dissenters were a small group in the early
1850s but were fortunate enough to number some of the richest and most
influential Blackheathens amongst their supporters. The Congregational
Chapel in Park Vista, Greenwich, had been the centre for the Blackheath
adherents and in 1852 James Peek of St. Germans Place (see above) purchased a plot from the railway company on the south side of the line, for a
new chapel.

The foundation stone for the Blackheath Congregational Church was laid
on 28 July 1853. It was built in a "richly ornamented Gothic style", in
Kentish ragstone and topped by two 73-foot towers, with quoins and dressings
in Bath stone. The architects were "Messrs Brandon and Ritchie, of Greenwich" - probably John Raphael Brandon (1817-1877) although there seems to
be no record of Mr. Ritchie in the Greenwich directories of the period.
Brandon and his brother, Joshua Arthur, had written on Gothic architecture
and in 1844 designed a station at Epsom for the atmospheric railway.

The Blackheath church cost £4,260 and was enormous, seating more than
1000. Fortunately the first two incumbents, the Revds Sherman and Beazley,
were able to win new supporters and there seems to have been no difficulty
in filling the pews. The Blackheath Congregational Church boasted only
seven ministers in its first hundred years and one, the Revd Thomas Wigley,
served the congregation from 1928 to 1961.

During the 1939-1945 war the church was badly damaged by blast and bomb and by 1945 the congregation were meeting in the hall on the west end of the building. In February 1957 a new church building, to the designs of Trevor Dannatt RIBA, had been raised within the walls of the old. Dannatt used much of the material from the ruined building to create a modern church in harmony with the remaining section of the 1850 structure.

Ecumenical progress in the 1960s saw the creation of the United Reformed Church out of the combined congregations of the Baptist Church and Congregational Unions. As a result there was much re-organisation of man power and assets and, because of dwindling congregations, the Blackheath Congregational Church was closed for religious worship in 1974.

The pastors at the Blackheath Congregational Church were as follows:

1854-1862 - Revd James Sherman (1811-1862)
1862-1875 - Revd Joseph Beazley (1812-1899)
1876-1881 - Henry Batchelor
1881-1895 - Revd Charles Wilson (1831-1915)
1895-1915 - Revd Robert Fotheringham MA (1864-1920)
     1916   - Revd Dr Rowland (temporary pastor)
1917-1927 - Revd Ieuan Maldwyn Jones MA
1928-1961 - Revd Thomas Wigley (d. 1961)

Society of Friends

The Blackheath meeting of the Society of Friends (Quakers) joined the meeting at Woolwich in 1962 but subsequent increase in numbers from the Blackheath area dictated a return to SE3. Initially plans were made for the erection of a meeting house on the north west end of Blackheath Vale, but these were abandoned. The chapter met in the newly-restored Congregational Church and eventually purchased a small site on the south side of Independents Road opposite the Congregational building. A new meeting house was built there, again designed by Trevor Dannatt RIBA, and formally opened in November 1972.

South Vale House

The most westerly plot of excess railway ground, now covered by a London Borough of Lewisham housing estate, was the largest parcel to be let by the Railway Company. It stretched from the west edge of the Congregational church to the back gardens of the Glebe, and was sold freehold to G. Sowerby Herbert in 1852, who built himself a large two-storey house on the west end of the plot. This was South Vale House, a dwelling of 15 rooms standing in two acres of garden. In June 1863 Herbert sold the house to Edgar Rodwell who remained in the property until 1881 in which year it was acquired by John Knill, later Alderman Sir John Knill, bart, JP.

Knill (1856-1934) was a wharfinger, son of Stuart Knill (1824-1898) of The Crosslets, 14 West Grove. The Knill family, who had lived in Greenwich since the late 18th century, achieved an almost unique double ; both father and son became Lords Mayor of London. Stuart Knill, who was knighted, in 1892; son John, then Alderman Sir John Knill, moved to the Mansion House in 1909.

The family were devout Roman Catholics and made much contribution to

the church in Cresswell Park as well as to other secular causes and activities. Many Blackheath people felt their greatest appreciation of the Knills
when Sir John engaged Harry Lauder, the Scots comedian, to perform at
the Concert Hall in Blackheath for a charity show in 1912. The family
moved to Mayfield, Sussex, at the end of 1919 where Sir John died in 1934,
and his wife Edith (née Powell) died in 1944.

South Vale House was occupied by William Roxburgh from 1921 to 1927;
and by Albert Alfred Mead (1888-1940) in 1927. The Mead family only
lived here until December 1939, leaving the house then because of the
bombing risks.

The freehold had been re-acquired by the Collins Estate in 1935 and in
1940 they let the house to the then Lewisham Borough Council as a store
for furniture from bombed houses. In 1944 it was damaged by the V2 rocket
which hit The Glebe and was re-requisitioned in 1945 by the Council.

It is clear now that the Council had long intended to demolish the property
and develop the site for community housing and, despite protest, the house
was allowed to fall into further disrepair. In 1952, their compulsory
purchase order having been approved by the Ministry of Housing, the house
was demolished - exactly 100 years after its erection.

Lawn Terrace and Lee Terrace

The slip road called Lawn Terrace, which leads from the Village to Lee
Terrace at its boundary with The Glebe, was originally a footpath on the
boundary of a field. By the 1820s its status had grown somewhat and it
served as a mews road - called Collins Lane - to houses then being built
on the Lee Terrace frontage of the Collins Estate.

In 1834 building leases had been granted by the Collins Estate to William
Seager, then at 58 Tranquil Vale, to erect a row of semi-detached houses
fronting Lee Terrace (now numbered 47 to 61 Lee Terrace). The prime
site, facing Blackheath Village, had been leased to the Blackheath Proprietary School in 1831 and Seager, following the building line of the school
where it faced Collins Lane, later erected a row of seven two-storey
cottages, miniature versions of the houses known as St. Germans Terrace in
Shooters Hill Road (presently numbered 2-20 Shooters Hill Road). The
Collins Lane cottages took the title "Seager's Cottages", which name they
kept until the end of the 19th century. Four have survived and are presently
numbered 11, 13, 15 & 17 Lawn Terrace.

In 1863 a Mr. G. Moore built a terrace of 12 houses backing onto the
garden ground of South Vale House. These were sold later that year as
"brick-built carcases", a common practice then in that the builder would
obtain a short lease for a peppercorn rent, build the basic structure and
arrange the sewer connection (in this case with the sewer running past the
Congregational church) and then sell the house for completion to a party
who would then buy a long lease from the freeholder.

The name Lawn Terrace was in use for this development by 1864 and by
1866 there were 20 houses here, the paving of the pathway and road from
the Village to Lee Terrace being completed in 1867.

Seager's Cottages may have been intended as accommodation for the
domestic staff working in the Lee Terrace houses at the end of whose
gardens the small houses stood, but there is no evidence to support this.

No. 3 was the home and workshop of Carl Schonhardt, a watch and clock maker, and No. 7 was occupied from the 1860s to the 1890s by Henry Seager (1848-1895) the carpenter son of William.

The Lawn Terrace properties were highly popular with the working shop-keepers of the Village; John Goslin, the tobacconist of 50 Tranquil Vale (q.v.) at No. 3; James Jennings, the printer, lived at No. 5; Edgar Neve, the bookseller of Tranquil Vale, at No. 8; Charles Irish, the saddler, at No. 17, and so on. One remarkable tenancy was that of Charles Driver (1838-1915) at No. 12 (later No. 22); he was verger of St. Michael's Church in Blackheath Park from 1863-1915 and lived in Lawn Terrace from the early 1860s until his death.

In 1903 the numbering of Seager's Cottages and Lawn Terrace was regularised. Seager's Cottages became 1-7 Lawn Terrace; there were no houses numbered 8, 9 & 10 although there were stables and outbuildings here until they were demolished in 1938, and Nos. 1-20 Lawn Terrace became Nos. 11-30.

During the war Nos. 1 to 3 were demolished and Nos. 23 to 30 Lawn Terrace badly damaged by blast. In 1952 the remaining houses of the original Lawn Terrace were taken down as part of the clearance work for the new council estate. The four surviving Seager Cottages were subsequently re-numbered Nos. 11 to 15 and are all that remain of a once important domestic segment of the Village.

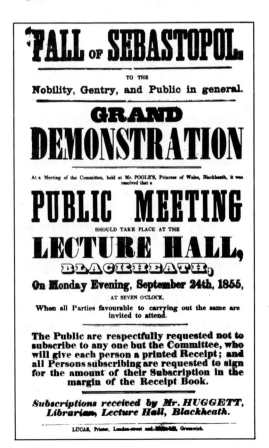

The front page of the first issue of Blackheath's own newspaper, January 1889.

136

11   Tranquil Vale (east) and Tranquil Place

The central triangle of the Village, bounded by Tranquil Vale, Montpelier Vale and Royal Parade was developed for building almost certainly because of the location of a public well - Queen Elizabeth's Well - on the edge of the waste of the Heath.

Much of the central section of the Village was enclosed from the Heath by the Earls of Dartmouth who, as freeholders, were Lords of the Manor. Whilst many encroachments on common land led to protest and anger, it is doubtful whether this particular enclosure gave rise to any real disquiet. The site was small, eventually no more than two thirds of an acre, and it was bounded on its two longest sides by the public roads to Lewisham and Lee from Greenwich and Woolwich. The land sloped quite sharply, and this, coupled with the activity which must have been drawn to the well area would have reduced the land's value as common grazing.

No buildings are shown on this site in the 1695 Survey of the Manor of East Greenwich but in 1741 a plan was filed to the Manorial Court sitting at the Green Man public house relating to Sir Gregory Page's alteration of a water course in Blackheath. This map shows a building or buildings roughly on the site of the present Three Tuns public house set in an enclosure with an area of about one third of an acre. The buildings are marked as "Richardson Headley's House land demised by the Earl of Dartmouth."

Headly's name appears in a number of local records, the first in 1719 when on 14 January he witnessed the will of John Clowser, the yeoman farmer living at the Six Chimneys, Blackheath. The Six Chimneys was a house which stood on the western boundary of the Wricklemarsh estate, probably at the top end of Montpelier Vale, south of Wemyss Road. It had been demolished by 1742.

Richardson Headly was the son of John Headly, a farmer who cultivated lands in the parish of Charlton, and there is good reason to suppose that he was a tenant of the Morden estate at Wricklemarsh. His son, Richardson (d. August 1737) married Ann, daughter of John Clowser, at Morden College on April 21 1720. In that year the younger Headly is listed in the Charlton parish churchwarden's account as paying £23. 6. 8 land taxes, almost as much as Lady Morden had paid previously, and this could mean that he had acquired, through marriage, an agricultural lease for much of the park land of Wricklemarsh, taking over John Clowser's tenancy.

Richardson's name is missing from the Charlton parish account books after 1722. But in 1724 Sir Gregory Page is mentioned for the first time, paying almost exactly the total land taxes paid by Lady Morden's tenants. It is probably safe to assume that he took on the responsibility of paying the local taxes but that the tenants remained.

Although Richardson Headly held lands in Charlton he lived in the parish of Lewisham until his death on 8 August 1737. The parish entry reads: "Richardson Headly from the Three Tuns at Blackheath, buried." It is because of these words that local historians have assumed that there was a pub in Blackheath Village, on the site of the present Three Tuns at 52 Tranquil Vale, by 1737 and that Headly was an innkeeper. But there is little evidence to support either claim. It is clear that Richardson was a farmer of substantial means but he describes himself in his will as a victualler. But curiously there is no record in the licensing returns for the period 1712-1726 of a Three Tuns pub in the Parish of Lewisham, nor that anyone called Headley was a licensed victualler in the district. What is interesting is that the 1741 plan which marked Headly's house on the Village triangle shows a ground plan of what could be a terrace of three buildings facing due south but at an angle to the road now called Tranquil Vale. At best, assuming the name Three Tuns has something to do with spiritous liquors, it could be presumed that Headly owned a brewery here but, once more, there is no evidence to support this assumption.

The Three Tuns makes only a handful of appearances thereafter until the last decade of the 18th century. Ann Headly died on July 3 1738; on 11 June 1739 Elizabeth Collett "from Blackheath the Three Tuns by Richd. Headly, buried". This last could mean that Richardson Headly named a son Richard and he lived at the Three Tuns after his father's death. Finally, in May 1744 the parish registers noted the death of John Maplesden from the Three Tuns, of Blackheath.

From that date and for 34 years there is a gap in our knowledge, for without the rate books (pulped in the 1950s) and the parish registers (most of which were destroyed in 1830), it has not proved possible to trace the owners or tenants of the building which certainly stood on the site of the present Three Tuns and is marked on Rocque's map of 1746 and Hasted's plan of 1778. Further, although many of the 18th-century leases for Dartmouth estate properties on and around Blackheath have survived there is nothing extant for the central triangle of the Village earlier than 1791.

By 1780 Headly's house was in the possession of Thomas Roberts, a builder who, eight years later, obtained a lease from John Cator for land in the vicinity of the Princess of Wales public house at the top of Montpelier Row. Roberts remained at the Three Tuns house until 1788 and the following year the building passed to John Harmsworth - whom we know from the licensing returns was a publican. It would not be unreasonable to assume that Roberts had re-built or re-fitted Headly's house and that Harmsworth had converted a domestic dwelling into a tavern - the Three Tuns public house which survived until 1884.

In 1788 another building in the vicinity of the Three Tuns appears in the tax returns - this time the house of a Mr. Stockbridge who remained there until 1797; in 1791 a further property, occupied by Thomas Miller had been built. And in 1798 the boundaries of the triangle that are defined today by Tranquil Vale, Montpelier Vale and Royal Parade, had been established. The Dartmouth Estate had, by then, enclosed about an acre of the common land. The southern section, below the line of Tranquil Passage, previously Headly's garden, became the Three Tuns garden with the pub and its stables on the north west corner. The northern section of the enclosure was bounded on the north and west by two rows of cottages or small houses, and on the east side leased to Matthias Ingram for stabling

and a new large property known as Phoenix House. On the land behind the
cottages and Phoenix House various outbuildings were erected over the
next seventy years, including a dairy, a Wesleyan chapel, the Village
school and a fire brigade station.

Ingram's lease and the building of Phoenix House as well as its subsequent
re-development as Royal Parade is dealt with in Chapter 1, and the section
that follows covers the buildings on the east side of Tranquil Vale from the
apex of the triangle (36 Tranquil Vale) to the edge of the Heath (74 Tranquil
Vale and Highland House), and the Three Tuns. The area covered presently by Tranquil Passage and Brigade Street is described in Chapter 12.

Developments from 1800

The east side of Tranquil Vale can be divided into three distinct sections
which were developed and re-developed quite independently from each other.

Nos. 38-50 Tranquil Vale   Originally a development of shops in 1822 by
Joseph Jackson on the garden of the Three Tuns.
Re-built 1885 in their present form.

Nos. 52-56 Tranquil Vale   The Three Tuns (No. 52) and its attendant outhouses and stables. The latter were altered
and much re-built to form shop premises. The
whole site re-built in its present form in 1884-5.

Nos. 58-74 Tranquil Vale   The origins of this group are obscure but they
(Tranquil Place)   were certainly in existence by 1802. No. 58
was much altered in 1878; Nos. 70-74 were
re-built in 1879-80 as Highland House.
The whole terrace was known as Tranquil
Place until 1882.

In an attempt to keep the narrative as clear as possible the scheme of the
following material follows the three sections listed above. A survey of the
developments behind Tranquil Vale, i.e. Tranquil Passage, Brigade Street,
and the small courts and alleys built during the first half of the 19th century
is covered in Chapter 12.

36-50 TRANQUIL VALE

The first buildings on the site of the present 38 to 50 Tranquil Vale were
built as a result of a lease granted by the Dartmouth Estate to Joseph
Jackson of Kidbrooke, in September 1822. Prior to that the ground had
been the gardens and probably the bowling green for the Three Tuns public
house, the lease of which was granted to the brewer William James Steward
in 1822, minus its garden ground.

Whether Steward was not interested in using the garden or whether Dartmouth wanted to increase the building potential of the enclosure from the
waste, we do not know, but development here would have been inevitable.

The Jackson lease was for a term of 61 years from 29 September 1822
at an annual rent of £8. Little is known about Joseph Jackson except that
he was living in Blackheath in the 1820s and built Kidbrooke Lodge,
St. Germans Place, where he lived from 1838 to 1840. There is no other
evidence that he was a speculative builder and this development in Black-

heath Village may simply have been a private investment. It is known that he was a Liberal in politics and he served as a magistrate and Overseer to the Poor in the Liberty of Kidbrooke during the 1830s. Jackson's head-lease had passed to James Watson, the butcher, of 12 Montpelier Vale, before 1852 and Jackson may have died before that date.

The Jackson buildings were probably planned as shops from the outset although the records do not show commercial tenants much before the late 1820s, and in some cases the late 1830s. And because these properties were not listed as separate assessments in the Land Tax returns it is now unlikely that we will ever know the names of the original occupiers.

Jackson's shops were not built as a harmonious terrace of buildings; each was different from its neighbour, some were weatherboarded, and No. 48 was taller than the rest, being a four-storey brick and stucco construction. Nos. 36 & 38 Tranquil Vale were built as a block with No. 1 Montpelier Vale (q.v.) looking south and with frontages on Tranquil and Montpelier Vales. It was as a result, the prime commercial site in the Village, and was occupied from at least the 1830s to 1972 by grocers and wine merchants.

When the 1822 lease expired in 1883 a new lease for 99 years was granted to the tailor Charles Bond, on condition that he demolished the Jackson development. The new shops built for Bond, which survive today, were completed towards the end of 1885. Some kept their old trades and, in one or two cases, the traders from the original premises, but the change was so drastic and the continuity so broken that the 1822 and the 1885 developments are dealt with separately.

THE 1822 DEVELOPMENT

36 & 38 Tranquil Vale (were 1 & 2 Tranquil Vale)

These shops, built as one and mostly occupied by a single tenant, became one of the best-known retail units in the Village. Leased from 1836 by Barber Tuck, a grocer and wine merchant, the premises were so familiar that the site became known as Tuck's Corner. Barber Tuck (1809-1865) was born in Edmonton, Middlesex, and set up in business in Blackheath when he was 27. It is likely that he took over an existing grocery, for the shop had been built by 1823, but there is no record of the earlier proprietor. For 50 years Tuck's grocery and wine shop was one of the most successful businesses in the Village and was so profitable that the family were able to rent a large house - Hillside, in Cresswell Park (since demolished) - and not live above the shop as was the case with most retailers at the time. By 1862 Barber Tuck's sons David and Henry (1834-1906) had joined the family business but in 1865 Barber Tuck died, choking to death over a fish supper. His funeral was a solemn occasion and the Village shopkeepers closed for its duration as a mark of respect, for Tuck had been not only a prosperous shopkeeper but had played an active role in local parish and social affairs. The business was then controlled by his widow, Sarah (1817-1874) and the two sons until 1885 when the shop was demolished for re-development. Tuck's name went back over the facia of the new premises but by 1890 the grocery business had been sold and Henry Tuck was acting as an insurance agent at 38 Tranquil Vale from where he retired in 1892.

Initially the Tucks had traded only from 36 Tranquil Vale - No. 38 was

31. Spencer Place (3-9 Tranquil Vale) in the 1970s

32. Spencer Place (right) and Osborne Place (left) in 1905

33.   Nos 19-21 Tranquil Vale just before the last war

34.   South Vale, later Nos 23-35 Tranquil Vale, in the Winter of 1939-40

35.   South Vale in the 1960s

36.   Upper Tranquil Vale in 1874. Morley's shop is now 47 Tranquil Vale

37.   Collins Square after restoration in the 1960s

38.   Nos 45-47 Tranquil Vale and the Crown; No 47 was once the post office

occupied from the 1830s to about 1855 by George Sherwood Hudson, a plumber and glazier. For a year or two the premises were leased by Charles and Charlotte Knight, stay and corset makers, but by the early 1860s the shop had been taken over by Barber Tuck and used for an iron-mongery department and coal order office.

40 Tranquil Vale (was 3 Tranquil Vale)

This building was the home and workshop of James Price (1792-1858) a shoemaker from before 1826 to 1858, and thereafter of his daughter-in-law Mrs. Emily Ann Price. She ran the shop solely as a warehouse and perhaps because she was not a cobbler the trade dropped and 40 Tranquil Vale was leased in the mid 1860s by Hannah and Lewis Upton. Mrs. Upton opened the shop for millinery although her husband Lewis was a jeweller by trade. They remained here until 1881 and in the following year the prem-ises had been acquired by Miss Emma Crumpton, a ladies outfitter, who was successful in applying for a new lease when the old shop was demolished. She spent six years in the present premises before selling the business to Mrs. Fanny Loader in 1892.

42 Tranquil Vale (was 4 Tranquil Vale)

The two buildings which have stood on this site have sold the same type of goods - china and glass - for more than 140 years to the date of writing although successive proprietors have sometimes had to diversify in order to balance the books.

The earliest recorded occupier was John Armstrong who was established here as a grocer by 1825. Before 1830 he had altered the emphasis of his business and was selling china, glass and other household supplies. In 1845 the shop was taken over by Stephen Trill who had been in partnership with his brother Thomas as silk mercers and drapers at 31 Tranquil Vale from 1832. The Trill family had owned drapery shops in London Street and Nelson Street, Greenwich, in the 1830s but never stayed at one address for long. Stephen Trill's venture into china and glass only lasted until about 1848-49 for, by 1850, the shop was being managed by Louisa Trill, described in the 1851 census as a widow supporting four children including Stephen jnr and Louisa jnr, which must have been very confusing when both parents were alive.

Mrs. Trill left the shop in 1852 and the lease and stock passed to William J. Price (1814-1908) who kept the tradition of china and glass dealing but combined it with a trade in curios. Price, who died aged 94 at 3 Montpelier Row, lived in Blackheath all his life. Towards the end he would reminisce about his youth and claimed to remember Tranquil Vale "...when it was market gardens with only wooden huts standing where the shops are now on the west side." This was either romantic licence, for the west side had been built up from No. 11 Tranquil Vale to Camden Row by 1810, or he was thinking of the ground behind the shops.

In 1883 Price negotiated a new 21 year lease on his premises at 42 Tran-quil Vale but this was cancelled when the re-development plans were implemented in 1884. Price took over the new building in 1885 but assigned the lease to Charles Lenn before 1890.

44 Tranquil Vale (was 5 Tranquil Vale)

The first known tenant of this shop was Henry Fletcher, a tailor, who had taken a lease some time during the 1830s. Nothing is known of Mr. Fletcher except that he managed to cram 17 people on to his premises on the day of the 1841 census, which was some feat considering the house consisted of not much more than five or six rooms. By 1850 the shop had passed to Charles John Bond (1811-1879) also a tailor and senior member of the Bond family of Blackheath, all of whom were hosiers, glovers and tailors. Charles Bond had started his business at 50 Tranquil Vale (q.v.) in 1830. He moved sometime between 1848 and 1850 to 44 Tranquil Vale and remained there until he retired in 1874. His son, Charles John Bond jnr (1836-1916) took on a lease of 3 Montpelier Vale (q.v.) and another son, George James Bond (1845-1899) traded from 18 Tranquil Vale (q.v.) until 1899. Charles Bond jnr sub-let 44 Tranquil Vale after his father's death to Mrs. Papworth, an upholstress, but in 1880 the shop had been converted to a dairy by Frederick George Boyton. He remained until 1882 when Jackson's original lease expired. Before the new, and present, building was erected by Charles Bond jnr, the lease had been assigned to Arthur Thynne, a baker and son of Samuel Thynne of 56 Tranquil Vale (q.v.).

46 Tranquil Vale (was 6 Tranquil Vale)

There were only two tenants in this shop in its 63 years and the first of these held the premises until 1879. This was William Charles Roe (1796-1860) and, subsequently, his widow Ann (1798-1879), both chemists and druggists. But William Roe's principal claim to interest the student of Blackheath history comes from his role as the Village postmaster, a task he took on when Ebenezer Larwill of 47 Tranquil Vale (q.v.) Blackheath's first postmaster, retired in 1852. Larwill had handled only the letter side of the task, but Roe actively developed the other side of the Post Office's activities, his shop becoming an official money order office in 1854. After his death in 1860 Mrs. Roe took over the role of postmaster, combining this with the principal job of dispensing medicines and remedies. In 1861 46 Tranquil Vale became a branch of the Post Office Savings Bank but the volume of business in Blackheath was growing very fast (postal codes for London had been introduced in 1859) and it is doubtful whether Mrs. Roe, then 64 years old, could have coped for much longer. The decision was, to some extent, taken out of her hands in that the Post Office decided to establish a district post and sorting office in Blackheath Village. This was opened in 1864 at Bank Buildings, on the corner of Tranquil Vale and Blackheath Grove, and Mrs. Roe was able to concentrate mostly on being a dispensing chemist, which task occupied her until she died in 1879, although her shop continued to be the letter office until 1869.

In the following year the tag end of the shop's lease was taken by John Henry Soper, a greengrocer, but he left the district when the old shop was demolished in 1885.

48 Tranquil Vale (was 7 Tranquil Vale)

This shop was much taller than the others in the terrace, being three

storeys high and built in brick and stucco. From the early 1820s it was
the headquarters of a prosperous building company, initially Woodgate &
Willcocks, painters and glaziers, but from the 1830s in sole proprietorship
of William Woodgate (1785-1851) and thereafter his son, William Henry
Woodgate (1810-?1875). During the 1850s and 1860s Mrs. Sarah Woodgate,
described as a plumber, lived here but whether she was William's widow
or William Henry's wife, is not recorded.

With the death of William jnr the old company ceased trading and the
premises were taken by Mrs. Elizabeth Papworth, an upholsteress, for
the remainder of the lease. During her tenancy part of the premises were
used by Henry Couchman, a builder and decorator, and he took on the lease
of the new building in 1885.

50 Tranquil Vale (was 8 Tranquil Vale)

This shop, as mentioned in the details on 44 Tranquil Vale, was the first
premises of Charles John Bond (1811-1879) a tailor and outfitter. He was
resident here from 1830 until 1848. Bond's business was inherited by his
sons, Charles jnr and George James, and continued in the Bond name until
1899, moving from 44 Tranquil Vale to 8 Montpelier Vale in 1878, with a
branch at 18 Tranquil Vale. In 1899 the goodwill was acquired by Sidney
Birdseye. In turn he sold out to William Morley Cheesewright (1883-1961)
after whose death the shop passed to H.H. Wagstaff, outfitters, presently
trading at 8 Montpelier Vale (q.v.) - thus maintaining an unbroken trade
of nearly 150 years from the opening of Charles Bond's first Blackheath
shop in 1830.

After Bond had moved from No. 50 Tranquil Vale the shop was acquired
by Edward J. Ford, a greengrocer, who also worked for William Roe at
46 Tranquil Vale as a postman. Before 1860 the shop was leased by Erith-
born John Goslin (1827-1901) a tobacconist who remained at No. 50 until
the end of the lease in 1885. Goslin was the principal Village tobacconist
of the time, almost certainly blending his own pipe mixtures, grinding
snuff and, probably grudgingly, selling cigarettes when they were still a
novelty and before they became a national addiction. With the rebuilding
of the old shop Goslin moved his business to 1 Blackheath Village (q.v.)
where it passed to Jude Silverstone on Goslin's death in 1901.

THE 1885 RE-DEVELOPMENT

Jackson's original building lease on Nos. 36-50 Tranquil Vale expired on
September 29 1883. When the original shops were built in 1822-23 they
were, no doubt, adequate for the volume of trade attracted to Blackheath
Village but, by the 1880s they were not - even with the development of
other shopping units in the Village at Camden Place, Royal Parade and
Osborne Place. Further, Jackson's buildings were deficient in drainage
and other services and by the 1850s most had had extensions and outbuildings
erected at the rear. There was much overcrowding and the service alley
entered through a courtyard at the back of the Three Tuns became a small
street in its own right, sometimes known as Pound's Mews after the licencee
of the Three Tuns.

In 1884 Jackson's lease was renewed to Charles John Bond jnr (1836-1916) the tailor and outfitter whose trading fortunes are dealt with elsewhere in this book. He was granted a 99-year lease on condition he tore down the old shops and re-built the same number on the site.

Clearance work started in 1884 and by the end of 1885 most of the present buildings were completed and occupied, some by the old tenants of the original Jackson shops but some by newcomers to the district determined to cash in on what was an extremely lucrative retailing catchment.

Blackheath had long been regarded as shopkeepers' paradise and the scheduled development of Westcombe Park with quality villas promised to increase an already brisk retail trade.

The post 1885 tenants of 36-50 Tranquil Vale were as follows:

36 Tranquil Vale

The new lease on this prime corner site was signed by the old tenants, the grocers and wine merchants, Tuck & Sons, by this time principally Henry Barber Tuck (1834-1906). Because of Henry's age the shop was placed in the hands of managers and by 1890 he disposed of his interest and the business passed to Alonso James Appleton who traded as the Central Supply Stores. Appleton was a poor business man and sold out at the end of 1891 to William F. Hamaton who changed the name of the shop to The London & Suburban Stores; he was followed by J. W. Chester in 1895. In 1900 Chester assigned the lease to T. Foster & Co., a chain of licenced grocers who were acquiring shops and off-licences all over London at the turn of the century. Foster's remained the owners of this shop until 1972, gradually switching the emphasis away from groceries and concentrating more and more on the wine and spirits trade.

During the post 1939-1945 mania for business expansion the company was taken over by a succession of larger and larger groups of wine and spirit retailing companies, eventually becoming part of the International Distillers and Vintners empire, but trading under the name of one of their subsidiaries, Peter Dominic. In 1972 the company left 36 Tranquil Vale and moved to No. 48 principally because of a shortage of cellar and retailing space, and thus brought an end to nearly 140 years of continuous trading as a wine shop on this site.

Messrs Foster were succeeded by the present tenants, Calvert, Hunt & Barden, estate agents.

38 Tranquil Vale

Before the re-building the shop on this site had been part of Tuck's corner and an integral part of No. 36 Tranquil Vale. The new building was a quite separate unit and was occupied by December 1885 by Mrs. Sarah Morton. Mrs. Morton was the widow of photographer Henry Morton of 47 Tranquil Vale (q.v.) and had occupied herself with the management of a fancy repository and toy shop at No. 47 from about 1866. The shop (known as Victoria House) had done well and Mrs. Morton took the lease on 38 Tranquil Vale to expand the business, concentrating on toys and games. She traded here until about 1905, latterly as Morton's Fancy Repository, and applied the old name - Victoria House - to the new shop.

On Sarah Morton's departure, the shop was divided into two units, 38a and 38b Tranquil Vale and has remained in two distinct halves ever since,

both sections being lock-up shops and the residential accommodation above
let separately. No. 38a became, for a few years, a tailor's shop owned
by Frederick G. Bond, grandson of the Charles Bond who has figured much
in this book, but by 1914 had passed to Achille Serre, dyers and cleaners,
as a receiving office. For a short spell it was a tobacconist and confectionery shop but its present use is as a dress shop. No. 38b was leased in
June 1915 by W. S. Shove, coal merchants, as an order office. Shove's had
been one of Blackheath's most successful corn and coal merchants from the
1840s until 1913 at 22 Tranquil Vale (q. v.) but the replacement of the horse
by the car and lorry had destroyed their principal business interest and it
was not necessary to maintain a large retail shop to deal in coal and coke.
Shove's became part of the Rickett, Cockerell group after the Great War
and the business was transferred to 1 Blackheath Village after 1945.
Through the 1950s and 1960s 38b Tranquil Vale became the shop window of
Lewis Pincombe, a watchmaker and jeweller, but in recent years has been
used as employment agency, florist, and reverted latterly to the sale of
watches, clocks and jewellery.

40 Tranquil Vale

The tenant of the old shop, Mrs. Emma Crumpton, a ladies outfitter, took
over the lease of the new building and continued to conduct her business
until 1891. It then passed to a Mrs. Fanny Loader who kept the shop until
1923 in the same trade. On her retirement the business was taken over
by a Mrs. R. E. Carter but in 1928 it was acquired by Ernest Henry Sanders
(1884-1960) and this surname has remained over the door ever since,
although Sanders retired in 1959 and the business passed to Mrs. Joyce
Smith.

42 Tranquil Vale

The previous shop here had sold china and glass from the 1820s, and from
1855 the business had been owned by William J. Price (1814-1908).
Despite his advancing years he took on the new lease in 1885 and kept the
old trading pattern but by the end of the 1880s he finally retired and sold
the shop to Charles Henry Lenn, then the owner of a china warehouse on
the Eltham Road. In 1907 he offered to sell the business and a 77-year
lease on the Tranquil Vale premises but does not seem to have found a
buyer immediately, because his company traded here for a further two or
three years.
   The shop remained empty from 1910 to 1912 but it was then taken over
by Carson & Co., the toy dealers who had owned Carson's Bazaar at 70-
72 Tranquil Vale (q. v.) from 1882 to 1912. Carson's remained at No. 42
until 1930 when they sold it to a milliner trading as "Jon". The shop
returned to its original use as a china and glass business but selling
building and domestic supplies in addition, in 1938. Initially it was known
as "Streek's, the builders", after W. John Streek (d. 1905) who had started
the business in 1876 at 57 Tranquil Vale (q. v.). Streek's successor,
William Alfred Rabson, kept his business going at 63 Tranquil Vale but
moved away from building materials towards domestic hardware and ironmongery after taking over 42 Tranquil Vale. By 1945 the shop at 42
Tranquil Vale was called Blackheath Builders Supplies and in 1949 was

controlled by William Rabson's son, Eric, on whose retirement in 1975 the shop was sold to Sparrow's Hardware Ltd.

44 Tranquil Vale

The present shop here was fitted out for a specific trade, bakery, for Arthur Thynne, a master baker and son of Samuel Thynne who had run a bakery at 56 Tranquil Vale (q.v.) from at least 1852 until the shop was burnt out in 1882. Arthur Thynne does not seem to have had the staying power of his father and he sold the business at No. 44 to Harold Shove, initially in his father's name, W. Spencer Shove, in April 1889. Shove continued trading under Thynne's name and the latter had to resort to the Courts to prevent this, claiming that Shove had purchased only the goodwill and equipment of Thynne's bakery, not the right to use the name. The use of Thynne's name was understandable, Shove's reputation had been made by the sale of coal and horse feed and his son's venture into baking and confectionery must have seemed a little odd. Despite strong trade rivalry from the other Village bakers, Riddington's, Jobbin's and Barrett's, Harold Shove made a success of his shop. In 1893 he opened a tea room, advertised as the first in Blackheath, in the rooms above the shop; in 1900 he took on the lease of No. 46 Tranquil Vale, next door, and extended the bakery, bread shop and the tea room, employing Leonard Hunt ARIBA, to redesign the upper rooms. The walls were decorated in very dark blue with a frieze of brown ground printed with water lilies in lighter blue, electric light was installed and new fitments and furnishings were added to make Shove's the most attractive tea rooms in the district. To encourage custom, Shove's confectioner was given full rein for his talents and huge tableaux in icing sugar were displayed in the windows; at Christmas 1900 a Royal icing replica of All Saints'Church illuminated from the inside; and to celebrate the end of the South Africa War in 1902, icing sugar models of Edward VII, the Imperial Crown, "Tommy Atkins", "Handyman", flags, banners and other patriotic symbols.

In 1907 Shove's business was taken over by Sidney Barrett & Son, the bakers at 63 Tranquil Vale (q.v.) who concentrated more on bread and buns and less on dainty teas and fantasies in icing sugar. They ran Nos. 44 & 46 Tranquil Vale in tandem until 1926, by which time the company had been absorbed by a retail chain of bakers who also controlled Jobbin's at 7 & 9 Blackheath Village.

From 1926 to 1940 No. 44 was used as a second hand furniture shop run principally by Alice Natali, wife of George Phineas Natali (1866-1939) a distinguished pianoforte manufacturer.

After a brief spell as a radio and electrical shop No. 44 went back to being a restaurant in 1948 when it was leased by Gerald Warner. He gave the business the name The Welcome Inn, which was retained when the restaurant passed to Mrs. C. Roberts in 1959. In 1963 there was a change of cuisine and The Welcome Inn became an Italian Restaurant, the Trattoria Franchini.

46 Tranquil Vale

The first tenant of the new building was William Hinds, a greengrocer and fruiterer who had traded at 9 Montpelier Vale (q.v.) from 1866 to the 1880s.

He stayed only until 1887 at No. 46 and moved back to Montpelier Vale in 1888, but this time to No. 1. For the next twelve years 46 Tranquil Vale was named Wemyss House by William Eve, a draper, who had worked for some years with Whittaker and Brown at 5 & 7 Tranquil Vale. Eve was a "fancy draper", selling stockings, gloves and costumes, but in 1900 he was nearing retirement and he accepted an offer from Harold Shove, the baker next door, to part with the lease. Eve moved to 43 Montpelier Vale (q.v.) where he set up a new Wemyss House for a further two years, finally retiring in 1902.

From 1900 to 1930 No. 46 was occupied by the principal tenants of No. 44 - from 1900 to 1907 by Shove, and from 1907 to 1930 by Barrett's, the bakers. In 1930 the shop was taken over by the United Dairy Co., originally an offshoot of the Express Dairy Company but later their fierce rivals. The UD surrendered their local milk rounds in 1940 when the doorstep retailing of milk was rationalised in order to save man power during the war, but kept their dairy shop until the early 1960s. Afterwards No. 46 was taken over by Messrs Stocker and Roberts, chartered surveyors and estate agents, for their Blackheath office, and they have stayed here ever since.

48 Tranquil Vale

The tenant here before the re-building was Henry Couchman, a builder, decorator and upholsterer. Couchman had taken over the long-established business of the Woodgate family and when the new shop was completed in 1885 he placed a stone plaque on the upper face of the building reading "Established 1800 - Rebuilt 1885". Whether this meant he thought there had been a building company on that site since 1800 or whether it referred to the Couchman family, who had been builders in Blackheath since the 18th century we do not know, but Henry was not a close relative of the Couchmans at 16 Montpelier Vale and his business had no link with them other than in name.

The retail section of No. 48 was sub-let from the early 1890s, firstly to the Misses West, ladies and children's outfitters, and afterwards to Eastman & Sons, dyers and cleaners; separate tenants occupied the upper rooms, including, in 1901, Madame Hart, a dressmaker, and in 1904 Esme et Cie, robes, who may in truth have been Mrs. Hart. From about 1908 to 1912 one third of the shop was taken as a separate unit by Constance Warwick, a florist, but thereafter the whole premises were used by Henry Couchman until 1917.

In 1919 the shop was re-styled by the Holloway family for the sale of antique and second hand furniture and they remained there until 1971, after which the premises were leased by Peter Dominic, the wine merchants who had traded previously at No. 36 Tranquil Vale.

50 Tranquil Vale

The re-building of the old tobacco shop on this site coincided with the re-building of the Three Tuns (q.v.) and the then enterprising licencee of the pub, William Frederick Walton, took over No. 50 as a retail off-licence. His successor, Charles Mead, was less interested in off-sales and No. 50 reverted to its old status as a tobacco shop. Only three families have conducted the business since 1895: Mr. & Mrs. Charles Aird from 1895 to 1909; Edward Brewin from 1910 to 1934; from 1934 to 1960 Frank Thomson Coultate (1897-1960) and thereafter his widow and their sons up until the present time.

The Three Tuns (52 Tranquil Vale)

The introductory paragraphs to this chapter outlined the few facts known about the 18th-century buildings on or near the site of the present Three Tuns and Nos. 54 & 56 Tranquil Vale.

In 1780 a building on the site of Headly's house is noted in the Land Tax returns as being held by Thomas Roberts and assessed at 12/-. Roberts is a curious but somewhat shadowy figure in Blackheath history. He was a builder, according to a lease of 1802, and held the Three Tuns house until 1788. In that year he signed a lease for a building on the site of the Princess of Wales public house at the east end of Montpelier Row. Because there is no evidence that he was a publican the author can only assume that his interest was as speculator, rescuing or redeveloping ancient and ruinous buildings, possibly for his own occupation.

Be that as it may, Roberts was replaced at the Three Tuns by John Harmsworth, who was a publican and remained here until 1800. During his tenancy the Dartmouth estate granted a lease on the Three Tuns by name on October 1 1791 to Richard Price and Abraham Constable, brewers, of Lewisham, for 31 years until 1822.

Abraham Constable was related to Michael and John Constable, millers, who had been in business as early as 1795 in Blackheath Vale and may have laid the foundations of the Blackheath Brewery which survived in the Vale until the 1870s. The Three Tuns lessees, Constable and Price, were probably linked commercially with two companies of brewers: Price and Jenkins of Church Street, Deptford; and Constable and Fordham of Lewisham. The latter's successors still hold the Three Tuns but by 1808 the Deptford company was known as Benjamin Price and Sarah Jenkins and listed as at Church Lane.

When Headly's house was re-built is not recorded but the plan attached to the 1791 lease shows a building the same shape as that on the 1843 map accompanying the tithe schedules for the Parish of Lewisham. It was a three-storeyed house, weather-boarded at the front with a cobbled passage-way through the middle leading to stables and a coach house at the rear. The Tuns would not have been a coaching inn, but it would certainly have boasted livery stables and been used by local carriers and horse bus proprietors as a pick-up point.

During the 19th century the Three Tuns was the principal village pub, much used by the local working men and shopkeepers. It was successful largely because of the continuity of its landlords, only two families from 1800 to 1884, under the overall control of the brewers who held the lease.

The Price and Constable lease was renewed in 1822 for a further 31 years, but this time the lessee was William James Steward & Co., who had taken over the Lewisham brewers sometime in the early years of the 19th century. By 1832 Steward had been joined by George Eagles Marsden but by 1837 the company was trading as Marsden and Nicholls at the Anchor Brewery on the Lewisham Road. Marsden controlled other local pubs including the Hare and Billett at Grotes Place, the Dukes Head at Dartmouth Row and

The George, which stood just north of Vanbrugh Castle on Maze Hill until 1905. By 1845 the brewery passed to the sole proprietorship of the brothers Harry and Vincent Nicholls and the company held leases on a large number of licenced houses making it inevitable that they would be taken over by one of the giant breweries. As early as 1877 the Three Tuns was selling Bass & Co. ales and when the house was re-built in 1885 it was as a Charrinton's pub.

But the character of a pub then, as now, was mostly created by the resident landlord and the success of the Tuns must be credited to the Ellisons and the Pounds.

In 1800 the licence of the Three Tuns passed from John Harmsworth to Timothy Ellison (1766-1834) and he, with his wife, Jane, were landlords there until 1824 by which time Timothy was also the landlord of the Hare and Billett, possibly with his brother Charles Moody Ellison as resident manager at that house. Timothy Ellison remained at the Hare and Billett until about 1830 but he retired to a house in Phoenix Place (q.v.) by 1832 and died there two years later.

His successor at the Tuns in 1824 was Thomas Pound (1785-1853) and he, his widow and his son William, held the licence here until 1884. Thomas encouraged trade by offering rooms for dinners and sports' clubs, provided facilities for carriers and horse buses and was no doubt instrumental in the development of the ground at the back of the pub for stabling and other commercial purposes. On his death the licence was transferred to his wife, Sarah, but in 1856 it had been assigned to his son William (1823-?1880). Thomas Pound's third son, John, became a builder and was the owner of brick fields in Burnt Ash Lane by the 1850s. He left his mark on Blackheath with various groups of buildings including some on the west side of Montpelier Vale and many of the houses on the north side of St. John's Park.

It cannot be denied that during William Pound's time the Three Tuns was not the most salubrious of hostelries. It became the haunt of the riff-raff after fairs and other entertainments on the Heath and the large crowds which congregated outside its doors would attract pick-pockets and cheats. In 1877 there was a riot in which 30 "roughs" fought a pitched battle with the police and more than 120 were involved. Despite these events there seems to have been no trouble in the renewal of the licence from year to year, perhaps because the Tuns was an essential part of the ordinary working life of the Village, with its slate clubs, dining room and livery stables, as well as its provision of Bass ales and Nicholls Entire.

The Dartmouth estate had readily granted a new lease in 1854 for 21 years, but when that expired the pub, along with other buildings in Tranquil Vale, was somewhat seedy, and the 1874 renewal was for a term of only ten years.

The old pub closed towards the end of 1884 and was torn down during the winter of 1884-85 along with the buildings on the site of the present 54 and 56 Tranquil Vale.

The re-building started in May 1885 and proceeded with a speed which was to cause disaster. In the July of that year the coping stones were added to brick work which was still green, and a cornice crumbled over, killing a stone mason and a labourer. The new design must have been a poor one for in 1892 and 1893 substantial alterations had to be effected to improve the usefulness of the building. Those of 1893 were made to cash in on the boom for billiards and the then proprietor, Charles Mead, added 500 sq. ft. of new cellarage, removed the tap room and passage and substituted a new public bar and a new dining room bar at the rear. The corner bar on the right of the main entrance was converted to a wine office with a separate entrance from the passage way next to No. 50 Tranquil Vale.

Mead's principal delight was his billiard saloon, 45ft. by 30ft. and 39ft. high with 60 sq. ft. of sky-light over each table, stained glass windows, and decorated with "flowering shrubs and fruit-bearing trees". A professional manager was engaged and exhibition matches by champions of the sport were arranged to encourage the customers.

Another change made by Mead was the renaming of the pub - he called it the Blackheath Distillery - but it is unlikely that any distilling took place here and the old name held.

Despite these changes, the installation of electric light in 1899, and other improvements, the Three Tuns lost much of its charm and character with the re-building, and there were frequent changes in landlord, some not staying more than a year or two. But whatever the state of its fortunes or popularity the Three Tuns is a link, perhaps the only link left in a chain which stretches back to the Blackheath Village of the early 18th century.

Landlords of the Three Tuns

The names before 1789 were tenants of a house on or near the site of the present Three Tuns but may not have been licencees of a public house.

?1719-1737	Richardson Headly (fl 1690-1737)
-1739	Richard Headly
-1739	Elizabeth Collett (d. 1739)
-1744	John Maplesden (d. 1744)
1780-1788	Thomas Roberts
1789-1800	James Harmsworth
1800-1824	Timothy Ellison (1766-1834)
1824-1853	Thomas Pound (1785-1853)
1854-1855	Sarah Pound
1856-1880	William Pound (fl 1823-1880)
1880	Thomas James Woolf
1882-1886	Edmund Charles Broom
1887-1891	William Frederick Walton
1892	George Thomas Riddall
1893-1894	Charles Mead
1895	W. J. Martin
1896	Robert Alexander Davy
1899	Henry Charles Collins
1901-1907	Jacob Traseger
1908-1910	Edward Hammett Osman
1912	Arthur Barker
1914	Thomas David Robert
1915-1917	Christopher Andrews
1921-1923	Walter Harris
1924-1930	Arthur Gregory
1931-1934	Victor Hope Cave
1935-1938	William F. Rogers
1965-1968	Douglas Seager
1969-1976-	Henry Charles Kaye and Gerald Robert Tuck

54 & 56 Tranquil Vale

The Three Tuns lease plan of 1791 shows nothing on this site except a small building facing into Tranquil Passage. Subsequently, larger buildings were erected here, principally as the coach house and stables for the public house. Whether these were later converted into shops on the Tranquil Vale frontage or were totally re-built in the 1820s is not known. Certainly the buildings revealed by the careful examination of photographs taken in the late 1860s or 1870s show that there were two substantial shops here and they may have been contemporary with the 1822 development to the south of the Three Tuns.

Their initial use was by builders, coopers and blacksmiths, but by the 1850s No. 56 had been converted into a bakery. The ground plan of the two buildings changed considerably over the years: in the 1840s No. 54 held a large workshop with a frontage on to Tranquil Passage, to the east of which were two small cottages. By the late 1860s the cottages had gone and the workshop had been split, the Tranquil Passage frontage being part of No. 56 Tranquil Vale. In 1871 the present 6 & 7 Tranquil Passage were built on the site of the two cottages mentioned above, and were held on the same lease as that for No. 54 Tranquil Vale.

Re-development would almost certainly have taken place with the expiry of the leases in 1883 but the process was confirmed in 1882 when No. 56 was gutted by fire.

Because the early buildings were held on the same lease as the Three Tuns by William Steward and his successors, no accurate details have come down of his sub-tenants. But from the late 1830s it is possible to allot tenants from information in the commercial directories and census returns.

54 Tranquil Vale (was 10 Tranquil Vale)

In 1822 the building on this site was a coach house attached to the Three Tuns, there was a dung pit at the back and a door leading to the stable yard behind the public house.

By 1835 the coach house had been turned into a cooperage, in the hands of William Chapman whose principal place of business was 66 Tranquil Vale (q. v.). It is possible that Chapman's predecessor at No. 54 was John Armstrong, also a cooper of Tranquil Vale, but this cannot be proved. Chapman remained here until the late 1840s and by this time the building had been sufficiently altered to make it suitable for domestic use; the tenant in 1851 was George Walton, a blacksmith.

In 1853 the Dartmouth Estate issued new leases for the Three Tuns site and the outbuildings, but this time No. 52 was afforded its own lease which was granted to William Neale, a Greenwich builder with premises in South Street. Neale (d. 1854) named his son William and because there are so few records of the family it is not possible to be sure which Neale was the leaseholder after William snrs death; also there was a dispute over his estate between his son and the widow, Anne Elizabeth.

Possibly as result of this rancour the shop was let to Mrs. Elizabeth Randle (or Randall) an upholstress, and her husband William, a cabinet maker, during the early 1860s although the name Neale & Sons remained over the door for some years thereafter.

In 1869 the premises were rented by Henry Dry (1835-1920) and Edward Norman, carpenters and builders, and in 1872 the lease on the shop was assigned to Edward Norman. Henry Dry left the partnership in 1870 and set up a carpenter's shop in Royal Parade, eventually earning a high reputation as carpentry instructor at the Blackheath Proprietary School and the Royal Naval School at New Cross.

Edward Norman stayed at 54 Tranquil Vale until 1875 and by the following year the lease had been assigned to John Urell. He sub-let the premises to James Mead, another cabinet maker and carpenter who stayed here until 1901 having taken on the responsibility for building the present shop on the site of the old coachhouse in 1884-5. Although the new building, integral with No. 56, was an imposing structure compared with the old premises, its most valuable use must have been residential. The shop, although large, did not attract the trades which might have benefited from the generous floor space. After its use as an upholsterer's work shop in the early years of this century, it was taken from 1910 to 1914 by a Mrs. Boydell, a print seller, working in concert with Arthur Rayner, a picture restorer.

In 1915 the whole shop was leased as a receiving office by Arthur S. Barton, trading as the Reliance Laundry, which kept this name until 1954. After a brief spell as a furniture showroom the premises were acquired by David Rae, turf accountants, and opened as a betting shop in October 1962. The application for a licence for this betting shop was the subject of fierce controversy in Blackheath and the view was expressed that such an institution was "out of character with the district". Counter petitions by enthusiastic punters helped ensure the establishment of the betting shop and it remains to this day.

56 Tranquil Vale (was 11 Tranquil Vale)

When No. 54 was the coachhouse for the Three Tuns, this site was the stables, but by 1838 new arrangements had put the horses elsewhere, probably in stalls behind the pub, and the old stables were taken over by William Green Pinhey (1795-1859). Pinhey was a builder, operating on a large scale and employing more than 30 men in the 1840s, and was responsible for much of the development of the Lee Park and Dacre Park estates in the early 1850s. He was the occupier of No. 56 from before 1837 until 1859 but by 1850 he had sub-let the frontage at Tranquil Vale, initially to William Short, a grocer, but in 1852 to Samuel Thynne, a baker and confectioner who traded from here until 1882. Pinhey obtained a new lease on the whole premises in 1853 for a further 31 years but after his death in 1859 the business passed to his son William Fox Pinhey (1856-1929) who moved the company elsewhere. Eventually Pinhey's lease was assigned to Edward Tompson but he remained no more than a landlord to Samuel Thynne (1811-1882) until the 1853 lease expired. The re-development was encouraged not only by the expiry of the lease but also by a fire which in 1882 gutted the old bake shop and may have been started in the ovens. Thynne's business passed to his son, Arthur, who re-opened the bakery at the then newly-built 44 Tranquil Vale in 1884.

When the re-built No. 56 Tranquil Vale was completed it was leased by Robert Lewis as the Tranquil Coffee and Dining Rooms. Lewis had owned a small café in Tranquil Passage in the early 1880s, one of the first of its kind in Blackheath, and his move in 1884 to the larger premises gave him the opportunity to cater for club dinners, socials and masonic meetings. His restaurant passed to Richard Hurst in 1904 and through a succession of proprietors until the late 1950s, providing rather solid plain cooking of the type demanded by working men. In 1962 the style changed and it became the Top Hat restaurant and delicatessen and a continental influence tinged the cooking. But by the end of the 1960s this venture closed. In recent years the old dining rooms has been refitted as an antique shop; the bow-windowed extension at the rear, fronting on to Tranquil Passage, being built in 1975.

ii Tranquil Place

58-74 Tranquil Vale

The buildings presently numbered 58 to 74 Tranquil Vale are, in part, the oldest surviving structures on the east side of Tranquil Vale and some of the oldest in Blackheath Village. Their mid-Victorian shop fronts and the overpowering out-of-character block known as Highland House (72-74 Tranquil Vale) have obscured the qualities of the terrace but the observer who stands on the west side of Tranquil Vale and looks at Nos. 66 & 68, or who views these same buildings from the rear in Brigade Street, will see certain signs of their antiquity.

It is likely that this group were built as early as 1799 and are nearly contemporary with Nos. 23-35 Tranquil Vale. Originally there were five dwellings here but by the 1840s all but the northernmost house had been divided into two, thus creating the nine basic premises that can be identified today. By the end of the 19th century Nos. 66 and 68 had each been split into two half shops but in recent years No. 66 has been converted back single unit.

During 1879 a new lease was granted for Nos. 1-3 Tranquil Place (74-70 Tranquil Vale) and the opportunity taken to demolish the original houses and build a four-storey mansion block - Highland House.

These factors, added to the complexities raised by the various leases granted during the 19th century, make it difficult to keep the historical narrative straightforward.

To aid the reader a table is given showing the change in street numbering in the 19th century, simple lease details and assignments. On the following pages is a list of the tenants of the original five houses from about 1800 to 1832; thereafter each building is dealt with separately as it was from about 1840 to the present day - as nine retail units.

Tranquil Place before 1840

The five-house terrace making up Tranquil Place seems to have been built between 1799 and 1805 - certainly not earlier and certainly no later. This doubt is because the only surviving record of the period is to be found in the Land Tax returns which show two of the houses (Nos. 2 & 5 - now 70 & 72 and 58 & 60 Tranquil Vale) in existence by 1799; No. 1 (74 Tranquil Vale) first appears in the tax returns in 1800; No. 3 (66 & 68 Tranquil Vale) in 1802; and No. 4 (62 & 64 Tranquil Vale) in 1805.

This does not necessarily mean that the houses were built at different times and the variation in dates may mean that some of the properties remained empty for a period or that the tenant of one may have paid the tax on more than the one property. No. 1 Tranquil Place may not have been part of the terrace originally but as the only known illustration of this

The development of Tranquil Place

Present style	1878-1885	1871	1851	1840
74a Tranquil Vale				
74 Tranquil Vale	1 Tranquil Place	1 Tranquil Vale	8 Tranquil Place	1 Tranquil Place
72 Tranquil Vale	2 Tranquil Place	2 Tranquil Vale	7 Tranquil Place	2 Tranquil Place
70 Tranquil Vale	3 Tranquil Place	3 Tranquil Vale	6 Tranquil Place	2 Tranquil Place
68 Tranquil Vale	4 Tranquil Place	4 Tranquil Vale	5 Tranquil Place	3 Tranquil Place
66 Tranquil Vale	5 Tranquil Place	5 Tranquil Vale	4 Tranquil Place	3 Tranquil Place
64 Tranquil Vale	6 Tranquil Place	6 Tranquil Vale	3 Tranquil Place	4 Tranquil Place
62 Tranquil Vale	7 Tranquil Place	7 Tranquil Vale	2 Tranquil Place	4 Tranquil Place
60 Tranquil Vale	8 Tranquil Place	8 Tranquil Vale	1 Tranquil Place	5 Tranquil Place
58 Tranquil Vale	9 Tranquil Place	9 Tranquil Vale	1 Tranquil Place	5 Tranquil Place

Demised to T.E. Couchman 25 March 1879 for Highland House ex 1-3 Tranquil Place. 99 year lease from 25 March 1879 to T.E. Couchman on 4-7 Tranquil Place.

Leases on Tranquil Place

Present style		Lease equivalent	Lease details
74 Tranquil Vale	}	= 1 Tranquil Place	Lease to Joseph Russell 31 years from 29 September 1840.
72 Tranquil Vale			
70 Tranquil Place		= 2 Tranquil Place	New lease to George Hockley as 1-5 Tranquil Place 14 years from 25 March 1865.
68 Tranquil Place	}	= 3 Tranquil Place	
66 Tranquil Place			
64 Tranquil Place	}	= 4 Tranquil Place	Lease to Peter Stepney 31 years from 29 September 1839.
62 Tranquil Vale			
60 Tranquil Vale	}	= 5 Tranquil Place	Lease to William Seager 31 years from 29 September 1840. Lease as 8 & 9 Tranquil Place to S. Riddington for 93 years from 29 September 1877.
58 Tranquil Vale			

building shows but part of the structure, we cannot be sure. From the start these houses were in domestic use although No. 2 may have been a bakery; but by the 1830s most had become shops, in which state they have remained.

Soon after the granting of the 1839 and 1840 leases Nos. 2, 3 and 4 Tranquil Place were divided into double shop units and the street numbers changed from 1-5 Tranquil Place to 1-8 Tranquil Place.

Sometime between 1875 and the 1890s, possibly as the result of the new leases granted to Riddington and Couchman in 1879 and the subsequent demolition of Nos. 1 & 2 Tranquil Place, the small windows on the roof line were re-modelled to their present style and, no doubt, the roofs were re-slated. Nos. 8 & 9 (now 60 & 58 Tranquil Vale) were more drastically altered and embellished and the windows changed from simple casements to three part lancets, in the style then popular on new buildings elsewhere in the district.

Despite these changes much of the old Tranquil Place has survived.

Prior to the granting of the leases in 1839 and 1840 the only reliable record of tenancies for these buildings will be found in the Land Tax returns. Unfortunately, the Land Tax was not always paid by the tenant and it was possible to redeem one's Land Tax obligation; thus for quite lengthy periods the names are repeated from year to year. But as this is the only information we have it is a useful guideline, and tenancies can sometimes be confirmed from other sources.

To avoid making a complicated matter more complicated the Land Tax tenancies for the 5 house terrace from about 1800 to 1832 are given below. This is followed by notes on the occupiers of the individual houses, but using their present numbers.

Tranquil Place tenancies 1800-1832

No. 1 (now 74 Tranquil Vale)

1803-1823	Mr. Dickens
1824	Mr. Dixon
1825-1832	Charles Brown, butcher

No. 2 (now 70 & 72 Tranquil Vale)

| 1800-1826 | Mrs. Bolt, possibly Mrs. Louisa Bolt, baker |
| 1827-1832 | Peter Stepney, bootmaker |

No. 3 (now 66 & 68 Tranquil Vale)

1802-1803	Joseph Wheeler
1804	Mr. Bailey
1805	Captain Cole
1807	Captain W. Brentford
1808	W. Brentford "or occupier"
1809-1824	Mr. Barrett
1825-1827	Mr. Morton
1828	Mr. Orsley
1829	Mr. Knight
1830-1832	Mr. Lowton

No. 4 (now 62 & 64 Tranquil Vale)

1805	Mrs. Manning
1806-1808	Mrs. Inglefield
1809-1832	Mrs. Major

No. 5 (now 58 & 60 Tranquil Vale)

1800-1806	James May
1808-1824	Mr. Harris
1825	Mr. Walker
1826	Mr. Hart, baker
1827-1832	Mr. Duncan

Tranquil Place from 1840 to the present day

The following pages contain information on the tenancies of the shops as they are numbered at present. Readers who are interested should refer to the table on page 155 for earlier designations and house numbers.

58 Tranquil Vale

This house was allied to No. 60 Tranquil Vale and, for many years, the lease embraced the two cottages at the rear fronting on to Tranquil Passage. Although William Seager (1801-1857), the builder, obtained the head lease in 1840 he had been the tenant here since 1832. Business success allowed him to move his home to 18 Montpelier Row before the 1850s and the shop and house at Tranquil Place were sub-let to a succession of tradesmen, principally grocers or greengrocers. In 1851 the occupier was William Short, a grocer; by 1855 there was the first in a line of greengrocers which lasted until 1878; in 1858, G. King; 1860-1874, George Smith; and from 1876 to 1878, John Henry Soper, by whose time the head lease had passed from the Seager family to Edward Tompson, a lawyer of Lincolns Inn.

In 1878 both head lessor and tenant changed. The new 93 year lease had been granted to Stephen Riddington (1811-1882), the baker of 9 Blackheath Village (q.v.) and brother of Joseph Riddington (1815-1873), the butcher at No. 60 Tranquil Vale (q.v.). Riddington's tenants initially were butchers: Heron Rawlings from 1878, and George Hutchinson in 1881-1882, but in 1885 the shop had passed to Mrs. Sarah Morley as an art needlework shop and had been re-named Appleton House. The Morley family worked from here until 1897 when their lease expired; they were directly related to the Morleys who traded as music and piano dealers at 45 Tranquil Vale (q.v.) from 1861 to 1888 and at 23 Tranquil Vale from 1888 to 1942. Two other Morley ladies were closely involved in the needlework shop: Mrs. Matilda Elizabeth Morley (1837-1909) and Emily Jane Morley (fl.1870-1925) a distinguished needlewoman who taught fine craft work at the Blackheath School of Art, in Lee Road, from 1898 until her death.

After the Morley's departure the shop remained empty for some years but in 1901 it was leased by Rawlings Bros., one of the many new companies in the early years of this century offering their skills as electrical engineers. They remained here until about 1905 when the shop was acquired by Symon and Patterson, who made blouses.

In 1912 and 1913 the premises were empty and there was some difficulty in finding a buyer but in 1914 the head lease was taken by Mr. & Mrs. E.R. Rayner, print sellers and picture restorers, although Mrs. Rayner traded as Mrs. E.R. Boydell from 1916 to 1921. It was in the 1920s that, for a few years, No. 58 was reunited with No. 60, as it had been in the early years of the 19th century. The tenant then was trading as "Phyllis, gowns and knitted wear" who, encouraged by her success at No. 60, took over a rival business, Royalties, then at No. 58. But by 1933 the shops had split once more, the gown shop remaining at No. 58 until the last war.

During the late 1940s and early 1950s these were premises of a poster and signboard company but by 1956 had been taken by E. Minassian, an oriental carpet dealer who used the shop for the sale of curios. It is with this name and use that the shop is trading presently.

60 Tranquil Vale

By 1845 William Seager had divided 5 Tranquil Place into two units which became 8 & 9 Tranquil Place. No. 8 (now 60 Tranquil Vale) was let to Joseph Riddington (1815-1873) as a butcher's shop. Riddington, who was born at Colnbrook, Bucks, was the younger brother of Stephen Riddington (1811-1882) the baker who had extended his trade into the Village in 1859 at 9 Blackheath Village (q.v.). Joseph was content to remain in business in a small way and stayed at Tranquil Place until his death in 1873, after which his widow took over running the shop until about 1876.

A new lease (allied to No. 58 Tranquil Vale) was granted to Stephen Riddington in 1877 who, the following year, let the premises as a fancy repository to Messrs Strachan and Songest. In 1880 the shop, titled Murillo House, was leased by the Misses Marianne and Emily Frame as an art materials shop and, appropriately, picture frame makers. In 1899 they took over No. 62 Tranquil Vale, trading from both until 1907 when the business was sold. The new tenant did not occupy No. 60 and this shop remained empty for many years, not being used until 1914. In that year the premises were taken by a Mrs. Shattock, a "wardrobe dealer" - in other words, second hand clothes - and in 1916 the business was taken over by Mrs. Florence Root who called the company "Royalties". This name held until 1932 but the proprietors changed periodically and the emphasis moved away from the dress agency trade to concentrate on tailor made costumes, latterly as Phyllis' gown shop at No. 58 Tranquil Vale embracing the Royalties tradename in 1929.

From 1933 to 1936 the shop became an estate agency, called Martin & Co., and from 1936 to 1938 it was held by Arthur Dill & Company, Ltd., builders and decorators. In October that year the premises took on its present use when it was leased to C.S. Russell, as a barber's shop. Russell remained here until 1959 and the business then passed to Edwin J. Bray, who was still cutting gentlemen's hair here at the time of writing, the last working barber in Blackheath Village, stoutly resisting the change in hairdressing habits.

62 Tranquil Vale

This shop, initially linked with No. 64, was leased to Peter Stepney, a shoemaker, for 31 years from 29 September 1839. It has not been possible to trace the occupants of No. 62 between 1832 and 1850 and this may indicate that the two units were not then separated. By 1849 No. 62 was occupied by a Mr. Hope, a boot and shoe maker and possibly Stepney's business successor. His tenancy was not to last long as the shop was consumed by fire in January 1850, the damage extending to Riddington's shop at No. 60 and to the Wesleyan chapel at the rear. After rebuilding the premises were leased to Miss Martha Littell for a fancy and Berlin wool repository and this trade remained here until 1868 but in the proprietor-ship of Martha and Johnson Brooks from about 1860 and Mrs. E. Roberts from about 1865.

In 1870 the premises were rented as a bible and tract depot, initially under the control of James Manchee, but also involving a Capt. Gordon Rippon and, from 1880 to 1899 William Coultas and Sarah Ann Andrews (1832-1917). Considering the strong religious bias in the bookstock at Burnside's (20 Tranquil Vale, q.v.) it is remarkable that the Village could support a religious bookshop even in those evangelical days.

To help with the rent, part of the premises were let to a succession of dressmakers. In 1899 the tract depot closed and the shop was acquired as a stationers by the Misses Frame, then trading as picture framers and art materials suppliers at 60 Tranquil Vale. In 1907 they sold the business at No. 62 to A.R. Knight and Co., who in turn passed it on to Harry Ernest Smith who traded from here from 1917 to 1930 as a picture framer.

During the early 1930s the shop was empty but in 1932 it was acquired by the present proprietors, Messrs A. Steward, as a greengrocery.

The Wesleyan Chapel

Before 1847 the headlease on Nos. 62 and 64 Tranquil Vale was assigned to Thomas Allen, a solicitor with strong Methodist leanings. He was a member of the small congregation of Wesleyan Methodists who met in one of the cottages in Phoenix Row (or Vale) facing the Heath and who had used that house for its church since 1814. The growth of the movement soon made it imperative for them to find larger premises and Allen offered them the garden ground of his house at 62 Tranquil Vale and paid for the erection of a chapel there in 1847. It seated 400 and must have been a major advance for their cause, but it was sited hard up against buildings in Tranquil Passage and what became Brigade Street and some parts of these were not particularly healthy.

The building survived for less than 20 years, mainly because it was outgrown by its congregation. In 1863 the foundation stone for a new Wes-leyan chapel was laid on a site in Blackheath Grove - and the new building would not only seat 1000 worshippers but was enhanced by schoolrooms and a parsonage. The Tranquil Vale chapel remained until 1866, when it was demolished along with the tumbledown and pestilence-ridden houses at the rear, but the entrance door in Tranquil Vale (marked as No. 62) remains to this day.

64 Tranquil Vale

The earliest known commercial tenant of these premises was William John Hunter (1820-c1860), a plumber and glazier who was here by 1847. In 1855 the tenant is shown in commercial directories as Charles John Hudson, plumber, but as Mrs. Emma Hunter was the proprietress of the business from at least 1858 to about 1862 there is a possibility that the Hudson reference was a mis-print.

Thereafter there have been a wide variety of tenants and trades here. It would serve no useful purpose to list every name but the principal users were Henry Jeffery (1828-1891), a fishmonger of Blackheath Vale from 1870 to 1879; Mrs. Annie Jackson (1850-1929), an antique dealer, from 1888 to 1895 and who moved to 32 Tranquil Vale where the company traded until 1936; from 1905 to 1918 No. 64 was a café and ice cream parlour owned by Peter Angelinetta who later owned the café at No. 72 Tranquil Vale (q.v.).

Since 1920 the shop has been a ladies hairdressers, and used for the sale of clothes and antique furniture. Its present use, as an art gallery, is comparatively recent.

66 Tranquil Vale

This shop and, for a few years, No. 68 Tranquil Vale, was the Village cooperage, owned by the Chapman family who lived here from as early as 1835 up until 1882. The first known proprietor was William Chapman (c1796-1859) who was joined by his sons - principally William Thomas Chapman (1828-1868) - as working coopers. On the death of William Chapman jnr the business was sustained by his widow, Annie, but as time went on she concentrated more on selling brushes and baskets and less on barrels. So much so that in 1874 half the premises had been let to Robert Edward Gibbins, then trading as the Peacock Steam Dye Works, and no doubt he took over the old workshop at the rear. Gibbins was here until 1880 and in the same year the Misses Porter and Charlotte Elizabeth Hardcastle set up a baby linen warehouse at what was then 5a Tranquil Place (66a Tranquil Vale). In 1892 the other side of the shop was being used by bootmaker James Lawrence and for many years this pattern applied, with shoemakers on one side and drapers or milliners on the other. During the 1920s and 1930s the Corrie family occupied one or other of the half units following both dressmaking and bootmaking interests.

Because these units were small and, therefore, attracted low rents, the tenancies were brief and there seems little point in recording in detail the trail of antique dealers, second hand booksellers, florists, bakers and others who were in occupation often for little more than a year at a time.

After the 1939-1945 war the two halves were re-united for John Venner, a cabinet maker who occupied No. 66 from 1948 to 1965.

After Venner the premises were empty for some time but in the last two or three years have been used as a charity shop by Oxfam.

68 Tranquil Vale

This shop was linked with No. 66 Tranquil Vale in its early years and there is no record of a commercial tenant trading solely from No. 68 until 1848. In that year the premises were leased by William Post Ayres, a nurseryman and florist with a national reputation for his pelargoniums. His nursery ground was rented from the Brooklands estate to the south of Blackheath Park and from there he developed a thriving horticultural business.

In 1853 he went bankrupt and in the April his stock was sold at public auction in the hall of the Blackheath Literary Institution next to the railway station. For the next ten years his old shop was occupied by glass merchants, tailors, hairdressers and drapers, but by 1866 was taken by Mrs. Emma Hunter, the cooper's widow from No. 64 Tranquil Vale. Mrs. Hunter's new shop was devoted to the sale of drapery, a more ladylike occupation than the selling of barrels and casks, in which trade she had been occupied during her husband's lifetime.

Mrs. Hunter kept the shop until 1888 but before this date had sub-let one half of the retail space to Gibbins and Everden, dyers and cleaners. From about that date and until the 1939-1945 war No. 68 was held by dyers and cleaners, from 1901 trading as Johnson Bros., and 68a was taken by a succession of greengrocers, florists, grocers and tailors. In 1937 the proprietor was Madeline Moore, a florist, who was succeeded in 1952 by Mrs. Constance Macklin who kept her predecessor's trade name. Shortly after the last war the two half units were linked under one proprietor and No. 68 became the flower shop, and 68a a grocery and dairy - the situation which applies today.

70-74 Tranquil Vale

In 1879 Nos. 1-3 Tranquil Place (74, 72 & 70 Tranquil Vale respectively) were leased for re-development to T. E. Couchman. Why Couchman did not rebuild Nos. 62 to 68 Tranquil Vale at the same time as Nos. 70-74 is something of a mystery. Be that as it may, Couchman demolished Nos. 70-74 Tranquil Vale in 1879 and built a massive four storey block on the site which he named Highland House.

This was the first of the major redevelopments in Blackheath Village which, if it had continued, could easily have destroyed its entire early 19th-century character. Encouraged, no doubt, by the rapid development of other suburbs and the re-building of the inner suburbs, builders and speculators were anxious to replace small retail units and rows of two storey cottages with three, four and five storey blocks which could contain shops at ground level, office accommodation above and profitable flats on the top.

Blackheath Village suffered three such redevelopments - none absolutely necessary in that the buildings they replaced were neither antiquated nor worn out: Bank Buildings on the corner of Tranquil Vale and Blackheath Grove in 1888; Beaconsfield Buildings in Lee Road in 1883-1886; and Highland House. Highland Mansions (18-20 Tranquil Vale) built in 1903 could be placed in the same category.

Highland House was erected by Edward Banks, a builder from Lewisham, and was completed for occupation in 1881. When the block was completed its name was applied principally to the shops facing Tranquil Vale. The Royal Parade frontage was known at various times as Balmoral House or Belle Vue House, but in 1887 the nomenclature No. 17 Royal Parade was fixed.

70 Tranquil Vale

Before the rebuilding in 1879 this shop enjoyed only three tenants for more than 50 years. By 1827, when it was part of 2 Tranquil Place with No. 72 Tranquil Vale, it was used by Peter Stepney, the boot and shoemaker, and occupied by him until 1839 when the new lease was granted. Stepney

divided the shop into two parts, remaining at 72 Tranquil Vale and sub-
letting No. 70 to Charles Collings, a cornchandler who traded here until ·
the early 1840s. By 1850 the tenant was Samuel Hopkins, a cabinet maker
and upholsterer and he worked here until the building was cleared for
demolition in 1879.

The tenants in the new block, from 1882 up until the present day, have
always been hosiers and outfitters. Initially it was the partnership of
Elizabeth and Harriet Lance who were at No. 70 until 1893; they sold out to
Adelaide and S. Jekyll who in turn sold the business in 1899 to a lady trading
as Madame Lemare. All these ladies had, of course, sold women's
and children's clothing but in 1903 the shop was acquired by Charles Perry,
a gentlemen's hosier and outfitter and this emphasis has remained to the
present day. Charles Perry (1839-1922) had started his business as a very
young man in Woolwich in 1862. In 1887 he moved to Blackheath, becoming
one of the first tenants at Beaconsfield Buildings (No. 11 Lee Road). In
1903 he sold his lease there to Messrs Hinds and Co., and moved to 70
Tranquil Vale where he continued in his business until his death at the age
of 83 - a working life of 60 years as his own master. The shop continued to
bear his name until 1935, trading as Perry & Sons, then as Perry & Co.
but it was taken over by Arthur John Wakelin in 1933 and by 1936 was trading
in this name. The business passed to his son, John Wakelin, and at the
time of writing trades as Bulmer and Wakelin - a span of 94 years as an
outfitter's shop.

72 Tranquil Vale

After Peter Stepney had left these premises there is a gap in the record
from 1840 to 1846, although the original house on this site may have been
the workshop of William Suter, a smith and ironmonger, in 1845. Certainly
by the following year, John Patman, a Suffolk-born blacksmith, had his
forge here and seems to have been the only smith in the Village not attached
to a particular livery stable. He had worked at 24 or 26 Montpelier Vale in
the late 1830s and 1840s but had left Blackheath by 1855 when the workshop
at 72 Tranquil Vale had been leased by William Short (1825-1880) a grocer
and cheesemonger. Short stayed here until the building was demolished
and his stock and fittings were sold in March 1879.

The new shop was taken by Thomas Mills & Co., tailors and outfitters,
who specialised in servants' liveries and uniforms. The company had been
established by the brothers Thomas and George Mills at Green End in
Woolwich in 1851 and their Blackheath shop was put into the hands of a
manager, Frank Smith. He looked after the Mills Bros. interests until
1895 at which date Smith (fl 1860-1922) bought out the branch at 72 Tranquil
Vale and traded on his own account here until 1904. In that year he moved
his business to 18 Tranquil Vale where a branch had been established in
1899 when he took over part of the Bond/Birdseye company. No. 18 Tranquil Vale was rebuilt in 1904 and Smith then gave up the shop at 72 Tranquil
Vale.

It was linked for a few years with Carson's Bazaar at 74 Tranquil Vale
(q.v.) but was eventually acquired by Peter Angelinetta, the cafe proprietor
from 64 Tranquil Vale (q.v.) and he managed the Café Como here up until
the beginning of the 1939-1945 war. The premises remained a café - of an
inexpensive kind - until 1970 when it was re-fitted as the Indian restaurant

it is now.

74 Tranquil Vale

The original early 19th-century building on this site is shown in the Land Tax returns as being held by Charles Brown, a butcher, from 1826 to 1832 At the same time the commercial directories list James Russell, a builder and carpenter in Tranquil Vale. The Russell family had established their reputation locally early in the 19th century and it is known that James' son, Joseph Russell, was in business at 1 Tranquil Place in 1838. The tithe schedule map of 1843 shows a substantial building at the rear of the shop and it is not unlikely that this was the builder's store and yard and that for a few years at least, the front was used for the butcher's premises.

Joseph Russell (1813-1874) was responsible for developing much of Granville Park and Vanbrugh Park, working from 74 Tranquil Vale until 1847 when he moved to the Manor House at Vanbrugh Fields.

He sold his business to George Willmot (1809-1859) in June 1847 but retained the head lease on this shop and Nos. 66-72 as well until 1863 when the unexpired portion was assigned to one George Hockley, but in the form of a new lease to run for 14 years from 1865. Before that, Willmot had died and in September 1859 his stock was sold at auction for the benefit of his widow, the daughter of George Weedon Bennett of 28 Tranquil Vale (q.v.) whom he married in 1850.

His successor was not a builder, but Henry Edward Thompson (1823-1892) a window blind maker who was to stay at 1 Tranquil Place until its demolition on the expiry of the lease in 1879, although the shop had to be rebuilt in July 1862 after a bad fire. Thompson moved to High House in Montpelier Row, on the east side of the Princess of Wales public house, and the business was continued by his son, Henry John Thompson, until 1917.

When Highland House was built, No. 74 Tranquil Vale was leased by William Carson for a toy shop and fancy bazaar. It became known as Carson's Bazaar and the shop as Carson's Corner, for it was clearly a well-loved toyshop in the Village and with the closure of the Blackheath Bazaar at 32 Tranquil Vale in 1892 was without rivals of any significance. Carson remained here until 1913 and in that year the company moved down the hill to No. 42 Tranquil Vale, where the name stayed over the shop until 1930.

Curiously, although Carson's Corner was a prime trading site in the Village it remained empty throughout the Great War and it was not until 1920 that it re-opened, this time as a second hand furniture shop owned by John Kelly. From 1927 to the early 1940s the corner section of the premises were used by Miss M. Davis for the sale of lingerie, but the Royal Parade frontage was held by Mary and Hilda Skinner from 1925 to 1935 as an arts and crafts showroom, this slip of a shop remaining a separate premises until the 1960s, used principally for antiques by Mr. & Mrs. E.A. Parker.

In 1949 No. 74 was leased by Jameson Benbrook for an antiquarian bookshop. After three years he sold the business to the Misses Atkins and Korn who built up a steady trade until they retired in 1962. Their successor was Mrs. May Roberts but in 1970 she sold the business to her manager, Louis Leff, and he remains proprietor to this day.

These premises are included in this section because they are an integral part of Highland House, although it is numbered as part of Royal Parade and has been since 1887.

There were two short-lived ventures here: the first was an artificial flower business run by one Benjamin Brain from 1885 to 1887; the second was Madame Henrietta Rosen's millinery shop which she called Belle Vue House from 1887 to 1888.

In 1890 the shop was re-opened as confectioners and tea-rooms, in which use it remains today. The first proprietor was W. Ellis, who claimed to be a French and English confectioner, and he was followed by a succession of owners, all following the same trade, until 1904 when the restaurant took the name Christy's Tea Rooms and boasted of its agency for Fuller's American confectionery. The name has been kept for more than 70 years although the proprietors have changed a number of times, and it is now known as Chrysty's Patisserie. Only one proprietor stayed here for a long period, Mrs. A.D. Brown (1878-1950) who owned Christy's from 1917 to 1947.

It would not be right to complete this history of Highland House without recording that the rooms above No. 74 Tranquil Vale have been used for ladies hairdressing since the 1920s.

12 The Village hamlets: Bath Place, Tranquil Passage and Camden Row

Although Blackheath Village developed in the early 19th century primarily as a string of houses and shops facing the main roads of Tranquil Vale and Montpelier Vale, a number of small communities grew up which were hidden behind the larger properties. They consisted of tight huddles of cottages, mostly wooden, usually occupied by labourers, artisans and washer-women. Because of poor sanitation and water supply they rapidly became unhealthy and were subject to clearance orders on health grounds from the 1850s onwards. Nevertheless, they have no small part in the history of the Village, for their existence demonstrates that even the most attractive and best-mannered communities could contain aspects which were, for the most part, no credit to their landlords. But it must be re-membered that the freeholders were not necessarily rapacious and exploitive men and that people in the early and mid 19th century would accept conditions which today we would find wholly intolerable. The law was on the side of the property owner, there were precious few regulations governing housing conditions, over-crowding and drainage, and the alternative to poor housing was no housing and reliance on parish relief, the workhouse and beggary.

There were five main groups of working mens' houses in or close to the Village of which the first three are dealt with in the following pages:

1. Bath Place, behind Montpelier Vale
2. Tranquil Passage
3. Camden Row
4. Blackheath Vale
5. Munro's Cottages, behind the Hare and Billet and on the east end of Eliot Place

Collins Square, most of which had been re-developed by the mid 19th century, and Phoenix Vale (Washerwoman's Row), demolished for Royal Parade, are described elsewhere. Blackheath Vale is covered in a separate chapter.

Bath Place

Until the development of Wemyss Road along its present course in 1880 it was possible to travel only a few yards along the road leading east from Montpelier Vale before the traveller came to the gardens and meadows held by the owners of Nos. 22 and 23 Montpelier Row. But at the end of this short roadway, in a dell to the south, was a cluster of cottages known as Bath Place. Some of the cottages were cleared by the end of the 1880s for the Express Dairy bottling depot but those in the bottom of the dell, behind the Wesleyan church, survived until 1939 when they were demolished on health grounds by the then Lewisham Borough Council. Had Lewisham not had the clearance order confirmed the cottages here would certainly have been razed by the V2 rocket which hit this section of the Village in March 1945.

The origins of the Bath Place houses are obscure. In 1798 the Land Tax returns show that a Mr. Dyer was the owner of four cottages in the locality described above and situated on John Cator's freehold. We know that much of Montpelier Row had been built by that date so it is probable that independent small trades would have been attracted to Blackheath by that development. But it is unlikely that the Bath Place cottages would have been built for servants as the large houses would have been serviced by resident staff.

Be that as it may, the number of dwellings grew and by the 1840s a small hamlet of 19 houses had been established. But in the early years of the 19th century development had proceeded along Montpelier Vale so that the Bath Place cottages were hidden from view by the 1820s or earlier. The 1841 census returns and other records show that there were two houses called 1 & 2 Ledgers Place (probably a tenant's name) roughly on the outside of the bend of the present route of Wemyss Road; on the dairy depot site were three houses called 1-3 Upper Bath Place; and at the bottom of what is now the service road behind Montpelier Vale were nine cottages, six in a terrace, called Bath Place, although the detached dwellings were sometimes known as 4 & 5 Upper Bath Place.

The name Bath Place first appears in commercial directories and other records in the 1830s and may have been adopted because of its proximity to John Hally's "commodious" swimming bath, fashioned from an overflow pond on the Upper Kid Brooke in 1836, but this is only conjecture, for the appellation 'Bath' was not uncommon for groups of cottages in the early 19th century.

The Bath Place houses soon became the homes of the labouring poor, the gardeners, laundresses and charwomen, matched by the tiny courts of Camden Row (q.v.) at the top of Tranquil Vale, Phoenix Passage in the heart of the Village, and Munro's cottages between Grotes Place and Eliot Place. They were ill-drained and poorly-served for water supply, this being available only from a common pump in the roadway. The General Board of Health report in 1853 quoted Dr. William Carr (1814-1877) as saying that between July and September 1849 there had been four cholera deaths in Blackheath, "...two at a filthy spot called Bath Place...unfit for habitation except for Twentyman's and Smith's cottages."

It is worth noting that the two houses declared healthy were not, in fact, in Bath Place but on the north side of the road which led from Montpelier Vale to the cut, and both were occupied by schoolteachers. They stood on a strip of land subsequently developed for the present 24 Montpelier Row (Heath End) and the stable building which, since the last war, has been used as an Express Dairy Co. depot. By the 1830s there were three size-able houses here: nearest the Village was Montpelier Cottage, occupied in 1832 by a Lt. Cook RN, but by 1841 was being conducted as a boarding house by James Ite. Ite's son, a pupil at Colfe's School, died in 1849 and the family left the district, Montpelier Cottage passing to John Youens, a fly, cab and omnibus proprietor who owned one of the many two horse coaches which took businessmen to the City each day. His son continued the business from 1 Collins Street when Montpelier Cottage was pulled down in 1874.

To the south east stood a small house known as Vale Cottage, also tenanted as early as the 1830s, and occupied during the late 1840s and the 1850s by Sophie Twentyman (or Twinterman), a schoolmistress. This was also demolished in 1873-4, the last occupier being George B. Ive, a carpenter.

On the site of the dairy depot, on the elbow of the road, was a more substantial house than the others known as Bath Cottage - a misnomer, for it was quite large and stood in a reasonable garden. The only known tenant was Thomas Smith (1804-?1870) who was resident there from at least 1845 to 1866. As there is no mention of this property in the 1871 census return, it is likely that it had been demolished by that time. Smith was the headmaster of St. Michael's Church School which met at No. 5 Paragon Place from its foundation in 1846 until 1901 when, primarily as a result of the reorganisation of the state education system, it closed. Smith was succeeded in 1859 by James Allen (1837-1916) who remained in the job for 42 years, during which time he was never absent from the school for a single day.

With the building of a new main sewer in 1855 along the line of the Kid Brooke and the railway metals, the drainage of Bath Place must have improved dramatically, but the householders would have had to rely on the pump for fresh water for many more years after that.

With the development of Wemyss Road in 1879-1880 the three cottages of Upper Bath Place were numbered 1-3 Wemyss Road, but when the Express Country Milk Company arrived in the Village and leased No. 22 Montpelier Vale (q.v.) they also purchased Upper Bath Place and, by 1885, had demolished these for the new bottling depot and creamery. Ledger's Place fell to the pickaxe for Nos. 5 & 6 Wemyss Road.

The end of Bath Place came in February 1939 after a public inquiry into clearance orders for 2, 5 & 6 Bath Place and some houses in Paragon Place which confirmed the proposal. What was left survived, almost derelict, until March 1945 when Adolf Hitler's rocket engineers completed the task.

Camden Row

At the opposite side of the Village from Bath Place, in Tranquil Vale beyond the Crown Public House and hidden by Lamb's buildings (q.v.) is a small street of neat Victorian villas built in the mid-1890s. This is Camden Row, once a collection of 22 dwellings of wooden construction and the nearest any part of the Village got to a slum. Yet the demolition of these unsavoury houses was not achieved until the leases expired and the property was due to revert to the ground landlord, in this case the Dartmouth Estate.

In the 1790s the site had been dominated by Thomas Rashleigh's house, and this property and the development of Camden Place is described in the Chapter 9 (Tranquil Vale (West)). By 1798 a row of at least four dwellings had been erected to the north east of Rashleigh's house, facing the pathway behind the newly-erected Lamb's Buildings. They occupied part of what had been Rashleigh's garden and are recorded as the property of a Mrs. Gormey. One of the tenants was William Molineaux, a watch and clock maker and his address is given as Camden Row as early as 1802. From 1814 the number of dwellings increased and by the 1830s there were more than 15 on the site, by the 1840s more than 25. As each house held, on average, four or more people, the overcrowding must have been atrocious.

In 1838 a 61-year lease (to run from 1836) was granted for the whole site to Charles Brown, a butcher then trading from 3 Camden Place (57 Tranquil Vale, q. v.). By then there were so many dwellings in Camden Row that they had to be identified in groups. About half way up the Row was a small court of eight houses known as Camden Cottages or Camden Square and, in 1861, Camden Court. At the bottom of the Square were two small dwellings usually identified as Camden Garden Cottages. In time Camden Square became known as Camden Passage. But those houses facing the row were usually known as Camden Row or Camden Cottages.

The whole group presented an uninviting picture by the 1850s and the Board of Health reports make dismal reading. Almost every house was ill-drained and butchers' and grocers' refuse was strewn about the roadway. None of the houses could boast a proper water supply as this had to be taken from pumps in the yards, often so close to open drains that the water was impure and clean water had to be scrounged in order to make tea. Most slops were emptied directly into the drains under the pumps so it was not surprising that the inhabitants were frequently ill and that some died.

Reports of cess pools not emptied for fourteen years, common sinks shared by twenty families, piles of rotting offal behind the butchers' shops and offensive privies, were common. Combined with the high density of population, five, seven or nine persons in two or three-roomed cottages, the picture is one which did no credit either to the freeholder - the Earls of Dartmouth - nor to the head lessors: Charles Brown and, for some houses, the local builder, Joseph Russell (1813-1874).

The building of the main sewer line through the Village in 1855 should have made a difference but no connection was made to the Camden Row dwellings, primarily because the Collins estate would not approve the laying of the pipes across their holding; thus it was not until 1866 when the law stepped in that Camden Row was properly drained.

Brown's lease was for 61 years, but the unexpired portion was offered for sale on many occasions. In April 1860 the whole street, along with some equally afflicted cottages and stables at the back of Grotes Place, were advertised for disposal and described as bringing in an annual income of £1085 on yearly rental agreements. The sale notice in 1863 refers to the properties as being brick built, which they may have been in part, but this did not prevent a summons against the owner in 1869, a Mr. Moult, for neglecting to provide proper drains.

Despite all the above, the tenancy records (census returns from 1841 to 1871 and details from leases) show a remarkable continuity in the tenancies, with families occupying the same house for more than 50 years. Charles Cutts, a shoemaker, lived in Camden Row more than 45 years from the 1830s to the late 1870s. His tenancy was so long that the Row was some-times known as "Cutt's Lane". The Cuthbert family (carpenters) were here more than 50 years; the Paynes - laundresses and fly proprietors and by no means destitute - from the early 1840s to 1902; the Coppins family and a Mrs. Denny, a laundress, and others all managed to survive periods of up to 40 years in houses which were condemned time and time again.

Camden Row was cleared in 1896 - not as a result of concern by the land-lords, nor as the result of pressure by a group known as the Blackheath Sanitary Committee, but simply because the leases expired.

Tranquil Passage

Tranquil Passage marks the north boundary of the enclosure from the Heath on which the original Three Tuns was built in the early years of the 18th century. It is likely that the Three Tuns catchment later included the land running north and presently defined on the north and east by Royal Parade, for by 1799 the Dartmouth Estate had granted leases for stables and a house (Phoenix House, q.v.) on the Royal Parade and north Montpelier Vale plot and for a development of five buildings which became Nos. 58-74 Tranquil Vale.

Once the garden ground of the Tuns had been developed in 1822 by Joseph Jackson, this left a hole within the central triangle of the Village, a hole which was however being rapidly filled with small dwellings, some clinging leech-like to the backs of the houses in Montpelier Vale and the lower numbers of Tranquil Vale. There is also evidence that some properties had been erected as early as 1800, for a Thomas Miller was paying a land tax of £6 for four cottages in 1806 and had paid the same sum in 1800. Miller also obtained a lease from the Dartmouth Estate in August 1804 to build two cottages behind the Three Tuns and roughly on the site of the back wall of the present Library (Tranquil Hall). Also, by then, a Mr. May had erected a building 45ft by 16ft on the site of the present 5 Tranquil Passage. During the 1830s further small developments were approved, including a lease for a dairy and cowstalls behind the west end of what became Royal Parade, to Thomas Seamark (1783-1858) who farmed 73 acres on the Shooters Hill Road.

Most of the building in the Tranquil Passage area was for stabling or builders' yards but in 1841 William Seager was granted a lease to erect eight dwellings on either side of a public passageway variously known as Three Tuns Passage, Phoenix Passage or Tranquil Passage, although this last name was properly only applied to that footway which survives as Tranquil Passage today. Seager's houses created a small square or court, and this was sometimes known as Phoenix Square - the narrow alleyway between taking the name Dartmouth Passage.

Shortly after the erection the Phoenix Square lease was assigned to another local builder, Joseph Russell (1813-1874). Why Russell bought these houses is a mystery, although Seager was in financial difficulties in the 1840s and Russell may have obtained the lease at an advantageous price. This would have been the only advantage, for the cottages were poorly built, lacked drainage and water supplies and, most extraordinary, had doors below the level of the passageway, which made them liable to flood. In 1849 a child died of cholera at No. 9 Phoenix Square and another case was recorded in the house opposite. The medical officer then recorded that the cesspool under the house was giving off a most offensive smell and declared that the houses were unfit for human habitation.

There had been no improvement by 1853 when the General Board of Health found that the condition of the houses in Phoenix Square endangered life. Russell had, by then, sold the lease and the new landlord (not named) claimed that he intended to remove the privies which, in the words of Dr. Milroy, overflowed with "horrible effluent which is poisoning the inhabitants." It was imperative that water closets and water be laid on to the houses. Yet, ten years later, a summons was served on the then landlord, Thomas Fox, the corn merchant of Phoenix Place and only 23 years old, for owning a cottage in an insanitary condition.

The 1853 outbreaks of infectious diseases, whilst not as bad as the 1849 cholera epidemic which had killed 89 people in Greenwich and Lewisham alone during the week ending August 28, saw the formation of a Blackheath Sanitary Committee. The Times, in October 1853, reported the death of a child at Phoenix Square as a result of cholera. This was firmly denied by the then Vicar of Lewisham, the Rev. the Hon. Henry Legge. He pointed out that the offending houses were now being drained and water laid on. Further, that the death was that of a woman and the condition had been "brought on by her own imprudence." The Rev. Legge (1805-1887), uncle of the then freeholder, the 4th Earl of Dartmouth (1784-1853) made a serious mistake by writing in such terms, for he unleashed a torrent of contradiction. Correspondents urged him to visit King Street, Loat's Pits and Essex Place in Lewisham, and Hanover and Silver Streets in Greenwich. Further, the Blackheath Sanitary Committee had arranged from contributed funds to improve the effluent drainage at Phoenix Vale and Blackheath Vale although, they felt, the responsibility was that of the freeholder, the Earl of Dartmouth.

Pound's Mews - the alley running behind Nos. 36-52 Tranquil Vale - was not much better: by the 1850s the privies were full and overflowing and there was no proper drainage. There was a large accumulation of dung from the Three Tuns stables and one heap was placed against a pump into which it drained. This pump was the only water supply for several families.

Salvation came in part with the development of Royal Parade and subsequent works. In 1866 there was a great clearance and the old Wesleyan chapel behind 62 Tranquil Vale, Seamark's dairy and outhouses and the odorous cottages of Phoenix Square were demolished and, until the development of Brigade Street, what had been a huddle of 30 overcrowded dwellings was reduced to nine, all with proper drainage and water supply.

The final clearances did not come about until the re-building of Nos. 36-52 Tranquil Vale and the Three Tuns in 1885, but before that date there had been a great improvement. It has been long believed that the Tranquil Passage area had been rebuilt in the 1870s after a major fire, but there is no reliable evidence for this. It is more likely that the wooden and other combustible materials from the demolished cottages were burned on the spot at this time because they were a health hazard. It would therefore be understandable for the dispossessed tenants to claim in later years that they had lost their homes in a conflagration rather than reveal the true cause.

With the exception of the building used as a branch library by the London Borough of Lewisham, none of the buildings presently to be found in Tranquil Passage are older than the 1870s.

Bridage Street arose on the foundations of Phoenix Square and was built on a lease to Mrs. Charlotte Seager in 1873. It was her father-in-law, William Seager, who had built the offensive houses on the site 40 years before, but the new properties - four cottages and a row of workshops on the north east - were not only brick-built but connected to a proper water supply and drainage system.

Thus, in the 1870s a new village within the Village had been created, a collection of small, neat houses, a few small shopkeepers, and some service trades. The Royal Parade Mews housed farriers, blacksmiths, builders and decorators, carpenters and joiners. The Brigade Street workshops were occupied by Henry Seager, the carpenter son of William Seager, and from the mid-1880s by James Slater, a smith and gasfitter. His son, Frank, joined Charles Fawcett as a builder and decorator, and their company traded here until 1973. From 1899 to the 1920s Butcher, Curnow made photographic apparatus here and the workshop on the east side of Brigade Street was used as the All Saints Mission Room and Men's Club from the 1890s until 1926 when the new parish hall was built in Tranquil Vale.

Since the mid-1960s there have been many changes: some of the small shops have been converted into offices, the barbers have retired, and mock bow windows out of architectural character have been built. But there remains enough of the old Tranquil Passage in the form of upholsterers, clock menders, cobblers and the Heathvale Press printshop, to have maintained something,at least of its Victorian aspect.

But there are two buildings here which require more than passing attention, for they played an important part in the social welfare of Blackheath Village for many years. These were the Village school and the fire brigade station and are dealt with below.

Brigade House and the Blackheath Firemen

Facing the Royal Parade entrance to Brigade Street is a tall, three-storey building presently used as a photographic laboratory (Lab One) and previously, for many years, used for photographic work by Messrs Butcher, Curnow of 33-35 Tranquil Vale (q.v.).

This was erected as a fire brigade station in 1871 on the site of Thomas Seamark's dairy and cowsheds, and marked the arrival of an important and much-needed service for Blackheath.

Throughout the first half of the 19th century the demand for an organised and professional fire brigade in Blackheath, Greenwich and Lewisham had been loud, especially after a major conflagration. In the early years the only answer to a domestic fire was the hope that your neighbours would turn out in sufficient numbers to save your possessions and that there was a reasonable supply of water nearby.

By the 1830s some parishes and local insurance offices maintained fire fighting equipment and some organisations possessed hand pumps. One such was Morden College and it was pressed into use on a number of occasions when hayricks at the Kidbrooke farms caught fire. In January 1834 there was a new demand for better fire fighting arrangements when a major conflagration at Deptford burned merrily because the Kent Insurance Company's engine could not be released until the fire chief (who lived in Blackheath) gave his consent. The crowd did not wait, they broke into the shed just before engines arrived from the London and Sun insurance brigades.

There were a number of serious fires in Blackheath Village in the 1830s and John Hally's swimming bath often provided the water source for their extinction. Pumps and escapes would be fetched from Lewisham and Greenwich for there was no adequate equipment any nearer. In 1851 No. 3 Montpelier Row was gutted and Nos. 2 & 4 seriously damaged. Once more there was the cry that it was a scandal that a wealthy parish like Lee* lacked a fire appliance. In 1862 No. 74 Tranquil Vale burned down and in July 1864 a severe blaze destroyed the Colonnade stables near to the Princess

*Montpelier Row was in the Parish of Lewisham

of Wales tavern in Paragon Place. The engines to tackle this last blaze came from Morden College, Mr. Penn's factory at Greenwich, and from as far away as Tooley Street.

Probably the district's most serious fire of the decade had been the destruction of Eastcombe in December 1860, for this was a fine early 18th century mansion, and irreplaceable.

Once more, Blackheathens decided to take matters into their own hands and a meeting was convened at the Alexandra Hall in July 1865 to establish a volunteer fire brigade for the Village, to be based at the Princess of Wales. The meeting was attended not only by interested shop keepers but also by landowner/industrialist John Penn (1805-1878), then living at The Cedars on Belmont Hill, as well as other influential local residents. There seems to be no record that the Blackheath Volunteer Fire Brigade ever turned out, but a Greenwich Amateur Fire Brigade of 30 men and an engine were stationed at the top of Hyde Vale in 1869 ready to do duty in the district.

But work was already in hand on a much wider scale and the Metropolitan Fire Brigade Act of 1865 had established the London brigade as a municipal responsibility. As a department of the Metropolitan Board of Works it was run with extrovert flare by Captain (later Sir) Eyre Massey Shaw (1830-1908), a splendid Victorian of great vision and energy, friend of the Prince of Wales (later Edward VII) and immortalised in Gilbert and Sullivan's Iolanthe. At the age of 29 he had been appointed Chief Constable of Belfast and organised the fire brigade there with such skill and success that he was offered the post of Fire Chief in London in 1861.

The decision to open a brigade station in Blackheath was made in November 1869 but it took a further two years to find a suitable site and complete building works. The Earl of Dartmouth made available the plot of ground in Royal Parade Mews at a virtually nominal rent of £15 a year on a 99 year lease. The occurrence book of the London Fire Brigade records, in the neat copperplate of Capt. Shaw (he kept all the records personally, including those on the individual firemen) that: "A new fire station will shortly be opened at Tranquil Vale, Blackheath. It will be called Blackheath Station and will bear the number of 46. It will, for the present, be manned by one officer and two firemen and be provided with one manual engine and the usual appliances."

The Blackheath station, erected by builders Scrivenor & White at a cost of £1372, opened on January 1 1872. The single officer and two men quickly became an establishment of 12 (1 officer and 11 men) with one horse escape, two hand escapes, one horse cart and one van. Fire alarms were placed around the district at the junctions of 14 main roads (and some minor ones) including the Old Dover Road, Granville Park, The Paragon and Vanbrugh Terrace. The appliance room door was 11 ft high, there was no brass pole, but the Blackheath Brigade could, in May 1872, turn out, horses harnessed and ready for action in 3mins 30secs.

The first chief officer at Blackheath was John Marshall, with the rank of sub-engineer, and he stayed at Blackheath until 1876. Born in 1842, Marshall did well in the brigade but his career ended when he resigned from the Poplar station to escape punishment not only for being under the influence of drink when on duty but for disobeying a senior officer. While at Blackheath he had behaved himself, which is more than can be said for some of his men. The records show that the ordinary firemen did not stay long in the service - whether this was because they did not like the

39.   The Crown in the 1830s

40.   No 1 Collins Street

41.   Collins Street (west)

42.   South Vale Terrace

43.   Camden Place, the morning after the Zeppelin raid, August 14 1916

44.   Nos 63-5 Tranquil Vale; the remaining fragment of Lamb's Buildings

45a. Tuck's Corner in the early 1850s

45b. Tuck's Corner in the early 1870s

work or whether Blackheath was an unpopular posting we cannot say.

Thomas Hill, who stayed at Blackheath only four months, had to be cautioned for drunkenness, Henry von Beenan, a native of Saxony, stayed two months before taking a job with the Opera Comique in Paris; Thomas Ashford stayed at Tranquil Vale for four years and rose steadily through the ranks, but not without misdemeanour, including being absent from the station and missing an engine. He died at the Royal Alhambra Theatre fire in 1882. Matthew Rowland was fined 19/6d for being found with two females in his watch box in Tranquil Vale in August 1872.

The history of the local brigade proved singularly uneventful although it did, of course, back up other stations outside the district to fight large scale fires. Their relative proximity to their catchment meant that appliances could arrive within minutes of an alarm and the only major blaze in Blackheath that they had to tackle was in January 1880 when 61 Granville Park was destroyed. Unfortunately the calamity was made far worse because volunteer fire fighters claimed they were hampered by the local professionals and the building blazed away while rivals stood on the pavement and argued.

During the 1870s and 1880s more and more brigade stations opened and as they did, the work of the Blackheath station declined. Although improvements were made to the Tranquil Vale station in 1893 and one of the first telephones in the district installed there in that year, the establishment of brigades at Lee Green in 1895 and Lewisham in 1899 reduced the work load on Blackheath.

What really closed the Tranquil Vale station was the advent of the motorised fire engine. Initially, a fire station was needed for a catchment not much bigger than where a few minutes dash by a horse-drawn vehicle would bring the firemen to the blaze with a reasonable chance of putting it out. The petrol motor increased that distance by miles even in the traffic-congested streets of London.

The initial decision to close Blackheath was made in 1906, coinciding with the retirement of Mr. Levi George, the officer-in-charge, although the LCC vowed to keep Blackheath in operation until the Charlton station was working. There were petitions and delegations pleading a reprieve, but the LCC only delayed their decision until December 1908 when the Charlton station was made up to 12 men. The closure of the Blackheath and Shooters Hill stations came in October 1909 and the Village thereafter had to depend on the Charlton and Lee Green brigades.

Those who knew the ways of the bureaucrats could tell from the decision in 1906 not to install electricity, although current was available, that the Blackheath station would close whatever the local people might do to try to prevent it.

The empty fire station was not vacant for long. It made an ideal repository and was leased by Ebenezer Smith of 43 Tranquil Vale (q.v.) for his upholstery works and for storing furniture. It has remained in a variety of commercial uses ever since, but most recently as a photographic printing works.

The Village School

What is most surprising about the Village school is that before 1851 the

Village did not possess such an institution for the education of the children of the ordinary working people. There were any number of private and proprietary schools in the neighbourhood for those who could afford the fees, and a few places in the charity schools, e.g. Colfe's and Roan's, for a bright child nominated by the parish. There were also a few dame schools but no records of these has survived.

St. Michael's church in Blackheath Park, then still a proprietary chapel in the Parish of Charlton, established a church school in Paragon Place in 1846 but there was no schoolroom in the Blackheath ward of Lewisham. The need was met by Augusta, the Countess of Lewisham, in 1851 when she paid for a schoolroom to be built in Tranquil Passage on a site donated by the Dartmouth Estate. The building involved the demolition of two small cottages and the removal of the last traces of the head of the old public well - Queen Elizabeth's Well - which had been marked on Traver's survey of East Greenwich of 1695. The new school had two rooms, was declared to be large enough for 120 pupils, and was supplied with a basement play area opening to a small court yard at the back.

The Tranquil Passage school was essentially for the teaching of infants, probably up to the ages of about nine or ten. Until compulsory education to the age of 12 was introduced in 1870, the boys would, no doubt, become apprenticed to local tradesmen or become messengers or shop boys, if they were not bright enough to gain a place at one of the charity schools. The girls mostly went to be trained in the domestic arts at the School of Industry in Blackheath Vale, although some worked for dressmakers and in drapers' shops.

With the establishment of All Saints' as a Chapel of Ease in the Lewisham Parish and, eventually, as a parish in its own right in 1857, the responsibility for the school fell totally on the parish, but it was not until 1878 that the Dartmouth family finally vested all interest in the building with the parish officers. This coincided with the conveyance of land in Blackheath Vale for the erection of a girls' school which was established to provide a sounder, broader education than that offered by the old School of Industry.

The first mistress of the Infant School was a Miss Martha Rice, and she was succeeded by a line of ladies, some of whom were very young, like Anne Pitt who was in charge at the age of nineteen in 1861, although assisted by the 15-year old Eliza Bull. There were about a dozen teachers at the school in its 88 years of service to the community, mostly unmarried and certainly dedicated.

The teachers at the Tranquil Passage Infants School were as follows:

1851-1855 - Martha Rice
1860   - Ellen Buller
1861-1874 - Ann Pitt; also Eliza Bull (1861); Miss Maule (1869); Sarah
            Fry (1871)
1878-1891 - Mary Hambleton
1894-1924 - Mrs. Enefer; also Miss M.M. Battell from 1905-1934
1924-1939 - Dora Harris

In the 1930s the Infant School was proving too small. There was an average attendance of more than 80 pupils and eventually the All Saints' Church Hall in Tranquil Vale had to be pressed into service as an extra classroom. In June 1939 the old building was sold and three extra classrooms built on to the Girls' School in Blackheath Vale. The enlarged building there re-opened in September 1939 as a junior mixed and infants school. It promptly closed again with the outbreak of war and the bulk of the pupils were evacuated to Bexhill-on-Sea.

The empty Infants School in Tranquil Passage was sold, and used thereafter as a meeting and exhibition hall. In 1962 it was leased to the London Borough of Lewisham as a branch library.

W. BUTCHER & SON,

✳ ✳ ✳ ✳ ✳ PHOTOGRAPHIC STORES, ✳ ✳ ✳ ✳ ✳

BLACKHEATH, S.E.

1892. COMPLETE ILLUSTRATED CATALOGUE. OVER 100 PAGES. NOW READY. FREE ON APPLICATION.

W. BUTCHER & SON'S 1892 "MINIMUM" CAMERA.

Weight, ½-plate, 3 lbs.   Size, including all projections, 8 × 8 × 2¼.   Longest focus, 16 in.

THE PRINCIPAL ADVANTAGES OF THIS CAMERA ARE—

1st.—It is compact, light, durable, and economical in price.
2nd.—It combines all the improvements that are necessary for first-class work.
3rd.—It is simple in its construction, reducing the cost, and avoiding difficulties in using.

DESCRIPTION.

It is made in well-seasoned Mahogany, with Leather Bellows, Lined, Very Sperior Finish, Rising and Falling Front, with Good Range in each direction; Front Extension, with Rack and Pinion Adjustment, suitable for Longest Focus Lenses; Reversible Holder; Swing Back, &c. Back portion of the Camera is arranged to slide up close to the Front, for use with Wide Angle Lenses, so there is no projecting Baseboard to cut off Angle of the View. It is one of the most compact and lightest Cameras in the market. **PRICES** (Including Three best Double-hinged Dark Slides)—

| 6½ × 4¾ | **£4 5 0** | 8½ × 6½ | **£7 0 0** | 10 × 8 | **£9 9 0** |

"MINIMUM" PHOTOGRAPHIC SETS,

Including the above Camera, with Three Double Dark Slides, W. Butcher & Son's Leviathan Rapid Rectilinear Lens (Iris Diaphragm), Thornton-Pickard Shutter, and Best Light Four-fold Stand. Complete, with Waterproof Leather-bound Case.

| 6½ × 4¾ | **£8 12 0** | 8½ × 6½ | **£11 10 0** | 10 × 8 | **£17 0 0** |

The above Sets are guaranteed thoroughly reliable, and are the best possible value for money; specially designed for Tourists and others requiring a light and durable Instrument.

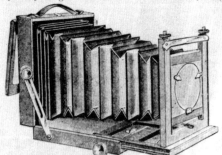

W. BUTCHER & SON'S
1892
POPULAR ½-plate SET.

This is a strong Portable Mahogany Camera, having Double Extension, Wide-fronted Leather Kinnear Bellows, Reversing Back, One Double Dark Slide, with Treble-hinged Shutters, Good Rapid Rectilinear Lens, and strong Two-fold Tripod Stand. As a medium quality Camera, it is sure to give satisfaction, both on account of its workmanship and superior finish.

Price £4 4 0, complete.

13 Blackheath Proprietary School and Selwyn Court

The development of Blackheath as a major residential suburb had started with a burst of building work on the Heath frontage of the Cator Estate with Montpelier Row and the Paragon, and the erection of some of the houses in Eliot Place by Alexandra Doull (fl.1760-1817). These works covered the years from about 1790 to 1805, but then there was a lull - occasioned perhaps by the costly war with France - and, with the exception of some isolated building, e.g. three or four properties on the Cator lands, nothing substantial was built in Blackheath until the 1820s. But then development proceeded with a rush and by the end of the decade there were a considerable number of houses in the Village, in St. Germans Place, on the Cator Estate, and building speculators were looking eagerly at Lee and south Greenwich.

Houses meant people, and people meant a demand for shops and schools. The shops were supplied with enthusiasm, and the Village grew quickly. But the provision of schools was less satisfactory. Greenwich was well-endowed, with a number of charities including John Roan's and the Bluecoat foundation for the bright but needy pupil, and there were a host of small teaching establishments for the middle classes, run for profit and usually owned by clergymen. The most distinguished of these was the Croom's Hill school conducted by Dr. Charles Parr Burney (1757-1817), which had been started as the Greenwich Academy in 1742 by earlier proprietors and came into Burney's possession in about 1789.

With the growth of Blackheath there was a movement up the hill possibly because the air away from the river was considered healthier, and many of the new properties facing the Heath were taken for educational purposes. They were mostly boarding houses, and mostly for boys. For some curious reason the girls' schools tended to be on Maze Hill, perhaps to avoid too much contact with the young gentlemen. The boys' schools ranged from the very bad (David Copperfield's Salem House was based by Charles Dickens on a school at Blackheath) to the not so bad, like the Revd William Greenlaw's academy in St. Germans Place, which he opened in 1823 and which survives today as Christ College; and the Revd John Potticary's school at No. 3 Eliot Place from 1805 to 1831, which boasted Benjamin Disraeli amongst its early pupils.

By the late 1820s the population of Blackheath was large enough for the inhabitants to become concerned at the lack of educational opportunity for their sons. What they wanted was a public day school, offering sound education which would prepare their children for the universities, the army and the church. To meet this need a group of influential residents banded together to consider the question. They included the Revd Andrew Brandram (1790-1851), then Joint Secretary of the British and Foreign Bible Society, John Meadows White (?1799-1863), a solicitor, and the Revd Joseph Fenn

(1791-1878), incumbent at Cator's proprietary chapel (later St. Michael's) in Blackheath Park.

The outcome of a meeting in January 1830 at White's residence (No. 14 The Paragon) was the establishment of a proprietary school, i.e. a school owned by share-holding proprietors who subscribed the initial capital in the form of 100 £20 shares. The method was not, then, novel but it was sufficiently unusual for Blackheath's subsequent success to encourage a host of imitators, including the present Cheltenham College. The owner- ship of a share entitled the holder to send or nominate a boy for the school. The shares were subscribed very rapidly and a further meeting at the Princess of Wales tavern in February 1830, attended by the new owners, confirmed the broad rules of the institution and elected a committee which included the above-mentioned Brandram and Fenn, Benjamin Engleheart of Park House, Cresswell Park (q.v.) and others; John Meadows White was appointed Honorary Secretary.

The first task was to find a site. Initially, plans were made for a building on the Heath between the east windmill (now Talbot Place) and the Greenwich Park wall. Negotiations which involved not only the Commissioners of Woods and Forests (the Crown) but also the Greenwich Vestry (the Manor) proved protracted and the committee kept its options by looking at altern- ative sites. The rules of the Blackheath Proprietary School (BPS, or the "Prop" as it quickly became known) allowed the use of temporary premises and the school was opened on January 31 1831 with 25 pupils on the books under the headmastership of the Revd Sanderson Tennant (1802-1872). The first home of the BPS was long thought to have been at Nos. 25-27 Tranquil Vale, but this theory was based on the reminiscence of Robert Tillett (1830- 1908) who was porter at the school from 1860 to 1904. In fact, the school committee rented some rooms in Tranquil Vale owned by a Mr. Cooper, and the only property-owning gentleman of that name in Tranquil Vale in 1831 was landlord of the Crown public house. It is likely, therefore, that the BPS rented a room at the Crown but, in later years when the temperance movement was in full cry, it would not have been politic to place the origins of a distinguished public school in a pub. But the stay in Mr. Cooper's rooms was brief. Negotiations for the Heath site had failed and so had those for some meadow land on the Cator Estate near Manor Way or Brook- lands Park because of conditions on both sides which neither the BPS committee nor the Cators could accept. Then as now, householders in residential roads were frightened of the prospect of a noisy school in the vicinity. Instead, after complex negotiation, a plot was found on the corner of Lee Lane and Blackheath Village, now the corner of Lee Terrace and the Village and covered by Selwyn Court. This was on the Collins Estate and a lease was granted for a 75-year term from March 25 1831 at an annual rent of £40.

The new building - possibly designed by George Smith (1783-1869) although there is no proof for this - was opened six months later in October 1831, not much more than 18 months after the birth of the scheme. The buildings were not extensive, being plain stock brick with some stone dressings, and took the form of a large hall (Big School) centred between two wings, with a gate house and a headmaster's house. In no time the premises were far too small, but overcrowding was not considered a hindrance to proper learning in those days and classes would be conducted simultaneously in different corners of the same room.

From the start the BPS was a success: of the first 25 pupils not less than seven achieved merit in later life and numbered a future Member of Parliament, an Archdeacon, and John Mason Neale (1818-1866) whose varied career as an author included writing one eighth of the titles in Hymns Ancient and Modern. It was the quality of its pupils that brought to the BPS a level of distinction that was to become unparalleled by any public school of its size, or indeed by many larger establishments. Of course, a great number started with advantages: Blackheath was from the beginning an attractive and convenient suburb for the captains of commerce and the military and naval men tied to London by reasons of employment but anxious to raise their families away from the City stink and overcrowding. They tended to be educated men, liberal in outlook and cultured, but with that streak of puritanism that by virtue of hard work and application, coupled with the spur of a devotion to God and the Monarchy, drove them to excel (or try to) in everything they did.

Tennant remained head of the BPS until 1847, the number of pupils climbing to 94 in 1835 and to 122 in December 1836. But the Prop's early history was not without incident and one event almost saw its end. In 1834 there was a fundamental disagreement over interpretation of the rules amongst members of the original committee. As a result, a breakaway movement, led by John Meadows White, was begun and, on the superficial grounds that the BPS was over-subscribed, the formation of the Blackheath New Proprietary School announced. Such was the climate of feeling, as well as the need for school places in the district, the scheme went forward and a building was erected in Lee Terrace in 1835 to the design of George Ledwell Taylor (1780-1873). The new school was as successful as the original BPS at the start and more than 100 pupils enrolled there by 1836. For a short term, the new Prop outstripped the old school when assessed on a pupil count.

Although the quality of the teaching and achievement at the BPS was sustained, with a satisfactory record of successes at the Universities, the late 1840s saw a depressing decline in the school roll. This was partly becuase of a growing interest in the great public schools and new foundations with their rich endowments, and partly because of over-provision of educational places in schools suited to the requirements of the middle classes. The BPS (and the New BPS enrolments) went into decline, and Tennant, headmaster since the opening, had his engagement terminated in June 1847 - for by then the school roll had fallen to 53. Curiously, the standards had not fallen and the general improvements in educational technique, the introduction of "modern" subjects - i.e. something other than Latin and Greek - had been copied by other schools. Following the Blackheath methods, there had been reforms too at some of the older, nationally-famous, places of learning.

Tennant was replaced by the 25-year old Revd Edward John Selwyn (1822-1893) by the Michaelmas term of 1847. When he took over, the school list was a meagre 48 pupils - when he resigned in 1864 the numbers had reached 275 boys and 15 masters, and in that time he placed the BPS among the leaders in British public schools. Of course, during those years the population of Blackheath had increased greatly, perhaps trebled, and so the potential catchment had improved. Also, the New Proprietary School, which had slumped along with the Prop in the 1840s, never recovered fully. It struggled along, no longer a proprietary school but called Blackheath College, and was conducted as a private grammar school by the Revd John Abraham Andras until its demise in 1866. Andras had previously been a master with the BPS but had left in 1846.

In Selwyn's days at Blackheath the Prop turned out large numbers of pupils who were to achieve distinction in diverse professions and callings: future Bishops, Generals, members of Parliament, civil servants, academics, and lads who were to find military glory in the campaigns of the Crimea and the Indian Mutiny as well as in other corners of the Empire, and two of whom were to be awarded the Victoria Cross. In the last two years of Selwyn's time every boy in the Upper VIth won an open scholarship to Oxford or Cambridge. Coupled with the academic triumphs was a great surge in prowess in organised sport.

Blackheath was pre-eminent in two games: football and hockey. They played lacrosse for a short time but dropped this when it became popular in girls' schools. But it was football, of the Rugby School variety, and their own brand of hockey, which the Prop boys had adopted, and the school was playing both on the Heath in the 1840s. The establishment of an Old Blackheathans club grew out of a desire to increase the opportunities to play these games, for, at the start, there were too few schools nearby to make a fixture card interesting and old boys had no club with which to play once they ceased to be schoolboys. Initially, the football and hockey players were members of the same organisation, but by 1861 they had split, and the two separate clubs pursued an independent existence. The Old Blackheathan Club, as an organisation designed solely to keep old boys in touch with each other, was re-formed on a properly constituted basis in the early 1880s, but the sports' clubs went their own ways, eventually recruiting playing members who were not old Prop School boys. Both clubs - the Blackheath Football Club and the Blackheath Hockey Club - flourish today, perhaps the oldest clubs of their type in the world. The Hockey Club has had its ups and downs of fortune, but the Blackheath Football Club enjoys a legendary past, many of its members (usually the old Prop boys) playing for England in the early decades of international competition. And it was old Prop players who were among the first, if not the first, to take the game to the Universities in the 1870s, and to Ireland, New Zealand and Australia. Until 1876 when the OBs rented a field at Charlton (not the Rectory Field, which was acquired in 1885 when the Blackheath Cricket, Football & Lawn Tennis Co. Ltd. was formed to regularise playing arrangements for Blackheath sportsmen) all school games were played on the Heath. The common was the playground for most of the local schools in Victorian times, as well as the major centre for amateur cricket, golf, and any other sport which took the natives' fancy. One cannot but admire this enterprise, for the Heath was not the smooth grass it is today - it was broken up by pits - the remains of gravel and sand workings - and much of the ground was uneven and still sprinkled with patches of gorse. Most sports' clubs had to clear and level their playing areas from season to season although the hockey players were less concerned because of the nature of the game.

This was the golden age for the Prop School. It was supreme in work and sport, and the school history* shows that the move to the army, Oxford or Cambridge and a brilliant military or academic career was the rule for most of its pupils. The school magazine was launched in the 1860s and a

* History of the Blackheath Proprietary School, by J.W. Kirby BA.
Blackheath Press. 1933.

modern student reading the old copies could be forgiven for wondering whether Blackheath was not the inspiration for the next generation of school literature, the Boys' Own Paper, the novels of G.A. Henty and others, and the poems of Henry Newbolt. The only missing ingredient in the Blackheath method was that it was not a boarding establishment so there could be no dorm feasts or similar japes. Nevertheless, some masters were allowed to take in boarders and this made the school attractive to parents who lived in the suburbs well away from Blackheath. But it was essentially the local day school for boys - for those who could afford the fees - and the names on the pupils' register closely match many of those to be found in the street directories of the 1860s and 1870s covering the Cator Estate, Vanbrugh Park and Shooters Hill Road areas. It could be argued that no family of influence and standing in Blackheath was without a member who did not, at some time, attend the Prop. But, despite this, the school experienced a continuing problem in that when boys reached the age for sixth form work many would be sent off to tutors (like Keiser's School in Dartmouth Row and, later, Wolffram's) which specialised in cramming for places at Woolwich and Sandhurst officer cadet schools. Other boys would spend two or three years at the Prop before moving to Rugby, Harrow or one of the other public schools with a wider curriculum or better facilities.

Selwyn resigned in 1864, having satisfied the governors by keeping the school strong by a mixture of stern discipline and moral example. His successor, the Revd John Kempthorne MA (1834-fl. 1890) who had been a master at St. Paul's School, was a less stern man and he reorganised the punishment system (in Selwyn's day this had consisted of solitary confinement!) as well as the teaching. He placed a greater emphasis on the teaching of English and the sciences, appointed new masters and encouraged the better staff amongst those he found on his appointment to stay. In his reforms he was well supported by a number of masters who had served the school for many years and who continued to do so with distinction. Of these, Roger Sueur (1806-fl 1876) who taught French from 1841 to 1875, and F. Osiander (1832-1893), a native of Wurtemberg, who had joined the Prop by 1863 to teach French, took over German classes and taught at the school until his death, must be mentioned. Osiander - whose name was based on two Greek words meaning 'Holy Man' - was one of the great teachers of the latter half of the 19th century, who earned the affection of his pupils at the same time as getting them to give of their best academically. He served the school for 31 years and the memoirs of Old Blackheathans and the BPS magazines are full of references to his kindness and sterling qualities - à remarkable achievement for a German among a nation then given to regarding foreigners as of little consequence.

Although Kempthorne took over a flourishing school he was answerable to a governing committee who were out of touch with the then modern attitudes towards teaching and educational management. The committee were ruled, as they had been 30 years before, by the Revd Joseph Fenn and consisted largely of retired generals and stockbrokers. They urged caution when brighter, younger, men would have supported the headmaster in schemes which meant improvement and change. For example, when the buildings of the New Proprietary School in Lee Terrace were, once again, for sale and offered to the BPS on advantageous terms, the committee yet again turned down the chance to buy the freehold and expand the overcrowded school. In the end the New Prop buildings were demolished and the house called Greylands, presently an old peoples' home, erected on the site in 1872.

In 1876 Kempthorne resigned after 12 years' service, in which time the prestige of the school had been enhanced by successes of scholarship and on the sports' fields. But his stewardship had not ensured a return to the numbers of pupils of Selwyn's days, and the committee were finding it increasingly difficult to attract staff of the necessary calibre to sustain the Prop's undoubted reputation. Kempthorne's successor was the Revd Edward Wilton South (1848-1927) who, although a young man, had some teaching experience at St. Paul's and a brilliant academic record at Trinity College. South came to the school when it had ceased to hold its position as the only well-known public school just outside London. St. Paul's, University College School, Dulwich and Tonbridge were exercising a strong attraction and all were larger, in terms of accommodation, than the BPS. But South's enthusiasm, classical scholarship and teaching abilities produced good results, with more University distinctions being achieved in his time than at any during the previous history of the school. One curiosity, although he was not an athlete he imposed compulsory games upon his charges. While this must have infuriated many of the boys it did ensure a good standard in cricket and football, and some pupils went on to earn county and international caps for their particular sports. The school also rented its first private playing field - in Manor Way - in South's days, primarily because the Heath was becoming less and less convenient a playground, due to increasing traffic and the growing number of schools wishing to use its pitches. In 1878 Dr Joseph Fenn died, aged 87, thus ending a connection of 48 years with the school. His nine sons had all been educated at the Prop and seven of them passed on to Trinity College, Cambridge - whence all the BPS headmasters had been drawn.

It was during the 1880s that the school registers reveal names of local families whose influence has not entirely gone from Blackheath, and some of whose descendants were living in the district until the last war: Spurling, Fraser, Ireland, Whately, Dyer, Poland, Previte, de Montmorency, Duckham, Prestige and McDougall. Mostly the sons of heads of leading commercial organisations, or stockbrokers, their futures were assured, but the Prop School brought out the best, both academically and on the sports' field, and helped most to complete their education at Oxford or Cambridge. At one time there were so many ex-BPS boys at Cambridge that they were able to form their own society - the Pagans - with a distinctive blazer and cap and the occasional dinner.

Attempts to reform the structure and management of the BPS were seriously considered in 1886 and it was further agreed that the committee should negotiate to purchase the freehold as the school lease was due to expire barely 20 years later. They also considered the possibility of transferring the controlling interest in the establishment to the Church Schools Company, for, although the BPS was not a religious foundation, Fenn and the early proprietors had been strongly influenced by their faith. It was laid down in the rules, for example, that the boys had to receive moral and religious instruction and that the headmasters must be ordained members of the Church of England. This last rule was changed in 1886, but they failed to buy their ground and the other reforms were not proceeded with, partly because of expense and partly because of the complicated legal requirements for altering the proprietary status of the institution.

Edward Wilton South resigned in 1887 and, following the examples of both Selwyn and Kempthorne before him, took up clerical work, becoming the vicar of several livings. He had worked hard for the BPS, added further lustre to the school's record of academic success and produced not only classicists but also good mathematicians and scientists. Perhaps his most treasured memory of the Prop was the production of a comedy by Aristophanes which his senior boys enacted in the original Greek at the Rink Hall (q.v.) in 1883, and the work he put in towards the establishment of a sister school - the Blackheath High School. This last is dealt with in the next chapter.

In 1887 the school fees were 25gns a year; a neighbouring boys' school offering much the same syllabus, Colfe's School, then on the corner of Walerand Road and Lewisham Hill, charged 9gns - but the BPS was a public school with a high reputation. On the recommendation of Selwyn's son, Revd E.J. Selwyn, the committee appointed Herbert Bendall (fl 1857-1927) as headmaster, the first not to be an ordained clergyman, and once vice-principal of Liverpool College. Bendall took over with a staff that had dwindled to nine. The relative smallness of the school did not however reduce its ability on the games field and the football team continued to win most of its matches against other public schools with four or five times the number of pupils from which to draw their teams. Bendall stayed until the end of 1894, initially bringing the roll up to 150 pupils but seeing it fall to less than 100. He was succeeded by Herbert Rivers Woolrych (1852-1917) who had been second master for ten years and was appointed head with the task of running the school with greater economy than hitherto. But many factors were against him, not least of which was the rapidly expiring lease on the buildings, the growth of other public day schools nearby and the enthusiasm for boarding schools. A few families still supported the Prop, old boys sent their sons, but an increasing number of Blackheathens were prepared to send their children away to be educated, partly following fashion but partly in order to guarantee a good mark in the army entrance or university examinations. The ailing Proprietary School, the parents thought, might not survive the span of their child's school career, however sound it might appear at the outset. Somehow, enthusiasm had waned and although there were more than 20 families within half a mile of Blackheath Village with Prop connections who could have restored the school's fortunes by donations, none came forward.

By 1904 the BPS was near to closing down, but a spirited rearguard action by committee chairman Arthur Thomas Whately (1851-1940), of 7 Pond Road, found enough funds to continue, though in a reconstituted form. The school became a limited liability company and the fees were reduced. Finally, the word Proprietary was dropped from the title. The BPS became the "Blackheath School", a name urged upon the committee many times over the years as the term 'Proprietary' was often confused with 'preparatory' or 'propriety'. The lease was extended for a further three year term as an experiment which, if it succeeded, would be repeated. But Woolrych resigned in the middle of 1905 and the committee found that their troubles were no further diminished. They were faced with the tragedy of a school with a distinguished reputation, with more than 100 pupils on the books, but with so uncertain a future that the better staff were fast leaving for more secure posts.

Yet the boys seemed oblivious to all these difficulties in the last half dozen years and the standards of work, scholastic achievement, and success on the rugby football and cricket field were maintained. The school Cadet Corps was enthusiastically supported and Blackheath won shields for shooting in Public School competitions at Bisley up to the very last term.

Woolrych's successor was Edward Provis (1850-1941) whose two years as headmaster ended a career as a mathematics teacher at the BPS which had started in the early 1880s. There was little he could do to prevent the closing of the school and he presided over its last terms with the same attention to work and discipline as if the school were destined to flourish for another 70 years. Provis lived to the immense age of 91, the last 20 years of his life being spent at No. 10 The Paragon (then a private hotel), but falling victim to the war when that house was severely blitzed in March 1941.

The Blackheath Proprietary School closed in December 1907. It had lasted for 77 years, and had built a golden record of scholastic achievement and success on the games' fields. It was one of the best public schools in Britain and the proportion of its pupils who were destined to become distinguished in their chosen professions was astonishingly high. Many of the names mean little now, although they were known internationally in their time and the pages of the Dictionary of National Biography and of Who Was Who contain a high percentage of old BPS pupils. Perhaps a few have remained household names to this day: the Duckham brothers, whose motor lubricants are brand leaders even today, but who distinguished themselves in aircraft production and ordnance during the Great War; McDougall, of the flour-milling empire; H. M. Tennent, the theatrical impresario, and, of all people, Donald McGill (1875-1962) the comic postcard artist who remained an enthusiastic supporter of the Old Blackheathans Club until his death.

It is of more than passing interest to remember that the two men who were most responsible for the invention and exploitation of the Tank as an instrument of war - Major General Sir Ernest Swinton (1868-1951) and Major General Sir Hugh Elles (1880-1945) - were educated at the BPS. Swinton conceived the ideas and convinced the War Office; Elles commanded the tanks at Cambrai in 1917, the first major battle in which they were to play a decisive role.

The story of most schools ends with their closure, but with the BPS this is not the case. The buildings passed into different uses, and these are described below, but the old boys kept the spirit alive for the next 60 years and even now some of the traditions established by the Prop still survive. The Old Blackheathan rugby football and hockey clubs flourish today; the Royal Blackheath Golf Club at Eltham still play annually for a medal instituted by the OBs; but, most remarkably, at the time of writing this paragraph (1976) the Old Blackheathans Club was still in existence, 69 years after the school closed its doors. Obviously, after such a great passage of time the membership has declined to a handful, but the Prop boys were bound with what The Times called "a most prehensile old school tie". The present body had been founded in the 1880s, primarily to lend support to the sports' clubs, but it gradually took on a different role, as a clearing house for information about old boys and the organisation of annual dinners, lunches and newsletters. When the school closed, the membership went into decline although many were eligible to join. But the lack of a school building to act as a focal point for their interest and the subsequent losses of OBs during the Great War (47 were killed and many wounded) caused a drop in support to about 70.

But in 1931 the OBs celebrated the centenary of the foundation of their school when, on October 31, more than 100 sat down for dinner at Gatti's Restaurant in the Strand. Old Blackheathan F. B. Malim, by then Master of Wellington, took the chair and there was an evening of justifiable congratulation and nostalgia: "Mr. Spurling said his mind went back that evening to those autumn afternoons of long ago, mist on the Heath, magenta-and-white jerseys swerving down the field of play, and he heard the cry once more, 'School! School!'"

It had been the intention that, after the centenary celebrations, the OBs club should wind up. But the new enthusiasm generated by the meeting of old friends gave the OBs a fresh impetus. Due almost solely to the immense energy of Donald McDonald, the last head monitor of the Black-heath School, who acted as Joint Honorary Secretary with W. F. Dyer (d. 1962), the OBs club flourished and, at one stage, membership was pushed up to the 500 mark. Until the last war the Club held annual dinners, often reported in The Times, but in the difficult years of 1939-1945 many of the, by then, aged membership were scattered, and with the coming of peace the dinners were reduced to lunches which continued until 1967. But there was always McDonald's newsletter to keep members up-to-date, and this was still being dispatched when the 1970s dawned.

It is a remarkable ending to a remarkable story that the Old Blackheathans Club was functioning in 1974 although the formal membership had declined to eight and it was doubtful whether more than three or four other ex-BPS pupils were still alive.

The Blackheath Proprietary School could not grow. It lacked room for expansion and its governors for the first 50 years lacked the ability to alter their views as the environment and the social world changed. But its spirit was so strong that it survived for nearly seventy years after the last pupil and master left the classrooms.

Two members of the staff lived on to the mid-1950s; both had been pupils at the BPS before their appointment as masters. Hubert William Ord, who died in April 1954, aged 84, entered the school in 1881 and returned, with a BA from London University, in 1895 to teach. Affectionately known as "Polly" Ord he taught at the BPS until 1904 and afterwards set up as a private tutor and crammer, returning to occupy his old room at the Prop long after the school had closed.

The last surviving BPS master was the Revd A. W. Smyth who died in 1956 in his early 80s. Smyth, who had been a pupil in 1888, taught at the Prop during its last eight years, setting up a boarding house in Aberdeen Terrace in 1902 to encourage enrolments from outside the district. The house moved to Heath Hill House (now Golf House) in Goffers Road in 1904 but closed with the shutting of the school in 1907.

The School Buildings after 1907

Once the Prop had closed the first task was to sell the contents, and the auctions took place in January 1908. The stained glass which filled the windows of the "Big" school was transferred, along with the honours boards and official portraits of the headmasters, to the Blackheath Concert Hall. All these have since disappeared but a few small lights with the school crest, motto and colours can be identified in some windows on the south elevation of the Hall. Many old boys acquired school fitments, desks and sports' shields, and the school records eventually passed to the Lewisham Public Libraries, in whose hands they remain today.

For the next two years the buildings remained empty, fit for few uses other than educational, but in August 1909 the BPS was leased by the Blackheath Press, then occupying part of the Alexandra Hall (q.v.). The Blackheath Press had been founded by Charles North (1847-1915) in 1881 in Lee. By 1887 he had taken over James Jennings' print shop at 3 Blackheath Village, under which heading more details of North and his business will be found. Expansion of the company dictated a move in 1892 to the old swimming bath area in the Alexandra Hall on the corner of Cresswell Park, and from that address North enjoyed no small reputation as the publisher of the local newspaper, the Blackheath Local Guide and District Advertiser.

The move to the BPS building - the big school room housed the machinery and the library became a jobbing shop and paper warehouse - was an occasion for solemn declarations. North, in his newspaper, wrote: "...a revered place...we will issue from the Press works that will in no way clash with the high scholarship and noble ideals associated with these buildings." The Blackheath Press must have been hard put to to keep this promise, for it printed everything, from greengrocer's paper bags to posters, visiting cards and books, many items not usually associated with scholarship and noble ideals, although the quality of the printing was always high.

By 1914 some of the outlying rooms had been let off for commercial purposes and until 1936 the buildings were known as the Blackheath Chambers, one of the principal occupants being Miss Helen Anderson who taught shorthand and typing, and H.W. Ord occupied one of his old classrooms where he crammed hopeful entrants for the public schools with the rudiments of Latin and other subjects.

North died in 1915, aged 68, and the business passed to Herbert Mitchenall but continued to trade with the somewhat awkward title; "Charles North - The Blackheath Press" for some years afterwards.

North's newspaper, the Blackheath Local Guide, was enjoying a circulation of 6000 copies when he died and his successors continued to produce the paper for it had become a vital instrument for the communication of news and social events among the people of Blackheath. It kept its distinctive size, $9\frac{1}{2}$in by 7in, but frequently reached 48 or 60 pages an issue. For some years a Royal edition on art paper was produced. From the beginning and up to the last war it was delivered free to every house in the district. The continued success of the paper was largely due to the efforts of Walter John Davis (1876-1963) who had been apprenticed to North in 1890. Davis worked for the Blackheath Press for 68 years, the business closing down in 1958 when he retired at the age of 82. He had edited the BLG through Mitchenhall's time and had built up an encyclopaedic knowledge of Blackheath families and institutions. The obituary sections of his newspaper were always meticulous and detailed and have been of inestimable value in the research for this book. Wartime economies in 1940 reduced the number of pages but the BLG continued publication until August 1957. Attempts to revive the journal, firstly as the Blackheath Reporter, in September 1959, and again in 1965, did not succeed, and Blackheath saw the last issue of a local newspaper in September 1966.

In 1936 the lease on the old BPS buildings expired and the Collins Estate granted a re-development lease to W. H. Vincent's Home Property and Investment Company. The ground was cleared but not before a new home had been built for the Blackheath Press close to the site of the old school porter's lodge fronting on to Lawn Terrace.

But the building which rose on the Village frontage and named Selwyn Court, after the great headmaster of the Blackheath Proprietary School, was to attract more attention than its promoters could have envisaged. The BPS buildings were unsuitable for most commercial purposes and useless for housing, so that demolition was inevitable. But the expiry of the lease coincided with a number of impending dramatic changes to the architectural quality of Blackheath, largely wrought by speculators who were destroying old houses and erecting blocks of indifferently-designed and poorly-built flats. Most of this re-building was to take place at the top of Crooms Hill or on the Dartmouth Place frontages of the Heath, but the developers had also gained a strong hold on Cator lands south of Black-heath Park and the St. Germans acres of Kidbrooke were disappearing under ribbons of concrete and brick. Eastnor House on the corner of Lloyds Place had been converted into a factory and industrial premises of lament-able appearance had been built in Eliot Place, Independents Road and Blackheath Grove.

The leases of many early and mid-19th century terraces in the district were shortly to expire. By unhappy accident these expirations coincided with a speculative building boom in London's suburbs. The period was, furthermore, one in which planning controls were slight and British arch-itectural design and building quality had reached their nadir. There was much disquiet, not only in Blackheath, and when the concrete shell of Selwyn Court - an example of architectural bad manners unparalleled in the district - appeared in the Village, there was a revolt.

It was led by Douglas Percy Bliss, the artist, then living in Lee Park, and he wrote in November 1936 to the Blackheath Local Guide, suggesting the formation of a local civic amenity society. Bliss said: "Can we any longer afford to sit by indignant but unprotesting while unenlightened public and rapacious private enterprise repeat here the disastrous blunder of Eltham, or let Blackheath sink to the level of Lee or Lewisham?"

Bliss's plea was not without some cause. Greenwich Council had only recently used what little power it had to prevent a filling station being built on the Heath, but it was doubtful whether Lewisham would be able to prevent the proposal to demolish some of the heart of the Village in order to widen the roadway. As a result of his letter, a public meeting was held in the All Saints' Hall on January 18 1937. It was attended by more than 100 people, including many who were prominent in the fields of architecture and urban history.

A resolution at the meeting gave life to the Blackheath Society, Bliss being appointed the Honorary Secretary, and Dr. Ernest A. Baker (1869-1941), a distinguished librarian and author, was elected its first Chairman. The 8th Earl of Dartmouth (1888-1962) accepted the Presidency and the committee included a number of local residents who were to serve the Society with great enthusiasm and effect for many years: Professor J. Bullocke (1898-1969) who served as Chairman from 1948 to 1969; Professor Michael Lewis CBE, DLitt (1880-1970); William R. Davidge FRIBA (d1961); Daniel Moir Carnegie FSA (d1949); and Alan Roger Martin FSA (1901-1974) who acted as Honorary Secretary for some years and was instrumental in sustaining the Society through the 1939-1945 war. Martin, Davidge and Carnegie backed their concern with money in 1938 by floating a company - the Blackheath Preservation Trust Ltd. - to purchase and secure historic buildings that were dilapidated or at risk from demolition.

There were a few dissident voices at the inaugural meeting of the new society in 1937 - principally from estate agents who felt that the Blackheath Society should concern itself with preserving the Heath and general amenities, leaving the natural process of the decay and re-development of buildings safely in the hands of those with professional knowledge of such matters. Fortunately for Blackheath, the Society did not heed their advice and pursued with vigour its declared aims of "preserving the beauty and amenities of the district and offering wise guidance on developments".

Ironically, the Society's strongest ally in the early years came from an unlikely quarter when war was declared against Germany in 1939 and all pending development and road schemes were abandoned. By the time the country had recovered from the austerity years the Society had new problems to tackle, but these are not part of this volume.

Neither the Blackheath Society nor the Preservation Trust could prevent the development of Selwyn Court, which was three quarters finished when Bliss wrote his letter. Most of the shops were occupied by 1938 and numbered as Blackheath Village. The north corner, No. 20, now a wine merchants' opened as a ladies and children's clothes shop; No. 22, now a hairdressers, 'Jeanne', was opened as an opticians by J. R. March (1911-1943) who was killed in action, serving as a pilot with the Royal Air Force; No. 26 has always been a greengrocers, trading initially as W. T. Vincent, but for the last 15 years owned by W. T. Amos; Nos. 28 & 28a have followed the same trades for more than 20 years, as a tailors and wool shop respectively; No. 32 has been a tobacconist from the outset, trading until the 1960s as Sparrow & Co., but in recent years as a branch of Finlay & Co.; No. 34 was the original Selwyn Court Estate Office but has been used as a branch office by Stocker & Roberts, the estate agents, as a dental surgery and, presently, the studio of John Sani, a photographer.

But Selwyn Court's major contribution to the history of Blackheath Village is its mute testimony to what most of the Village would have looked like if the people of Blackheath had not worked to ensure otherwise.

46. Tuck's Corner shortly after the 1885 redevelopment

47. Tranquil Vale in the late 1840s

48.　Tranquil Vale (east) in the early 1870s. Rebuilt in 1885

49.　Tranquil Vale and the Three Tuns 1872-4

50.　The same view as Illustration 49 — after the 1885 redevelopment

51.　Tranquil Place in 1874

52.   Outside No 70 Tranquil Vale in 1904

53.   Highland House in about 1910

14 Blackheath High School
and Wemyss Road

The previous chapter has covered in some detail the story of the Blackheath
Proprietary School, a public day school for boys which no longer exists.
On the opposite side of the Village, at the east end of Wemyss Road, stands
the Blackheath High School, a public day school for girls established in
1880 and markedly different from the BPS in its origins. The High School
functions today, an important member of a group of schools allied to the
Girls Public Day School Trust. The BPS failed after 76 years because its
committee lacked vision and because the philosophy of the 1830s was out of
date when changes were required to cope with the demands of the 1880s and
later years. The BHS survived because its foundation was vested firmly
with an organisation that had been quick to catch the mood of the times and
supply a service for which there was an urgent local demand - a secondary
education which would prepare girls for the universities, training colleges
and professions.

Before 1880 very few girls, outside exceptional and, perhaps, eccentric
homes, were educated to university entrance level; the girls of Blackheath
were no exception although there is enough evidence in the records of the
first half of the 19th century to show that some efforts were being made in
the district towards offering girls a sound education.

Girls' schools then were of two types: charity schools for the poor and
the Schools of Industry for the not quite so poor; and a host of private
schools, run for profit, often very small, and usually enjoying names like:
"The College for the Daughters of Gentlemen" or something similar. A
little mathematics, a little French (often taught by a penniless native of
Gaul living in the neighbourhood), callisthenics - exercises to develop
graceful movement and strength - and something called logic or natural
philosophy, seemed to be the sum of the curriculum. There would be
much sewing and Bible reading, and the pupil would be expected to supply
a silver knife, fork and spoon and six towels. Her father paid the fees,
which might range from 10gns to 50gns a year. The teacher would be the
school proprietor, usually the spinster daughter of a clergyman or a widow
with no other means of support, and certainly no qualifications.

The schools were of little use, but they kept the girls out of mischief
until they 'came out' at 17 and, with a modicum of luck and no small amount
of scheming on their mother's part, they would be married within the year.

Maze Hill was the favourite district for girls' schools in the 19th century,
and throughout those years there was at least one on its length and sometimes more. Douglas House (since demolished) on the corner opposite
Park Vista was a private school from the 1830s to the 1860s - initially for
boys, but by 1857 it was Mrs Harriet Horn's Ladies Boarding School. Two
doors to the south was the residence of John Le Gallois, professor of

languages, who must have made a reasonable living in the 1840s and 1850s as virtually no school prospectus is complete without him as visiting professor. No. 47 (with 49) was a ladies boarding school in the 1830s, owned by Mrs. Lewis Jeanneret. Buffar House (now the site of 53 & 55 Maze Hill) was conducted as a girls' school by Mrs. Mary Ann Cousins and Mrs. Leonora Ballantyne from the 1820s to 1838, but Mrs. Cousins' bankruptcy in 1841 led to the school's closure and the demolition of the house which had stood since the mid-17th century.

At the top of the hill stood two buildings which specialised in the education of girls but at opposite ends of the spectrum. A house known as Mayfield Lodge, tucked under Vanbrugh Castle on the north side, was owned by John Hooper Hartnoll in 1829. His best claim to local fame was as publisher of the newspaper which became the Kentish Mercury, but his wife, Mary, used part of the premises for her "Maize Hill Establishment", which offered board and instruction for young ladies. There were only eight pupils but in 1834 they paid 30gns a year for the privilege of being taught by Mrs. Hartnoll. The Hartnolls moved to Brixton in 1845 and the school passed to other proprietors. In 1863 the emphasis changed when the building was leased by the Rescue Society for Females, which took in and trained young women between the ages of about 16 and 25 in the art of domestic work: the 1871 census notes their occupation as "servants". The "servants" were probably rescued from prostitution, which must have alarmed the owners of the house next door - Vanbrugh Castle.

The Castle, which had been occupied as a private residence from when it was built in 1719 by Sir John Vanbrugh (1664-1726) until the early years of the 19th century, was destined, like so many large and awkward buildings, to become an institution. It found a great utility as an educational establishment up until the present day, although the tenant from 1838 to 1844 was Dr. John Holker Potts (1789-1850) who used the building as an Institution for Spinal Diseases.

When the Castle was put up for auction in 1845 the purchasers were the Hart family (the widow Mary with her spinster daughters Charlotte and Louisa). For the next 45 years Vanbrugh Castle housed schoolgirls: after the Harts came the Misses Henrietta, Martha and Ellen Nicholson who managed to make a living from only 17 pupils yet employed a teacher of French and seven servants. By 1884 their school was in the hands of Madame Russell Roberts (Vanbrugh Park High School) and by 1888, the Misses Gale, Shaw and St. Clare. They left in 1892.

But by no means all the major schools were on Maze Hill, and three, probably the best before the establishment of the High School, were at opposite ends of the Heath. The most distinguished in the early years of the 19th century was the school at Bryan House (2 South Row, demolished after extensive damage in 1940) which was conducted by Mrs. Margaret Bryan from 1799 to 1823. Mrs. Bryan was no ordinary teacher, for she published books on astronomy and mathematics, adorned with pictures of her attractive daughters on the frontispiece. Her school passed to Rebecca Nightingale in 1826, and she stayed at Bryan House until at least 1841.

Probably the most advanced teaching for Blackheath girls was to be found in Dartmouth Row. A house on the site of Nos. 22a-26, which became the College of Greyladies in 1895, was once a boarding school owned by Miss Louisa Browning from the 1830s to 1861. Miss Browning was the aunt of the poet, Robert Browning (1812-1899), and some of her pupils were destined to enjoy fame as pioneers for women's rights: Elizabeth Garrett (1836-1917), Britain's first woman doctor, and Emily Davies (1830-1921), a tireless champion for higher education for girls.

Further south, on the corner of Dartmouth Row and Morden Hill, was the girls' school called Cedar Lodge which had been founded in Lee Park in 1857 by the Misses Mary and Kate Maberley. They conducted their school in Dartmouth Row from 1859 to 1895 when they retired to No. 2 The Orchard - Kate Maberley living there until her death in 1922 at the age of 95 years. The school had been sold in 1895 to Mary Addison (1861-1944) and her sister, who altered the status to that of a day school, but in 1909 they moved Cedar Lodge School to 1 Talbot Place where it functioned until 1918.

The above paragraphs, a brief survey of educational provision for Blackheath girls, have been set out simply to show the state of female schooling in 19th-century Blackheath. The provision for boys was much stronger, for, with the establishment of the BPS, there was at least one school which was more than adequate and seemed, in the late 1870s, to be secure. But this was for the boys only, and the passing of the compulsory education legislation in the 1870s caused Blackheath parents to consider the education of their daughters more seriously than before. A surprising number were taught at home by governesses and none of the local schools could have coped with the sheer numbers of young women needing more than the rudiments of literacy.

Reform, however, was in the air: the success of Frances Mary Buss (1827-1894) in the foundation of the North London Collegiate School in 1850 had shown what could be achieved. Cheltenham Ladies College in 1853 and the Royal School for the Daughters of Officers of the Army in 1864 were some of the first in a growing number of public schools, but they were essentially boarding establishments.

What Blackheath wanted was a day school of the same calibre. For once, local enterprise was slow to respond and the incentive came partly from outside the suburb. For many years parents had been pressing the headmasters of the BPS to open a section of their school for girls, and it was not until Edward Wilton South's appointment in 1876 that the pleas were listened to with any seriousness. By then, an organisation entitled the Girls Public Day School Company had been established for four years and had opened schools at Oxford, Nottingham, Croydon, and elsewhere. Local effort had to supply the building fund but the organisation, staffing and curriculum was firmly in the hands of the Company.

In Blackheath the parochial movement was led by Edward South and his wife Frances Julia (nee Green) who had been one of the first students at Newnham College, Cambridge, and had declined a teaching post at Cheltenham Ladies College offered to her by Dorothea Beale (1831-1906).

A "drawing room" meeting was held in 1878 at the South residence (41 Lee Terrace, since demolished) at which more than 100 supporters were present including Mrs. William Grey of the GPDSCo, a Miss Shirreff, and Mrs. Helen Taylor, the niece of John Stuart Mill (1806-1873) who had been a keen supporter of women's rights and had lived at 113 Blackheath Park from 1852 to 1871.

The local committee made a formal request to the Company (later to be known as the Girls Public Day School Trust Ltd., and hereafter referred to as the Trust) to open a school at Blackheath, and this was agreed but for the lack of a suitable building. It was pointed out to the citizens of Blackheath that it would be necessary to build a school and that they would have to pay for it. The Blackheathens, led by the Revd George Meyrick Jones, proprietor of the boys' school at No. 4 St. Germans Place, were able to find subscribers enough to take up an issue of about 600 £5 shares which would show a return of 5 per cent; although in 1927 it was alleged* that a number of prominent families refused to subscribe on the excuse that there was no point in spending money on educating girls.

The choice of a designer was simple, for it was singularly fortunate that a member of the committee was Mrs. Robson of No. 2 The Paragon and wife of Edward Robert Robson FSA (1835-1917). He was a distinguished architect, and designer of the new buildings for the London School Board for whom he was official architect from 1871 to 1903. His plans for the Blackheath High School were published in 1879 and work commenced early that year. The quick settlement on a site was another stroke of fortune for, unlike the BPS nearly fifty years previously, there proved to be no difficulty in finding the ground and no protracted negotiations. In 1877 the Cator Estate had granted a development lease for the paddock and meadow which ran behind Nos. 22 & 23 Montpelier Row to a Lee builder, George W. Gorrum. He named the new street Wemyss Road, but for what reason it has not been possible to uncover. Construction work began on the houses on the south side of the road in 1879, some being held by Gorrum though Nos. 6 & 7 were on a headlease to Mrs. Charlotte Seager (1800-1889) the widow of William Seager (1798-1857), then living at No. 18 Montpelier Row. The High School site on the corner of Wemyss Road and Paragon Mews (now Paragon Place) had been a gravel pit in the 18th century and was used for this purpose as late as the 1790s by James Lee, who may have been the builder of Nos. 22 & 23 Montpelier Row. The original lease with Cator for the School site came into effect on 26 April 1880 although the school had, by then, been open for three months.

Robson's buildings were completed by the end of 1879, the contractors being Walls Brothers, of Lee, and the bill came to £5,500. The principal structure, the central block at present, was designed to accommodate 300 pupils, with a half acre playground at the rear. It was the first purpose-built school in the Trust's stable and, as such, warranted a ceremonial opening. The Trust was fortunate in being supported in its aims by HRH Princess Louise, then Marchioness of Lorne (1848-1939). She was the sixth child of Queen Victoria and generally held to be the most attractive and most intelligent. The Princess had married the Marquess of Lorne (heir to the Dukedom of Argyll) in 1871 and had been the first member of the Royal family to marry a British subject for more years than most could remember. Both were more interested in intellectual and artistic pursuits than in joining the stiff and hum-drum life at Court. The Trust had been founded in 1872 under Princess Louise's aegis, and she had taken an active part in promoting female education through the National Union for the Higher Education of Women, also founded in 1872.

It was arranged that she would formally open the new High School at Blackheath, a decision that was extremely helpful for the new institution because, while some Blackheath families had scorned the idea of a serious secondary school for their daughters, they were also some of those most conscious of the need to move in "fashionable" directions. Once news

* In the Book of the Blackheath High School.

spread that a member of the Royal family would be visiting the Village there was an unseemly rush for reserved places on the route of her procession and enrolments were so brisk that there were 68 pupils waiting for their desks before the first term began.

The High School was declared open on January 7 1880 and the Village put on an enthusiastic and colourful display to greet the Princess: "...the first ever visit to this rising locality by a Royal Personage..." To celebrate, the town was dressed overall, with banners in yellow and green stretched across the roads and a large board on the shop fronts of Mr. Sullivan and Mr. Hale (Nos. 30 & 32 Montpelier Vale) bearing the legend: "Welcome to the Princess". So excited were the populace that shopkeepers, whose premises were well hidden from the Royal gaze, declared their loyalty in bunting and flag. A strong force of police constables under the control of Superintendent McHugo was employed to keep order, and 200 members of the Volunteer Militia lined the route, acting as a Guard of Honour from the railway station to the new school.

The Blackheath High School commenced its first full term on January 19 1880 and by 1881 had reached its full compliment of 300 pupils. Robson had presented the School with a cast copy of the Venus de Milo and this stood on a pedestal at the end of the main hall - its undressed state not finding complete favour with one or two of the parents.

The School's first headmistress was Miss S. Allen Olney, who had taught at South Hampstead High School of which her sister had been headmistress. The new school was the largest of the Trust's properties and the 17th establishment to be opened under their auspice. Unlike the Proprietary School for Boys the BHS experienced few, if any, real difficulties in maintaining a high intake and recruiting staff. It was not, then, fashionable or considered necessary to send girls away to boarding school, as was happening more and more to their brothers, and the competition to catch pupils was not particularly fierce, despite the proliferation of small private day schools in the district. Staff recruitment was aided because well-educated young women were beginning to graduate from universities and training colleges and many were anxious to become teachers, as, despite constant agitation to break the barriers, most other professions remained closed.

Miss Allen Olney resigned her post in 1886, having supervised the task of establishing a sound pattern of teaching, discipline and administration. From the start the BHS had entered its pupils for the Cambridge Local Examinations (the then equivalent of the GCE) and within two years of its foundation the School could mark its honour boards with scholarships to Lady Margaret Hall, Girton College, and Bedford College in Regent's Park. Miss Olney was succeeded by Florence Gadesden MA (d. 1934) from Leamington, who served the School for 33 years until her retirement in 1919. Miss Gadesden, who was elected President of the Head Mistresses Association, must be credited for the successful development of the Blackheath High School and for ensuring its future - for not all the Trust's schools did survive.

As in the case of so many prospering institutions, the original buildings quickly proved inadequate, and as early as 1882 extra accommodation had had to be provided. And by 1898 when the school roll was past the 400 mark, the Trust authorised the building of a science block, which was completed to the designs of architect J. Osborne-Smith, in that year.

From the start the school had enrolled small girls (and a handful of very
small boys) in its preparatory department, but pressure on space had caused
the school to transfer this activity by the 1890s to No. 33 Wemyss Road.
In 1904 a short lease was taken on Stone House (15 Montpelier Row) for
domestic science and preparatory pupils for, by this time, the school was
teaching over 450 girls and the demand for places was brisk. More than
2,400 pupils had passed through the school by 1901, in which year the
Blackheath High celebrated its jubilee. Among the celebrations was a
grand concert which was particularly notable for being an all-female occasion, both in respect of performers and audience. The only male present
was orchestral conductor Alfred Burnett, since the school had not been
able to produce a musician of the necessary quality and of the right sex.

   By 1907 the inconvenience of maintaining a separate department in Montpelier Row led the Trust to take the important step of purchasing Nos. 26
& 27 Wemyss Road, to the west of the main building, for a permanent
extension. No. 26 had been the headmistresses' official residence in the
school's first decade, but it had later reverted to private occupation. To
derive the greatest benefit from the addition the two houses were demolished
and a new wing built on the site to house the kitchens, science laboratories,
and domestic science practice rooms.

   These were some of the best years for the suburb of Blackheath, not
solely because of its educational establishments, although the Village
boasted three public schools between 1880 and 1907: the Prop, the
High School and the School for Missionaries Sons in Independents Road.
The 1890s saw a flowering of intellectual and artistic activity unparalleled
in towns three times the size, with the establishment of the art schools,
the Conservatoire, the Concert Hall, and other ventures. The Village was
a quality shopping centre and the raw new estates of the 1860s: Granville
Park, Vanbrugh Park, Kidbrooke and St. Johns, were softening as the
gardens and trees which made no small contribution towards the character
of the district, began to attain a natural maturity and attractiveness which
was aided by high incomes and cheap servants.

   The period and the place have been immortalised in the fiction of Edith
Nesbit (1858-1924), who set half-a-dozen of her most popular works in the
Blackheath of the turn of this century. The 'Treasure Seekers' and the
'Wouldbegoods' (the Bastable family) moved from Lewisham Road when
father's business prospered, to the Red House on Blackheath - probably
the Red House in Dartmouth Place, long since torn down.

> "And when we were taken to the beautiful big Blackheath house we
> thought now all would be well, because it was a house with vineries,
> and pineries, and gas and water, and shrubberies and stabling, and
> replete with every modern convenience, like it says in Dyer &
> Hilton's list of Eligible House Property."

> "We went to live at the Red House at Christmas. After the holidays
> the girls went to Blackheath High School, and we boys went to the
> Prop. (that means the Proprietary School)."

The Wouldbegoods - 1901

Nesbit's books were fiction, based on her local knowledge, and whether
she "sent" the Bastable girls to the High School because its methods were

194

in harmony with her Fabian philosophy, which supported women's rights and education for girls, or whether she simply caught the atmosphere and social idiom of middle-class late 19th-century Blackheath, it is hard to tell. The High School played its part in the campaign for women's suffrage, both ex-pupils and staff, including Florence Gadesden, speaking at local rallies and supporting the London Society for Women's Suffrage. One such meeting, in 1909, took place at the Woodbegood's Red House, then the home of the Duckham family, when the Blackheath chapter of the Suffragettes numbered 115. A later meeting, in the October of that year, was held at the Concert Hall, and such was the hooliganism, with stink bombs, fireworks and the blowing of horns, perpetrated by a rowdy opposition, that the police were forced to eject many of the audience and the meeting was abandoned in uproar.

Although High School personalities were in favour of female suffrage, they were not militants and the smooth progress and development of the school were not interrupted. The new wing, built in 1908, served the school well enough for the early years of the 20th century and through the Great War. When peace came in 1919 Florence Gadesden retired after a generation's service to the Blackheath School, during which it was not impossible that she may have taught three generations of the same family.

Her successor was Margaret Gale (1881-1953), previously headmistress of Ipswich High School, who found a school that was crammed to the attics and with no room left on the original site to expand without a total loss of the small playground. Nos. 28 & 29 Wemyss Road had been purchased as an extension but these had proved barely adequate. In 1926 the High School took over No. 14 The Paragon for its junior department. The house had been used for a boarding school since 1918, when it had been approved as an official boarding house for the High School under Mrs. Percy Dale. In 1920, that arrangement ceased and No. 14 was subsequently used by Miss F.M. Barnes as a private boarding and day school for girls. From 1926 until it was severely damaged by a bomb in May 1941, No. 14 was an important annexe to the Blackheath High School, although it was little used once war broke out in 1939. Miss Gale left in 1931 to take charge of the Trust's school at Oxford and she was succeeded by Alice Kathleen Lewis MA (1888-1976) one-time headmistress of the Brighton High School.

Miss Lewis (who died as this chapter was being drafted) had the extra task of supervising the school during the 1939-1945 war which, with the outbreak of hostilities, had been evacuated to Tunbridge Wells. Initially, the main buildings in Wemyss Road were closed and, at the same time, the official boarding house at No. 66 Westcombe Park Road (Stanley House) was shut. But, by 1940, a handful of pupils, including some unable to join the evacuation, were back at Wemyss Road, following a basic curriculum, without science or games, for a fee of 10gns a term.

When the school returned from Tunbridge Wells and the Wemyss Road buildings had been put in order, the staff and pupils picked up most of the threads of the pre-war days, but Miss Lewis retired in 1945 and her place was taken by Miss J.S.A. Macaulay MA, BLitt. The BHS continued to thrive, rebuilding its roll to about 500-530 in all departments and still offering an education which was designed to lead a girl to the universities or the professions. The High School revived the concept of a separate junior department with its purchase, in 1945, of No. 13 Morden Road, a rambling house that had been the home of the surgeon John Flint South

(1797-1882) during the years 1865-1882. South, the uncle of Edward Wilton South, had been a keen supporter of the High School in Blackheath and, despite his advancing years, had been helpful to the movement in the late 1870s.

Miss Macaulay left Blackheath in 1955. Her successor, Miss S. M. Wheatley MA, served only six years as headmistress, for she did something quite unique for a Blackheath High School principal - she married, becoming Mrs. Stoker in April 1960, and retired from teaching at the end of the Christmas term in 1961.

Miss F.M. Abraham MA, the present Head, previously at Liverpool High School, was appointed in 1962 - only the seventh head teacher in the school's 96 year history.

The Blackheath High School suffered few of the traumas and upsets of the Proprietary School. It was based on a strong financial ground and its purpose was clear - to educate girls to university standards regardless of income and social status. This last concept was aided by a system whereby the parent paid fees according to means and by the granting of places to bright girls from local authority schools where the authority paid the fees. There had always been enough girls of sufficient calibre to fill the desks of the High School but the post war years saw great changes both in educational opportunity for all social groups and a shifting attitude among the middle classes towards state schools. Increasing provision of comprehensive education in the district and the lavish facilities provided by the state for sixth form study tempted parents who, traditionally, would have regarded the High School as their first choice. But the relatively modest fees of the BHS attracted pupils from a wider and wider catchment area and the recent decline in choice for secondary education with the abolition of the traditional grammar schools, created a new generation of pupils whose parents preferred their daughters to be educated in traditional methods at a neighbourhood high school. There seems little doubt that the system and the Girls Public Day School Trust will flourish for many more years and that the Blackheath High School will celebrate its centenary in 1980.

Of the remainder of Wemyss Road, the history is brief and uneventful until the last war. All the present Victorian houses were built between 1880 and 1883 by George Gorrum to a single design; only No. 36, of an unusual shape in order to cram the house on to the small site, broke the pattern. Unfortunately, the presence of the High School and the use of the Village end of the road by the Express Dairy Company for a bottling depot reduced the amenity of the street and many of the buildings had been turned into flats or lodging houses before the 1914-1918 war.

The building on the north side of Wemyss Road at the west end, presently a food depot for the Express Dairy milk floats, was built as a stable and used by the Blackheath Riding Academy during the 1930s. Nos. 1-3 Wemyss Road were originally part of Bath Place (see Chapter 12) and demolished at the end of the 19th century. Nos. 4-9, three pairs of semi-detached houses built to the same style as the other houses in Wemyss Road, were severely damaged in March 1945 by the rocket bomb which fell on the Wesleyan church in Blackheath Grove. The cleared site was acquired by the police authority in 1951 and blocks of flats built there in 1954 to the design of architects Westwood, Son & Harrison; the building contractor was Leslie Bilsby. In 1975 these flats were sold to the London Borough of Lewisham for the municipal housing stock.

15 Blackheath Vale

Until the beginning of this century Blackheath Common was extensively
covered with pits and hollows, much like those close to Vanbrugh Park,
which were the remains of old gravel and sand pits. For centuries this
part of south east London had been systematically worked for gravel, sand,
lime and chalk deposits, especially around the Heath, the Point and Maid-
enstone Hill, and the Loampit Vale areas. The development of houses
around the Heath in the middle of the 18th century brought pressure on the
Crown (who granted the leases for quarrying) and the Lords of the Manors
in whose freehold much of the Heath fell, to reduce what had become a
nuisance. For the empty workings rapidly filled with gorse, rubbish and
water and, as well as being dangerous, they were also the hiding places
for footpads and highwaymen. There was a never-ending stream of newspaper reports in the 18th and early 19th century of brigands leaping from
gravel pits to rob and injure unwary travellers, and law-abiding citizens
were constantly tumbling into the pits and breaking their limbs.

But sand and gravel were valuable building materials and much in demand
for the development and re-development of London. An unidentified newspaper cutting of 1788 made the point quite well: "The gravel of this country
and particularly that of Blackheath and Kensington, is said to be superior
in quality to that of any other. Louis XIV offered to Charles II as many
cubic stones to pave London on condition of his receiving in exchange as
much gravel as would be necessary to gravel the gardens of Versailles. The
exchange did not take place: but as the late Commercial Treaty has already
produced some advantageous speculations, it is confidently said that in the
spirit of trade the gravel pits will not be overlooked."

Despite these excavations a large part of the Heath remained relatively
flat and the influx of population and the use of the Common for sports,
games and public meetings, made it clear that the Heath had an amenity
which overweighed its commercial possibility as a gravel quarry. The
ground was commonland and, as such, was free grazing, although this
had not prevented a creeping process of encroachment whereby freeholders
and Lords of the Manor would fence in quite large tracts for building purposes.
The earliest such encroachment, other than Greenwich Park, was the development of Dartmouth Row in the 1690s by the widow Susannah Graham
and her nephew William Legge, 1st Earl (2nd Baron) Dartmouth (1672-1750).
But throughout the 18th century a gradual encroachment had "tidied up"
various estate boundaries and there was also a dispute over the exact line
of the ancient Manor of East Greenwich which had been defined, as accurately
as the then standards of cartography would permit, in Samuel Traver's
survey of 1695.

Many of the old gravel pits remained to scar and add interest to the Heath
until quite recent times: Marr's Ravine (between Goffer's Road and Hare
and Billet Road) was filled in with spoil from the major sewer works of
1905, and the pits known as Crown Pits (between Charlton Way and Shooters

Hill Road, now the site of the funfairs) and the Washerwomen's Pits opposite Royal Parade, were not filled in and grassed over until the 1939-1945 war when they were deemed suitable for the disposal of bomb rubble. Only Vanbrugh Pits have been allowed to remain in their original state.

But the principal pit, which seems to have been excavated in the mid-18th century for sand, was so large that it eventually attracted commercial premises to its rim, and a large hamlet of houses grew up in its shelter. This was Blackheath Vale, an unusual village, quite cut off by the Heath from the rest of the Village and, perhaps, unique in metropolitan London.

Blackheath Vale is not marked on the Rocque survey of 1746, nor on the survey published in Hasted's 'Hundred of Blackheath' published in 1778. A plan of Blackheath drawn by Robert Barker in 1748 showed some gravel pits on the Heath (unlike Rocque and Hasted which showed none) but not on the site of Blackheath Vale. Nevertheless, that there was a sandpit on the site can be deduced from leases granted by the 3rd Earl of Dartmouth (1731-1801) for building. There were at least two windmills on or close to the Heath in the late 17th century: one close to the fence of Hollyhedge House, on the Heath towards Dartmouth Place, and another near Morden Hill.

By 1770 Hollyhedge House, in the Dartmouth freehold, had been released to one Charles Newton and by then the mill had been pulled down. But there was still enough work for more than one windmill. The river Ravensbourne had enough speed of current to drive a grinding wheel but the farms of Kidbrooke and Lee as well as the local demand for cattle and horse feed would have been more than sufficient to keep a host of millers busy. Further, the Heath was an ideal site for a windmill, with wide sweeps of high open land which would allow the mill sails to catch even a slight breeze.

Thus, with the closing of the Hollyhedge mill, Dartmouth granted new leases to millers for plots on the edge of what is now Blackheath Vale. The first, to William Basden (or Basdon) was dated 3 November 1770 and was for a term of 61 years from September 29, thus expiring in 1831. This lease included a windmill on a site very close to the two existing houses called Mill House and Golf House. The other mill, which may have been built at about the same time, stood near Talbot Place, just outside the back garden of the present All Saints' vicarage in Duke Humphrey Road.

Whether the mills were built on the edge of a large sandpit or whether excavations took place after the mills had been erected, we cannot tell, for the want of licence records and plans of permitted gravel and sand excavation rights.

But from the years 1789 to 1804 such was the depth of the pit that some building works had taken place within it and a sizeable livery stables erected on the south side of the entrance path, while the first of a number of cottages had also been built there. Further, by 1805, the ground behind the west mill dropped down sharply like a cliff face, much as the west end of Blackheath Vale does presently, although now the cliff is retained by a concrete buttressed wall.

The tenancies of the windmills can only be guessed at presently, despite evidence from the Dartmouth leases, the Land Tax returns and, towards the end, the commercial directories. This is because none of the above sources give a complete picture - for all lack, in some respect, important linking clues.

The West Mill: This was held by Basden on the lease of 1770; a cottage close by was in the tenure of Edmund Bull in 1771 and he is shown in the

Land Tax returns until 1783 and Mrs. Bull by 1784-5. Bull was at the Holly-hedge House mill before 1770 and may have been the working miller at Bas-den's new mill. In 1792 a 40-year lease was given to Mrs. Eleanor Under-wood; and Richard Underwood appears in the Land Tax returns for the period 1786-1794. The west mill was held by Mrs. Anne Peace in 1804 and she may have worked it from 1793 since the name Peace is listed in the Land Tax returns from that date.

In 1820 the returns show the west mill to be occupied by Mr. Daniels (or Daniel). There was a Charles Henry Daniel in the area in 1816 and this may be the same man. But Henry Daniels (sic) appears in the Land Tax returns from 1784 to 1801 and Mrs. Daniels from 1802 to 1819, being jointly assessed "for the mill" with Mrs. Peace from 1809 to 1819. The Daniels are named on the lease as late tenants for the mill site when it was granted to Thomas Whitmarsh in 1835-6 (see below). An aquatint (in the Lewisham Local History Library) is captioned in a contemporary hand: "Taken down in November 1835".

The East Mill: It is easier to work backwards for the tenancies of the Talbot Place mill although it is likely that the head lessor was not always the work-ing miller. This was the case when in 1825 the east mill ground and the house at the back, East Mill Cottage (see below), were let to the Hon. Mrs. Foy. The tenants from 1795 were members of the Constable family, named by 1800 as Michael and James, who were described as millers on a lease of 1807. But who held the mill before 1795 will be a subject for conjecture until more evidence is found. The Land Tax returns offer two possibilities: John Bond from 1780 to 1784, and Christopher Lance from 1780 to 1783, were both assessed at £2 in the tax lists, which might indicate they were the millers at the east and west mills. Moving on to 1825 and Mrs. Foy's tenancy, there is no known record of the working miller for the east mill, though the Pigot commercial directories list John Holloway from 1826 to 1832 and Joseph Hills in 1826 and 1828, as millers of Blackheath. Both mills were still standing in 1832, for this was when John Gilbert, later Sir John Gilbert RA, PRWS (1817-1897) made some ink sketches of the scene.

The east mill may have been standing as late as September 1842, when the Kentish Mercury reported a covey of partridges "running past the wind-mill". This must refer to the east mill since the west mill had been taken down by 1836. After the main structure had been demolished the stump remained for some years, but it had been removed by 1850.

Both mills occupied land which many thought were illegal encroachments, but the erection of a utility such as a windmill would have caused less offence than a straightforward building speculation. The most dramatic of these was in 1803, when John Julius Angerstein (1735-1823) and Thomas Moore enclosed about 35 acres of common between Shooters Hill Road and the Charlton and Old Dover Roads, for which they were fined in the form of annual donations to the Parish funds. These fines, although trivial, seemed to discourage further encroachments on the Heath until the late 1840s and the demolition of the east mill. In November 1847 the site of Talbot Place was defined by a railing with a boundary some feet forward of the curtilage of the old mill ground. Once more there was an outcry, and this proved to be the last of the illegal encroachments by private landowners, though there have since been a number by the municipal authorities.

Temporary encroachments in the form of gravel digging, turf cutting and rubbish dumping continued well into the 1860s, all to be followed by public complaint. In 1865 a 60ft by 75ft pit was enclosed for further excavation

opposite the park wall, much to the annoyance of the local boards of works.
Such excavations, coupled with fears that the Heath was being spoiled by
lack of care, led to the formation of the Blackheath Improvement Association
and the Blackheath Preservation Society who petitioned to the Metropolitan
Board of Works and the Home Secretary to preserve the qualities of the
common. In June 1868 the government made it quite clear that no more
gravel should be taken from the Heath and by 1869 Parliament had tabled
legislation to take London's commons into public ownership for ever. Even
this did not prevent one last act of encroachment in October of that year.
The Greenwich District Board of Works announced that they strongly dis-
approved of the removal of gravel from the Heath by the Trustees of Sir
Gregory Page Turner's estate for building work in the Vanbrugh Park area.

The Development of Blackheath Vale

With the establishment of the windmills and abandonment of the sand pit by
the excavators, the Dartmouth Estate granted leases for the development of
stables and artisans' cottages on sites mostly below the rim of the Vale.
But a few houses, on a more generous scale, were built on the edge of the
pit, initially within the boundaries of the mill sites.

   The oldest of these was East Mill Cottage, so called because of its proximity to the mill and not, necessarily, because it was allied to it in any way.
The name was a misnomer, for it was a sizeable double-fronted house, with
four bedrooms, two reception rooms and the usual offices. The earliest
reference to a property which is without doubt East Mill Cottage was in 1795
when it was held by Mr. Constable. By 1800 the Tax Return is more specific and lists the tenant as Michael and James Constable, millers, kin to
Abraham Constable who was a brewer and had been granted, with Richard
Price, a lease on the Three Tuns in Tranquil Vale in 1791. From 1805 to
1824 East Mill Cottage is shown in the tenure of James Constable. In 1825
the property passed to the Rt. Hon. Lady Sophia Foy (d. 1845), widow of Lt.
Col. Nathaniel Foy (1764-1817) who had been based at Woolwich. Lady Foy
resided at East Mill Cottage for the next two decades and during her residence and for many years afterwards the house became better known as Foy
Cottage. On Lady Foy's death the property passed to Benjamin Smith jnr
(1804-1862) who negotiated a new lease for it in 1846 for a term of 31 years.
This lease was in addition to the old east mill site, held by Smith, who
issued the tenancy leases for Talbot Place, built there in 1851.

   Benjamin Smith was the son of the corn merchant and baker, also Benjamin
(1769-1822), whose commercial career is described in those pages covering
the history of Lamb's Buildings (Chapter 9). It was not surprising that
Smith jnr leased Foy Cottage, for the family had a successful connection
with Blackheath Vale since about 1800 and were the head lessors of a row
of cottages called Union Vale (see below) built between 1806 and 1810.

   Smith jnr died at Foy Cottage and the unexpired portion of his lease was
offered for sale in January 1863. The next tenant was Charles Archibald,
a civil engineer, but in 1873 the property was taken by George William
Wood (1820-fl. 1904), the fishmonger of 13 Tranquil Vale (q. v.), who lived
there until the lease expired in the early 1880s.

   The old house was demolished in 1885 to be replaced by a vicarage for
All Saints' Church. The vicarage was built during the years 1885 and 1886
to the design of architect Benjamin Tabberer FRIBA, FSI (1831-1910) a one-
time district surveyor for Greenwich, who designed No. 21 Montpelier Row

(Alverstoke House) for himself in the same year as the new vicarage.

Benjamin Smith's occupancy and lease of Foy Cottage clearly included a development right for the ground in front of the old mill enclosure, whether or not the local populace regarded this as an encroachment. In 1850 work started on two pairs of three storey semi-detached houses which were given the name Talbot Place. The title was chosen to honour the memory of the first wife of the then freeholder, William, 4th Earl of Dartmouth (1784-1853). He had married Francis Charlotte, daughter of the 2nd Earl of Talbot, in 1821 but she had died in October 1823 at the early age of 22; their first child, George, died in the same month, aged but one year.

The original lease for Talbot Place had been granted to Smith on a 61-year term from Christmas 1851 although work had started before this. Smith, in turn, sub-let his new houses on 21-year leases; the whole group was eventually assigned to Frederick Heritage in October 1872, by which time the head lease had been extended to a 99-year term.

Only No. 1 seems to have been given a name: Rockingham, and this house enjoyed a reputation as a girls' school when it was occupied by Miss Mary Addison (1861-1944) and her sister. They had purchased the school known as Cedar Lodge in Dartmouth Row from the Misses Maberley in 1896 but moved the institution to Talbot Place in 1909 as Rockingham - a "Day School for the Daughters of Gentlemen". The school closed at the end of 1918 and the house reverted to private use.

The west mill site

The original lease on the west mill expired in 1831 and the mill had been demolished by 1835. At the same time, all the outbuildings and the Daniels' family house (Ivy Cottage) were removed and the empty ground let for development. The speculator here was Thomas Whitmarsh, and he was granted a lease on September 1 1836 for a 31-year term, to run from September 1835. Whitmarsh lived at the Green Man public house which stood on the corner of Dartmouth Row and Blackheath Hill. There is some doubt as to which Thomas Whitmarsh took the Blackheath Vale lease because father and son had the same forename: Thomas Whtimarsh snr (1780-1847) was landlord of the Green Man from 1822 until his death in 1847; his son, Thomas Henry Whitmarsh (1805-1862) also resided at the Green Man although his mother, Ann Whitmarsh (1784-1871), held the licence after Thomas snr's death.

One or other Whitmarsh borrowed £500 from Dr. Hollis of Lewisham and built two houses to a curious plan in that they were semi-detached but joined by a long party wall running north west to south east. The half to the north west, which took the name Windmills and, later, Mill House, was sub-let to William Morley, a merchant with interests in Manchester. Morley (1787-1884) lived in the house for 46 years and his daughter, Miss L. Morley, completed the half-century by remaining for a further four years after her father's death. The property passed to Robert Craig McKerrow, a commission agent, in 1890 but he quit in 1897 when he compounded with his creditors. During the Great War the house was empty for a period, but from 1915 to 1917 it was used as a hostel for some of the Belgian refugees who had been welcomed to Blackheath in great numbers and given temporary lodging in a number of empty mansions. Between the wars Mill House was occupied by Robert MacDonald Wilson (1868-1929), an explosives expert; and from 1937 to 1956 by Air Vice Marshal Sir George Laing KCB, CBE, RAF (1884-1956) who had been AoC 41 Group from 1939 to 1944. By Laing's time the house had been divided into two flats, one of which was occupied in recent years by Gerald Raffles (d. 1975), the theatrical manager.

The south east house of the pair was leased initially to William Wilson (1781-fl. 1844) and the name Windmills was also applied to this property. It passed through various tenancies during the 19th century and in 1855, when occupied by Dr. Richard Dawson MRCP, it was known as Heath Hall.

In 1904 the building was leased by Revd A.W. Smyth (d. 1956) as a boarding house for the Blackheath Proprietary School (see Chapter 13) but was closed in 1907 when the institution was wound up. By 1910 Heath Hall (or Heath Hill House as it was sometimes known) had been let to the Royal Blackheath Golf Club as a club house. The Royal Blackheath was, and still is, the oldest golf club in the world, claiming to have been founded as early as 1608 when James I (VI of Scotland) is alleged to have played a Scots game, goff, on Blackheath. This is most unlikely, but the legend is worth supporting until more positive evidence of origins comes to light, although as the Club's early records were destroyed in a fire towards the end of the 18th century, this is proving difficult. There is some circumstantial evidence that the Club existed by 1766 and a letter written in 1831 said that the Club had "kept together...for nearly a century".

Be that as it may, the Club leased various premises around the Heath for their Club House and had occupied 93 Blackheath Hill from 1865. The move to Heath Hill House, now called Golf House, came only a few years before the Club ceased using the Heath as their links. Increasing traffic and municipal control during the early years of the 20th century had made play somewhat difficult, and with the occupation of the Heath by baggage trains and troops during the 1914-1918 war the golfers were driven away. They joined the Eltham Club at that time and amalgamated with them in 1923.

Despite this move, the Golf Club kept Heath Hill House as a social club and this use continued until the 1939-1945 war when the building was requisitioned. In 1951 the house was restored to private use. The stables at the rear, facing Goffer's Road, were built in 1858 but between the wars were converted into a dwelling house.

Union Vale and Talbot House

Outside the mill sites the general development of Blackheath Vale took place within the boundary of the old sand pit and below the level of the Heath. This was probably because the digging of the pit had been an act of encroachment but, once dug, the exposed ground could no longer be claimed as common. It certainly would have been no use as grazing, for the thin top soil would have been removed and, in the normal course of events, the hollow would have filled with storm and drain water to create a pond.

But Blackheath Vale did not fill with water. Either there was natural drainage into the pebbles of the Blackheath gravel beds, or the sand digging had revealed an underground stream which was able to cope with additional water. The Vale, being dry and sheltered, attracted a small population and there may have been some small dwellings for sand and gravel diggers in the pit before the end of the 18th century.

Serious development and the building of workmen's cottages started at the beginning of the 19th century with the erection of four cottages before 1804, although a livery stables had been established on the south west side of the central roadway through the Vale possibly by 1789.

One particular development had a 172ft frontage on the Heath, but the houses were built at the bottom of the slope into the Vale - a curious arrangement which may have been made to avoid the charge of encroachment being laid at the door of the Dartmouth family. This was Union Vale, a row of nine cottages set down in the Vale on the south west side of the road but running parallel with Duke Humphrey Road. The gardens stretched up the slope towards the Heath, which in bad weather cannot have given much joy to the residents, as the incline of the ground would have drained the surplus water into the foundations of the cottages.

Union Vale was built by Benjamin Smith snr, the baker of Lamb's Buildings, between 1806 and 1810, although his lease for the plot - a 53-year term from September 1811 - was not signed until January 1812. Eight of the houses were artisans' cottages, rented by coachmen, laundresses, gardeners and cowkeepers, but the ninth - Union Cottage - was larger than the rest and became the headquarters of Smith's corn dealing business. This was run parallel with his bakery, a natural adjunct, but when Smith snr died (in 1822) the bakery passed to his eldest son, also Benjamin, while the corn merchandising business went to his widow Catherine (1773-1840) and his younger son William Smith (1808-1842). In time they added coal to their stock in trade, as was common practice in the 19th century, and on William Smith's death the business was sold to Mrs. Mary Lonsdale, a widow, who traded here with her son until the mid-1850s.

Although the terrace of Union Vale continued to be occupied mostly by ordinary working folk, including a cowkeeper with the extraordinary name of Saving Luckcuck, Union Cottage was leased to a solicitor, John Scard (1802-fl. 1880). Scard formed himself into a one-man preservation group in 1864 when the All Saints' Vestry drew up plans to site a new parish school on the Heath between Blackheath Vale and the new church. He won his fight and was presented with a snuff box by the grateful residents of Blackheath Vale, as a token of their appreciation.

Smith's original lease on Union Vale expired in 1864 but the houses survived another ten years, although by then then they were in a dilapidated condition and, along with many other groups of cottages in the Vale, ripe for redevelopment.

Union Vale was torn down in the early 1870s and a development lease for the site granted to Henry Edward Joyce, of Princes Road (now Rise), Lewisham, from Christmas 1876. The replacement properties were not laid down until the late 1870s and when they were, Joyce, sensibly, sited the houses on the Heath frontage, with the back gardens sloping into the Vale. The new group, four substantial properties, were built as two pairs of semi-detached dwellings and given the name Talbot Houses. The largest pair, Nos. 1 & 2 (The Hollies and The Maples respectively) were completed by 1880 and occupied the corner site nearest the Hare and Billet pond. Nos. 3 & 4 (Rosslyn and Heathside Villas) were assigned by Joyce to two prosperous Village tradesmen: No. 3 to Charles John Bond, and No. 4 to William Butcher, but neither lived in their properties and the acquisition of the leases must have been solely as an investment.

Talbot Houses was renamed Duke Humphrey Road in 1933, in order to dispel confusion between the Houses and Talbot Place, but in earlier years the Post Office had imposed the appellation Nos. 1-4 The Vale, although this was during a time when the houses in the Vale proper were known by their old terrace names.

In March 1939 much excitement was created for the tenants of Talbot Houses when Herr Behlan, a Second Secretary of the German Embassy, landed a light aircraft on the Heath, partly for lack of fuel, but also because he thought he was in the vicinity of Croydon airport. His machine ran on to the pavement in front of No. 2 and quickly attracted a crowd of enthusiastic onlookers. The next time the Germans came so near to Talbot Houses was on 21 July 1944 when Nos. 1 & 2 were blown to smithereens and Nos. 3 & 4 so badly damaged they had to be demolished.

The owner of No. 2 since 1929, Frank Thwaites Bush ARIBA, was granted a redevelopment permit for the whole site after the last war and drew up plans for a tactful replacement which harmonised with the architecture in the vicinity both in appearance and height. Unfortunately, after consent had been granted the then Lewisham Borough Council served a compulsory purchase order for the site with a view to building a block of municipal flats. A spirited action by local residents and the Blackheath Society forced a public enquiry which led to the Secretary of State refusing to confirm the compulsory purchase order. Bush was able to proceed with the development and Goffer's House was erected on the site - the third development on that parcel of land in 150 years.

The original Talbot Houses, as a street name, was extended in the 1880s to cover a small plot of land on the north east side of the entrance to Blackheath Vale and facing the Village. Until the early 1870s this land had been the Heath end of the garden or waste ground attached to a house or pair of cottages held by the Millward family. With the redevelopment of Blackheath Vale the plot was sold at the end of the 1870s and a pair of large semi-detached houses built on the Heath frontage. Initially they were known as Nos. 1 & 2 The Retreat, possibly because one of the Millward houses had this name in 1871, but were later renumbered as Nos. 5 & 6 Talbot Houses. They were large and not very convenient properties and had been converted into flats by the early 1930s, if not before.

The heart of Blackheath Vale

The development of the hollow of Blackheath Vale started in earnest in 1804 with leases to William Stepney and George Millward to erect a pair of cottages apiece on the south west side of the footpath which led from the Heath to the bottom of the old sand pit. By 1810 there were at least 20 dwellings there and the number did not increase to any appreciable degree until the late 1870s when most of the original dwellings were torn down and the street almost totally redeveloped.

Although Blackheath Vale was largely a village of working mens' houses, three important facilities were sited there - a girls' school, a brewery and a livery stables - which played no small role in the history of Blackheath.

By the end of the first decade of the 19th century there were groups of cottages in the Vale in the ownership of Robert Jennings, John Blow, a builder, and Messrs Bryant, Edward Davies, Neale and Mortimer. Some held only a single dwelling, no doubt their own houses, but others owned three or four cottages, some of which they sub-let. As the years went by the head leases were bought and sold and some lessees added further houses to their plots or improved the existing properties and added stables and outhouses.

The Millward family were one of these and after George Millward died, possibly in 1823, his lease was taken over by his widow, Ann, who lived in Blackheath Vale until 1858, reaching the great age of 102.

During the early years of the 19th century the name "Blackheath Vale" does not seem to have been much used - identification of particular houses was usually by the names of the tenants or lease holders and the residents of the Vale would be described as of: 'Blow's Buildings' or 'Bryant Place', or whatever.

In 1826 a number of the cottages had passed to William Wright (1785-1874), a carpenter and builder, and brother of Thomas Wright (1797-1883), a livery stable keeper who was living in the Vale by the mid-1830s. The Wright family and the Blow family (to a lesser extent) dominated Blackheath Vale for three quarters of the 19th century, and their sons and nephews occupied more than a fair share of the cottages. By 1851 the official address for the central street of Blackheath Vale was 'Wright's Pits'. Members of the Blow family, who had a business connection with Messrs Couchman of 16 Montpelier Vale (q. v.) from the early years of the 20th century, were resident in the Vale from at least 1806 until the deaths of Edwin Blow (1827-1895) and his brother Joseph (1820-1904). Both followed their fathers as carpenters and builders, and the family name lived on in Blackheath in the company known as E. F. Blow & Co., at 16 Montpelier Vale, until 1963 although the Blow family ceased to have any connection with the business long before.

Most of the inhabitants of the Vale were employed by Wright and Blow as carpenters, bricklayers, and building labourers. And the few who were not probably worked for Thomas Wright as cab drivers or in his livery stables.

These stables were alleged to have been established in the Vale, at the bottom of the slope behind Union Vale, as early as 1789, but there is nothing in the Land Tax returns nor in the Dartmouth leases to support this. There may have been some slight substance to the story, in that one of the local coach proprietors, possibly Matthias Ingram of Phoenix Place (q. v.), may have parked his carriages in the protection of the sand pit and that eventually he was allowed to erect stables there. Certainly, the Millward family paid a relatively large tax (£25) for stables in 1825 and by 1830 Thomas Pinnock was in business in the Vale as a livery stable proprietor. Before 1838 Thomas Wright had taken over Pinnock's stables and was to remain the owner until 1878. The business boasted 40 stalls, four loose boxes, a 20-carriage 60ft by 25ft coach house and a six-roomed house. In 1878 it was purchased by Edwin Davis Moore, one-time licencee of the Railway Hotel (q. v.) in Blackheath Village, who had maintained a small livery stable at the back of the pub since his father had been granted the first licence in 1851.

The livery stable in the 19th century served the same purpose as today's petrol filling stations, motor works and bus garages. Not only would the proprietor employ a number of the cabmen who waited at the ranks opposite the railway station and in Tranquil Vale, but he would deal in carriages, traps and domestic horse-drawn vehicles. The trade in Blackheath was extremely lucrative and there were at least half a dozen fly proprietors making a good living there between the 1840s and 1900. Although a good number of the houses boasted stables and a carriage house and could afford coachmen, many had neither the facility for housing the horses nor the men needed to drive them.

Before the building of the railway in 1849, Blackheath businessmen had to rely for their journey to the City on the livery stable proprietors who ran omnibus services from the public houses to Gracechurch Street close to the Bank of England. The choice was wide: Clarke's omnibus, from the Princess of Wales; Youen's City Coaches, from Blackheath Park; Hubble's coach, from the Hare and Billet; Scudd's bus, from the north end of Pond Road; and Collins' coaches, which picked up at the Three Tuns; but the largest company was Wheatley's, which called at the Three Tuns, Tuck's Corner and the Hare and Billet and ran a quarter hour service from the Green Man to the City every day. This last was part of a major network of horse bus routes owned by a Greenwich family, Thomas (1802-1866) and John Wheatley. Their business dropped sharply when the railway came and their profitable omnibus system, "The Nelson", was reduced to the short routes between the new railway stations.

Blackheath Station was served from the 1850s by a number of local small bus operators: Scudd's bus ran a round journey from Footscray via the Station, and a Mr. Staples supplied a bus service from the Red Lion, Shooters Hill Road, to Blackheath Station. But the most useful route was the Eltham run which was operating several services a day from the mid-1850s. In 1867 the Blackheath-Eltham omnibus service was a distinctive, green-painted 3-horse bus and the service continued until 1907, although in 1894 the then owners, Thomas Tilling, purchased a new vehicle, with seats in green plush, from Messrs Lines of Clapham: it could seat 12 inside and 16 outside and was driven by one Harry Stamborough, who was the principal driver on the route for more than 30 years.

Two other services earned the affection of Blackheathens: the yellow, one-horse bus with iron-shod wheels, which plied from the Station to the Charlton Road, and Blaker's Station-Shooters Hill Road service. The former took eight passengers - six inside, and two next to the driver; the inside passengers passed their fares up through a trapdoor in the roof. The driver of this bus was Charles Morgan, who was at the reins every day without fail for 20 years, driving 26 journeys each day and achieving a total of 313,000 miles. When he retired in 1912, grateful residents collected a purse of £117.15.0 to help him in his old age. Robert Blaker (1862-1923),who drove between Blackheath Station and Shooters Hill Road, equalled Morgan's record in length of service, but managed to achieve 424,320 miles in his career. When he retired in 1913 he was given a testimonial and a collection of £83.

The old horse buses survived in Blackheath longer than on most routes, although as early as 1904 motor buses were taking over some of the journeys and the Catford-Southend (Lewisham) run had been motorised as early as 1902. The last horse bus in Blackheath ran on December 7 1912, by which time the local bus operation was firmly in the hands of Thomas Tilling and the National Bus Company. In October 1933 the private bus companies were taken over by London Transport.

But the horse cabs took much longer to disappear from the Blackheath roads: the cabmen had been part of the scene since the building of the railway station and were regarded with mixed feelings by the populace. Despite constant reports of drunkenness, rudeness, over-charging and unhelpfulness by the cabmen, it was surprising how splendid they were when the weather was bad and the horse bus was late. In August 1890 grateful citizens presented the cabbies with a shelter for the rank in Tranquil Vale. It was a miniature restaurant on wheels, built by carpenter Henry Dry and painted in chocolate and stone. There were lockers and coat hooks, a cooking stove, unbreakable enamel crockery and other comforts. With some difficulty it was wheeled up the road to its resting place half way up the hill. Within three months, residents successfully petitioned for its removal higher up the Village, on the corner with Royal Parade. Here it stayed until 1919, when it was moved to the station yard. With the decline of the cab ranks the hut was less and less used, although it survived in the yard until well after the last war.

The improvement in the bus services, the advent of the motor taxi and private car ownership between the wars saw a rapid decline in the local cab rank until only the Ewins family remained. But one man kept a link with the past - Albert Dorville, of Auckland Lodge stables in Shooters Hill Road (behind No. 50), continued to maintain his horse cab until 1947, when he retired after 55 years on the Blackheath station rank.

The Blackheath Vale livery stables' link with the local horse bus and cab system lasted until the beginning of the Great War, by which time the premises had been taken over by Tillings, mostly for garaging. After the war the old stables were used for a variety of light engineering purposes, eventually being leased by Standard Telephones Ltd. What was left in 1939 was largely damaged and demolished as a result of bombing which destroyed 10 of the houses on the south side of the Vale.

The School for Girls

The All Saints' Church of England School, at the end of the Vale, and an important part of the local educational system today, was largely built in 1878 but has origins which stretch back to 1825.

According to Bagshaw's Directory of 1847, a National School of Industry in Blackheath Vale had been founded in 1825. While this may have been true, no other evidence has come to light to support this institution before 1838. There is no doubt that a National School of Industry for Girls had been founded in 1815 in Church Passage, Greenwich, and the Blackheath Vale school may have followed the Greenwich example 10 years later.

Whatever the case, we know that by 1838 the school was well-established, teaching 100 girls (the daughters of the working people) the skills of the servant: dressmaking, cookery, laundering, housework, as well as the rudiments of literacy. The school was supported by donations and subscriptions as well as a nominal payment by the pupils. It was probably sited behind the houses on the north side of the Vale, although no detail has come down to us in the form of leases or site plans, and the building is not named as such on maps of the mid-19th century.

The headmistresses of the National School at Blackheath Vale were as follows: Mrs. Martha Castle in 1838; Charlotte Baker in 1841; Mrs. Harriet Hadley from 1847 to 1860, although Charlotte Baker was still teaching there in 1851; and Mrs. Francis Elizabeth New from 1860 to 1866.

In 1867 the National School was taken over by the Parish, and became the All Saints' Girls School, being put in the charge of Miss E. Jones (fl. 1840-1915) who was to serve as headmistress of her school for 43 years, until her retirement in 1910.

But long before that, in 1878, the old building was torn down and the Parish took a lease for the present school site, remaining there ever since. There was little change until the late 1930s, when over-crowding of the Infants' School in Tranquil Passage saw a transfer of schooling to the Parish Hall on the west side of Tranquil Vale. In 1939 the infant schoolroom was sold and three extra classrooms, cloakrooms and a staff room were built at Blackheath Vale. The old girls' school then became a junior mixed and infants' school, still a Church of England School, but aided by the state.

The Blackheath Brewery

One of the surprises in Blackheath's commercial history is its lack of local breweries before the 1820s. Not one of the pubs ever boasted that it brewed its own beer although the Hare and Billet, which was in existence with that name by 1765, must have produced a house ale, judging by the vast quantities sold on fair days and holidays. By the start of the 19th century the Village pubs were already under the control of brewers from Lewisham, principally the Constable family and, later, Steward and Marsden. But this did not prevent the establishment of a local brewery in Blackheath Vale, although the exact date of its foundation is not known.

The Constable family, who lived at East Mill Cottage (q.v.) from 1795 until 1824, may have had some hand in the brewery, but the first surviving record of the sale of alcoholic drink in the Vale came on September 1823 when Mary Wheatley petitioned the local justices for a licence for a house in Bryant's Place, Blackheath Vale. Her plea was rejected, but the 1826 Pigot Commercial Directory lists one Paul Chitts as a brewer in Blackheath Vale. Chitts must have been a sub-tenant, for his name does not appear in the Dartmouth leases for Blackheath Vale or in the Land Tax returns.

The establishment of a brewery here meant a generous, clean water supply, and this lends support for the development of a hamlet in the Vale in the early years of the 19th century. But whether the water came from underground streams or had to be pumped or hauled up in buckets from wells we do not know.

Chitts is listed in the 1828 Pigot, but as this directory seems to be little more than a reprint of the 1826 edition it is not possible to be sure that he was still in the Vale at that date. By 1832 the brewery was owned by Thomas Ingle (1782-1846) who described himself as a "pale beer brewer". He remained the Blackheath brewer until his death in 1846, supplying, no doubt, the beer carts and beer tents which were set up on the Heath on summer days and when the Bank Holiday crowds thronged the Heath and Greenwich Park.

After Ingle's death the brewery was held, briefly, by Charles Wright - he was a carpenter but also the head lessor of the building, and possibly wanted to keep the business going until a new tenant brewer could be found. He was not to wait long, for by 1850 the Blackheath Brewery was in operation once more, in the proprietorship of James Peacock. Peacock (1812-fl. 1875) was to be the last 'Blackheath Brewer', producing his own ales, stouts and porter until 1875 when the brewery closed.

Peacock's beers could be purchased for 1/6d a gallon, and no doubt he mostly supplied the retail trade, but he enjoyed a brisk boost to the profits in the summer when the Heath was packed with visitors. His speciality then was "Peacock's Swipes", a special beer brewed for the holiday trade. Swipes was a weak beer, possibly only barely brewed because of the speed needed to keep up supplies, and its sale was encouraged by the local justices of the peace who wished to keep drunkenness within reasonable bounds. For a few years Peacock held a retail beer house licence and named his pub 'The British Queen', but it was probably no more than a room in his home or works set aside for retail sales on the premises.

James Peacock, who had at least 11 children, left Blackheath Vale when Wright's leases expired and most of the street was redeveloped. He seems also to have left the district, for no further information about him has been gleaned. In 1878 a James Peacock, beer retailer, is listed for 97 Greenwich (High) Road, and he was still there in 1882; but in 1885 and 1887 the tenant was Mrs. Elizabeth Peacock. We cannot be certain that this is the right man because the Blackheath brewer had a son, also named James; furthermore, James snr's wife was Harriet Knight. The departure of the Peacocks from Blackheath Vale marked not only the end of the Blackheath Brewery but the end of an era - by 1879 hardly a single building from the original developments in the Vale was left standing.

The south side of the road was totally re-built, taking the numbers 2 to 26 Blackheath Vale, on a 99-year lease to Miss Harriet Pinnock of Dalston; she was possibly the daughter of Thomas Pinnock, who had held the livery stables in 1832. Some of these houses survive today, the exceptions being Nos. 18 to 26 which were severely damaged during the last war. The site was acquired by the Lewisham Borough Council in 1949 and, subsequently, new bouses were built, generally in keeping with the surviving terrace in height and volume.

The north side of the Vale was sold to Stephen Riddington, the baker of Brunswick Place (q.v.); Nos. 1-9 Blackheath Vale were originally Nos. 1 - 5 Patshull Villas and leased from September 1872 for 99 years; Nos. 9 & 11 at the rear were Nos. 1 & 2 Fern Villas; Nos. 15 to 27 (originally Nos. 1-7 Windsor Villas with the sequence starting at the Heath end of the terrace) were leased to Riddington for 92 years from December 1879.

Blackheath Vale has remained remarkably unchanged since that time and still retains some of the pattern established in the early years of the 19th century: the footpath and steps leading to Goffer's Road is marked as a passageway on an 1815 lease to one Richard Neale; the site of Benjamin Smith's Union Vale is clearly defined by the fence behind Goffer's House; and the Stone Restoration Company hugging the north embankment harks back to the 1830s when Aquila Newman traded from Blackheath Vale as a stone mason.

All Saints' Church

It was a remarkable fact of local history that, until the building of All Saints' Church in 1857, a few hundred yards to the east of Blackheath Vale, the inhabitants of Blackheath within the parish of Lewisham had no parish church nearer than St. Mary's, Lewisham for divine worship. Of course, this was a technicality, for the devout Christian who embraced the established faith could use the proprietary chapels of St. Germans (founded in 1823) in St. Germans Place, the church in Dartmouth Row (now the Church of the Ascension), which had been established as long ago as the 1690s, and, from 1829, the Cator's church (now St. Michael's and All Angels) in Blackheath Park.

The lack of an Established Church in Blackheath Village, despite the fact that most of it lay within the boundary of the Parish of Lewisham, was partly because these acres were on the very edge of the parish. Until the late 1870s Lewisham was largely open country, and close to Blackheath were the parish churches of Lee and Charlton - not too far in the early 19th century, when people were prepared to walk quite considerable distances to work and worship.

But the rapid development of Blackheath led to a drift of worshippers to chapels outside the parish for lack of their own church, and there was clearly a need to establish a chapel of ease for Lewisham. Furthermore, the church authorities knew that Blackheath was an ideal place for a new church, as not only was there a large enough population to support a living, but it was a prosperous suburb and its parishioners would be able to afford the cost of the building works. The idea of a new church for Blackheath was formally discussed at a meeting at the Green Man in February 1854 which was attended by the then Bishop of London, Dr. Charles James Blomfield (1786-1857) and various church and lay representatives of both the Parishes of Lewisham and Greenwich. The meeting resolved that an "Established Church be erected on Blackheath near to that part usually called the Village", and a committee was formed to see this project through. It was led by the then Vicar of Lewisham, the Revd and Honorable Henry Legge (1805-1887), 5th son of George, 3rd Earl of Dartmouth (1755-1810), and the second of the family to hold the living. Furthermore, he resided at Hollyhedge House, a mansion of the Heath, close to Dartmouth Place and within the proposed parish. Other members of the committee included local businessmen, Henry Couchman, the builder of 16 Montpelier Vale (q.v.), and Walter Bagnall (1798-1867) of 33/35 Tranquil Vale.

The committee was stiffened with other local representatives, and further discussions on the question of the site for the new church and the means to raise the funds for its erection took place from March 1854 onwards. It was the site that proved most difficult. It was clear that the ground would be donated by the freeholders - the Dartmouth family - and soon obvious that it would be taken from the common land of Blackheath. Initially, a triangle close to the Hare and Billet and Goffer's Road was chosen, later the ground opposite Phoenix Place (q.v.), and later still a plot between Eastnor House on the corner of Lloyds Place and the present corner of Royal Parade and Tranquil Vale. Finally, the committee settled on the site on which the church was eventually to be built, having abandoned the others principally for structural engineering reasons. Meanwhile, the funds flowed in: £600 by 1854, including generous donations from members of the Legge family living in Blackheath, and by 1857 the building fund had reached nearly £1120. In 1855 an architect had been chosen - he was Benjamin Ferrey FSA, FRIBA (1810-1880), an ex-pupil of Augustus Charles Pugin (1762-1832) and, by 1855, a consultant architect to the Church Building Society.

The committee accepted a tender of £3497 from Messrs Holland, of Bloomsbury, and work started in October 1857 despite the building fund being short by about £500. On October 26 1857 the foundation stone was laid by William, 5th Earl of Dartmouth (1823-18), but by the time the church was nearing completion about nine months later, not only had the scheme to build a tower and spire to be put back but the construction costs had risen, leaving the building fund short by nearly £1000. It took an increase in the endowment as well as a further donation by the Earl of Dartmouth and a bank loan at 4 per cent to cover the remaining costs. Dartmouth was not prepared to give more than he did on the grounds that the congregation likely to be attracted to the church was quite rich enough to repay quickly any outstanding loans.

When the new church of All Saints' was consecrated and opened for worship in November 1858, it was the centre of a new ecclesiastical district in the Parish of Lewisham, with a population of about 1700. It lacked its tower and spire, the Greenwich District Board of Works had protested that it was an illegal encroachment on the commonland, and the new Parochial Council were in debt. Nevertheless, All Saints' prospered, the debts were rapidly amortised, and so skilfully had the church been placed near, but not in, the Village, that even the Board of Works stopped grumbling.

The style was Gothic revival, the materials Kentish ragstone with soft stone dressings - and the setting superb. To some eyes the church looked like a toy, set down on a giant green carpet and, when covered with snow, like the perfect subject for a Christmas card.

The first incumbent was the Revd James Sanderson Clarke (1820-1911) who had been a curate at St. Mary's, the parish church of Lewisham, before his appointment in 1857. Clarke stayed only six years at All Saints' having accepted the living at Goudhurst in 1864; he held this until his death 47 years later. His successor at All Saints', the Revd Charles Abbot Stevens (1818-1908) saw the completion of the main fabric of the church in 1867, when the spire was finally added, thus ending the jibes that the tower-less church looked like nothing more than three barns.

All Saints', as well as being the Blackheath 'parish' church, also took on responsibility for the local schools, firstly the infant school in Tranquil Passage and, later, the girls' school in Blackheath Vale. The congregation supported their place of worship whenever required and two further additions were made to the church. The first was in 1890, with the addition of new vestries; and the second, a new porch in 1899, put the final touch to a building that had been started 46 years before. It is interesting to note that the porch was designed by Sir Arthur William Blomfield FRIBA (1829-1899), probably his last commission. Blomfield was the son of Dr. Charles Blomfield who had chaired the meeting at the Green Man in February 1854 which had resolved to build the church at Blackheath.

The incumbents at All Saints' after the resignation of the Revd Stevens, were as follows:

1880-1882:	Revd Frederick George Holbrooke (d. 1911)
1883-1892:	Revd Edward Foyle Randolph (1837-1909)
1892-1907:	Revd Henry Welsford Snell MA (1835-1908)
1907-1915:	Revd George Isaac Swinnerton MA (d. 1925)
1915-1925:	Revd Charles Jasper Palmer MA (d. 1931)
1925-1934:	Revd Albert Palmer
1934-1941:	Revd Alan James Sutherland Symons
1941-1943:	Revd Reginald Morgan Pitches MA
1943-1945:	Revd Eric Walter Garnham Lunn (induction June 1944)

1945-1953:   Revd Norman William Gowing
1954-1959:   Revd H.A. Lewis Jefferson
1959-1971:   Revd Thomas Percival Clarke
1972 to date: Revd Canon Stanley John Ashby

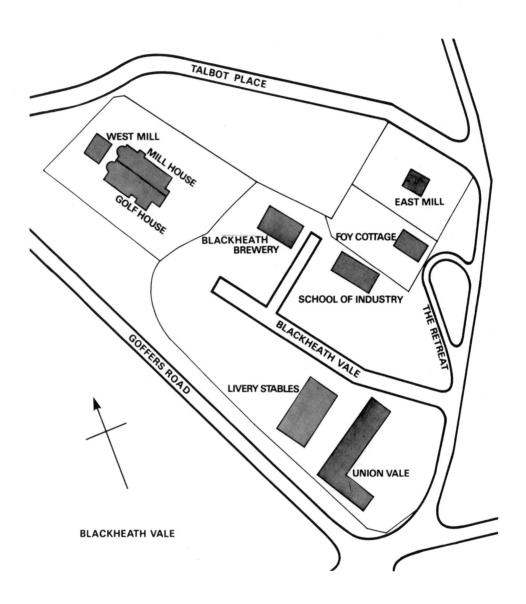

16 Art, Music and Community Life

At the beginning of the 19th century Blackheath people had no meeting place outside their own homes other than the Green Man assembly rooms on Blackheath Hill, the church at Lee and the chapel at Dartmouth Place. This was probably no real hardship as the population was small and there had been little development other than Montpelier Row, and the houses there had drawing rooms large enough for a modest dance or secular meeting.

The Green Man was much used for political meetings and entertainments and gentlemen would meet there for most social purposes - indeed the Blackheath Golf Club ate its weekly dinners there, having moved from the Assembly Rooms of the Chocolate House on the north side of the main road in the 1790s.

Thus, the demand in Blackheath was adequately catered for, in that the population was too small to warrant special facilities. But during the early years of the 19th century the population of Greenwich was growing and the beginnings of professional theatre were being established. By the 1820s the Green Man rooms were in increasingly greater demand, principally for private dances, recitals, concerts and general entertainments.

The pressure on the space - the room could seat 400 - was such that there seems to have been some function or other at the Green Man almost every night in the 1830s. If it was not the first Blackheath Assembly of the season "where 250 of the gentry including officers from Woolwich danced quadrilles, waltzes and the gallopade to Mr. Payne's band until 2am" (February 1834), then it was the world-renowned violinist Signor Paganini playing his own works, or a Mr. Young who caught bullets in his fingers, a Blackheath Golf Club Dinner, an exhibition by Madame Tussaud of her waxworks, or a demonstration of Carter's Oxy-Hydrogen Microscope which would show the visitor 12ft dragons in drops of water for payment of 1/-.

But as the number of households grew, so did the need for purpose-built cultural centres and meeting halls.

In 1834 the Greenwich Philharmonic Society had been formed and they hired the Green Man in February for an orchestral concert, but had to stiffen the orchestra desks with members of the Royal Artillery Band from Woolwich. This body was one of the first groups in the district whose standards were sufficient to attract a paying audience, and one of the earliest local examples of the Victorian enthusiasm for the organisation of leisure and the pursuit of culture and knowledge. Although the Greenwich Philharmonic Society did not last long (at least, with that name) the formation of that and similar groups gave impetus to the foundation of the local literary institutions: in Greenwich in 1835 and in Blackheath in 1842. The literary institutions, usually enjoying grandiloquent titles like The Society for the Acquisition and Diffusion of Useful Knowledge, provided libraries, lectures, opportunities for further education and, most popular, reading rooms and meeting halls, long before the provision of such services became a municipal responsibility.

The foundation of the literary institutions in Blackheath and Greenwich was largely due to the efforts of the Bennett family, watch and clock makers whose business had been founded in Cheapside in 1765. A branch of the company had been established in Stockwell Street, Greenwich, and the family concentrated much of their interest in south east London, the Greenwich shop becoming the family home.

In 1825 John Bennett, son of the founder, took the lease of Park House in Cresswell Park, thus establishing a financial interest in property in the Village. It was his three sons - George, William and John - who were to make an important impact on Victorian Blackheath and Greenwich, which survives today in various street names.

The Bennetts entered wholeheartedly into the social, political and cultural life of Greenwich and Blackheath. John (1814-1897) was marginally more loyal to the city, maintaining control over the Cheapside establishment - buying the front page of the Great Exhibition Catalogue in 1851 to advertise the family business - and achieving distinction in City circles, moving through the Court of Common Council to be elected Sheriff and receive a Knighthood in 1873.

William Cox Bennett (1820-1895) was essentially a poet and journalist rather than a shop keeper and the Stockwell Street shop was closed in December 1858 because of this. He was active in local politics and persuaded his fellow Liberals to adopt William Ewart Gladstone as their prospective MP in 1868. During his lifetime he enjoyed a high reputation as a poet, admired by John Ruskin among others, but earned his daily bread for many years as London correspondent of Le Figaro. Perhaps his best contribution to local matters were his efforts during his time as Honorary Secretary of the Greenwich Society for the Acquisition and Diffusion of Useful Knowledge towards the building in 1843 of the Greenwich Literary Institution in Royal Hill. His Society survived until 1896 and the building, acquired at that time by the then Greenwich Borough Council, was kept in use as a meeting hall until 1938, in which year the site was cleared for the erection of the new Town Hall.

George Weedon Bennett (1816-1861) established a branch of the family business in Blackheath in 1835 at 3 Blackheath Village (q.v.) and moved in 1840 to 28 Tranquil Vale (q.v.). The story of his trading success will be found under those headings and what is of interest here is his activity as honorary secretary of the Blackheath Society for the Acquisition and Diffusion of Useful Knowledge. The Society had been founded in 1842, clearly inspired by the Greenwich Society under the supervision of brother William. Its members met in a small room over a Village shop and paid subscriptions of 10/- a year for adults and 5/- for children. The reading room was open from 6pm to 10pm in winter and 7pm to 10pm in winter, by 1843 was employing a librarian, John Huggett (1805-1870), and published a catalogue of books. These were mostly donations and, to judge by the titles, consisted largely of discards from the libraries of elderly clerics. Nevertheless, the movement was under way and well-supported by many influential tradesmen and the Church. In 1844 plans were drawn up for the erection of premises and a site found next to a footpath that became, five years later, the Blackheath Station yard.

In 1845 a terrace of new shops was erected which took the name Spencer Place but is now numbered 3-9 Tranquil Vale (q.v.). At the rear of these, on an irregularly-shaped piece of ground the Blackheath Literary Institution was built at a cost of £1500 - the first purpose-built meeting hall and lecture room in Blackheath. It was almost certainly designed by George Smith FIBA (1783-1869), who had been architect to the Greenwich Institution when William Bennett was honorary secretary to that body, and who lived in Blackheath. Smith, the son of William Smith, a Greenwich architect and surveyor, had been taught at the RA schools in 1801 and established a practice in the City. By the age of 27 he had been appointed District Surveyor of the South Division of London and was, from time to time, surveyor to the Coopers Company, the Mercers Company and, during the 1840s, to the Trustees of Morden College. He was an early member of the Institute of British Architects and served on its Council. Smith designed Brooklands in Brooklands Park (where he lived from 1825 to 1838), a house called Bellefield in Foxes Dale (demolished for a Span estate in 1965), the original London Bridge Railway Station, Woodbastwick Hall in Norfolk for the Cator family, St. Michael's church in Blackheath Park, and many other buildings in the Home Counties and the City. He is credited with the design of Blackheath Station in 1849 and the Blackheath Proprietary School in 1831 - but there is no certain proof of his involvement with these buildings.

The Literary Institution was a large lecture hall, with a gallery at one end and a platform at the other. Mock doorways situated on either side of the platform were fitted to give the impression that the building was much bigger than it really was.

The declared objects of the Blackheath Society were self-education and improvement, but there seems to be no record of formal classes, as with the Greenwich Institute, although the library and reading rooms were popular with the subscribing members and the book stock rose steadily each year. By 1849 the reading room was opened at 8am so that commuters could have a quick glance at The Times and other daily papers before they caught their morning horse bus or train to the City.

But the prime use of the building was as a place of entertainment or meeting hall and the reported events tended to be those whereby the lecturers and readers hired the hall and charged for admission to cover costs and make profits. For Blackheath people at least, the Village now boasted a substitute for the Green Man rooms, not as large perhaps, but somewhere easier to reach on cold winter nights, and without the taint of drink.

In its time the Blackheath Institution was the venue for ventriloquists, children's tea parties, lectures on the dramatic works of Schiller, instrumental and song recitals, meetings to protest at the squalid conditions of some of the workmen's cottages in Tranquil Passage, to inaugurate the local volunteer militia, for learned dissertations, juvenile entertainments, exhibitions, sales and magic lantern shows. In 1848 the Blackheath Sacred Harmonic Society gave its first concerts there, conducted by Mr. Ricketts "...who for some time, conducted concerts by the Greenwich Sacred Harmonic Society which has broken up a short time since owing to internal disorder amongst its members." A not unusual turn of events amongst the amateur choral and dramatic societies over the following 50 years.

The Blackheath Literary Institution enjoyed a short life. The Society had collapsed, along with similar groups elsewhere in London suburbs, in the mid-1850s, and in 1858 the lecture hall had been purchased by a local tradesman, probably Thomas Whittaker, the draper of 5 & 7 Tranquil Vale (q.v.) for it was certainly in his hands in the 1870s. The rooms were kept as a newspaper reading room and lecture hall* until the mid-1860s, available for hire on a strictly commercial basis and with none of the pious intentions of the original promoters of the enterprise. Bennett had died in 1861, brother William was busy with politics in Greenwich and the spirit of the movement was broken. The new railway track could carry people up to London for far more sophisticated entertainments than the Literary Institution could provide. Furthermore, the hall was too small and lacked many facilities, not the least among its deficiencies being the single earth closet.

Between 1845 and 1860 the population had increased considerably, with the development of the Lee Park and Lee Terrace area, Granville Park and Vanbrugh Park. The Heath side of Kidbrooke was about to be developed and all this lent reason for the establishment of a larger auditorium.

Although it was much altered over the intervening years, the old Institution remained part of the workshop premises for 5 & 7 Tranquil Vale until 1940 when it was damaged by bomb blast. The rocket bomb in March 1945 hastened its decay and by 1946 the building was a rubbish-filled shell, part of the walls having to be demolished. In 1952 it was purchased by the Blackheath Preservation Trust Ltd. with the intention of restoration, but the Greater London Development Plan motorway schemes prevented that and it was not until the safeguarding was lifted in 1973 that the Trust was able to implement its plans.

The new building, to the design of the architects Carden, Godfrey and Macfadyen, followed the basic style of the old institution in that it retained some of the original walls and shape, and the lancet windows, an important feature of the earlier structure, were replaced. It was not the intention to build a pastiche of the 1845 structure but to create a new building which would harmonise with the surrounding scene in design and materials. It is now occupied by the Mary Evans Picture Library and Colin Banks and John Miles, a graphics design partnership.

The Alexandra Hall (Lloyds Bank, Cresswell Park)

With the demise of the Literary Institution and the growing demand occasioned by the influx of middle class professional and commercial families to Blackheath in the late 1850s and early 1860s, the need for a meeting centre became even more urgent. The new churches in the district were not, then, the possessors of parish halls and the use of the ecclesiastical buildings for secular purposes would not have been entertained.

By chance, it was, in part, the Bennett family who supplied the answer. From 1825 they had held the lease on the old Park Hall estate centred on Cresswell Park. In 1860 they were granted a new 99-year lease for land and this allowed for development and redevelopment.

The first section to be built up was the south west end of Bennett Park and the corner with Cresswell Park through a building lease granted to William Harding. He realised that there were two facilities lacking in Blackheath with the decline of the Literary Institution and the loss, some

*Local legend claims that Charles Dickens delivered one of his dramatic readings here but, although he once lectured at the Greenwich Literary Institution, there is no evidence he spoke at Blackheath.

years before, of John Hally's swimming bath (see the section on Frederick's Place: Chapter 7). Harding supplied the swimming bath as well as a large meeting hall and theatre in the shape of the Alexandra Assembly Lecture and Reading Rooms, a building which was described in October 1872 (when it was for sale) as "A well-built and noble block of modern architecture of the Grecian style... ornamental external appearance... flight of stone steps which lead to the spacious and handsome Hall or Concert Room..."

The construction work took place early in 1863 and coincided with the celebrations attached to the announcement of the betrothal of the then Prince of Wales (Edward VII) to Princess Alexandra of Denmark. Harding, in a fit of patriotism, named his new hall The Alexandra Assembly Rooms and the name stuck until the mid-1920s when the building passed out of public use.

The other attraction was Harding's Blackheath Tepid and Swimming Baths which he opened on 17 June 1863. The main pool measured 56ft by 20ft and held 60,000 gallons of water; in addition there were several private hot and cold baths. Open from 6am to 10pm every day except Sundays, the charge was 1/-, but season tickets which allowed 16 sessions a month cost 10/-, and for a daily bath the season cost was 15/- a month. For swimming, a professional instructor was engaged. Coupled with the meeting hall, the swimming and bathing facilities were described by the Kentish Mercury as "...the most desirable and complete public establishment in the County of Kent."

The proprietor or lessee of the Alexandra Hall was Edgar Drewett, the photographer who traded from 3 Blackheath Village (q.v.) from 1861-1885, and he was not slow in promoting the new enterprise. The first concert took place on 12 January 1864 with a song and instrumental recital by a variety of artists, led by the constructor (sic) Signor Alberto Randeggri. The newspapers wrote that: "The concert proved the rooms to be admirably adapted for musical entertainment and facilities are thus afforded to the residents of the surrounding neighbourhood of attending really first rate music near their own homes."

The events that followed were as various as had been those at the Green Man and the Literary Institution but in July 1864 the rooms were let out during the day as a school - the Alexandra College "for the daughters of Gentlemen only" run by a Mrs. West. There was a long list of professors teaching a variety of subjects, including Italian, the Harp, philosophy, dancing and callisthenics. The general courses cost 30gns for girls over 12 years and 25gns for the younger ones. Alexandra College was typical of many such "schools" - little more than a high-principled prospectus attracting insufficient pupils - and it disappears from the records shortly after the opening announcement.

During the 1860s Blackheathens found the Alexandra Hall a useful central venue not only for entertainment but also for meetings of protest. A typical occasion was the meeting called in February 1865 to float a new gas company - The Kent Consumers Gas Co. - as an alternative to the Phoenix Gas Co., which had supplied the district since the 1830s. Phoenix gas was impure, the new company's promoters claimed. But the local public were not convinced, especially as the enabling legislation provided for works to be built at Hither Green, then clean and rural, and one protester pointed out that a member of the Board of the new gas company was also a director of the Kent Water Co., whose product was "the filthiest in London".

The Bill enabling the new company to go ahead was thrown out of the Commons and the local people felt they had won a sound victory. But it was hollow - the South East Railway Company obtained the site and covered it with engine sheds and sidings.

Such was the activity at the Hall during the 1860s that it started to take business away from the Greenwich Lecture Hall in Royal Hill; the inhabitants of Greenwich, already using Blackheath shops to the detriment of their own tradesmen, were prepared to brave the journey across the Heath for the more generous seating and better facilities.

One extraordinary enterprise that started here was the Blackheath Mendicity Society, which was established with the express aim of discouraging professional beggars. The founder was the Reverend Henry Martyn-Hart (1838-1920) then a school teacher at 22 Montpelier Row and later incumbent at St. Germans Chapel in St. Germans Place and, from 1880 to 1920, Dean of Denver, USA.

Blackheath, along with other relatively well-to-do suburbs, was plagued by professional mendicants in the 1860s and Hart devised a system whereby householders would refuse to give alms but hand the beggar a ticket and direct him or her to the Mendicity Society room at the Alexandra Hall where an officer would investigate the claim. In the Society's first year it dealt with 2002 cases of which 1241 were passing tramps, 117 were referred to the relieving officer of their parish, and more than 700 were proved to be imposters.

The scheme was an immense success and local contributions were sufficiently in surplus to clothe urchins, pay them a weekly wage for sweeping crossings and blacking shoes, and generally encourage them to improve their lot.

The Blackheath Mendicity Society was enthusiastically received and reduced the begging frauds; The Times, in a leading article in January 1869, praised the scheme, but The Standard was not so sure. It wrote: "The (Village) is not exactly of the rustic order...we doubt whether a thatched roof, a hayrick or a pigsty could be found in all the place. The windows of the houses - we dare not call them cottages - are festooned with muslin and shaded by Venetians.

"The gardens have the choicest flowers and in the highways are the most elegant of shops. Of the Villagers it may be said they walk in silk attire ...and not unfrequently vary their outdoor enjoyments by riding instead of walking. Blackheath is a Village of the upper middle class."

The Standard went on to sneer at the Mendicity Society's method of displaying the daily tally of beggars helped or turned away, and concluded that the scheme only pushed beggars out of Blackheath - it was not real charity.

Despite such comments the scheme worked and spread, not only in this country but also abroad. It eventually became part of the Charity Organisation Society - now the Family Welfare Association - but continued in Blackheath until the late 1870s, by which time other voluntary groups were organising charitable relief.

The Mendicity Society left the Alexandra Hall early in the 1870s and took over a house behind the Crown public house in Tranquil Vale (q.v.). By this time the Hall was managed by Thomas Simpson (1815-1875) who also controlled the hall and baths in Nelson Street, Woolwich.

Of the principal events at the Hall during the 1870s, three stand out: the meetings of the Blackheath Preservation Society which pressed the Metropolitan Board of Works to take over the management of Blackheath to ensure its preservation for all time and prevent encroachments and despoilation, the first performances of the Blackheath Dramatic Club, and the meetings of a small group of young intellectuals who later established the Art Club, the Blackheath School of Art and Science, the Conservatoire of Music, and built the Blackheath Concert Hall.

These organisations are dealt with below, but it is worth noting that the pattern of events at the Alexandra Hall changed somewhat with the opening of the roller skating rink and its attached rink hall in 1876. The new structure in Blackheath Grove was not a purpose-built concert hall but it could be readily adapted to seat 1000 spectators and upwards of 200 performers at a squash, whilst the Alexandra Hall could seat not much more than 500, although there was a fixed stage and other facilities.

Yet the effect was not as disastrous for the older building as had been the opening of the Alexandra Hall on the Literary Institution.

The principal reason probably lay with the various purposes to which the Hall could be put. The swimming bath continued to flourish and was much used by local schools, while the smaller rooms lent themselves admirably to educational uses during the day.

Users included local charities and the annual meetings of the East Greenwich Ragged Schools board of trustees took place here. The school had been founded before 1849 and by the 1870s was helping more than 270 pupils each year, supplying them with shoes and shirts as well as the rudiments of literacy. Many of the boys came from the Bear Lane area of East Greenwich, a place described as "the dirty fringe of the rich garment" of Blackheath and Royal Greenwich, by one of the school's trustees.

Drewett returned as proprietor during the 1870s but from 1878-1886 the management was in the hands of Alfred Budds.

During the 1880s the Hall's prime use moved towards religious evangelism, although other events were staged there, including, in 1885, a dinner of the Vegetarian Society (founded in 1847) and presided over by Dr. Allinson. The rate payer from 1886 to 1890 was John Septimus Rivolta (1833-?1890), a merchant with interests in South America who lived at 102 Manor Way from 1863 to 1889. Why Rivolta took on the Alexandra Hall is not known for it cannot have been a lucrative investment, but in 1891 the property had passed to Dr. Robert McKilliam MD (1837-1915) a homeopathic doctor and religious zealot then living at 13 Blackheath Village.

McKilliam's involvement was, to a great extent, the salvation of the Hall as well as of the souls he wished to convert. The main room was kept for religious meetings and the old swimming bath - by then eclipsed by the new public baths at Ladywell - was converted into commercial accommodation.

This latter was rented by Charles North, the printer and publisher of the local newspaper, The Blackheath Local Guide and District Advertiser, which North had launched in 1889. Details of North's background and success will be found in the notes concerning 3 Blackheath Village (q.v.) so it must suffice here to record that the new premises in the Alexandra Hall gave North room to install up-to-date equipment and increase the staff of his Blackheath Press, as well as employ a trained journalist to edit the newspaper, which had grown from eight pages to forty by 1893.

The Blackheath Press remained here until 1910 by which time the company had outgrown its once spacious premises and it moved to the vacant rooms of the old Blackheath Proprietary School which had closed its doors in 1907.

During McKilliam's last years parts of the Hall were let for a variety of commercial purposes, to antique dealers, dress makers and so on, and on his death it should have been sold. By then, however, the country was at war and the building was requisitioned by the Royal Army Pay Corps as a canteen for some of the 1000 girl clerks then employed in Blackheath at the various public buildings taken for the duration.

In 1921 the old Alexandra Hall was sold to the Kent Cinema Circuit Co., Ltd., but they did not use it for a cinema and eventually the building passed to Lloyds Bank who made substantial alterations to its interior in May 1928. From the outset there were three small shops in the Cresswell Park frontage but these were eliminated after the war and the facade restored.

The present appearance of the banking hall dates from the extensive alteration and restoration work made during January 1970.

THE ART AND MUSIC SCHOOLS

During the mid-1870s the Alexandra Hall was the meeting place of small groups of Blackheath men, some artists and musicians, but mostly local residents interested in cultural matters and deeply conscious of the lack of proper facilities to meet the growing enthusiasm for art, music and the theatre.

Among these were Edward Onslow Ford RA (1852-1901), the sculptor and an old boy of the Blackheath Proprietary School, Ernest Waterlow RA, later President of the Water Colour Society; George Corner, the artist; William Claude Johnson, the electrical engineer of Johnson & Phillips; William Webster; and John Blaxland Jameson, an art teacher.

Of these, William Webster (1856-1910) was, undoubtedly, the most dedicated to the cause, and he became a great benefactor to Blackheath, being almost solely responsible for the establishment of the Conservatoire of Music, the Art School and Art Club and the erection of the Concert Hall.

He was a versatile man of genius, distinguished in whatever field excited his attention and he was fortunate enough perhaps to have lived in an age when it was not considered a disgrace to describe oneself as having "no occupation" but simply be rich enough to do as one pleased. Born in Wyberton, Lincolnshire, Webster was the son of William Webster (18   - 1888), the civil engineer largely responsible for the construction of the Thames Embankment, major drainage and water schemes and other large-scale works. Webster snr had settled in Blackheath in 1870, building for himself an enormous mansion - Wyberton House in Lee Terrace, which is now the main building of St. Joseph's School. Young Webster was trained as a chemical engineer but devoted himself to all manner of scientific and artistic interests. As a violinist he had sufficient talent to play Beethoven string quartets with professionals in public concerts, he possessed a fine voice (trained by W.H. Cummings, later Principal of the Guildhall School of Music) and his paintings found a place at the Royal Academy Summer Exhibitions in 1885 and 1899. But these activities were simply dilettante accomplishments to be used for the benefit of others, and most of his appearances were at concerts from which the profits were handed to charity.

54.   Blackheath Congregational Church in the 1860s

55.   South Vale House in the 1920s

56.   Bath Place Cottages, about 1904

57.   School for the Sons of Missionaries in 1857

58.   Blackheath Station in 1850

59.   Blackheath Station in the 1970s

60. The railway sidings before the last war

61. Blackheath Proprietary School before 1857

Webster's real work was in the world of science; he was elected a Fellow of the Chemical Society for his pioneer experiments with X-Rays and in 1887 he perfected a system for the electrolytic purification of sewage, which effectively turned seawater into a disinfectant. His pioneering work with X-Rays (with Thomas Moore FRCS (1838-1900)) was not only some of the most important in this country - being undertaken only three months after Rontgen's discovery - but led to Webster's early death. He was unstinting in demonstrating the technique, carrying the equipment to local hospitals in times of emergency, and prepared to attend any worthwhile charitable function in order to help draw the crowds. The dangers of using X-Rays were not then known and there is no doubt that constant exposure to the rays led to Webster's acute illness in 1899 and eventually to his untimely death.

Webster's memorials were the Blackheath art and music schools that he not only helped establish but for which he was instrumental in laying down the administrative rules, as well as the building of the institutions and their subsequent management. He helped raise the initial capital investment, found teachers of the highest calibre, and was able, through his authority and moral scrupulousness, to ensure that others maintained their interest and pursued ambitions to their conclusion.

All four of the institutions described below owed their origins to Webster and the meetings at the Alexandra Hall in the 1870s, but they are dealt with as separate entities for the sake of narrative flow.

The Schools of Art

Although Webster and his colleagues were to build their Blackheath arts centres from scratch, they were aided to some extent by the fact that one of their number, John Blaxland Jameson, an instructor at the Royal Military Academy, Woolwich, had established the Blackheath Academy of Art in rooms at the Alexandra Hall by 1877. This did not prevent the setting up of another art school, the Government School of Art, linked to the South Kensington Schools, at 41 Bennett Park by 1881 under the supervision of Joseph Hill (1852-1895) who was also principal of the art department at the Goldsmiths' Institute in New Cross. The Bennett Park School soon acquired the title, the Blackheath, Lee and Lewisham Government School of Art and moved to 27 Bennett Park in January 1884.

Art schools were by no means a new idea in the district. Professors of drawing had taken private pupils throughout the 19th century and in the 1860s Cormack Brown's School of Fine Art flourished at Blackheath Road, where for 7/6 a month the pupil could choose from a wide variety of courses, including Flemish and French - Mr. Brown was a citizen of Antwerp. In the 1880s there was a private institution called the Blackheath School of Art, in Lansdowne Place at the top of Blackheath Hill. But it was the schools in Blackheath Village which achieved success despite their initial rivalry. The courses they offered were more than simply ways of passing time for amateur painters, they were a means of learning craft skills, obtaining certificates of efficiency from the Government Schools and, for many, a means of achieving a teacher's diploma. Both schools were run on non profit-making bases and governed by locally-recruited committees, usually members of Blackheath's leading families.

On the death of Joseph Hill, his assistant John Howard Hale

was appointed headmaster and discussions instituted with the trustees of Jameson's school at the Alexandra Hall of which William Webster was chairman. Plans were already well advanced for the erection of a music school and concert hall and Webster's ambition was to include an art school on the same site. The joint resources of the two schools would be needed to achieve this end and the Trustees of both parties agreed to merge and create one art school - The Blackheath, Lee and Lewisham School of Art and Science - to occupy purpose-built premises behind the Conservatoire.

The new building (which still stands but is in Government requisition) was designed by James Edmeston & Edward Gabriel, the architects of the Blackheath Concert Hall and Conservatoire (q.v.) who were commissioned by the Blackheath Art Extension Co., Ltd., a holding company floated by Webster and others to erect buildings and hold the head lease granted at most favourable terms for 90 years by Albemarle Cator (1836-1906).

When the new school opened in 1896 with John Hale as Principal and Jameson as his assistant, there were 300 pupils attending not only the usual life, figure and landscape classes but enthusiatic for a wide range of applied arts courses, in such subjects as pottery, modelling, carving and sculpture, wood engraving, art needlework and graphic design.

The success of the school warranted extensions and a new studio block in 1911 (now partially hidden by temporary buildings) added considerably to the scope of the curriculum.

The Great War of 1914-1918 affected the School of Art much as it did the other public institutions in Blackheath Village. Military occupation gradually embraced most of the large non-domestic buildings and by 1918 the pay clerks in the Blackheath Concert Hall spilled over into the Art School studios. There was some compensation in that the War Office paid for the temporary removal of the Art School to 5 Lee Terrace but the then London County Council decided to cancel the School's grant aid in order to force a merger with the art departments of the Woolwich and Goldsmith's colleges. Blackheath supporters engaged in a spirited battle with the authorities, mainly on the ground that the Blackheath School was the largest of the three and that the handcraft courses then in train would be important contributions to the post war reconstruction. The appeal was successful and, despite a last minute move by the Royal Army Pay Corps to remain in Blackheath permanently, they quit Blackheath in 1921 and the Art School buildings were returned to their rightful owners in 1922.

Hale retired in 1929 and the new Principal was John Platt ARCA, FSAM, one time Principal of the Leicester College of Art and a skilled wood engraver. Platt remained at Blackheath until its forced closure in 1941 when the buildings, once again, were requisitioned for government use. Platt worked hard for Blackheath, he raised standards by recruiting the best staff he could find and encouraged his pupils to exhibit their work. The emphasis was essentially on the acquisition of skills rather than experiment, but this did not prevent Platt and James Woodford ARCA, his assistant, from attracting modern artists to Blackheath. He was particularly fortunate to engage the distinguished engraver and typographer Eric Gill to deliver a series of lectures in 1939.

It was the intention of the Art School trustees to re-open their school after the last war but the circumstances prevented this. The buildings were still occupied by government departments and there had been radical changes in the structure of further education and art teaching in London which combined to hinder the restoration of small private art schools.

At the time of writing the Art School trustees were actively considering the possibility of using their buildings for art purposes once the Government lease finally expires.

Blackheath Conservatoire of Music

Alone of all Webster's creations, the Conservatoire of Music he founded in 1881 still flourishes, busier at the time of writing than it has been through the 95 years of its foundation.

Unlike the Art Schools there was no private foundation upon which to base a music school although there must have been half a hundred private teachers of pianoforte, singing and instrumental technique, to judge from the small advertisements of the local newspapers. Further, the organists at the local churches and most of the private schools offered music lessons, and this showed that there was strong musical interest in the district. Various choral and orchestral societies had flourished from the early 1830s but they rarely lasted long, either because the principal organiser died or left the district or because the members bickered amongst themselves over policy in the choice of works or lead singers.

By 1877 a Blackheath Musical Society was in existence but, more important, the violin teacher and orchestral conductor Alfred Burnett (1839-1918) was living in Blackheath and organising amateur music making of a very high standard.

Burnett knew Webster and in 1880 they, along with William Hayman Cummings (see below) and Isaac Adolphus Crookenden (1832-1907) a chartered engineer and Company Secretary to the Phoenix Gas Company, living at 138 Shooters Hill Road, formed a Musical Guild. The aim of the Guild was to establish a school of music and this was achieved in an astonishingly short time. Within a year of the formation of the Guild the committee had leased 28 Bennett Park and enrolled 60 pupils in the new Blackheath Conservatoire of Music. Henry Hersee (1820-1896), music critic of The Observer, was chairman, Webster took on the task of Secretary, supported by Ormond James Yearsley (c1850-1927).

The strength of the new Conservatoire and its future success lay with the quality of the men who supervised its inception. They were nearly all practicing musicians and in most cases, influential in the politics of London's musical life. Hersee was critic for The Observer from 1871 to 1894, had been a close friend of Charles Dickens and written for a variety of illustrated and cultural weeklies as well as translating the libretti of many operas including Carmen. His family included a daughter, Madame Rose Hersee (1845-1924) who enjoyed a long and distinguished career as a principal singer with the Carl Rosa Company.

William Hayman Cummings (1831-1915) was a noted tenor, singing both in concerts and churches, especially Westminster Abbey and the Chapel Royal. He taught at the Royal Academy from 1879 to 1896 and held the post of Principal at the Guildhall School of Music from 1896 to 1911, during which time he helped found the Purcell Society and edited volumes of Purcell's music, as well as writing a biography of that composer.

But it was Alfred Burnett who unified music making in Blackheath and encouraged professional colleagues to come to Blackheath to staff the new Conservatoire and add lustre to the ever-improving amateur orchestras who performed under his baton. Burnett was a violinist by profession, and had been taught by Henryk Wieniawski (1835-1880) the distinguished Polish fiddle player and teacher. Burnett earned three national reputations, as a solo violinist and teacher of the instrument, as a conductor, but principally as an orchestral leader. He was much in demand as concert master for the main festivals in this country: the Birmingham, Worcester, Hereford Three Choirs festivals, various series and festivals of music at the Royal Albert Hall, and so on. In Blackheath his talents were employed in schooling and performing with good amateur forces, and by the mid-1870s he had recruited a 64-piece orchestra playing under various titles but principally as the Blackheath Orchestral Society, and was confident enough to sponsor a benefit concert of his own music in 1877. In 1880 this particular society was disbanded, for although their concerts were well attended Burnett suffered personal loss running to about £275 over the three years of the operation.

The huge success of the Conservatoire gave a fresh impetus in that the new talents amongst its pupils and professors could be recruited to supply performances of major works hitherto available only in the large London halls and at Crystal Palace. The Alexandra Hall in Blackheath was proving too small to satisfy the existing taste for big choirs and bands but the Rink Hall in Blackheath Grove (q.v.) could just hold about 1000 persons. Further, Burnett's success gave encouragement to Webster's dream to build a new concert hall in the Village.

In 1889 a new orchestral group was formed, the Blackheath Philharmonic Society, attached to which was a choir of 120 voices. For the next five years the society was to be triumphant, with performances of Mozart's Requiem, Mendelssohn's Elijah, Handel's Judas Maccabaeus, Gounod's Solemn Mass, and the latter's Faust in 1893 with a professional orchestra and the versatile William Webster in the main role. But alas, as with previous attempts to conduct a harmonious music society and satisfy all its members as well as its audiences, disagreements were expressed. No one was forced either to join the Philharmonic, or attend its concerts, but it was such a dominant part of local social life - other than the Blackheath Club, the Golf Club and the West Kent Carlton Club at Point Hill, all of which were for gentlemen only - that it was inevitable that criticism should be made.

Matters came to a head when dissidents wrote to the Blackheath Local Guide in May and June 1894 on the question whether the Society should or should not perform secular as well as sacred music. Certain factions in the choral society were fearful that they would be called upon to sing Wagner, Bizet, Rossini and even Gilbert and Sullivan, although the new Blackheath Amateur Operatic Society, to judge by their programme, had a monopoly on the last. The argument led to bitter dispute and comment from outsiders, including one gentleman who signed himself "Philistine". He wrote that minority interests dominated the Society's work and that, personally, he preferred smoking concerts and glees and that he "looked upon Mr. Burnett as my natural enemy". The Secretary of the Philharmonic at that time was the young George Mackern (1866-1923), later Principal of the Blackheath Conservatoire, and he resigned his office as a result of the controversy. But in July 1894 he had married Burnett's daughter, Alice, at St. Margaret's, Lee, and spent the honeymoon at Bayreuth - so it was clear where his sympathies lay.

The Philharmonic died - but Burnett and Webster simply recruited its old membership into the Blackheath Conservatoire of Music Choral Society and placed that body on a secure political and financial basis which survived without major problems for the next generation.

The new Society, coupled with the immense success achieved by the Conservatoire, heralded the opening of the Blackheath Concert Hall in 1895 and the completion of the Conservatoire's new home in 1896. This last body had rapidly outgrown its original premises at 28 Bennett Park and had leased No. 30 in 1883 and No. 32 in 1890. Some classes had been held in the Alexandra Hall at the outset and the completion in 1886 of the Blackheath Art Club Studios (see below) at the end of Bennett Park allowed for the use of its exhibition hall as a rehearsal and recital room.

In 1890 Webster commissioned some designs for a purpose-built conservatory from the architects Higgs and Rudkin who had designed the Art Club, but this scheme proved too expensive and was shelved.

But in 1895 a site had been leased from the Cator Estate for not only a conservatory but also for the concert hall and the Art School buildings, to be built under the auspices of the Blackheath Art Extension Co. Ltd., which had been launched by Webster and others with a share capital of 2000 £1 shares.

The Conservatoire was designed by James Edmeston (c1830-1898) and Edward Gabriel (d1928) of Old Broad Street, in a rather plain "Queen Anne" style as a series of small rooms with double doors for sound insulation and perfect for its purpose.

The Conservatoire opened with nearly 1000 pupils on its books and 50 visiting professors, mostly teachers from the Royal Academy, the Royal College of Music and Guildhall School of Music. Burnett was the doyen, being then Professor of Violin at both the Royal Academy and the Royal College, and his conducting capabilities were drawing the London critics to Blackheath.

Initially, the management of the Conservatoire was in the control of Hersee as President, Webster as Honorary Secretary and Ormond Yearsley, but in 1893 the day to day work was placed in the hands of a full-time employee known as the Lady Superintendant - Miss Mary Botting (d1924) who held the post until her retirement in 1920. Eventually Webster was appointed Honorary Director but was forced to resign the position in 1909 because of ill-health. The managers then appointed George Mackern FRAM (1856-1923) as Principal, with a salary, overall control over teaching and performing standards, and the right to continue an independent musical career.

Mackern was a professional pianist and conductor. He had been educated at George Valentine's school at 9 Eliot Place and the Royal Academy of Music and studied piano in Germany with Clara Schumann. From the early 1890s he entered into the musical life of Blackheath with some enthusiasm, conducting the Blackheath Philharmonic, the orchestra of the Blackheath Amateur Operatic Society and other groups with seemingly unflagging energy. He had assisted Webster at the Conservatoire, especially in the arrangements of the BCM concert series, and was able to secure the services of internationally-distinguished artists to play and sing under his baton.

More details of Mackern's concert promotions will be found in the pages concerning the Concert Hall. He remained Principal at the Conservatoire until his death in 1923, having inherited Webster's mantle and managed to wear it with distinction. He raised the Blackheath Conservatoire's status to a high level, opening a branch in Eltham in 1913, and maintained standards during the difficult years of the Great War.

Until the outbreak of the 1939-1945 war the Conservatoire retained its links with the originators through the continuity of its teachers and administrators. Mary Botting was succeeded as Lady Superintendent in 1920 by her assistant since 1900 - Miss Edith S. Dealy, who kept the post until her death in May 1937. Mackern was succeeded as Principal by George H. Wilby who had been connected with the Blackheath Conservatoire as a teacher since the 1890s, and he held the post until 1930 when he emigrated to South Africa. Wilby was succeeded by his brother, an orchestral conductor, Edgar Ronald Wilby (1879-1955) who remained in charge of the Conservatoire until his death.

It is no reflection on Edgar Wilby's abilities that he took over the institution at a time when musical interest in Blackheath and elsewhere was in decline. The days of the major orchestral concerts at the Blackheath Concert Hall were over and the press were interested in the standards of the Conservatoire only when it proved to have trained such child stars as Nova Pilbeam and Beryl Laverick (now Mrs. Reginald Maudling) or composers and conductors of light music like Sidney Torch, Reginald King and Harry Farjeon. Of the less well-known but equally distinguished pupils who had tried for a concert platform career in a musically-disinterested climate, only Heddle Nash (1896-1961) and Edward York Bowen (1884-1961) achieved more than parochial reference.

In 1956 Dr. Geoffrey Leeds, DMus, FRCO, ARCM, LRAM, was appointed Principal and he was succeeded in 1968 by the present incumbent, organist Robert Munns, FRAM, ARCM, ARCO.

Presently, the Conservatoire is the only fully-functioning institution founded by William Webster, but it is a tribute to him and the work of successive Principals and the honorary officers of the School that it is busier now than it has ever been and will shortly celebrate its centenary.

The Blackheath Art Club

Although Webster and his friends had been instrumental in establishing the art and music schools for Blackheath on a non-profit making basis, they also created one institution to be run on strictly commercial lines, possibly in order to subsidise the Art School and the Conservatoire.

This was the Blackheath Art Club which was built on the site of a small lecture hall and billiard room at the far end of Bennett Park.

The aim was to provide studios for working artists - somewhere they could work, teach and hold exhibitions and also provide space for extra artistic activities such as recitals, dances and displays.

The Blackheath Art Club was founded in 1883 to "promote social intercourse among gentlemen interested in science, literature, painting and music in Blackheath and the neighbourhood." Although the building was designed for the Art Club it was erected and paid for by a company called the Art Club and Studio Building Co., and the building and studios let to the Art Club and to individual artists. It was designed by Higgs and Rudkin and completed in 1886; the same architects designed No. 112 Westcombe Park for W. Claude Johnson (1847-1928), the electrical engineer, in the following year.

The Art Club members were quick to use their building and artists equally quick to rent the studios. The President of the Club was Sir Frederick Abel (1827-1902), the inventor of cordite, whose brother, Charles Denton Abel (1831-1906), the President of the Chartered Institute of Patent Agents, had helped supply the funds to establish the Conservatoire of Music. The Club furnished two main opportunities: a place where artists could meet and work, and a venue for their admirers to see what was new in the visual arts and have the chance to purchase. The buildings were also much used for recitals, poetry readings, chamber music and rehearsals, small dances and the like.

From 1886 to 1916 the Art Club mounted two annual exhibitions, one in Spring and the other in the Autumn, which can best be described as Blackheath's alternative to the Summer Exhibition of the Royal Academy. There was always a good display of work by the local professionals and from the teachers and pupils of the Blackheath Art School, but the bulk of the exhibits came from amateurs and weekend painters and local topographical subjects and portaits always excited much attention.

The reputations of most of the artists then working in Blackheath have not survived outside the brief entries in reference books, but some had a national following in their time. The leading figure was Terrick John Williams RA, PRI (1860-1936), who was elected President of the Royal Institute of Painters in Water Colour in 1933, and a full Royal Academician in 1934. He took studios in Blackheath in the early 1890s and remained there, working and teaching, sometimes at the Art School, until the 1930s. Other leading figures included: Arthur Acland Hunt (1841-1914), professor of painting at the Royal Naval College from 1873 to 1909, his brother Aubrey H. Hunt - both related to William Holman Hunt (1827-1910); Adam Duncan Carse; Hugh Bellingham Smith; George Edward Corner (1853-1891); Cecil Hunt, son of Arthur Acland Hunt; and Reginald Jones.

Among the various clubs and societies which met at the Art Club was the Blackheath Camera Club, from 1892; the Blackheath Essay and Debating Society, whose honorary secretary was Hubert Bland (1856-1914); and the Blackheath Badminton Club. Before the Concert Hall was completed the exhibition hall was often hired for tableaux vivants and soirees musicales. One of the former was reported in the Strand Magazine of July 1891: "It was noticed in one of the tableaux that the audience did not consider it a success on account of a young lady who was supposed to be putting on her shoe, but who was in reality pinching out a large piece of burning soot which had fallen on her dress."

And when Madame Rose Hersee, the distinguished soprano, gave a soiree musicale in December 1891, more than 200 friends accepted her invitation and the local newspaper reported that "some very rich toiletries were worn and in many cases costly diamonds."

The Art Club functioned well until the Great War. The last exhibition it arranged was the Spring Show in April 1916 which contained the works of many of the Club's keenest supporters, but, by then, few of the founders were still alive or active on its behalf and many of the younger members were in the forces or had left the district. The last public use of the buildings was a meeting arranged by the London Society for Promoting Christianity among the Jews, in October 1916, and by the following year the building had been requisitioned for government use.

In December 1920 the Art Club was released but the organisation was wound up on the grounds of lack of support and the high cost of rates, gas and the usual services necessary for the upkeep of the building, and it was no longer possible for the Art Club to continue its activities.

In 1921 the premises were put up for auction, but the purchaser, after allowing it to be used for furniture auctions and following an abortive negotiation with a local boy's preparatory school (Belmont House), eventually let it to Squire Sanders Ltd., a company of manufacturing milliners.

There were attempts to revive the Art Club, encouraged by demands which were expressed throughout the 1920s. In 1933 the Blackheath Art and Craft Society was formed, with John Howard Hale, the Principal of the Blackheath Art School, and Terrick Williams on the committee. The BACS kept going, based to a great extent on the Art School, until the 1939-1945 war, when along with many other groups, it foundered. The present Blackheath Art Society was formed in 1948.

In 1931 the Bennett Park studios were once more empty and, for a brief period, the exhibition hall was available for hire, but from 1934 to 1943 the buildings became the headquarters of a most remarkable enterprise. Although the commercial directories list the tenants as the GPO Film Studio, that uninformative title conveyed nothing of the pioneering work done by the men and women who worked at the old Blackheath Art Club rooms, nor the fact that without their vision the cinema and television we watch today would be considerably worse than it is.

The cinema had not gained a place in Blackheath commercially. William Butcher seized on the novelty of moving pictures in the 1890s (see Chapter 9) but the closest any picture palace came to the Village was at Lee Green when the Imperial opened in December 1913. The Globe at Hither Green, with cerise and gold decor, opened the same month, and in the previous February the Kings Hall at Lewisham had opened with a performance of Max Reinhardt's The Miracle, with an orchestra and choir to perform Humperdinck's incidental music. In 1921 the Alexandra Hall had been taken by the Kent Cinema Circuit Co., but any plans they may have had for converting it into a cinema did not go forward.

In 1928 the Government set up an organisation called the Empire Marketing Board to promote research into the production, preservation and transport of the Empire's food supplies. Every conceivable form of activity was catered for and the plans budgeted for posters, printing, publicity and, lastly, films. Hoardings appeared everywhere - some on Blackheath, but these were removed after public protest. One of the EMB's employees was Stephen Tallents (later Sir Stephen) who acted as public relations officer to the Board, and it was because of his encouragement that a full-time film unit was created. Its first director was John Grierson (1898-1964). But the Board had not reckoned to be landed with such vigorous talent and were astonished by the quality of the first production, an account of the work of the North Sea herring fleet - called Drifters.

Drifters was arguably the first proper use of an art form for propaganda and the EMB boasted the first government-sponsored film company outside Soviet Russia.

By 1933 the Board had been wound up as a failure but Tallents, determined that the unit should not disintegrate, convinced the Post Office that they should employ a film unit and that the old EMB unit was all ready to go into action on the GPO's behalf.

In that year they took the lease on the Blackheath Art Club studios as their main centre, although administration was kept at Soho Square, London. From 1934 to 1941 the unit made dozens of films; some were shot in and around Blackheath, some in the studio itself on sets built by the unit and others were made on location but edited and made up in the Blackheath Studios.

The people who worked at Blackheath add up to a golden list in the history of the cinema: John Gillet, Pat Jackson, Richard McNaughton, Ken Cameron, Harry Watt, John Grierson, Humphrey Jennings, Cavalcanti, Basil Wright and William Coldstream. Enrolled into supplying their own special skills were musicians and writers, of whom Benjamin Britten, W.H. Auden, E.M. Forster, Constant Lambert and J.B. Priestley are probably the best known. Among the long list of films, Nightmail, Coalface, BBC - Voice of Britain, and The King's Stamps (an early colour film) were important landmarks in the history of documentary film making. The film about the BBC included a sequence shot outside the Railway Hotel (q.v.) in Blackheath Village.

With the outbreak of the 1939-1945 war the pattern of film making changed and a number of projects were casualties of this alteration in emphasis. In 1938 plans were laid for a film about the infant television service and John Logie Baird, the television pioneer, journeyed to Blackheath with some of his equipment. In September 1939 the television service was withdrawn for the duration and the GPO film scrapped.

In 1940 the GPO film unit, then part of the Ministry of Information, became the Crown Film Unit and, although the unit moved to Beaconsfield in 1943, some of the best wartime documentaries had been produced from Blackheath: Britain Can Take it, Target for Tonight, most of the Humphrey Jennings' documentaries, Coastal Command, Western Approaches, and Desert Victory.

The studios were also used as a clearing house for captured German and Italian films and all the new films from the USA earmarked for screening to the Prime Minister at Chequers.

After the Crown Film Unit (disbanded in 1952) moved to Beaconsfield the Art Club rooms were leased to Elliot Bros., the electrical engineers, and used for the assembly of aircraft instruments. This use ceased in 1953 and the building sold freehold the following year, since when it has been used as a hostel for students and as a boarding house, although there have been attempts to purchase it and put it back into community use.

Blackheath Concert Hall

Until 1895 two halls served the needs of the Blackheath music and dramatic societies: the Alexandra Hall from 1864, and the Rink Hall from 1876. But the former was too small and the latter inconvenient and too thinly insulated against outside noise.

William Webster and his fellow committeemen and directors had launched the Blackheath Conservatoire and established the Art Schools with every intention of providing them with permanent purpose-built homes. But there were problems over cost and siting. Ideally they had to be close to the Village - the heart of the Blackheath community - but land in the centre was not available and, even if it had been - probably too expensive. In 1893 the Cator family were able to offer a solution. On the corner of Lee

Road and Blackheath Park was a row of terrace houses known as Park Place, which had been built in 1809 by William Dyer; running behind these was Blackheath Park Mews which contained the building used as the St. Michael's Church School for Girls, and the Martin fly and carriage stables. The leases had expired in 1883 and had not been renewed except on a short term basis. There were ten houses all told with No. 1 Park Place nearest the Village and, with its entrance in Blackheath Park, No. 10 which stood on the site of the present 1 Blackheath Park; Nos. 1 & 3 were doctor's surgeries; No. 2 the home of Henry Dry, the carpenter, from 1879; No. 9 the home of a builder named Thomas Smith for more than 30 years.

Albermarle Cator (1836-1906) agreed to lease the site for 90 years from 1893 for the erection of a music and art school and a concert hall, to Webster's Blackheath Art Extension Co. Ltd., for £100 a year.

The Art Extension Company had been funded by Webster, C.D. Abel and William George Barnes (1833-1911), a provision merchant and Sheriff of London, who lived at 115 Blackheath Park. But, wealthy though they were, they could not pay for the erection of a large concert hall, and so another company was floated - The Blackheath Concert Hall Co. Ltd., with a capital of £12,000 in 2,400 £5 shares. Enough of the stock had been taken up by November 1893 for the Committee confidently to instruct architects to proceed with their plans, some of which had been prepared as early as 1889 in anticipation of finding suitable ground.

The practice given the task was that of the well-established architects and surveyors James Edmeston and Edward Gabriel. Edmeston was the son of James Edmeston snr (1791-1867) who had been in practice since the 1820s (employing Sir George Gilbert Scott (1811-1878) when a pupil), but who was known locally only for the Greenwich Tannery in 1864 and an involvement in the development of Westcombe Park estate. Be that as it may, Edmeston & Gabriel (d1928) were sound craftsmen and it is likely that Gabriel had the greater hand in the design, Edmeston then being elderly and near retirement.

The site was cleared in May 1894 and the contract given to J.O. Richardson of Peckham. The sculptured frieze in gesso duro work and other decorations were entrusted to a Mr. Searle. Webster, as with all the projects in which he was involved, acted as unofficial clerk of works. The original contract price was just under £9000 but the final cost with pictures and furniture came to £11,500. A small sum by today's standards but expensive in its time, although it is a tribute to the quality demanded by perfectionists like Webster that the fabric of the Hall is in such good condition today.

By September 1895 the company was advertising two halls for private bookings: the main hall 94ft by 58ft, seating more than 1200 people; a small hall seating about 300. The main stage was 29ft wide and had a rake of 1: 15ft and could accommodate 200 performers. There was also a generous provision of dressing rooms, a kitchen, box office, cloak rooms and administrative offices as well as a caretaker's house overlooking Blackheath Park. The floor of the main auditorium was sprung and laid on concrete; the ceiling was panelled in goloach moulding similar to that used in the Louvre in Paris; and the building originally was lit by two gas illuminators, each holding 109 burners. A clock was supplied by Robert Fielding of 13 Montpelier Vale (q.v.).

Webster had spread the risk on the venture by the issuing of shares, and most of these had been taken in small lots by local people, many of them active in the music and dramatic societies for whom the Concert Hall had, to a great extent, been built.

One of these, the Blackheath Philharmonic, had been dissolved within a few months of the Hall's opening ceremony but, as has been recounted above, Burnett and George Mackern regrouped the forces under the wing of the Conservatoire of Music.

The other two main participants were the Blackheath Dramatic Club and the Blackheath Amateur Operatic Society, both distinguished in their time but casualties of the 1939-1945 war and changes in taste and circumstance.

The Blackheath Dramatic Club was in existence in 1870 although a group of local people had mounted amateur theatricals in aid of the Royal National Lifeboat Institution as early as 1867 in the Alexandra Hall. This was at a time when the public theatre was not considered wholly respectable by a middle class that indulged its passion for the stage in private theatricals.

The earliest known performance by the Blackheath Dramatic Club was of T.A. Bayley's The Spitalfield's Weaver and took place at the Alexandra Hall (q.v.) in aid of the funds of the volunteer militia. The Club continued to mount two or three productions a year, all profits being channelled to charitable purpose, usually the North Kent Dispensary (later the Miller Hospital) until at least 1880 although some presentations took place at the New Cross Hall in Lewisham Road. Despite professional help, good audiences and its increasing contribution to good works, the Club lapsed in the 1880s and it was not until 1893 that, encouraged by the success of the Blackheath Amateur Operatic Society, it was revived. The chief architect of its new life was George Seymour Brocklebank (1854-1927), a stockbroker, whose father, also George, had founded the Greenwich & Blackheath Amateur Musical Society in 1843. The Club soon picked up the threads again and rapidly became a strong part of the cultural life of the district, still funnelling its surplus funds to charity but confining its repertoire to comedies, thrillers and other works of a rather lightweight nature in order not to overtax its audiences. Brocklebank remained with the Club until 1927 and it was largely his efforts which kept the standards high and encouraged professional actors to join the company and produce some of the plays. One of the youngest members in its early days was Harry Moncrieff Tennent (1879-1941) who was to become one of Britain's leading theatrical impresarios and whose company still exists, the largest of its kind in the UK. In all, the Blackheath Dramatic Club mounted 88 productions between 1893 and 1939 - the last year of its activity. Although in any case the war would have curtailed this activity the Club was suffering financial difficulty towards the end of 1939 and the cost of producing plays of a standard to fill a 1200-seat hall for three nights in a row must have been a strain.

In 1947 there were discussions to merge the Dramatic Club with the Blackheath Amateur Operatic Society, also moribund, but times and tastes had changed and the Blackheath Dramatic Club, one of the oldest and best amateur companies in Britain, faded away.

The Blackheath Amateur Operatic Society was formed in 1893 as a lighter side of the musical activity based essentially on the Conservatoire. Many of the performers were the same as those in the Conservatoire Choir and orchestras, and the conductor was George Mackern. Their early performances (almost always Gilbert and Sullivan operettas) were given at the Rink Hall where Pirates of Penzance, HMS Pinafore, Patience and The Mikado were staged in elaborate productions and were well reviewed. After the opening of the Concert Hall the BAOS pursued their policy of offering light music and operettas, a single production every year except for the period when the Hall was in government use, until 1939. By 1900 more than £1000 in profits had been donated to the Miller Hospital.

The last production, Millocker's Maid of the Mountains, was staged in January 1939, and although there was an attempt to revive the Society after the 1939-1945 war, it, like the Blackheath Dramatic Club, was eventually wound up.

The formal opening of the Concert Hall took place on October 26 1895 with a ceremony performed by Lord Hugh Cecil; during most of the day the Band of the Royal Artillery played selections from the popular classics, 3000-4000 people came to look and Stephen Jobbins of Montpelier Vale catered for the special ceremony which took place in the early evening when a great many congratulatory speeches were delivered.

The first performance in the Hall, like so many thereafter, was for charity. The honour fell to the Blackheath Amateur Operatic Society who repeated three performances of their production of HMS Pinafore, conducted by Mackern and directed by Walter Hersee, son of Henry Hersee. Every performance was sold out and every local family of importance boasted a member in the orchestra, the chorus, or among the principals.

From the outset the Hall was a popular success, it had been booked solid for six months even before it opened and the concerts and entertainments well-subscribed. Members of the booking organisations took the bulk of the tickets before the general public had a chance and many Blackheathens must have heard much of the major orchestral repertoire for the first time in the Concert Hall.

It was Alfred Burnett, George Mackern and their semi-professional orchestras and amateur choirs who brought to the Blackheath Concert Hall 20 years of quite exceptional music making. Over the years they gave full-blooded performances of all the major oratorios and cantatas, The Messiah, Elijah, St. Paul, Dream of Gerontius, Gounod's Faust and Redemption, the Verdi Requiem, Berlioz' Damnation of Faust, symphonies by Beethoven, Dvorak, Tchaikovsky and Mendelssohn. After one concert in 1897 a local critic was moved to write: "The audience generally were greatly interested and stayed till the end of the performance, which is rather unusual at Blackheath concerts." There was always a full house for Wagner but a performance of Beethoven's Emperor Concerto was notable for the empty seats.

In 1909 Burnett made his farewell after 35 years of acting as Blackheath's concertmaster. A celebration concert was staged and many distinguished musicians including Harry Plunkett Greene (1865-1936), the concert baritone, and pianist Leonard Borwick (1868-1925), another pupil of Clara Schumann, gave their services free - well-wishers gave Burnett a testimonial and a cheque for £250, after a programme of Mendelssohn, Chopin and Schumann.

George Mackern pursued Burnett's policy and encouraged star performers to add Blackheath to their engagement lists. Thus Coleridge-Taylor (1875-1912) attended a performance of his Hiawatha, Madame Greig was in the audience when Percy Grainger (1882-1961) performed works by Greig as well as himself in 1909. Mark Hambourg, Clara Butt (1873-1936) and her husband Kennerley Mumford appeared at the Concert Hall on many occasions as did Plunkett Greene and Percy Grainger. Mischa Elman, Vladimir de Pachman (1848-1933), Fritz Kreisler, Wilhelm Backhaus, Irene Scharrer, Myra Hess and Elena Gerhardt graced its platform. And in 1914 the 11-year old piano prodigy, Solomon, took over from an indisposed concert pianist. During the years before the Great War Mackern hired the then newly-formed London Symphony Orchestra, many members of which had played at Blackheath Conservatoire concerts in previous seasons.

The Concert Hall was not, of course, solely for the use of the Blackheath musical establishment. It was an ideal venue for all types of meeting, from religious convocations to lectures on gas cookery, for those who could pay the hire charges. One of the earliest functions was a meeting and concert of the newly-formed Purcell Society in November 1895, there were tableaux vivants, Hungarian string bands, private dances (for which the Hall could be divided into card rooms and supper rooms), lectures on X-Rays by Webster in February 1898 and dancing classes by the Misses Sutton Moss on Fridays in the same year. Charity bazaars, at which every family supervised a stall, would see the Hall elaborately decorated to look like a Bedouin encampment or an Indian market; and during the South African war, concerts in aid of casualty funds roused audiences to such heights of jingoistic fervour that some Blackheathens were converted to the Boer cause.

In 1908 Albert Chevalier sang "My Old Dutch" for the umpteenth time; in 1909 Harry Lauder attended a charity concert, and Edward Shackleton lectured on the Antarctic; in 1911 George Bernard Shaw pleaded the case for a National Theatre. In that year a grand Coronation Ball was mounted, attended by 300 members of the "leading families". The vestibule was decorated in red, white and blue, the Hall proper in "art shades of pink and green", there were carpets from the carriage way to the main door, fairy lights and flowers. It was, perhaps, the last truly grand and near aristocratic event in Blackheath and the last time the poor would crowd around the Hall to watch the carriages and motor cars of the rich and privileged arrive for the evening's entertainment, bearing occupants clad in elegant clothes and adorned with diamonds.

Perhaps more democratic were the Tango Teas in 1913, when Pete and Pepita from the "London Opera House" gave afternoon demonstrations of dances to housewives with nothing else to do.

The Blackheath Concert Hall Company paid no dividend to its shareholders for it was under-subscribed initially, despite enthusiasm for the venture. As late as 1898 632 shares were still waiting for a buyer. After seven years operations the total profit reached £25 and attempts to force the directors to "make the hall pay" were resisted on the grounds that this would mean music hall and moving pictures.

In 1902 electric light was installed and the following year the building was totally re-decorated in green, pink and brown by Collins Bros. of Montpelier Vale "who exercised their usual taste in the scheme of decoration, art colours having been utilised with great effect."

During 1908 there were grumbles at the programmes, although outside the control of the Hall's directors, and a plea for more British composers: "I suppose we may not hear them because they have not enough discord and intellectual noise in their work. Most of the concerts I have been to in Blackheath have been deadly dull and the people apathetic."

In April 1915 the Hall was requisitioned by the War Office for the Royal Army Pay Corps, the first of Blackheath's public buildings to be taken in this way. More than 400 clerks and masses of documents filled the building which the authorities said they wished to keep until six months after the end of the hostilities. But when peace came it was evident that the army intended to stay put and there were disquieting rumours that they would be quite happy to remain in Blackheath for ever. In November 1919 a public petition forced a change of mind and the Pay Corps quit in 1920. After three months work to bring the building back to its pre-war condition and with the floor ("the best dance floor in London") re-planed and polished, the Blackheath Concert Hall re-opened on January 18 1921 with a performance of Lionel Monckton's Miss Hook of Holland by the Blackheath Amateur Operatic Society.

For the next 19 years the Blackheath Concert Hall continued to be the local centre for concerts, meetings, dancing and entertainment, although the standard and variety of music never reached the heights of the old Burnett concerts before 1910.

One problem for the Concert Hall Company was finding day-time users and this was partly solved by the formation in 1924 of the Blackheath Children's Holiday Club under the supervision of Captain John George Gibson of 6 St. Germans Place. This was a hugely successful scheme, offering organised games, badminton and a reading room, although there was some element of discipline in that the boys were not admitted except in white shirts and grey shorts.

In 1939 the military authorities remembered how useful had been the Blackheath Concert Hall in 1915, and the building was once more requisitioned. It has remained so ever since, eventually passing to the Department of Health and Social Security.

The only known view of the Alexandra Hall when still used for public meetings.   Taken c1905.

Bibliography

Periodicals

The Architect, 1869-1900.
Blackheath Local Guide and District Advertiser, 1889-1957.
Blackheath Reporter, 1959-1966.
Greenwich, Woolwich & Deptford Gazette, 1833-1839, later the Kentish
    Mercury (1840-1964); later the South East London Mercury (1964-
    1968); later the South East London and Kentish Mercury (1968-1975)
Kentish Independent, 1843-1975.
The Times, 1788-1976.
Transactions, later the Journal, of the Royal Institute of British Architects.

Directories

Samuel Bagshaw: History, Gazetteer & Directory of the County of Kent,
    1847.
Green's Court Guide & Commercial Directory & Gazetteer. Green & Co.,
    London, 1874.
Mason's Greenwich & Blackheath Shilling Directory and Handbook.
    Greenwich, 1852.
Melville's Directory & Gazetteer of Kent. W.H. Collingridge, London,
    1858.
Greenwich, Eltham, Lee, Blackheath & Lewisham Directory, 1869 and
    1870. J.H. Muzzall & Co., Brighton.
J.G. Harrod & Co's Postal & Commercial Directory of Kent, 1867.
Holden's Triennial Directories of London and 10 miles radius: 1799, 1802,
    1805, 1808, 1811.
Kelly's (Buff Book) Directories of Blackheath, Lee, Lewisham and
    Greenwich: 1881, 1883-1937/8.
Pigot & Co's National London & Provincial Commercial Directory: 1823-
    1840.
Post Office Directory of Kent: 1845-1891.
Post Office Directory of London: 1880-1970.
William Robson: Commercial Directory of London & Six Home Counties.
    1838.
Wakefield's Merchants & Tradesmens General Directory of London. 1790.
Underhill's London Directory: 1817, 1822.
Blackheath, Lee & Lewisham Directory for 1878-9. Ebenezer Wilmhurst,
    Blackheath, 1878.

Official and Unpublished Records

Registers of the Parish of Charlton 1653-1820.

Leases and counterparts from the Blackheath estate of the Earls of Dartmouth in the Martin Collection, London Borough of Greenwich Local History Library.

Minutes of the Blackheath and Divisional Petty Sessions: 1710-1726; 1743-1866.

Enumerated Census returns: 1841, 1851, 1861, 1871.

Rate books of the Parish of Greenwich: 1743-1900.

Rate books and Churchwardens' Accounts for the Parish of Charlton: 1710-1900.

Land Tax Returns for the Parishes of Lewisham and Greenwich: 1780-1832.

Poll books for the County of Kent: various, between 1730 and 1869.

District Board of Works minutes for Greenwich, Lewisham and Lee.

Tithe Schedules for the Parishes of Greenwich (1844), Lee (1839), Lewisham (1843) and Charlton (1839).

Books, Pamphlets, etc.

Material from the L. A. J. Baker Collection, London Borough of Lewisham Local History Library.

Blackheath Society: Annual Reports and other publications, 1937-1975.

Frederick Bingham: The "Borough" Pocket Guide to Blackheath. Edward J. Burrow, Cheltenham, 1909.

Frederick Boase: Modern English Biography (and Supplement) 1851-1900. Reprint by Frank Cass & Co., 1965.

William Bonwitt. A History of the Paragon, Blackheath. (Not yet published) 1976.

Colin Buchanan & Partners: Greenwich and Blackheath Study. Greater London Council, 1971.

H. M. Colvin: Biographical Dictionary of British Architects 1660-1840. John Murray. London, 1954.

Dictionary of National Biography, and Supplements. Oxford University Press.

Leland Lewis Duncan: History of the Borough of Lewisham. Blackheath Press, 1908. Reprinted with Supplement, London Borough of Lewisham, 1963.

Leland Lewis Duncan (editor): Parish Registers of St. Mary, Lewisham 1558-1750, being such portions as saved from the fire of 1830. Lewisham Antiquarian Society. Charles North, Blackheath, 1900.

Leland Lewis Duncan & Arthur Oswald Barron: Register of all the Marriages, Christenings and Burials in the Church of St. Margaret, Lee, 1579-1754. Lewisham Antiquarian Society. Charles North, Blackheath, 1889.

Leland Lewis Duncan & Herbert Charles Kirby: Monumental Inscriptions in the Church and Churchyard, St. Mary, Lewisham. Charles North, Lee, 1889.

John Evelyn's Diary. Edited by E. S. de Beer. 1955.

Alan Glencross: The Buildings of Greenwich. London Borough of Greenwich, 1974.

Transactions of the Greenwich and Lewisham Antiquarian Society: 1920-1976.

Transactions of the Greenwich Antiquarian Society: 1905-1914.

London Borough of Greenwich: Greenwich and Blackheath Conservation

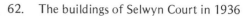
62. The buildings of Selwyn Court in 1936

64. The Alexandra Hall, built in 1863;
    converted for Lloyd's Bank in 1928

63. The Art Club, Bennett Park

65. Blackheath Literary Institution in 1846

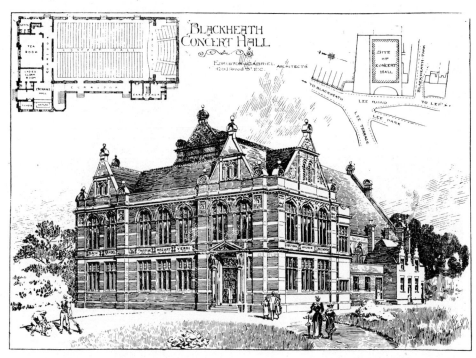

66. Original plans for the Blackheath Concert Hall

67. Talbot Houses, Blackheath Vale, December 1939

68. East Mill Cottage (Foy House) — demolished for All Saints' Vicarage in 1884

69.   The windmills on Blackheath in 1829: Talbot Place (left); Mill House site (right)

70.   All Saints' Church, before 1884 and the building of 21 Montpelier Row.

area. 1970.

Francis Hosier Hart: History of Lee and its Neighbourhood. Charles
    North, Lee, 1882.

Edward Hasted: History and Topographical Survey of the County of Kent.
    1778.

Edward Hasted: History of Kent: Volume 1 - The Hundred of Blackheath;
    edited by Henry Holman Drake. Mitchell & Hughes, London, 1886.

W. E. Hughes: Chronicles of the Blackheath Golfers. Chapman & Hall,
    London, 1897.

T. Bavington Jones: Kent at the Opening of the 20th Century - Contempor-
    ary Biographies: Pike's New Century Series, No. 10. W. T. Pike,
    Brighton, 1904.

John Kimbell: An Account of the Legacies etc., appertaining to the Church
    and Poor of the Parish of St. Alphege, Greenwich. Greenwich, 1816.
    (Includes a reprint of Samuel Traver's Survey of His Majesty's Lord-
    ship or Manor of East Greenwich, begun on 24 February, 1695,
    completed 27 May 1697).

John W. Kirby: The History of the Blackheath Proprietary School. Black-
    heath Press, London, 1933.

Henry Lansdell: Princess Aelfrida's Charity (A History of the Charity of
    Sir John Morden). Burnside, Blackheath, 1916.

Proceedings of the Lewisham Antiquarian Society: 1887-1912.

London Borough of Lewisham: Blackheath Conservation Area - an initial
    study. 1969.

Revd Daniel Lysons: The Environs of London. 1796.

Mary Charlotte Malim & Henrietta Caroline Escreet: The Book of the
    Blackheath High School. Blackheath Press, London, 1927.

Material from the Martin Collection, London Borough of Greenwich Local
    History Library.

Sir Leslie Monson: Notes toward a history of the Blackheath windmills.
    (not yet published) 1976.

Bryan Morgan: Express Journey 1864-1964 (Centenary history of the
    Express Dairy Co., Ltd.) Newman Neame, London, 1964.

Hubert William Ord: The Adventures of a School Master. Blackheath
    Press, 1936.

Beryl Platts: A History of Greenwich. David & Charles, Devon, 1973.

Neil Rhind: Blackheath Centenary 1871-1971. Greater London Council,
    1971.

Neil Rhind: Martin House; a short history of the Blackheath Literary
    Institution. Blackheath Preservation Trust Ltd., Blackheath, 1975.

John Smith: A History of Charlton , Volume 1. Charlton, 1970.

William Thomas Vincent: Records of the Woolwich District. Woolwich,
    1890.

Dora Ware: Short Dictionary of British Architects. Allen & Unwin,
    London, 1967.

Clifford Witting (editor): The Glory of the Sons - a history of Eltham
    College, the School for the Sons of Missionaries. Eltham College,
    London, 1952.

Who Was Who: 1897-1970. Adam & Charles Black. London.

Proceedings of the Woolwich & District Antiquarian Society, Woolwich,
    1954.

Index

The index below contains all the places and the principal names in this volume. A complete index of all names, places and subjects will be printed in the second volume.

Smith, Thomas, schoolmaster - 167
Smith, William - 203
Smith, W.H. & Sons, newsagents - 124
Smyth, Revd A.W. - 185
Soames, Revd William Aldwin - 122
Society for Acquisition and Diffusion of Useful Knowledge - 214
Society of Friends - 133
South, Edward Wilton - 182, 183, 191
South, John Flint - 195, 196
South Eastern Banking Co. - 64, 97
South Eastern Railway Co. - 79, 89, 121 et seq, 130
South Vale - 90 et seq
South Vale Cottage - 88, 113
South Vale House - 133
South Vale Mansions - 114
South Vale Road - 113
Spackman, Arthur John, oil and colourman - 23
Spencer Place - 91 et seq
Sports Clubs - 180
Stambury, Isaac & family, publican - 3
Stansby Street - 113
Station Masters - 126, 127
Stepney, Peter - 155, 158, 161
Stepney, William - 204
Stevens, Revd Charles Abbott - 211
Steward, William James, brewer - 139, 148
Stidolph, Maria, schoolmistress - 2, 56
Stidolph, William - 56
Stocker & Roberts, surveyors - 147, 188
Stoker, Mrs. (nee Wheatley) - 196
Stone and Marten, furriers - 37
Stone House, Montpelier Row - 194
Streek, William John, builder and plumber - 115 et seq, 145
Sueur, Roger, schoolmaster - 181
Suffragettes in Blackheath - 195
Sun-in-the-Sands public house - 112
SWIMMING BATH
   Alexandra Hall - 217
   Hally's nursery - 71
Swiss Cottage, Blackheath Park - 125

T

Tabberer, Benjamin, architect - 200

Talbot, Earl of - 200
Talbot Houses - 202
Talbot Place - 198, 199, 201
Tallents, Sir Stephen - 228
Tate, Dr. Robert Stark - 63
Taylor, George Ledwell, architect - 179
Taylor, Joseph Henry & family, bootmakers - 23, 36, 41
Taylor, William, shoemaker - 107
Tennant, Revd Sanderson - 178
Tennent, Harry Moncrieff, theatrical impresario - 231
Thompson, Henry Edward & family, blindmakers - 163
Thorpe Bros., grocers - 10, 46
Three Tuns Passage - 169
Three Tuns public house - 1, 31, 138, 148 et seq, 178, 206
Thynne, Arthur & family, bakers - 146, 152
Tidman, Revd Arthur - 130, 131
Tilling, Thomas, omnibus proprietor - 206
Todd, Dr. William - 51
Top Hat Restaurant - 153
Tract Depot - 159
Tranquil Passage - xiv, 1, 6, 153, 169 et seq
Tranquil Place - 137, 154 et seq
TRANQUIL VALE
   Nos. 1 to 63 - 87 et seq
   Nos. 16 to 20 - 67 et seq
   Nos. 22 to 34 (Osborne Place) - 39 et seq
   Nos. 36 to 50 - 139 et seq
   Nos. 52 to 74 - 154 et seq
'The Treasure Seekers' - 194
Tremlett, J.R., novelist - 132
Triggs, Robert Waddington & family, jewellers - 94, 101
Trill family, mercers and drapers - 57, 70, 92, 102, 141
Two Steps - 110
Tuck, Barber & family, grocers - 53, 140, 144
Tuck's Corner - 33, 140, 206
Turner, Ernest, antique dealer - 110
Turner, Ernest, grocer - 10, 11
Tunnard, William - 20
Tussaud, Madame - 213
Twentyman's Cottage - 166

Woodgate family, plumbers and glaziers - 142, 143
Woodlands, Mycenae Road - 132
Wookey, Edgar, estate agent - 7
Woolwich Equitable Building Society - 100
Wray, Titus, wine merchant - 10
Wray, Alfred Hughes, bookseller - 93
Wricklemarsh - xi, 19, 49, 67

Wright, Charles, carpenter - 208
Wright, Thomas & William, carpenters & livery stable keepers - 205
Wyberton House, 7 & 9 Lee Terrace - 220

Y-Z

Youens, John, coach proprietor - 166, 206
Zeppelin bombing, 1916 - 114, 116

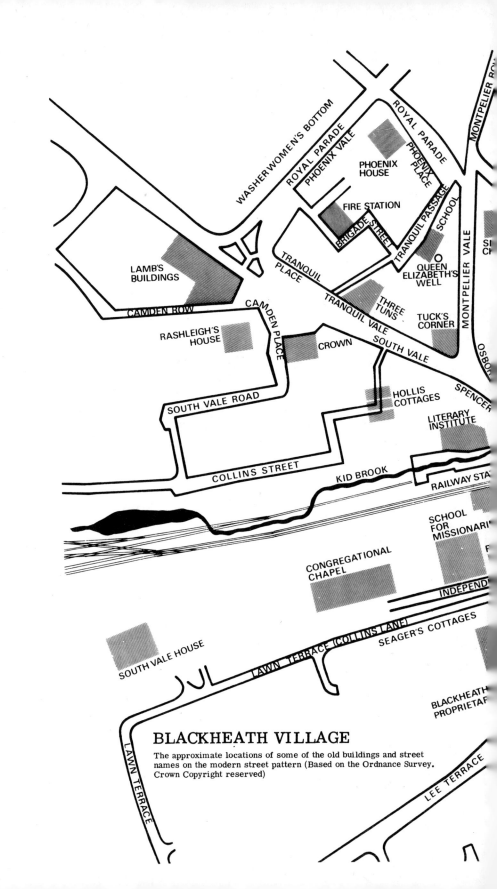

BLACKHEATH VILLAGE

The approximate locations of some of the old buildings and street names on the modern street pattern (Based on the Ordnance Survey. Crown Copyright reserved)